D1541589

BRITISH POLITICAL OPINION 1937–2000

THE GALLUP POLLS

UNIVERSITY OF
TORONTO AT
MISSISSAUGA
LIBRARY

BRITISH POLITICAL OPINION 1937–2000
The Gallup Polls

edited by Anthony King
compiled by Robert J. Wybrow
foreword by Alec Gallup

 Politico's
PUBLISHING

First published in Great Britain 2001
Politico's Publishing
8 Artillery Row
Westminster
London SW1P 1RZ

Tel 020 7931 0090
Fax 020 7828 8111
Email publishing@politicos.co.uk
Website http://www.politicos.co.uk/publishing

First published in hardback 2001

Copyright © The Gallup Organization 2001
Editorial apparatus © Anthony King
Compilation © Robert J. Wybrow

The right of The Gallup Organization, Anthony King and Robert J. Wybrow to be
identified as the authors of this work has been asserted by them in accordance with the
Copyright, Designs & Patents Act, 1988.

A catalogue record for this book is available from the British Library.

ISBN 1 902301 88 9

Printed and bound in Great Britain by Creative Print and Design Ltd.

All rights reserved. No part of this publication may be reproduced or
transmitted in any form or by any means, electronic or mechanical including photo-
copying, recording or information storage or retrieval system, without the prior permission
in writing of the publishers.

This book is sold subject to the condition that it shall not by way of trade or
otherwise be lent, resold, hired out, or otherwise circulated without the
publishers' prior consent in writing in any form of binding or cover other than that in
which it is published and without a similar condition being imposed on the subsequent
purchaser.

Contents

Foreword

ALEC GALLUP

The Gallup Poll, Britain's first public opinion poll, made its debut in the weekly news magazine *Cavalcade* in October 1937. A year later the daily *News Chronicle* began publication of a column based on Gallup Poll findings. Following the demise of the *News Chronicle* in 1960, Gallup moved to the *Daily Telegraph*, where its findings have been published ever since.

Henry Durant, a recent graduate of the London School of Economics, founded the British Gallup Poll in collaboration with the man who founded the Gallup Poll in the United States, George H. Gallup. Initially the British organization was known as the British Institute of Public Opinion. Durant, like his American colleague and mentor George Gallup, believed that 'the axiom that policy must be harmonized with public opinion is not an argument for the referendum':

> It is the business of a statesman to lead; and with his ear to the ground he is in no posture of leadership. The honest leader determines his course by the light of his own conscience and the special knowledge available to him, not by ascertaining the views of his necessarily less well-informed followers, in order that he may meekly conform. Having decided for himself what is right, he has then to convince the rank and file, knowing that if he fails to win or hold their support they will dismiss him and transfer their trust to another. That, and that only, is the sanction for the ultimate control of public opinion over policy.

The first topics about which the Gallup Poll sought the views of the British public included whether the grounds for divorce should be made easier, mercy killing, the Spanish civil war and whether or not Britain could remain neutral in any future war in Europe (most people thought not). Gallup in 1937 also asked whether, following the abdication of King Edward VIII, the former King and his wife should be invited to return to England to live (a substantial majority thought that they should). In the more than six decades since then, the Gallup Poll in Britain has recorded the public's opinions about every major news event, from the Churchill government's conduct of the Second World War to the more recent conflicts in the Balkans. It has also tracked the public's opinion about virtually every social, political and economic issue, including such enduring matters as religious beliefs, international travel, the ideal income and family size.

Probably the most visible aspect of Gallup's polling efforts, however, has been its measurements of voting intention, the standings of the major political parties, the performance of governments and the standings of Prime Ministers and other political personalities. In the fifteen general elections between 1945 and 1997, the British Gallup Poll has achieved an unmatched record of accuracy. For example, the average discrepancy between Gallup's published eve-of-election-poll findings for the three main political parties and the actual election results has been only 1.6 percentage points.

The US Origins of the Gallup Poll

To fully understand the story of the Gallup Poll in Britain, one needs to know something of the history of Gallup in the United States. The Gallup Poll, the world's first poll based on scientific sampling methods, made its debut in America on October 20, 1935 as a syndicated newspaper column. The technical methods used by the poll were based on procedures that George Gallup had developed based on experiments during the 1934 congressional election and the presidential election of 1932.

Gallup set out his views concerning the need for a national opinion poll to guide political leaders in terms very similar to those later used in Britain by Henry Durant:

> Without polls and therefore without adequate knowledge of the views of the people, a leader is in the hapless position of a military commander who must go into battle without knowing the strength or the deployment of the enemy troops he faces. If, through negligence or lack of understanding, he fails to obtain this kind of intelligence, he courts defeat. By the same token, the civil leader who attempts to carry out a programme without bothering to learn all he can about public opinion is equally derelict.

However, he continued:

> It is not incumbent upon a leader, . . . even in a democracy, to follow the wishes of the people slavishly. But the very nature of democracy makes it imperative that public opinion be taken into account in reaching decisions about legislative goals. The final responsibility rests, obviously, with the leader. He must be guided by his own best judgement and conscience.

Since its founding in 1935, the US Gallup Poll column has been released to the media on a continuous, once a week, or more frequent basis. Today the Gallup Poll is carried worldwide by the American national newspaper *USA Today* and by Cable News Network (CNN). Gallup's column is also distributed by the *Chicago Tribune* Syndicate to major news-papers in the U.S., including the *New York Times* and the *Washington Post*. In addition, the Gallup Poll's findings are reported daily on Gallup's internet site, *www.gallup.com*.

As in Britain, the US Gallup Poll is best known for its efforts in the political arena. The poll is probably most visible in connection with its continuous tracking of the comparative strength of candidates for political office in so-called trial-heat polls which Gallup introduced during the 1936 Roosevelt–Landon presidential election. In 1938, Gallup also originated the continuous measurement of how Americans rated the performance of their presidents. These presidential 'approval' ratings are the US equivalent of the British Gallup Poll's long-term monitoring of the British people's 'satisfaction' with their prime ministers.

The Gallup Poll in America was an almost immediate popular success, but at the start it encountered scepticism, even hostility, in most quarters, including among government officials. Critics questioned, for example, how it was possible to determine the opinions of the entire American public on the basis of only 1,500 interviews. They also questioned the likelihood of those interviewed actually telling the truth. However, the credibility of public opinion polls was enhanced significantly in 1936 when the Gallup Poll correctly predicted that FDR would easily defeat his Republican opponent, Alfred Landon, in the presidential election of that year. Gallup's findings, which were based on a carefully drawn representative sample of the US population, and 1,500 personal interviews, directly contradicted those of the *Literary Digest*, the well-reputed poll of record at that time. The *Digest*, whose figures were based on a biased sample frame and several million self-administered post-card interviews, claimed that Landon would win the election in a landslide. However, FDR won in a landslide and Landon was trounced. Gallup and the two other polls that relied on scientifically based samples, Roper and Crossley, were vindicated.

Over the subsequent decades, the scientific polls – although they have been off the mark from time to time – have nevertheless gained acceptance to the point where they are used today to investigate practically every aspect of human existence. To a significant extent, their present level of acceptance is due to the record of accuracy achieved by the Gallup Poll in its pre-election surveys in the United States. In the sixteen presidential elections since 1936, the deviation between Gallup's final pre-election survey figures and the actual election results has averaged only 2.2 percentage points, and since 1960 only 1.5 points. Similarly, in the seventeen congressional elections since 1936, the deviation between Gallup's final survey figures and the actual results has averaged only 1.5 percentage points.

George Gallup's Contribution

The introduction of the Gallup Poll on the American scene in the 1930s occurred while George H. Gallup was serving as the research director of Young and Rubicam, the well-known advertising agency. After receiving his PhD in psychology from the University of Iowa in 1925, Gallup spent several years conducting experiments to discover a scientific method for accurately measuring readership of newspapers' editorial and advertising content. After successfully developing and validating such a method, he submitted an article describing his new technique to *Editor and Publisher*, the main trade publication in the newspaper industry. The article made such an impression on Raymond Rubicam, co-founder of Young and Rubicam, that he invited Gallup to leave his position as acting dean of the Medill Journalism School at Northwestern University to become the agency's first research director.

As research director at Y & R, Gallup originated many of the basic methodologies and technical procedures used in marketing research, advertising research and media and audience research, all of which were based on the same scientific sampling principles on which the Gallup Poll was subsequently based. These included the 'recognition' (or 'reading and noting') and the 'impact' methods for gauging the effectiveness of advertisements as well as the principal methods for measuring radio listenership and subsequently television viewership. Gallup, in collaboration with David Oglivy, also developed virtually all of the methods and procedures used to determine the attitudes and behaviour of motion picture audiences.

Gallup's research innovations significantly increased the effectiveness of Young and Rubicam's advertising campaigns, contributing directly to the agency's rapid growth. Indeed, within a decade of Gallup's arrival as research director, Young and Rubicam had grown from a small New York-centred advertising agency to the third largest in the world. Ultimately, the new research methods that George Gallup developed at Young and Rubicam enabled the US Gallup Poll, the British Gallup Poll and other Gallup organizations around the world to expand from firms devoted exclusively to public opinion polling to full-service companies offering a wide range of survey research services.

Introduction

ANTHONY KING

Between 1937 and the year 2000 the Gallup Poll conducted something in the order of four million interviews with adults across Great Britain, asking them for their views on the political parties, on contemporary political personalities and on the political issues of the day. The purpose of this book is to make a large portion of Gallup's data available to students of British politics and political historians.

The phrase 'a large portion' is important, because the data set out in this book by no means constitute the whole of Gallup's data. In the first place, Gallup over the years has asked hundreds of questions about transient political events, episodes that caused a considerable stir at the time but had no lasting consequences. Those questions and the responses to them are recorded in the *Gallup Political and Economic Index* (until 1991 the *Gallup Political Index*) but have not been included in the tables below.

In the second place, the phrase 'a large portion of Gallup's data' is important because this book reports only Gallup's political data. But Gallup has also conducted a myriad of surveys on non-political topics, ranging from religious beliefs and practices to the countryside and consumer confidence. If the present volume, concentrating on politics and especially party politics, finds favour, a companion volume may be published later covering these other matters.

The data here were compiled by Robert J. Wybrow, who worked for Gallup from 1956 to 1998 and was in charge of the organization's political polling operations from 1972 to 1997. His was not an altogether easy task, despite the active cooperation of those who now run the Gallup Organization in Britain. Gallup has moved its headquarters on a number of occasions since 1937 – for example, from Regent Street to the Finchley Road in London and most recently from New Malden, Surrey, to Kingston-upon-Thames – and on several of these occasions a few data have gone missing. In addition, some of the data survive only in the form of one-off reports produced on someone's old-fashioned typewriter, and a small proportion of these data contain manifest errors (such as columns that sum to 105 per cent instead of 100 per cent and numbers that appear simply to have been repeated). Nevertheless, it has proved possible to reassemble the findings from the great bulk of Gallup's political surveys, and we believe the figures in the tables below to be substantially accurate. In the few cases where the data could not be found or struck us as being unreliable, the affected row in the relevant table has simply been left blank. A blank row may also indicate that, for some reason, the question was not asked in that particular month.

Users of this volume should bear in mind that the Gallup Organization, while it has inherited a strong sense of mission from its American founder, George H. Gallup, is nevertheless a commercial organization, most of whose political polling has always been undertaken in response to commissions from its media clients, notably the *Daily Telegraph* since 1960. Maintaining continuous time-series on a wide range of questions has always had to be subordinated to the need to economize on questionnaire length and to the related need to be able to meet clients' immediate journalistic requirements. Inevitably, too, considerable numbers of questions have been added or dropped in response to changing political circumstances. For example, no one today is much interested in the nationalization (i.e. state ownership) of British industry; it would therefore be perverse, and a waste of money, to ask about that. Conversely, given the importance of 'sleaze' as a political issue, beginning in the 1990s, it would be perverse not to ask people today whether they regard the government of the day as honest and trustworthy or not.

What is impressive, against that background, is not the inevitable stops and starts and the occasion lacunae in this body of data but the very long time spans over which some of the most important political questions have been asked. The Gallup series on voting intention goes back to 1937 and has been continuous since 1949. The series on satisfaction and dissatisfaction with the incumbent Prime Minister goes back to 1938 and has been more or less continuous since 1965. And there are similar series on Chancellors of the Exchequer and their Budgets. Gallup's data are, by a wide margin, the richest single source for the study of British political attitudes over more than half a century.

The editor and compiler of the present volume had, of course, to make a large number of decisions about which specific data should be included and which left out. On the whole, we operated a rule of thumb to the effect that the data would be included whenever a question (or a very similar question) had been asked on half a dozen occasions or more, or when the same subject had been investigated on half a dozen occasions or more (albeit with possibly different question wording). But it seemed to us more important to be useful than to be consistent, and some more *ad hoc* data have been included on that basis. In particular, Chapter 17 covers most of the major crises in British political life since the late 1930s, beginning with the Second World War and ending with Britain's participation in the recent Kosovo conflict.

There are a number of other general points that users of this volume will want to bear in mind. The first and perhaps the most important concerns the one major change that Gallup has made in its research methodology since its inception in 1937. Between 1937 and 1997 Gallup, in common with most other British polling organizations, conducted face-to-face interviews – employing the familiar man or woman with the clipboard – and based its samples on the so-called 'quota' method, with each interviewer instructed to obtain interviews with so many men and so many women, with so many unskilled manual workers and so many clerical workers, and so on.

However, the experience of Gallup and many other companies in the early 1990s, especially at the time of the 1992 general election, suggested that this methodology was flawed: that, for reasons that are still not entirely clear, it was tending to tilt survey samples in an anti-Conservative, pro-Labour direction. In any case, many in the survey-research industry had never been entirely happy, on theoretical grounds, with the quota method.

Gallup accordingly switched, in January 1997, from face-to-face interviewing to telephone interviewing and from quota sampling to something approaching pure random sampling. Interviewers now use a method known as random digit dialling, which excludes business numbers but includes ex-directory numbers. The method is designed so as to ensure that almost every adult in Great Britain – Northern Ireland has always been excluded – has an equal probability of being selected for interview. The introduction of random sampling had the effect, as expected, of eliminating the slight but politically significant anti-Conservative, pro-Labour tilt that had existed before. The switch to random sampling also had the effect, which had not been expected, of tending to reduce the number of respondents replying 'don't know' to a wide range of questions, though not to the voting-intention question.

It would be far too strong to say that the 1997 change of methodology renders the Gallup time-series since 1997 incomparable with those that went before; but the person using the tables below needs to be aware that the change did take place and to be wary, therefore, of making over-precise comparisons between pre- and post-1997 data. Reports of major shifts in opinion will have remained largely unaffected, but smaller-scale shifts will need to be interpreted with caution.

Most of the findings reported in these pages are drawn from surveys with approximately 1,000 respondents: usually in the region of 1,000-1,200. In some cases, the sample sizes are somewhat smaller (though never less than 800); in some cases, they are a good deal larger. Towards the end of general election campaigns, in particular, Gallup has usually increased the size of its samples to 2,000-2,500. The results reported here have, in most cases, been rounded either to the nearest whole number or to the nearest half. (Halves were dropped in 1997.) However, beginning in 1986, Gallup and the *Daily Telegraph* decided, with respect to a number of questions, including voting intention, to merge each of a number of weekly surveys to form a monthly composite or 'cumulative' sample. This monthly composite, which was called initially the Gallup 9000, is now known simply as the Gallup Index. The figures reporting the Gallup 9000 and the Gallup Index have been rounded to one place of decimals. In the tables that follow, the use of decimals in and of itself indicates that four or more surveys have been merged, yielding a total sample size of, usually, between 4,000 and 9,500.

Occasionally Gallup's samples comprise everyone aged sixteen and over; but the surveys relating to politics are almost invariably – for obvious reasons – confined to people who have reached voting age. Until 1969 the voting age in the United Kingdom was twenty-one and Gallup therefore interviewed only people aged twenty-one or over. In 1969, however, the voting age was lowered to eighteen and since then Gallup's samples have comprised people aged eighteen and over.

A proportion of Gallup's respondents, usually roughly 10–15 per cent, always reply 'don't know' to the voting-intention question or refuse to answer the question altogether. These respondents have been omitted from the voting-intention tables in Chapter 1 in the sense that the figures for the parties have been recalculated to sum to 100 per cent (or thereabouts, allowing for rounding). However, the figures in all the other tables have not been recalculated in this way and the proportion of 'don't knows', including refusals, has been indicated. As may be imagined, the proportion of 'don't knows' varies markedly depending on the nature of the question. Familar topics, about which most people have views, attract few of them; unfamiliar topics, about which large numbers of people do not have views, attract many, occasionally more than 40 per cent.

It goes without saying that, over a period of more than six decades, the wording of many of Gallup's questions, including its standard 'tracking' questions, has changed and that the order in which the questions are asked has also changed. Almost all of these changes are indicated either in the headnotes to the various chapters that follow or in footnotes. In the great majority of cases, minor modifications in the question wording or slight alterations in the order in which questions are asked is most unlikely to have affected the pattern of responses; but, in the few cases where there may have been such an effect, that possibility is signalled clearly in the headnotes.

To make some of the tables easier to interpret, horizontal lines have been employed as follows:

——————— indicates general election
----------------- indicates change of Prime Minister
—·—·—·—·— indicates change of Opposition leader.

The dates of general elections, changes of Prime Minister and changes of Opposition leader since 1937 are listed on pages xv–xvi.

Every effort has been made to ensure that the data in this book have been reported accurately, but the occasional error may have crept in. Anyone believing that he or she has spotted such an error is invited to write to Professor Anthony King, Department of Government, University of Essex, Wivenhoe Park, Colchester CO4 3SQ. However, matters of interpretation are, of course, solely a matter for the user.

DATES OF GENERAL ELECTIONS

5 July 1945

23 February 1950

25 October 1951

26 May 1955

8 October 1959

15 October 1964

31 March 1966

18 June 1970

28 February 1974

10 October 1974

3 May 1979

9 June 1983

11 June 1987

8 April 1992

1 May 1997

DATES ON WHICH PRIME MINISTERS CAME TO OFFICE

Clement Attlee, 26 July 1945

Winston Churchill, 26 October 1951

Sir Anthony Eden, 6 April 1955

Harold Macmillan, 10 January 1957

Sir Alec Douglas Home, 18 October 1963

Harold Wilson, 16 October 1964

Edward Heath, 19 June 1970

Harold Wilson, 4 March 1974

James Callaghan, 5 April 1976

Margaret Thatcher, 4 May 1979

John Major, 28 November 1990

Tony Blair, 2 May 1997

DATES ON WHICH LEADERS OF THE OPPOSITION WERE ELECTED (other than defeated Prime Ministers who became Leaders of the Opposition)

Hugh Gaitskell, 14 December 1955

Harold Wilson, 7 February 1963

Edward Heath, 2 August 1965

Margaret Thatcher, 11 February 1975

Michael Foot, 10 November 1980

Neil Kinnock, 2 October 1983

John Smith, 18 July 1992

Tony Blair, 21 July 1994

William Hague, 19 June 1997

CHAPTER I
Voting Intentions

Gallup first asked a voting-intention question in the autumn of 1937 on behalf of a magazine called *Cavalcade*. The question, as reported in *Cavalcade* on 30 October 1937, read simply: 'For whom would you vote today?' As they appeared in the magazine, neither the question nor the responses made any reference to the political parties. Instead the responses read simply, 'For the government, 68 per cent; for the Opposition, 32 per cent.'

Between 1943 and the mid-1990s Gallup's standard voting-intention question read, 'If there were a general election tomorrow, which party would you support?' In the mid-1990s, the question was revised slightly to read, 'If there were a general election tomorrow, which party would you vote for?' Also, until the time of the 1992 general election, the voting-intention question was asked only after the respondent had already been asked to express his or her views about the major party leaders (see Chapters 7-8 below). The possibility clearly existed that asking about the leaders first might affect the responses to the voting-intention question. For that reason, from June 1992 onwards the voting-intention question was asked in advance of any other political questions. In the event, it is doubtful whether either this repositioning of the voting-intention question or the subsequent rewording of the question affected in any substantial way the pattern of responses.

Table 1.1 reports the results of each month's snapshot survey, usually based on a sample of roughly 1,000–1,200. Table 1.2 reports the results, to one decimal place, of the monthly composite survey introduced in 1986 and described in the Introduction. Because the Gallup Index, as it is now called, is based on considerably larger whole-of-the-month samples, the amount of random variation it exhibits is substantially reduced. For that reason, the data reported in Table 1.2 show less month-to-month variation than do those reported in Table 1.1.

The so-called 'forced choice' question reported in Table 1.3 was introduced in August 1996 and since the beginning of 2000 has been asked in every monthly snapshot survey. Its purpose is partly to detect any changes in attitude towards the two major parties that may not be picked up by Gallup's other measures and partly also to see which, if either, of the two major political parties is preferred by the supporters of other parties and of none.

The 'who will win?' question reported in Table 1.4 was asked frequently between the mid 1960s and the late 1990s but has now fallen largely into abeyance. Its original purpose was to break into what some poll analysts call the 'spiral of silence': namely, the tendency of supporters of unpopular parties either to refuse to answer the voting-intention question or, less commonly, to claim that they support a party other than the one they actually do. A subsidiary purpose was to give respondents an opportunity to report, irrespective of their own party preference, what they were hearing in the pub or on the bus. The question is now asked less often because of a fear that respondents may simply be reflecting back to Gallup's interviewers the findings of the current opinion polls, which are now much more widely reported than they once were.

TABLE 1.1: THE SNAPSHOT 1943–2000

Q. If there were a general election tomorrow, which party would you vote for?
Q. If don't know: Which party are you most inclined to vote for?

		Cons	Lab	Lib	Other	Cons lead	Lab lead	
1943	Jun	36	44	10½	9½	–	8	A
	Jul	33	47½	11	8½	–	14½	
	Dec	31½	46½	11½	10½	–	15	
1944	Jan	28	45	12	14½	–	17	
1945	Feb	27½	47½	12½	12½	–	20	
	Apr	28	47	14	11	–	19	
	May	33	45	15	7	–	12	
	Jun	32	45	15	8	–	13	
	Jun	41	47	10	2	–	6	B
1946	Jan	32	52½	11	4½	–	20½	C
	May	40	43½	13	3½	–	3½	
1947	Jan	41	44½	12	2½	–	3½	
	Mar	43½	43½	10½	2½	0	0	
	Jun	42½	42½	12½	2½	0	0	
	Jul	42½	42½	12½	2½	0	0	
	Aug	44½	41	11	3½	3½	–	
	Sep	44½	39½	11½	4½	5	–	
	Nov	50½	38	9	2½	12½	–	
1948	Jan	44½	43½	10½	1½	1	–	
	Feb	46	42	8½	3½	4	–	
	Mar	46	43	8½	2½	3	–	
	Apr	42½	41	10½	6	1½	–	
	May	45	41½	11	2½	3½	–	
	Jul	48	39½	9	3½	8½	–	
	Aug	48	41	8½	2½	7	–	
	Sep	47½	41½	10	1	6	–	
	Oct	46½	41½	9½	2½	5	–	
	Nov	46	43	8½	2½	3	–	
1949	Jan	44	40½	13	2½	3½	–	
	Feb	44½	43½	9½	2½	1	–	
	Mar	41½	43	13	2½	–	1½	

cont'd . . .

		Cons	Lab	Lib	Other	Cons lead	Lab lead
	Apr	42	43½	13	1½	–	1½
	May	46	40	11	3	6	–
	Jun	46	41½	10	2½	4½	–
	Jul	44½	40½	12½	2½	4	–
	Aug	46½	40½	11½	1½	6	–
	Sep	46	40	12	2	6	–
	Oct	45½	39½	12½	2½	6	–
	Nov	43½	40	14	2½	3½	–
	Dec	45	41	12½	1½	4	–
1950	Jan	44	41½	12½	2	2½	–
	Feb	43	44½	12	½	–	1½
	Mar	43½	45½	8½	2½	–	2
	Apr	45½	47	7	½	–	1½
	May	43½	46½	9½	½	–	3
	Jun	43½	46	9	1½	–	2½
	Jul	42	43½	11	3½	–	1½
	Aug	44½	46	8½	1	–	1½
	Sep	43	45½	10	1½	–	2½
	Oct	42½	45	10	2½	–	2½
	Nov						
	Dec	43	44	11½	1½	–	1
1951	Jan	51	38	10	1	13	–
	Feb	51½	37½	9½	1½	14	–
	Mar	51	36½	10½	2	14½	–
	Apr	50½	38½	9	2	12	–
	May	49	40	9½	1½	9	–
	Jun	48	41	10	1	7	–
	Jul	49	39	10½	1½	10	–
	Aug	50½	38	10½	1	12½	–
	Sep	52	41	6½	½	11	–
	Oct	50½	44	4½	1	6½	–
	Nov						
	Dec	47	45	6½	1½	2	–
1952	Jan	44½	48	6	1½	–	3½
	Feb	41	47	10½	1½	–	6
	Mar	41½	48	9½	1	–	6½
	Apr						
	May	43½	49	7	½	–	5½
	Jun	40½	49	9½	1	–	8½
	Jul	40	50	8½	1½	–	10
	Aug	40	48	10½	1½	–	8
	Sep	41	48½	9	1½	–	7½

cont'd . . .

		Cons	Lab	Lib	Other	Cons lead	Lab lead
	Oct	41½	48	9	1½	–	6½
	Nov	43½	46½	9	1	–	3
	Dec	44	45½	9½	1	–	1½
1953	Jan	42½	46	10	1½	–	3½
	Feb	42½	46	10	1½	–	3½
	Mar	46½	44½	8	1	2	–
	Apr	47	45	7½	½	2	–
	May	47	45	7½	½	2	–
	Jun	46	46	7	1	0	0
	Jul						
	Aug	45	46	8	1	–	1
	Sep	44½	47½	7	1	–	3
	Oct	45	47½	7	½	–	2½
	Nov						
	Dec	45	47	7	1	–	2
1954	Jan 21–31	45½	46½	7	1	–	1
	Feb 26	45½	47	7	½	–	1½
	Feb 18–29	45	44½	9	1½	½	–
	Mar 20–31	46½	45½	7	1	1	–
	Mar 31	46	45½	7	1½	½	–
	Apr 16–27	46½	46	7	½	½	–
	May	45½	47½	6½	½	–	2
	Jun	45	47½	7	½	–	2½
	Jul						
	Aug	42½	48½	8	1	–	6
	Sep	43	48	8	1	–	5
	Oct	45	45½	8	1½	–	½
	Nov	46	47	6	1	–	1
	Dec						
1955	Jan	46½	45½	7	1	1	–
	Feb	46½	44½	8	1	2	–
	Mar	46½	44½	8	1	2	–
	Apr	48	44	7	1	4	–
	May 1–3	48½	47½	3	1	1	–
	May 8–10	49½	47	3	½	2½	–
	May 15–17	50½	47	2½	0	3½	–
	May 17–20	51	47	2	0	4	–
	May 21–24	51	47½	1½	0	3½	–
	Jun						
	Jul 2–13	47	43	9	1	4	–
	Aug	44½	47½	7	1	–	3
	Sep 9–19	48	44	7	1	4	–

cont'd . . .

		Cons	Lab	Lib	Other	Cons lead	Lab lead
	Oct 19–26	46½	44½	8	1	2	–
	Nov 24–Dec 4	44½	45½	9	1	–	1
	Dec 17–30	45½	46½	7½	½	–	1
1956	Jan 14–26	45½	46½	7½	½	–	1
	Feb 11–20	44	46	9	1	–	2
	Mar 24–Apr 4	44½	47½	7	1	–	3
	Apr 20–29	43	48	8	1	–	5
	May 19–27	43	47	9	1	–	4
	Jun						
	Jul 13–23	42	49	8	1	–	7
	Aug 16–24	43½	49½	6	1	–	6
	Sep 7–18	43	46½	10	½	–	3½
	Oct	42½	47	9½	1	–	4½
	Nov 10/11	46	45	8	1	1	–
	Nov 22–25	45	46	8½	½	–	1
	Dec 1/2	45	46	8	1	–	1
1957	Jan 12/13	43½	48½	7	1	–	5
	Feb	42	48	8½	1½	–	6
	Mar 15–22	40	51½	7½	1	–	11½
	Apr 12–16	41	51	7	1	–	10
	May 24–Jun 1	41½	50	7½	1	–	8½
	Jun						
	Jul 5–11	41½	49½	8	1	–	8
	Aug 16–27	41½	49	8½	1	–	7½
	Aug 29–Sep 10	40½	48½	10	1	–	8
	Sep 19–25	33½	52	14	½	–	18½
	Oct 4–8	37	49	13	1	–	12
	Nov 2–6	36	48½	14½	1	–	12½
	Nov 22–26	38½	49	12	½	–	10½
	Dec	41½	47½	9½	1½	–	6
1958	Jan 17–23	40	47½	12	½	–	7½
	Feb 14–19	36	44½	18½	1	–	8½
	Mar						
	Apr 19–23	38	46½	15	½	–	8½
	May 3–7	34	47	19	0	–	13
	May 30–Jun 6	39	45½	15	½	–	6½
	Jun 20–25	39½	43	17	½	–	3½
	Jul						
	Aug 1–6	42½	42	15	½	½	–
	Sep 19–23	44	43	13	0	1	–
	Oct 10–14	45½	41½	12	1	4	–
	Nov	46½	42½	10	1	4	–

cont'd . . .

		Cons	Lab	Lib	Other	Cons lead	Lab lead
	Dec 6–10	47	42½	9½	1	4½	–
1959	Jan 10–14	45½	45	8½	1	½	–
	Jan 24–28	44½	46½	8½	½	–	2
	Feb	43	47	8½	1½	–	4
	Mar 13–18	45½	47	6½	1	–	1½
	Apr 10–15	44½	44	10	1½	½	–
	May						
	Jun 6–10	45	43½	11	½	1½	–
	Jul 4–7	45½	41½	12½	½	4	–
	Jul 17–22	46	42	11	1	4	–
	Jul 23–27	46½	43	9½	1	3½	–
	Aug 7–12	47½	41½	10	1	6	–
	Sep	50½	43½	5½	½	7	–
	Sep 11–15	49	44½	6	½	4½	–
	Sep 25–28	46	46½	7	½	–	½
	Sep 29–Oct 2	45	47	7½	½	–	2
	Oct 3–6	46½	47½	5½	½	–	1
	Oct	48	46	5	1	2	–
	Nov	48	44	7	1	4	–
1959	Dec	47½	44	7½	1	3½	–
1960	Jan 1–6	47	43½	8½	1	3½	–
	Jan 9–20	47	42½	9½	1	4½	–
	Feb 5–24	47	43½	9	½	3½	–
	Mar 11–26	47	42	10	1	5	–
	Apr 6–27	45	42½	11½	1	2½	–
	May 1–29	45½	42½	11	1	3	–
	Jun 3–29	45½	43	10½	1	2½	–
	Jul 1–27	47	43	9	1	4	–
	Aug 25–Sep 5	47½	42	10	½	5½	–
	Sep 8–Oct 4	47½	40½	11	1	7	–
	Oct 20–Nov 2	50	37	12½	½	13	–
	Nov 3–29	46	40½	13½	0	5½	–
	Dec	47½	37½	14	1	10	–
1961	Jan	45	41½	12½	1	3½	–
	Feb	44	42	13	1	2	–
	Mar	44	40	15	1	4	–
	Apr 21–26	43½	40½	15	1	3	–
	Apr 28–May 9	44½	40½	14	1	4	–
	May 30–Jun 7	43½	40	15	1½	3½	–
	Jun 29–Jul 5	44	41½	14	½	2½	–
	Aug 2–9	38	43	17	2	–	5
	Aug 30–Sep 4	40	45½	13½	1	–	5½
	Sep 24–Oct 2	42½	45	12	½	–	2½

cont'd . . .

		Cons	Lab	Lib	Other	Cons lead	Lab lead
	Oct 12–16	43½	43½	12	1	0	0
	Nov 2–7	41½	43	14½	1	–	1½
	Nov 9–14	39	40	20	1	–	1
	Nov 30–Dec 6	38½	43	17½	1	–	4½
1962	Jan 5–14	42	42	15	1	0	0
	Feb 2–9	40	42½	17	½	–	2½
	Mar 1–7	39½	44	16	½	–	4½
	Mar 14–21	33	40	26	1	–	7
	Apr 7–16	33	41	25	1	–	8
	Apr 18–27	33½	40	26	½	–	6½
	May 3–9	34½	39½	25½	½	–	5
	Jun 1–6	35½	39	25	½	–	3½
	Jun 29–Jul 4	35½	41½	22	1	–	6
	Jul 6–11	37½	39½	22	1	–	2
	Jul 20–25	36	40½	22½	1	–	4½
	Aug 3–10	34	43	22	1	–	9
	Sep 12–19	34	45	20	1	–	11
	Sep 20–26	36½	45	17½	1	–	8½
	Oct 5–13	34½	43½	20	2	–	9
	Oct 12–20	40	41½	17	1½	–	1½
	Nov 2–9	39	47	13	1	–	8
	Nov 9–16	36	42½	20	1½	–	6½
	Nov 16–24	34½	44½	20½	½	–	10
	Dec 4–21	37	46	16	1	–	9
1963	Jan 11–18	35	48	16½	½	–	13
	Feb 1–5	32½	48	18½	1	–	15½

	Mar 1–12	33½	50	15½	1	–	16½
	Mar 29–Apr 10	34	49½	16	½	–	15½
	May 10–17	36	47	16	1	–	11
	Jun 7–14	31	51½	16½	1	–	20½
	Jun 22–26	36	50	13	1	–	14
	Jun 28–Jul 2	34½	51½	13	1	–	17
	Jul 5–10	34	52	13	1	–	18
	Jul 18–23	32	52	15	1	–	20
	Jul 25–30	33	50½	15½	1	–	17½
	Aug 1–6	35	49½	14½	1	–	14½
	Aug 22–27	33½	49½	15½	1½	–	16
	Aug 29–Sep 3	33½	50½	15	1	–	17
	Sep 5–10	34	50	15	1	–	16
	Sep 26–Oct 1	35½	46½	17	1	–	11
	Oct 3–8	35	47½	16	1½	–	12½

D

	Oct 17–22	38	49	12	1	–	11

cont'd . . .

		Cons	Lab	Lib	Other	Cons lead	Lab lead
	Oct 24–28	36	50	13	1	–	14
	Oct 31–Nov 5	37	49	13	1	–	12
	Nov 21–26	38	49½	12	½	–	11½
	Nov 29–Dec 3	39	48	12½	½	–	9
	Dec 3–9	39	47	13½	½	–	8
	Dec 12–16	37	50	12	1	–	13
	Dec 28–Jan 7	39	50	10½	½	–	11
1964	Jan 9–14	39½	48	12½	0	–	8½
	Jan 16–21	40½	46½	12½	½	–	6
	Jan 23–28	38	48	13	1	–	10
	Jan 30–Feb 4	38	50	11	1	–	12
	Feb 6–11	39	48½	12	½	–	9½
	Feb 13–18	40	48	11½	½	–	8
	Feb 20–25	42	45	11½	1½	–	3
	Feb 27–Mar 3	39½	47½	12	1	–	8
	Mar 5–10	37	50	13	0	–	13
	Mar 12–17	38½	46½	14	1	–	8
	Mar 19–24	40	49	10½	½	–	9
	Mar 25–31	38½	49½	11½	½	–	11
	Apr 2–7	37½	49½	13	0	–	12
	Apr 9–14	41	49	9½	½	–	8
	Apr 15–21	39	51½	9	½	–	12½
	Apr 24–28	36½	52	10½	1	–	15½
	May 1–5	35½	55	9½	0	–	19½
	May 7–12	38	51	10½	½	–	13
	May 13–19	41	48	11	0	–	7
	May 21–26	39½	51½	8½	½	–	12
	May 27–Jun 2	42	47	10½	½	–	5
	Jun 4–9	38½	51½	9	1	–	13
	Jun 10–16	42	49½	8	½	–	7½
	Jun 17–23	42	49	8½	½	–	7
	Jun 25–30	41½	51	7	½	–	9½
	Jul 2–7	38½	50½	10½	½	–	12
	Jul 9–21	42	49½	8	½	–	7½
	Jul 22–28	41	48½	10	½	–	7½
	Jul 30–Aug 4	43	48½	8½	0	–	5½
	Aug 6–11	42	49	9	0	–	7
	Aug 13–18	41½	49½	8½	½	–	8
	Aug 20–25	45	49½	5½	0	–	4½
	Aug 27–Sep 1	41½	50	8	½	–	8½
	Sep 2–9	44	46½	9	½	–	2½
	Sep	44½	47	8	½	–	2½
	Oct	44½	46½	8½	½	–	2

cont'd . . .

		Cons	Lab	Lib	Other	Cons lead	Lab lead
	Nov	38½	50	11	½	–	11½
	Dec	40	50½	9	½	–	10½
1965	Jan	42½	46½	10½	½	–	4
	Feb	45½	45	9	½	½	–
	Mar	43½	46	9½	1	–	2½
	Apr	39½	47½	12½	½	–	8
	May	44	43	12½	½	1	–
	Jun	47	42½	9½	1	4½	–
	Jul	46½	45	8	½	1½	–
	Aug	49	41½	8½	1	7½	–
	Sep	42	48½	8½	1	–	6½
	Oct	41½	49	9	½	–	7½
	Nov	42	48½	8½	1	–	6½
	Dec	40½	48½	10	1	–	8
1966	Jan	42	47½	9½	1	–	5½
	Feb	42½	50	7	½	–	7½
	Mar	40	51	8	1	–	11
	Apr 14–19	35½	54½	8½	1½	–	19
	May 6–10	35½	53½	10	1	–	18
	Jun 3–7	39½	52	7½	1	–	12½
	Jul 14–19	41	48½	8½	2	–	7½
	Jul 29–Aug 2	44½	44	10½	1	½	–
	Sep 2–6	42½	45	11½	1	–	2½
	Oct	43	44½	11½	1	–	1½
	Nov 7–13	44	42	12½	1½	2	–
	Dec 5–11	42	46	10½	1½	–	4
1967	Jan 9–15	42½	45½	10½	1½	–	3
	Feb 6–12	37	48½	13	1½	–	11½
	Feb 27–Mar 5	42½	42½	12½	2½	0	0
	Apr 12–16	45½	41½	11	2	4	–
	May 8–14	46½	40	12	1½	6½	–
	Jun 5–11	48	41	9½	1½	7	–
	Jul 2–9	43½	41	13	2½	2½	–
	Aug 6–13	43	42	13	2	1	–
	Sep 3–10	45	41½	10½	3	3½	–
	Oct	45	38	14	3	7	–
	Nov	46½	36	11½	6	10½	–
	Dec 9–17	49½	32	12	6½	17½	–
1968	Jan 6–14	45	39½	11	4½	5½	–
	Feb 3–11	52½	30	12½	5	22½	–
	Mar	50	31	15	4	19	–
	Mar 30–Apr 7	54½	30	12½	3	24½	–

cont'd . . .

		Cons	Lab	Lib	Other	Cons lead	Lab lead
	May 10–13	56	28	11	5	28	–
	Jun 7–9	51½	28	14	6½	23½	–
	Jul 4–7	50	30	13	7	20	–
	Aug	49½	34½	11½	4½	15	–
	Sep 12–15	47	37	11½	4½	10	–
	Oct	47	39	9½	4½	8	–
	Nov 7–10	50½	32	14	3½	18½	–
1968	Dec 5–9	55	29½	11	4½	25½	–
1969	Jan 9–12	53	31	11½	4½	22	–
	Feb 13–16	54½	32	11	2½	22½	–
	Mar 14–16	52½	34	10	3½	18½	–
	Apr 18–22	51	30½	13	5½	20½	–
	May 15–18	52	30½	13½	4	21½	–
	Jun 13–16	51	35	12	2	16	–
	Jul 10–13	55	31½	11	2½	23½	–
	Aug 14–17	47	34½	15½	3	12½	–
	Sep 11–14	46½	37	13	3½	9½	–
	Oct 16–19	46½	44½	7	2	2	–
	Nov 13–16	45	41½	10	3½	3½	–
	Dec 11–14	50	39½	9	1½	10½	–
1970	Jan 15–18	48½	41	7	3½	7½	–
	Feb 12–15	48	41	9	2	7	–
	Mar 13–15	46½	41	9½	3	5½	–
	Apr 17–19	47	42½	7½	3	4½	–
	May 5–9	41½	49	7½	2	–	7½
	May 13–17	42½	49½	6½	1½	–	7
	May 23–26	44½	50	4½	1	–	5½
	May 31–Jun 4	44	49½	5	1½	–	5½
	Jun 7–11	45½	48	5½	1	–	2½
	Jun 14–16	42	49	7½	1½		7
	Jul						
	Aug 13–16	47	43½	7½	2	3½	–
	Sep 10–13	46½	44	8	1½	2½	–
	Oct 16–18	46½	46½	6½	½	0	0
	Nov 12–15	43½	48	6½	2	–	4½
1970	Dec 10–13	46	44½	6	3½	1½	–
1971	Jan 14–17	42½	47	8½	2	–	4½
	Feb 8–14	41½	49	8	1½	–	7½
	Mar 11–14	38½	50½	8	3	–	12
	Apr 1–4	44½	48	6	1½	–	3½
	Apr 8–13	44	45½	9½	1	–	1½
	May 13–16	38	50	9½	2½	–	12

cont'd . . .

	Cons	Lab	Lib	Other	Cons lead	Lab lead
Jun 10–13	36	54	8	2	–	18
Jul 9–12	33½	55	8½	3	–	21½
Aug 11–15	42	48½	7	2½	–	6½
Sep 16–20	35	54	8½	2½	–	19
Oct 13–17	40	50	8	2	–	10
Nov 10–14	42½	48½	7	2	–	6
1971 Dec 8–12	42	48	7½	2½	–	6
1972 Jan 12–16	40½	48	9	2½	–	7½
Feb 9–13	40½	49	8½	2	–	8½
Mar 8–12	39½	48½	9½	2½	–	9
Apr 12–16	43½	44½	10	2	–	1
May 11–14	40½	46½	11	2	–	6
Jun 8–11	41	47	10	2	–	6
Jul 12–16	39	49	9½	2½	–	10
Aug 9–13	40	49	7½	3½	–	9
Sep 3–17	38½	49½	9½	2½	–	11
Oct 18–22	40	48	8½	3½	–	8
Nov 9–12	37½	45½	15	2	–	8
Dec 6–10	38	46½	12½	3	–	8½
1973 Jan 10–14	38½	44	15½	2	–	5½
Feb 8–11	38	47	12½	2½	–	9
Mar 9–12	39	43	16	2	–	4
Apr 11–15	38	41	17½	3½		3
May 10–13	38	43½	14½	4	–	5½
Jun 6–10	41	42	14½	2½	–	1
Jul 11–15	35½	45	17½	2	–	9½
Aug 8–12	31½	38	28	2½	–	6½
Sep 5–9	33½	43	22	1½	–	9½
Oct 17–21	33	39½	25½	2	–	6½
Nov 14–18	36½	38½	22½	2½	–	2
Dec 12–18	36	42½	18½	3	–	6½
1974 Jan 8–13	40	38	19	3	2	–
Feb 1–4	39½	42½	16	2	–	3
Feb 8–11	44½	43	11	1½	1½	–
Feb 12–14	42½	41½	14	2	1	–
Feb 16–18	41	40½	16½	2	½	–
Feb 18–21	42	40	16½	1½	2	–
Feb 26/27	39½	37½	20½	2½	2	–
Mar 13–18	35	43	19	3	–	8
Apr 9–16	33	49	15½	2½	–	16
May 8–13	33	46½	17	3½	–	13½
Jun 12–17	35½	44	17	3½	–	8½

cont'd . . .

		Cons	Lab	Lib	Other	Cons lead	Lab lead
	Jul 10–15	35	38	21	6	–	3
	Aug 8–12	35½	39½	21	4	–	4
	Aug 28–Sep 4	37½	40½	18	4	–	3
	Sep 11–17	34	42	20½	3½	–	8
	Sep 19–22	37½	42½	18	2	–	5
	Sep 19–26	39	44	15	2	–	5
	Sep 27–30	35	42½	19	3½	–	7½
	Sep 28–Oct 3	37	42½	17½	3	–	5½
	Oct 3–7	36	41½	19	3½	–	5½
	Nov 14–18	35	46½	14½	4	–	11½
	Dec 11–16	33	47	16½	3½	–	14
1975	Jan 9–13	34	48½	13	4½	–	14½
	Feb 13–17	45	41	11	3	4	–
	Mar 12–17	42	44	11	3	–	2
	Apr 9–14	43	45	10	2	–	2
	May 14–19	45½	39½	11	4	6	–
	Jun 11–16	44	40½	13	2½	3½	–
	Jul 11–14	43	40½	12½	4	2½	–
	Aug 13–18	40½	42	14	3½	–	1½
	Sep 17–22	38½	41½	16½	3½	–	3
	Oct 16–20	42½	40½	13½	3½	2	–
	Nov 12–17	39	44½	12½	4	–	5½
	Dec 11–16	40½	41	14	4½	–	½
1976	Jan 15–19	40½	42	14	3½	–	1½
	Feb 11–16	45½	40½	10½	3½	5	–
	Mar 10–15	44	41½	9½	5	2½	–
	Apr 8–12	41	46½	9	3½	–	5½
	May 12–17	44	41	10½	4½	3	–
	Jun 9–14	44	40½	11	4½	3½	–
	Jul 7–12	41	41	13	5	0	0
	Aug 11–16	44	41	10	5	3	–
	Sep 15–20	42½	42	11	4½	½	–
	Oct 14–18	48	36½	11½	4	11½	–
	Nov 10–15	55	30	11½	3½	25	–
	Dec 8–13	49½	34	11½	5	15½	–
1977	Jan 12–17	47	34	14½	4½	13	–
	Feb 9–14	46	33½	14	6½	12½	–
	Mar 9–14	49½	33	13	4½	16½	–
	Apr 13–18	49	33½	11½	6	15½	–
	May 11–16	53½	33	8½	5	20½	–
	Jun 9–13	47½	37	10½	5	10½	–
	Jul 13–18	49	34½	10½	6	14½	–

cont'd . . .

		Cons	Lab	Lib	Other	Cons lead	Lab lead
	Aug 10–15	48½	37½	9	5	11	–
	Sep 7–12	45½	41	8½	5	4½	–
	Oct 19–24	45	45	8	2	0	0
	Nov 9–14	45½	42	8½	4	3½	–
	Dec 7–12	44	44½	8	3½	–	½
1978	Jan 11–16	43½	43½	8½	4½	0	0
	Feb 8–13	48	39	9	4	9	–
	Mar 15–20	48	41	8	3	7	–
	Apr 13–17	45½	43½	7½	3½	2	–
	May 11–15	43½	43½	8½	4½	0	0
	Jun 7–12	45½	45½	6	3	0	0
	Jul 12–17	45	43	8½	3½	2	–
	Aug 9–14	43½	47½	6	3	–	4
	Sep 6–11	49½	42½	6	2	7	–
	Oct 17–23	42	47½	7½	3	–	5½
	Nov 8–13	43	48	6½	2½	–	5
	Dec 5–11	48	42½	6	3½	5½	–
1979	Jan 10–15	49	41½	6	3½	7½	–
	Feb 7–12	53	33	11	3	20	–
	Mar 7–12	51½	37	8½	3	14½	–
	Mar 21–28	47½	40½	9	3	7	–
	Mar 28–Apr 2	49	38½	9	3½	10½	–
	Apr 6–9	50	40	8	2	10	–
	Apr 14–18	47½	42	9	1½	5½	–
	Apr 19–21	46½	41½	10	2	5	–
	Apr 23–25	48	40	10½	1½	8	–
	Apr 30/May 1	43	41	13½	2½	2	–
	Jun 13–18	42	43½	12	2½	–	1½
	Jul 11–16	41	46	11½	1½	–	5
	Aug 8–13	41½	44	12½	2	–	2½
	Sep 12–17	40½	45	12	2½	–	4½
	Oct 17–22	40½	45	12½	2	–	4½
	Nov 7–12	39	43½	15½	2	–	4½
	Dec 4–10	38	42	18	2	–	4
1980	Jan 9–14	36	45	16	3	–	9
	Feb 6–11	37½	42	18	2½	–	4½
	Mar 11–17	37	49½	11½	2	–	12½
	Apr 10–14	36½	45	15	3½	–	8½
	May 15–19	39	43½	15½	2	–	4½
	Jun 11–16	40½	45	11½	3	–	4½
	Jul 10–14	40	43½	14	2½	–	3½
	Aug 14–18	38½	44	14½	3	–	5½

cont'd . . .

		Cons	Lab	Lib	Other	Cons lead	Lab lead
	Sep 10–15	35½	45	16½	3	–	9½
	Oct 1–6	40	43	13½	3½	–	3
	Oct 15–20	40	43	13½	3½	–	3
	Nov 12–17	36½	47	15	1½	–	10½
	Dec 10–15	35	47½	14½	3	–	12½
1981	Jan 14–19	33	46½	18½	2	–	13½
	Jan 28–Feb 2	36	35½	26½	2	½	–
	Mar 12–16	30	34	32	4	–	4
	Apr 8–13	30	34½	33	2½	–	4½
	May 6–11	32	35½	29	3½	–	3½
	Jun 10–15	29½	37½	30½	2½	–	8
	Jul 8–13	30	40½	26½	3	–	10½
	Aug 12–17	28	38½	32½	1	–	10½

		Cons	Lab	Lib	Other	Cons lead	Lab lead	Lib/SDP lead
	Sep 9–14	32	36½	29	2½	–	4½	
	Oct 21–26	29½	28	40	2½	1½	–	10½
	Nov 11–16	26½	29	42	2½	–	2½	13
	Dec 9–14	23	23½	50½	3	–	½	27
1982	Jan 13–18	27½	29½	39½	3½	–	2	10
	Feb 10–15	27½	34	36	2½	–	6½	2
	Mar 11–15	31½	33	33	2½	–	0	0
	Apr 7–12	31½	29	37	2½	2½	–	5½
	May 5–10	41½	28	29	1½	13½	–	
	Jun 9–14	45	25	28½	1½	20	–	
	Jul 7–12	46½	27½	24	2	19	–	
	Aug 11–16	44½	26½	27½	1½	18	–	
	Sep 8–13	44	30½	23	2½	13½	–	
	Oct 20–25	40½	29	27	3½	11½	–	
	Nov 10–15	42	34½	21½	2	7½	–	
	Dec 8–13	41	34½	22	2½	6½	–	
1983	Jan 12–17	44	31½	22½	2	12½	–	
	Feb 9–14	43½	32½	22	2	11	–	
	Mar 17–21	39½	28½	29	3	11	–	
	Apr 7–11	40½	35	22½	2	5½	–	
	May 4–9	49	31½	17½	2	17½	–	
	May 11–16	46	33	19	2	13	–	
	May 20–23	48	33	18	1	15	–	
	May 24–26	49	31½	18	1½	17½	–	
	May 25–30	47½	28	23	1½	19½	–	
	May 31–Jun 2	45½	31½	22	1	14	–	
	Jun 7/8	45½	26½	26	2	19	–	
	Jul 7–11	44	28½	26	1½	15½	–	
	Aug 10–15	44½	25	29	1½	19½	–	

cont'd . . .

		Cons	Lab	Lib	Other	Cons lead	Lab lead	
	Sep 7–12	45½	24½	29	I	21	–	
	Oct 19–24	42	35½	20½	2	6½	–	
	Nov 9–14	43½	36	19½	I	7½	–	
	Dec 7–12	42½	36	19½	2	6½	–	
1984	Jan 11–16	41½	38	19½	I	3½	–	
	Feb 8–13	43	33½	21½	2	9½	–	
	Mar 15–19	41	38½	19½	I	2½	–	
	Apr 11–16	41	36½	20½	2	4½	–	
	May 9–14	38½	36½	23	2	2	–	
	Jun 6–11	37½	38	23	1½	–	½	
	Jul 11–16	37½	38½	22	2	–	I	
	Aug 8–13	36	39	22½	2½	–	3	
	Sep 5–10	37	36	25½	1½	I	–	
	Oct 17–22	44½	32	21½	2	12½	–	
	Nov 7–12	44½	30½	23½	1½	14	–	
	Dec 5–10	39½	31	27½	2	8½	–	
1985	Jan 9–14	39	33	25½	2½	6	–	
	Feb 6–11	35	32	31½	1½	3	–	
	Mar 21–25	33	39½	25½	2	–	6½	
	Apr 17–22	34	37½	26½	2	–	3½	
	May 8–13	30½	34	33½	2	–	3½	
	Jun 12–17	34½	34½	30	I	0	0	
	Jul 10–15	27½	38	32½	2	–	10½	
	Aug 7–12	24	40	34	2	–	16	Lib/SDP lead
	Sep 11–16	29	29½	39	2½	–	–	9½
	Oct 16–21	32	38	28	2	–	6	–
	Nov 6–11	35	34	29½	1½	I	–	–
	Dec 4–9	33	32½	32½	2	½	–	–
1986	Jan 8–13	29½	34	35	1½	–	–	I
	Feb 5–10	29½	35½	33½	1½	–	6	–
	Mar 20–24	29½	34	34½	2	–	–	½
	Apr 9–14	28	38½	31½	2	–	10½	
	May 8–12	27½	37	32½	3	–	9½	
	Jun 11–16	34	39	24½	2½	–	5	
	Jul 9–14	33	38	27	2	–	5	
	Aug 6–11	30	36½	30	3½	–	6½	
	Sep 10–15	32½	38	27½	2	–	5½	
	Oct 16–20	37½	37½	22	3	0	0	
	Nov 12–17	36	39½	22	2½	–	3½	
	Dec 10–15	41	32½	23½	3	8½	–	
1987	Jan 14–20	34½	39½	23½	2½	–	5	
	Feb 11–16	36	34½	27½	2	1½	–	
	Mar 19–23	37½	29½	31½	1½	8	–	

cont'd . . .

		Cons	Lab	Lib	Other	Cons lead	Lab lead
	Apr 8–13	40½	28	29	2½	12½	–
	May 8–13	39	28	30	3	11	–
	May 19/20	42	33	23	2	9	–
	May 26/27	44½	36	18	1½	8½	–
	Jun 2/3	40½	36½	21½	1½	4	–
	Jun 8/9	41	34	23½	1½	7	–
	Jul 8–13	44½	33	20½	2	11½	–
	Aug 12–17	45½	35½	17½	1½	10	–
	Sep 16–21	44	33	20	3	11	–
	Oct 14–19	52	31½	13½	3	20½	–
	Nov 11–16	46½	33	17	3½	13½	–
	Dec 2–7	46½	34½	16	3	12	–
1988	Jan 13–18	45½	37	15	2½	8½	–
	Feb 11–15	46	36	15	3	10	–
	Mar 17–21	42	36½	19½	2	5½	
	Apr 13–18	40½	41½	15	3	–	1
	May 11–16	45	36	14½	4½	9	
	Jun 9–13	42	43	11	4	–	1
	Jul 13–18	41½	39	16	3½	2½	–
	Aug 10–15	45½	33½	17	4	12	–
	Sep 7–12	43	36½	17½	3	6½	–
	Oct 19–24	45½	34	17½	3	11½	–
	Nov 8–14	42½	36	17	4½	6½	–
	Dec 6–12	43	32	19½	5½	11	–
1989	Jan 12–16	42½	34	14	9½	8½	–
	Feb 9–13	40½	39	11½	9	1½	–
	Feb 15–20	39	39½	11½	10	–	½
	Feb 23–27	37½	37½	11½	13½	0	0
	Mar 29–Apr 3	37½	40	10	12½	–	2½
	Apr 27–May 1	40½	37½	10	12	3	–
	May 31– Jun 5	36½	43½	8	12	–	7
	Jun 28–Jul 3	34	47	6	13	–	13
	Aug 2–7	34	44½	5½	16	–	10½
	Aug 31–Sep 4	36½	43	6½	14	–	6½
	Sep 20–25	36½	42	7½	14	–	5½
	Sep 27–Oct 2	35	41½	8½	15	–	6½
	Oct 5–9	38	47½	4½	10	–	9½
	Oct 25–30	35	44	8	13	–	9
	Nov 29–Dec 4	37½	43½	9	10	–	6
1990	Jan 5–8	35	45½	7½	12	–	10½
	Jan 24–29	32½	48	8	11½	–	15½
	Feb 20–26	31	49½	7	12½	–	18½
	Mar 28–Apr 2	28	52½	7½	12	–	24½

cont'd . . .

		Cons	Lab	Lib	Other	Cons lead	Lab lead
	Apr 25–30	32	47	7½	13½	–	15
	May 30–Jun 4	29½	53	7½	10	–	23½
	Jun 27–Jul 2	36	47	9	8	–	11
	Jul 24–30	33½	48	11½	7	–	14½
	Aug 29–Sep 3	35½	48	8½	8	–	12½
	Sep 26–Oct 1	31½	46	14	8½	–	14½
	Oct 24–29	31½	46	15½	7	–	14½
	Nov 24–26	44½	41	10	4½	3½	–
	Dec 4–10	43	40½	10½	6	2½	–
1991	Jan 4–7	43	41½	10	5½	1½	–
	Jan 30–Feb 4	42	42½	10	5½	–	½
	Feb 25–Mar 1	45	36½	13	5½	8½	–
	Mar 25–30	39½	34½	18	8	5	–
	Apr 29–May 6	38½	38	18	5½	½	–
	May 27–Jun 3	33½	41½	21	4	–	8
	Jun 25–Jul 1	37	40½	17	5½	–	3½
	Jul 31–Aug 5	36	41	16½	6½	–	5
	Aug 24–Sep 2	39½	35	19½	6	4½	–
	Sep 24–30	42	38	15	5	4	–
	Oct 3/4	39½	41½	15	4	–	2
	Oct 29–Nov 4	36	44	15½	4½	–	8
	Nov 27–Dec 2	39½	37	19	4½	2½	–
1992	Jan 8–13	42	37½	16	4½	4½	–
	Jan 14–21	40	38	16½	5½	2	–
	Jan 21–28	38	39½	17½	5	–	1½
	Jan 29–Feb 3	42½	37½	14	6	5	–
	Feb 5–11	40	37½	17½	5	2½	–
	Feb 12–18	39	37	19	5	2	–
	Feb 19–25	37	37½	20	5½	–	½
	Feb 26–Mar 2	38½	38½	18½	4½	0	0
	Mar 4–10	37	38	20	5	–	1
	Mar 17/18	40½	38½	18	3	2	–
	Mar 24/25	40	40½	16½	3	–	½
	Mar 31/Apr 1	38	37½	20½	4	½	–
	Apr 2/3	37½	37½	22	3	0	0
	Apr 7/8	38½	38	20	3½	½	–
	Apr 29–May 4	41½	39	16½	3	2½	–
	May 28–Jun 1	44½	36½	16½	2½	8	–
	Jul 1–6	42	37½	15½	5	4½	–
	Jul 29–Aug 3	40½	45	12	2½	–	4½
	Sep 2–7	43	40½	12	4½	2½	–
	Sep 23–28	37	44	15	4	–	7

cont'd . . .

		Cons	Lab	Lib	Other	Cons lead	Lab lead
	October 7–12	36	45	13½	5½	–	9
	October 14–19	29	51	13½	6½	–	22
	Oct 28–Nov 2	32½	50	13	4½	–	17½
	Nov 25–30	29	52	14	5	–	23
1993	Jan	33½	45½	14½	6½	–	12
	Jan 27–1 Feb	33½	46	15½	5	–	12½
	Feb 24–Mar 1	32	49	14	5	–	17
	Mar 30–Apr 5	30½	49	15½	5	–	18½
	Apr 27–May 3	30	47	17½	5½	–	17
	May 26–31	25	49	23	3	–	24
	Jun 30–Jul 5	24½	43	26½	6	–	18½
	Jul 28–Aug 2	23	44½	27	5½	–	21½
	Sep 2–6	25½	46½	23	5	–	21
	Sep 22–27	23	44½	27	5½	–	21½
	Oct 27–Nov 1	24	46½	25½	4	–	22½
	Dec 1–6	27	48½	20	4½	–	21½
1994	Jan 6–11	25½	46½	20½	7½	–	21
	Jan 26–31	26	45½	23	5½	–	19½
	Feb 22–28	25	48½	21	5½	–	23½
	Mar 29–Apr 3	26½	51½	17½	4½	–	25
	May 4–9	24½	45½	25	5	–	21
	May 25–30	21	54	21½	3½	–	33
	Jun 30–Jul 4	26½	51	17½	5	–	24½
	Jul 27–Aug 1	23	56½	14½	6	–	33½
	Sep 1–5	22	56½	17	4½	–	34½
	Sep 22–27	21	57½	15½	6	–	36½
	Sep 28–Oct 3	25½	54	16½	4	–	28½
	Oct 26–31	21½	56½	17	5	–	35
	Nov 30–Dec 5	21½	61	13½	4	–	39½
1995	Jan 4–9	18½	62	14	5½	–	43½
	Jan 25–30	23½	59½	13	4	–	36
	Feb 22–27	20½	60½	15	4	–	40
	Mar 29–Apr 3	23	57½	15	4½	–	34½
	May 3–8	23	55½	16½	5	–	32½
	May 31–Jun 5	20	59½	14½	6	–	39½
	Jun 28–Jul 3	25½	57	13	4½	–	31½
	Jul 25–31	22½	57½	14½	5½	–	35
	Aug 31–Sep 4	26½	54½	14	5	–	28
	Sep 27–Oct 2	25½	55½	14	5	–	30
	Oct 25–30	21½	61	14½	3	–	39½
	Nov 29–Dec 4	23	62	12	3	–	39
1996	Jan 4–8	21	60½	14½	4	–	39½
	Feb 1–5	28	54½	14½	3	–	26½

cont'd . . .

		Cons	Lab	Lib	Other	Cons lead	Lab lead	
	Feb 29–Mar 4	23	57½	16	3½	–	34½	
	Mar 27–Apr 1	26	55½	15½	3	–	29½	
	May 1–6	24½	55½	15½	4½	–	31	
	May 30–Jun 3	22½	57	16	4½	–	34½	
	Jun 27–Jul 1	26	54½	14½	5	–	28½	
	Jul 31–Aug 5	25	59	11	5	–	34	
	Aug 28–Sep 3	25½	58½	11	5	–	33	
	Sep 18–24	27	54	13½	5½	–	27	
	Sep 26–Oct 1	27½	52	15	5½	–	24½	
	Oct 30–Nov 5	28	55	11	6	–	27	
	Nov 27–Dec 2	22	59	12	7	–	37	
1997	Jan 11–15	32½	50½	10½	6½	–	18	
	Jan 30–Feb 4	34	49	12	5	–	15	
	Feb 28–Mar 4	28	54	12½	5½	–	26	
	Mar 26–Apr 2	31	52	11	6	–	21	
	Apr 4–6	30	57	9	4	–	27	E
	Apr 5–7	30	58	8	4	–	28	
	Apr 6–8	29	56	9	6	–	27	
	Apr 7–9	28	56	10	6	–	28	
	Apr 7–10	29	56	10	5	–	27	
	Apr 8–11	32	54	10	5	–	22	
	Apr 9–12	32	51	12	5	–	19	
	Apr 10–13	32	48	14	6	–	16	
	Apr 11–14	31	50	13	6	–	19	
	Apr 12–15	28	53	12	7	–	25	
	Apr 13–16	31	52	10	7	–	21	
	Apr 14–17	32	50	11	7	–	18	
	Apr 15–18	33	50	12	5	–	17	
	Apr 16–19	31	50	12	7	–	19	
	Apr 17–20	31	49	13	7	–	18	
	Apr 18–21	32	49	12	7	–	17	
	Apr 23–25	32	50	11	7	–	18	
	Apr 24–26	32	49	12	7	–	17	
	Apr 25–27	30	50	14	6	–	20	
	Apr 26–28	29	53	13	5	–	24	
	Apr 27–29	30	52	12	6	–	22	
	Apr 29/30	33	46	16	5	–	13	
	April 30	33	47	14	6	–	14	
	May 1	31	44	17	7	–	13	
	May 29–Jun 4	23	59	13	5	–	36	
	Jul 2/3	23	61	13	3	–	38	
	Jul 31–Aug 6	25	58	12	4	–	33	

cont'd . . .

		Cons	Lab	Lib	Other	Cons lead	Lab lead
	Aug 27–Sep 3	26	58	12	5	–	32
	Sep 25–Oct 1	22	60	14	4	–	38
	Oct 30–Nov 4	23	63	11	4	–	40
	Nov 27–Dec 3	21	57	17	5	–	36
1998	Jan 5–7	26	56	12	5	–	30
	Jan 28–Feb 4	29	54	11	5	–	25
	Feb 26 –Mar 4	29	51	14	6	–	22
	Mar 26–Apr 1	26	54	16.	4	–	28
	Apr 23–29	25	54	16	4	–	29
	May 28–Jun 3	28	54	12	6	–	26 ·
	Jun 25– Jul 1	28	52	14	6	–	24
	Aug 26–3 Sep	28	54	12	6	–	26
	Sep 24–30	23	57	15	5	–	34
	Oct 29–Nov 4	28	54	14	5	–	26
	Nov 26–Dec 2	29	55	11	5	–	26
1999	Jan 4–6	29	52	13	5	–	23
	Jan 28–3 Feb	29	53	13	5	–	24
	Feb 26–Mar 4	30	52	11	6	–	22
	Mar 30–Apr 7	27	54	13	7	–	27
	Apr 21–28	29	52	13	7	–	23
	May 26–Jun 2	24	52	16	8	–	28
	Jun 23–30	27	51	14	8	–	24
	Jul 28–Aug 4	30	51	12	6	–	21
	Aug 25–Sep 1	27	52	13	7	–	25
	Sep 23–29	29	52	13	7	–	23
	Oct 27–Nov 2	28	52	14	6	–	24
	Nov 25–Dec 1	27	53	15	5	–	26
2000	Jan 5–12	30	53	12	5	–	23
	Feb 2–6	28	49	15	8	–	21
	Mar 1–7	31	51	11	6	–	20
	Apr 5–11	32	50	12	5		18
	May 3–9	31	47	14	7	–	16
	May 31–Jun 6	30	49	15	6	–	19
	Jul 5–11	35	45	14	6	–	10
	Aug 2–7	32	47	14	6	–	15
	Sep 7–12	32	45	16	6	–	13
	Sep 20–26	36	39	20	5	–	3
	Nov 1–7	34	45	14	6	–	11
2000	Dec 6–13	32	47	14	6	–	15

A Question in June 1943 read, 'If there were a general election tomorrow, how would you vote?'

B Second series of figures for June 1945 based on two questions: 'Have you definitely made up your mind how you intend to vote at the general election?' If Yes: 'For which candidate do you intend to vote?'

VOTING INTENTIONS // 21

C Question in January 1946 read, 'If you had to vote today, for which party would you vote?'
D Change of Prime Minister on 18 October 1963, during the polling period.
E Figures for April 1997 are 'rolling daily' based on 'definite' voters.

TABLE 1.2:   THE GALLUP INDEX, 1986–2000

Q. If there were a general election tomorrow, which party would you support/vote for?
Q. If Don't know: Which party would you be most inclined to vote for?

		Cons	Lab	Lib	Other	Cons lead	Lab lead	
1986	Jan	29.9	35.4	32.7	2.0	–	5.5	Lib/SDP lead
	Feb	29.2	34.3	34.8	1.9	–	5.1	0.5
	Mar	30.3	34.5	32.9	2.3	–	4.2	
	Apr	31.4	37.5	28.6	2.5	–	6.1	
	May	30.6	38.5	28.8	2.2	–	7.9	
	Jun	32.4	38.2	27.2	2.4	–	5.8	
	Jul	31.8	38.2	27.8	2.2	–	6.4	
	Aug	31.4	38.3	27.9	2.4	–	6.9	
	Sep	33.8	37.5	26.4	2.4	–	3.7	
	Oct	37.2	38.6	22.0	2.2	–	1.4	
	Nov	37.7	38.3	21.6	2.6	–	0.6	
	Dec	38.2	35.0	24.3	2.6	3.2	–	
1987	Jan	37.4	36.6	23.8	2.3	0.8	–	
	Feb	37.6	33.6	26.5	2.4	4.0	–	
	Mar	36.5	29.4	31.6	2.5	7.1	–	
	Apr	38.0	29.6	30.1	2.4	8.4	–	
	Jun	42.0	34.8	21.7	1.6	7.2	–	A
	Jul	44.2	34.9	18.4	2.5	9.3	–	
	Aug	44.9	34.3	19.8	2.1	10.6	–	
	Sep	46.5	33.5	17.5	2.4	13.0	–	
	Oct	47.8	33.7	15.9	2.6	14.1	–	
	Nov	46.3	36.4	14.6	2.7	9.9	–	
	Dec	45.7	35.7	16.0	2.6	10.0	–	
1988	Jan	45.4	37.0	14.9	2.7	8.4	–	
	Feb	44.7	38.2	14.6	2.5	6.5	–	
1989	Jan	42.6	35.5	16.7	5.3	7.1	–	
	Feb	41.0	36.4	17.9	4.7	4.6	–	
	Mar	38.9	37.7	17.9	5.4	1.2	–	
	Apr	39.1	38.4	17.0	5.5	0.7	–	
	May	40.9	40.8	12.8	5.4	0.1	–	
	Jun	38.2	41.3	11.0	9.4	–	3.1	
	Jul	35.5	43.3	10.0	11.1	–	7.8	

cont'd . . .

		Cons	Lab	Lib	Other	Cons lead	Lab lead
	Aug	36.8	42.6	9.3	11.3	–	5.8
	Sep	36.4	41.2	11.5	10.8	–	4.8
	Oct	36.2	47.0	8.3	8.6	–	10.8
	Nov	36.3	46.5	9.3	8.1	–	10.2
	Dec	37.3	46.2	9.4	7.1	–	8.9
1990	Jan	36.1	45.0	10.7	8.4	–	8.9
	Feb	32.7	47.3	11.6	8.5	–	14.6
	Mar	28.5	52.0	10.9	8.6	–	23.5
	Apr	28.1	51.8	11.6	8.4	–	23.7
	May	32.7	47.5	12.3	7.5	–	14.8
	Jun	33.7	49.5	8.8	8.1	–	15.8
	Jul	34.4	47.9	9.9	7.8	–	13.5
	Aug	35.1	47.6	9.3	7.9	–	12.5
	Sep	34.6	46.6	11.1	7.6	–	12.0
	Oct	34.3	46.4	13.0	6.3	–	12.1
	Nov	37.9	42.1	13.7	6.6	–	4.2
	Dec	44.6	39.1	10.5	5.8	5.5	–
1991	Jan	44.3	39.2	10.8	5.7	5.1	–
	Feb	44.3	39.3	11.0	5.4	5.0	–
	Mar	41.2	36.2	17.3	5.2	5.0	–
	Apr	40.9	37.1	16.5	5.6	3.8	–
	May	37.2	38.3	19.4	5.1	–	1.1
	Jun	36.5	39.7	18.7	5.0	–	3.2
	Jul	38.3	39.1	17.6	4.8	–	0.8
	Aug	38.5	38.8	17.1	5.5	–	0.3
	Sep	40.5	36.9	17.1	5.5	3.6	–
	Oct	41.0	40.4	13.8	4.8	0.6	–
	Nov	39.5	38.9	16.6	5.0	0.6	–
	Dec	40.6	38.9	15.0	5.6	1.7	–
1992	Jan	39.0	39.2	16.8	5.0	–	0.2
	Feb	38.9	27.6	18.3	5.5	11.3	–
	Mar	37.4	37.8	19.7	5.1		0.4
	Apr	38.5	38.0	20.0	3.5	0.5	–
	May	40.6	39.3	16.1	3.9	1.3	–
	Jun	39.8	40.4	15.2	4.5	–	0.6
	Jul	39.1	41.4	14.8	4.6	–	2.3
	Aug	38.4	42.6	14.1	4.9	–	4.2
	Sep	36.9	44.5	14.2	4.5	–	7.6
	Oct	32.0	48.4	14.4	5.3	–	16.4
	Nov	30.2	51.5	13.5	4.8	–	21.3
	Dec	32.2	48.1	14.6	5.1	–	15.9
1993	Jan	33.0	47.9	13.9	5.2	–	14.9

cont'd . . .

		Cons	Lab	Lib	Other	Cons lead	Lab lead
	Feb	31.9	47.4	15.4	5.4	–	15.5
	Mar	30.0	48.3	15.8	6.0	–	18.3
	Apr	30.9	47.4	16.0	5.8	–	16.5
	May	26.8	44.2	23.6	5.5	–	17.4
	Jun	24.2	45.8	24.5	5.6	–	21.6
	Jul	25.4	44.7	24.7	5.2	–	19.3
	Aug	23.7	42.9	28.3	5.1	–	19.2
	Sep	24.3	45.0	24.7	6.0	–	20.7
	Oct	26.2	45.6	22.6	5.5	–	19.4
	Nov	25.4	46.2	22.4	6.0	–	20.8
	Dec	26.8	46.4	21.3	5.4	–	19.6
1994	Jan	25.5	48.2	20.8	5.5	–	22.7
	Feb	26.3	47.6	21.0	5.1	–	21.3
	Mar	25.9	47.7	20.4	5.9	–	21.8
	Apr	24.4	48.3	22.3	4.9	–	23.9
	May	22.8	49.2	23.1	4.9	–	26.4
	Jun	21.6	51.8	20.3	6.3	–	30.2
	Jul	22.0	54.7	17.4	5.9	–	32.7
	Aug	23.0	55.5	16.6	5.0	–	32.5
	Sep	22.8	55.5	16.7	5.0	–	32.7
	Oct	22.8	56.7	15.5	5.1	–	33.9
	Nov	23.2	57.4	15.0	4.3	–	34.2
	Dec	20.4	60.9	14.3	4.4	–	40.5
1995	Jan	22.7	59.0	13.7	4.6	–	36.3
	Feb	21.8	59.5	13.7	4.9	–	37.7
	Mar	23.4	58.0	13.9	4.7	–	34.6
	Apr	22.5	57.2	15.3	5.1	–	34.7
	May	21.3	57.4	16.6	4.7	–	36.1
	Jun	22.6	58.2	14.8	4.5	–	35.6
	Jul	25.5	57.2	12.9	4.5	–	31.7
	Aug	24.7	55.5	15.0	4.8	–	30.8
	Sep	26.2	54.4	14.6	4.7	–	28.2
	Oct	24.3	58.9	13.0	3.9	–	34.6
	Nov	24.3	59.5	12.3	4.0	–	35.2
	Dec	24.7	58.0	13.0	4.3	–	33.3
1996	Jan	23.1	55.6	16.8	4.4	–	32.5
	Feb	25.4	55.4	14.9	4.4	–	30.0
	Mar	23.9	57.3	15.1	3.7	–	33.4
	Apr	23.8	57.2	14.3	4.6	–	33.4
	May	24.3	54.8	16.0	5.0	–	30.5
	Jun	26.1	54.9	14.5	4.4	–	28.8
	Jul	27.0	54.1	14.0	4.9	–	27.1
	Aug	26.9	53.3	13.8	6.0	–	26.4

cont'd . . .

		Cons	Lab	Lib	Other	Cons lead	Lab lead
	Sep	27.0	54.1	13.9	5.0	–	27.1
	Oct	25.8	54.7	15.0	4.6	–	28.9
	Nov	25.8	55.8	12.6	5.8	–	30.0
	Dec	26.0	56.0	12.5	5.4	–	30.0
1997	Jan	33.0	50.5	11.3	5.1	–	17.5
	Feb	32.8	50.9	10.8	5.7	–	18.1
	Mar	29.8	53.7	10.8	5.8	–	23.9
	Apr	31.0	50.0	12.6	6.4	–	19.0
	May	23.3	56.9	14.7	5.0	–	33.6
	Jun	24.2	60.4	11.5	3.9	–	36.2
	Jul	25.3	58.5	12.0	4.2	–	33.2
	Aug	26.8	57.6	11.4	4.3	–	30.8
	Sep	23.1	62.0	11.0	3.9	–	38.9
	Oct	23.2	63.2	9.7	4.0	–	40.0
	Nov	23.6	58.6	13.0	4.9	–	35.0
	Dec	24.6	56.6	13.8	5.0	–	32.0
1998	Jan	26.8	54.9	13.1	5.2	–	28.1
	Feb	28.1	54.4	12.9	4.8	–	26.3
	Mar	29.3	51.1	14.0	5.6	–	21.8
	Apr	26.5	53.8	15.3	4.5	–	27.3
	May	25.9	55.2	13.8	4.9	–	29.3
	Jun	27.1	54.1	12.8	6.0	–	27.0
	Jul	27.8	53.9	12.7	5.5	–	26.1
	Aug	28.0	54.9	12.0	5.1	–	26.9
	Sep	28.0	54.1	12.6	5.3	–	26.1
	Oct	25.3	56.5	13.0	5.3	–	31.2
	Nov	27.2	54.3	13.1	5.5	–	27.1
	Dec	27.1	55.5	12.3	5.0	–	28.4
1999	Jan	27.8	53.7	13.1	5.4	–	25.9
	Feb	27.5	53.9	13.6	5.0	–	26.4
	Mar	28.5	53.3	12.8	5.4	–	24.8
	Apr	26.1	55.4	12.9	5.6	–	29.3
	May	26.7	53.6	13.8	6.0	–	26.9
	Jun	26.7	50.2	15.2	8.0	–	23.5
	Jul	27.6	51.5	14.0	7.0	–	23.9
	Aug	27.7	51.6	14.4	6.3	–	23.9
	Sep	27.6	52.8	13.3	6.4	–	25.2
	Oct	27.6	53.2	12.7	6.5	–	25.6
	Nov	27.4	52.8	14.3	5.5	–	25.4
	Dec	27.0	54.2	13.3	5.5	–	27.2
2000	Jan	28.3	52.5	13.5	5.6	–	24.2
	Feb	29.1	51.3	12.9	6.7	–	22.2

cont'd . . .

	Cons	Lab	Lib	Other	Cons lead	Lab lead
Mar	29.8	50.9	12.7	6.7	–	21.1
Apr	30.4	49.5	13.1	7.0	–	19.1
May	32.5	47.3	13.4	6.9	–	14.8
Jun	31.7	46.7	15.2	6.4	–	15.0
Jul	32.0	48.9	12.7	6.4	–	16.9
Aug	29.7	50.6	13.3	6.4	–	20.9
Sep	35.5	40.6	17.0	6.9	–	5.1
Oct	34.8	44.1	14.7	6.4	–	9.3
Nov	33.3	46.4	14.1	6.2	–	13.1
2000 Dec	32.7	47.3	13.8	6.3	–	14.6

A Actual dates of fieldwork: May 19–June 9

TABLE 1.3:   'FORCED CHOICE'

Q. If you had to choose, which would you prefer to see after the next election, a Conservative Government led by Mr ..... or a Labour Government led by Mr ..... ?

		Cons	Lab	Neither	DK
1996	Aug	24	59	12	5
	Sep	25	58	12	5
	Sep	26	57	11	6
	Nov	28	55	10	7
	Dec	25	60	10	6
1997	Jan	37	59	3	1
	Feb	36	56	3	5
	Mar	31	60	5	3
	Apr	32	58	4	5
1998	Apr	28	61	6	5
2000	Jan	31	56	7	7
	Feb	32	56	9	4
	Mar	36	54	7	3
	Apr	36	54	6	4
	May	35	54	5	5
	Jun	33	55	7	4
	Jul	39	48	8	5
	Aug	38	53	5	4
	Sep	39	51	6	4
	Sep	43	46	8	3
	Nov	37	51	8	3
	Dec	39	53	5	3

TABLE 1.4:   WHICH PARTY TO WIN?

Q. Irrespective of how you, yourself, will vote, who do you think will win the next general election?

		Cons	Lab	Lib	Other	DK	
1947	Jun	32	46	3	1	18	A
1948	Jul	36	42	1	0	21	B
1949	Oct	30	46	1	0	23	C
1951	Aug	45	32	1	0	22	D
	Sep	44	30	0	0	26	E
1952	Jun	16	63	0	0	21	
	Aug	25	55	0	0	20	
1954	Sep	33	39	0	0	28	
	Nov	44	26	0	0	30	
1955	Apr	52	22	0	0	26	
1958	Nov	44	29	1	0	26	F
1959	Feb	39	28	0	0	33	
	Mar	46	24	1	0	29	
	Sep	50	28	2	0	20	
	Oct	49	22	1	0	28	
	Oct	51	21	2	0	26	
1961	Oct	51	24	6	0	19	G
1962	Feb	51	23	2	0	24	
	Mar	41	17	16	1	25	
	May	36	36	9	0	19	
	Jun	31	42	6	0	21	
	Jul	28	42	10	0	20	
	Sep	30	39	8	0	23	
	Oct	37	37	7	1	18	
1963	Mar	26	52	2	0	19	
	Apr	24	55	4	0	17	
	May	25	57	2	0	16	
	Jun	17	58	1	0	24	
	Jul	16	68	2	0	14	
	Aug	22	55	0	0	22	
	Sep	26	55	1	0	18	
	Oct	23	55	1	0	16	
	Nov	30	53	1	0	16	
	Dec	28	48	1	0	23	

cont'd . . .

		Cons	Lab	Lib	Other	DK
1964	Jan	29	45	0	0	25
	Feb	27	57	1	0	15
	Mar	31	47	0	0	21
	Apr	30	50	0	0	20
	Apr	17	66	0	0	17
	May	16	67	0	0	17
	Jun	20	63	1	0	16
	Jul	25	59	0	0	16
	Jul	25	54	0	0	21
	Aug	30	48	0	0	22
	Aug	27	54	0	0	18
	Sep	38	42	0	0	20
	Sep	39	42	0	0	19
	Oct	41	37	1	0	21
	Oct	34	38	1	0	27
1965	Jan	27	46	1	0	26
	Feb	49	28	0	0	22
	Mar	41	34	0	0	24
	Apr	41	38	1	0	20
	May	40	34	1	0	25
	Jun	58	24	0	0	18
	Jul	44	30	1	0	25
	Aug	57	24	0	0	19
	Sep	56	24	0	0	20
	Oct	39	39	0	0	22
	Nov	35	44	1	0	20
	Dec	35	46	1	0	18
1966	Jan	32	42	0	0	25
	Feb	20	62	0	0	18
	Mar	16	69	1	0	14
	Jun	27	48	0	0	25
	Jul	25	55	0	0	20
	Sep	37	37	0	0	26
	Nov	41	34	1	0	24
1967	Oct	56	19	2	0	23
	Oct	55	27	1	0	17
	Nov	62	23	1	1	13
1968	Apr	78	7	0	0	14
	Jun	73	11	1	1	15
	Jul	76	13	0	0	10
	Oct	55	25	1	0	19

cont'd . . .

		Cons	Lab	Lib	Other	DK
1969	May	76	9	0	0	14
	Oct	46	33	1	0	20
	Nov	48	31	0	0	21
	Dec	54	26	0	0	20
1970	Jan	54	25	0	0	21
	Feb	53	24	0	0	22
	Mar	54	27	0	0	19
	Apr	47	31	1	0	22
	May	25	56	0	0	18
	Jun	13	69	0	0	17
1972	Mar	23	57	0	0	20
	May	35	40	1	0	24
	Sep	23	57	0	0	20
	Oct	28	53	1	0	18
	Nov	28	52	1	0	19
	Dec	32	42	2	0	24
1973	Jan	31	46	2	0	21
	Feb	31	46	2	0	21
	Apr	26	50	0	0	24
	May	26	51	2	0	21
	Jun	33	47	1	0	19
	Jul	22	55	3	0	20
	Aug	26	47	6	0	21
	Sep	23	51	4	0	22
	Oct	29	47	4	0	20
	Nov	35	36	5	0	24
	Dec	31	43	3	1	22
1974	Jan	40	35	3	0	22
	Feb	60	20	2	0	18
	Feb	54	26	2	0	18
	Apr	19	52	2	0	27
	May	26	48	2	1	23
	Jun	25	51	2	0	22
	Jul	32	36	4	1	27
	Sep	27	44	3	1	26
	Sep	18	55	2	1	25
1975	May	45	29	1	1	24
	Jun	44	29	1	1	25
	Jul	46	28	1	1	24
	Aug	46	30	2	0	22
	Sep	44	29	2	1	24

cont'd . . .

		Cons	Lab	Lib	Other	DK
	Oct	45	32	2	0	21
	Nov	43	35	1	1	20
	Dec	45	29	2	1	23
1976	Jan	45	32	1	1	22
	Feb	46	30	1	1	23
	Mar	49	30	0	1	19
	Apr	41	33	0	0	25
	Apr	44	37	1	0	19
	May	35	36	1	1	28
	May	51	28	1	1	20
	Jun	48	29	0	1	22
	Jul	44	32	1	1	22
	Aug	45	33	1	0	21
	Sep	44	34	1	0	20
	Oct	57	20	0	1	22
	Nov	66	18	1	1	15
	Dec	62	17	0	1	20
1977	Jan	57	21	1	0	20
	Feb	62	18	1	1	18
	Mar	62	20	1	1	16
	Apr	67	16	1	1	15
	May	74	12	0	0	14
	Jun	69	15	0	1	14
	Jul	71	13	1	1	14
	Aug	64	19	0	1	16
	Sep	54	28	1	1	17
	Oct	49	31	1	0	19
	Nov	46	35	0	0	18
	Dec	48	32	0	0	20
1978	Jan	46	38	0	1	15
	Feb	40	40	0	0	19
	Mar	52	30	1	0	17
	Apr	45	38	0	1	17
	May	48	33	1	0	18
	Jun	39	43	0	1	17
	Jul	40	42	0	0	17
	Aug	42	36	0	0	21
	Sep	42	36	0	0	20
	Oct	47	35	1	0	17
	Nov	36	41	0	0	22
	Dec	41	40	0	0	19
1979	Jan	44	35	0	0	20
	Feb	65	20	0	0	15

cont'd . . .

		Cons	Lab	Lib	Other	DK
	Mar	61	23	1	0	16
	Apr	56	26	0	0	18
	Dec	28	44	3	0	25
1980	Jan	29	45	1	0	24
	Feb	29	45	2	0	24
	Mar	27	55	2	0	16
	Apr	25	52	3	0	20
	May	24	57	1	0	18
	Jun	28	55	1	0	15
	Jul	28	55	1	0	17
	Aug	28	50	2	1	19
	Sep	22	58	2	0	18
	Oct	30	53	2	0	15
	Nov	22	60	0	0	17
	Dec	18	67	1	0	15
1981	Jan	17	65	2	1	16
	Feb	25	42	3	5	25
	Mar	17	50	4	7	23
	Apr	20	44	13	1	22
	May	18	56	6	1	19
	Jun	18	60	4	0	17
	Jul	13	63	5	1	19
	Aug	18	52	13	1	16
	Sep	19	46	13	0	22
	Oct	14	39	24	1	22
	Nov	17	31	33	1	18
	Dec	12	23	43	1	21
1982	Jan	16	27	37	0	20
	Feb	21	35	24	1	20
	Mar	32	33	15	1	19
	Apr	23	27	26	1	23
	May	43	21	14	0	22
	Jun	68	13	5	0	14
	Jul	66	12	7	1	15
	Aug	58	17	7	0	17
	Sep	58	19	5	0	18
	Oct	58	20	6	0	16
	Nov	55	22	4	1	18
	Dec	54	25	3	1	17
1983	Jan	61	19	3	0	16
	Feb	62	19	3	1	15
	Mar	66	11	7	0	16

cont'd . . .

		Cons	Lab	Lib	Other	DK
	Apr	59	21	4	0	16
	May	76	11	0	0	12
	May	78	11	1	0	10
	May	79	11	0	0	9
	Jun	81	9	3	0	8
	Jun	87	5	2	0	6
	Jul	49	16	8	0	26
	Aug	56	10	12	0	22
	Sep	64	12	6	0	18
	Oct	48	28	6	0	18
	Nov	53	26	3	0	18
	Dec	49	27	4	1	20
1984	Jan	58	22	2	0	17
	Feb	59	23	2	0	15
	Mar	50	35	3	0	13
	Apr	52	28	3	1	17
	May	50	30	5	0	16
	Jun	49	31	3	0	16
	Jul	43	37	4	0	16
	Aug	49	29	4	1	18
	Sep	54	28	4	0	14
	Oct	64	19	4	0	14
	Nov	67	17	2	0	14
	Dec	67	16	3	0	14
1985	Jan	65	16	5	0	14
	Feb	63	19	6	0	13
	Mar	53	28	5	1	14
	Apr	54	28	4	0	15
	May	46	26	8	1	18
	Jun	44	31	10	1	14
	Jul	37	27	14	2	21
	Aug	34	33	13	1	20
	Sep	41	25	12	2	19
	Oct	39	28	11	2	19
	Nov	47	25	7	2	19
	Dec	47	24	8	2	19
1986	Jan	40	27	10	2	21
	Feb	35	30	12	2	22
	Mar	45	27	8	2	19
	Apr	36	40	4	2	17
	May	28	49	6	2	14
	Jun	35	43	4	1	17

cont'd . . .

		Cons	Lab	Lib	Other	DK
	Jul	43	38	4	0	15
	Aug	38	39	6	1	15
	Sep	43	38	3	2	14
	Oct	49	32	2	1	15
	Nov	55	28	1	1	14
	Dec	65	18	3	0	14
1987	Jan	63	19	2	2	13
	Feb	65	19	2	2	13
	Mar	69	10	5	1	15
	Apr	74	8	5	1	12
	May	87	6	1	0	6
	May	83	8	1	0	7
	May	81	11	1	1	7
	Jun	82	9	1	0	9
	Jun	77	11	1	2	9
	Dec	69	15	1	0	15
1988	Jan	74	12	1	0	13
	Feb	71	14	1	0	14
	Mar	70	14	1	0	15
	Apr	74	16	1	0	9
	May	68	17	0	0	14
	Jun	71	17	1	0	11
	Jul	78	11	1	0	10
	Aug	79	9	1	0	11
	Sep	80	11	1	0	9
	Oct	83	8	0	0	9
	Nov	73	14	1	0	12
	Dec	78	13	1	0	8
1989	Jan	79	9	1	0	10
	Feb	74	10	2	0	14
	Mar	68	15	2	1	13
	Apr	70	17	2	1	11
	May	64	22	1	0	13
	Jul	47	40	1	0	12
	Aug	52	34	1	0	13
	Aug	56	32	0	0	11
	Oct	59	29	0	0	11
	Oct	45	42	0	0	12
	Dec	52	36	2	1	10
1990	Jan	51	36	0	0	13
	Jan	50	36	1	0	13
	Feb	38	48	0	0	13
	Mar	26	62	0	0	11

cont'd . . .

		Cons	Lab	Lib	Other	DK
	Apr	33	56	1	0	10
	Jun	38	52	0	0	9
	Jul	48	41	0	0	11
	Jul	45	42	1	0	13
	Aug	48	40	1	0	12
	Sep	47	41	1	0	11
	Sep	43	40	3	0	14
	Dec	60	27	1	0	12
1991	Jan	55	33	0	0	11
	Feb	62	27	0	0	11
	Mar	65	24	1	0	10
	Mar	54	27	3	0	15
	Apr	53	32	2	1	13
	May	38	46	2	1	14
	Jun	42	43	1	0	14
	Aug	48	36	1	0	15
	Aug	52	31	2	0	15
	Sep	58	25	1	0	15
	Nov	47	37	1	0	15
1991	Nov	45	37	2	1	15
1992	Jan	47	36	1	0	16
	Feb	56	26	0	0	18
	Feb	48	30	0	2	19
	May	55	22	2	0	21
	Jun	63	15	2	0	19
	Jul	62	16	2	0	19
	Aug	56	23	1	0	19
	Sep	56	26	1	0	16
	Oct	43	37	2	1	17
	Oct	38	41	3	1	18
	Nov	34	44	1	0	21
	Nov	29	50	1	0	18
	Dec	33	46	2	1	18
	Dec	41	40	1	0	17
1993	Jan	45	37	2	0	17
	Feb	45	35	2	1	17
	Mar	39	43	2	0	16
	Apr	45	37	1	0	17
	May	52	32	2	0	13
	May	36	39	7	1	16
	May	35	42	7	2	15
	Jul	40	39	6	2	14

cont'd . . .

		Cons	Lab	Lib	Other	DK
	Aug	36	37	10	1	15
	Sep	38	36	6	1	20
	Sep	41	34	7	2	16
	Nov	40	39	5	1	15
	Dec	41	38	3	1	18
1994	Jan	46	38	3	1	12
	Jan	34	51	3	0	12
	Feb	34	43	3	1	19
	Apr	35	45	4	1	15
	May	31	49	5	1	14
	May	25	57	3	0	14
	Jul	21	66	2	0	10
	Aug	22	66	1	1	10
	Sep	25	61	2	0	11
	Sep	26	59	2	1	13
	Oct	23	60	2	0	14
	Dec	25	61	1	0	13
1995	Jan	20	67	1	0	12
	Jan	24	64	1	0	11
	Feb	22	65	1	0	11
	Apr	23	63	1	0	13
	May	17	71	1	0	11
	Jun	14	75	1	0	9
	Jul	23	65	1	0	11
	Jul	25	62	1	0	11
	Sep	25	60	1	0	14
	Oct	28	57	1	0	14
	Oct	28	58	2	0	12
	Dec	25	62	1	0	12
1996	Jan	20	65	1	1	12
	Feb	25	63	1	0	12
	Mar	24	62	1	0	13
	Apr	23	63	2	0	12
	May	20	69	1	0	11
	Jun	21	66	1	0	12
	Jul	25	61	1	0	13
	Aug	27	62	1	0	11
	Sep	30	58	1	0	11
	Oct	29	59	1	0	10
	Nov	28	61	0	0	11
	Dec	26	61	1	0	11
1997	Jan	27	66	1	0	6
	Feb	31	60	0	0	8

cont'd . . .

		Cons	Lab	Lib	Other	DK
	Mar	22	71	0	0	6
	Apr	18	73	0	0	7
	Jun	11	69	1	0	17
	Jul	13	72	1	0	14
	Aug	16	72	1	0	11
	Sep	18	67	2	0	13
	Oct	8	78	2	0	12
	Nov	12	74	1	0	12
1997	Dec	9	78	3	0	10
1999	Sep	14	75	2	1	7
2000	Sep	37	51	2	2	8

A Question in June 1947 read, 'Regardless of your own political views, which party do you think will win the next general election?'

B Question in July 1948 read, 'Irrespective of how you yourself feel, which party do you think will win the next general election?'

C Question in 1949 read, 'Which party do you think will win?'

D Question in August 1951 read, 'Which party do you think will win the next election?'

E Question in September 1951 read, 'Who do you think will win the next election?'

F Question in 1958 upto March 1959 read, 'Irrespective of how you, yourself, would vote, who do you think would win the next general election?'

G In 1961 and 1962 the Liberal figure relates to 'Liberals holding balance'.

CHAPTER 2
The Political Parties

This chapter reports a range of questions that Gallup has asked frequently about the political parties, especially the Conservative and Labour parties. Some of the questions ask the respondent to compare the various parties; others ask the respondent about the parties individually.

The 'party unity' questions reported in Table 2.1 have been asked frequently since the mid 1970s, and in most of the snapshot surveys since the 1980s, and are a response to the widespread belief that united parties are more likely to be successful at the polls than divided ones. Table 2.2 reports a wide variety of 'best to handle' questions, ones that invite respondents to say which party they think would best handle a problem or problems facing the country. Since the late 1980s and early 1990s Gallup has usually asked the 'best to handle' type of question in a standard format, beginning 'I am going to read out a list of problems ...'. The responses to these questions, grouped by topic, are reported from p. 59 onwards.

A similar but separate series of questions, reported in Table 2.3, focuses on the economy. These questions were asked only sporadically between 1964 and 1990 but have been asked in almost every survey since 1991. The question, as originally formulated, read: 'If Britain ran into economic difficulties, who do you think could handle the problem best: the Conservatives under Sir Alec Douglas-Home or Labour under Mr Wilson?' The phrase that opened the original version of the question, 'If Britain ran into economic difficulties', seemed appropriate during the booming 1960s but seemed less appropriate subsequently and, since the late 1980s, has taken the form, 'With Britain in economic difficulties'. The names of the party leaders in the question were initially changed as the party leaders themselves changed but have latterly been dropped. As in the case of minor changes to the wording of the voting-intention question (see p. 1), it is doubtful whether these changes to the wording of the 'economic competence' question have significantly affected the pattern of responses.

Tables 2.4–2.7 report the responses to a number of questions concerning which political party had the best leaders and policies, how much confidence respondents had in the various parties, and how competent they thought the parties were to manage the country's affairs. The different questions were asked at various times between the mid 1950s and the mid 1990s.

TABLE 2.1: CONSERVATIVE PARTY UNITY 1965–2000

Q. Do you think the Conservative Party is united or divided at the present time? A

		United	Divided	DK
1965	May	51	29	20
1965	Oct	48	27	25
1966	Feb	31	50	19
	Aug	47	33	20
	Oct	34	42	24
1967	Feb	30	50	20
	Mar	34	41	25
1969	Oct	40	42	18
1971	Oct	42	40	18
	Nov	38	46	16
	Nov	49	35	16
1972	May	45	39	16
	Sep	44	38	18
1972	Apr	42	38	20
	Jul	31	42	27
1974	Jun	33	41	26
1975	Feb	32	52	16
	Mar	38	47	15
	Apr	47	36	17
	May	42	38	20
	Jun	41	41	18
	Oct	37	50	13
1976	Feb	44	42	15
	Apr	42	37	21
	Apr	47	36	17
	May	44	37	19
	Aug	38	44	18
	Sep	36	44	20
	Oct	50	37	13
	Nov	54	30	16
1977	Sep	42	39	19
	Sep	37	43	20
	Oct	51	36	13
1978	Sep	38	40	22
1979	Sep	63	16	21

cont'd . . .

		United	Divided	DK
1980	Jul	56	25	17
	Aug	51	31	18
	Oct	61	24	15
	Oct	69	21	9
	Nov	56	33	11
	Dec	50	40	10
1981	Jan	49	39	12
	Feb	50	37	12
	Feb	56	33	11
	Mar	53	36	11
	Mar	36	55	9
	Apr	40	48	11
	May	51	36	13
	Jun	45	41	14
	Jul	44	45	11
	Oct	43	44	13
	Oct	33	60	7
1982	Mar	52	40	8
	Mar	55	36	10
	Apr	43	49	9
	May	65	27	8
	Jun	70	22	8
	Jul	68	25	7
	Aug	49	37	13
	Sep	67	26	7
	Oct	67	25	8
	Nov	65	26	9
	Dec	68	24	8
1983	Jan	70	21	9
	Feb	66	25	9
	Mar	76	17	7
	Apr	73	18	9
	May	71	18	10
	May	73	18	9
	May	75	17	8
	May	76	15	10
	May	76	17	7
	Jun	75	16	9
	Jun	82	12	6
	Jul	74	18	9
	Aug	76	17	7
	Sep	75	19	6
	Oct	64	28	8

cont'd . . .

		United	Divided	DK
	Nov	65	28	7
	Dec	59	32	9
1984	Jan	67	22	11
	Feb	58	35	7
	Mar	58	36	6
	Apr	54	38	8
	May	61	33	7
	Jun	57	36	7
	Jul	46	46	8
	Aug	51	38	11
	Sep	56	35	9
	Sep	46	42	12
	Oct	70	22	8
	Nov	69	24	7
	Dec	49	44	6
1985	Jan	51	40	9
	Feb	51	41	8
	Mar	50	44	6
	Apr	50	42	7
	May	46	47	7
	Jun	43	49	8
	Jul	44	46	10
	Aug	41	49	10
	Sep	49	41	10
	Sep	43	48	9
	Oct	54	36	9
	Nov	55	35	10
1985	Dec	60	31	9
1986	Jan	34	56	9
	Feb	22	72	6
	Mar	41	52	7
	Apr	43	49	8
	May	36	55	9
	Jun	43	49	8
	Jul	41	51	8
	Aug	34	56	10
	Sep	45	46	9
	Sep	38	52	11
	Oct	58	34	8
	Nov	58	32	11
	Dec	58	32	11
1987	Jan	58	31	10
	Feb	59	31	10

cont'd . . .

		United	Divided	DK
	Mar	70	21	10
	Apr	68	22	10
	May	77	15	8
	Jun	81	13	6
	Jul	75	17	8
	Aug	69	22	9
	Sep	71	22	7
	Sep	63	27	10
	Oct	73	18	8
	Nov	66	25	9
	Dec	70	22	8
1988	Jan	62	30	8
	Feb	66	27	8
	Mar	64	28	8
	Apr	58	34	8
	May	51	40	9
	Jun	63	28	9
	Jul	66	25	8
	Aug	65	25	10
	Sep	66	26	8
	Sep	58	32	10
	Oct	71	20	9
	Nov	61	29	10
1988	Dec	64	27	9
1989	Jan	66	22	12
	Feb	63	27	10
	Mar	60	29	11
	Apr	61	29	10
	Apr	58	31	11
	May	59	30	11
	Jul	39	52	8
	Aug	39	52	9
	Sep	47	42	11
	Sep	51	39	10
	Oct	52	38	10
	Oct	28	65	7
	Dec	29	62	9
1990	Jan	32	57	10
	Jan	34	56	10
	Feb	32	59	9
	Apr	18	76	6
	Apr	23	68	10
	Jun	27	65	7

cont'd . . .

		United	Divided	DK
	Jul	37	55	9
	Jul	30	61	9
	Sep	41	46	12
	Sep	45	45	11
	Oct	33	56	11
	Dec	41	51	8
1991	Jan	46	44	11
	Feb	63	27	10
	Feb	66	25	9
	Mar	29	64	7
	May	36	55	8
	Jun	30	61	9
	Jun	23	70	7
	Aug	35	55	10
	Sep	47	43	10
	Sep	50	37	13
	Sep	55	34	11
	Nov	41	48	12
	Dec	20	71	8
1992	Jan	35	54	11
	Feb	48	41	11
	Mar	48	41	11
	May	66	25	9
	May	63	26	11
	Jul	44	45	11
	Aug	48	40	12
	Sep	42	46	11
	Oct	14	79	7
	Nov	13	80	7
	Nov	19	73	8
1993	Jan	26	63	11
	Jan	30	59	11
	Feb	27	62	11
	Apr	24	67	9
	May	27	63	10
	May	15	77	8
	Jul	14	80	6
	Aug	11	80	9
	Sep	11	80	9
	Sep	10	81	9
	Nov	16	77	8
	Dec	26	63	11
1994	Jan	20	72	8

cont'd . . .

		United	Divided	DK
	Jan	12	77	11
	Feb	14	76	10
	Apr	9	84	7
	May	8	85	7
	May	11	80	9
	Jun	12	80	8
	Jul	14	75	10
	Sep	15	74	11
	Sep	17	68	15
	Oct	15	74	11
	Dec	9	84	7
1995	Jan	6	88	6
	Jan	10	81	10
	Feb	7	85	8
	Mar	9	85	7
	May	10	81	9
	Jun	7	85	8
	Jul	5	90	6
	Jul	12	81	7
	Sep	21	71	9
	Sep	17	72	11
	Oct	21	68	11
	Oct	18	71	11
	Dec	17	73	9
1996	Jan	7	85	8
	Feb	12	79	9
	Mar	10	81	9
	Mar	12	77	11
	May	9	81	10
	Jun	9	82	9
	Jun	12	76	12
	Aug	11	79	10
	Sep	15	75	10
	Sep	12	76	12
	Sep	15	76	9
	Nov	16	74	10
	Nov	15	76	10
1997	Jan	14	83	3
	Feb	18	78	4
	Mar	15	80	4
	Apr	17	78	5
	Apr	12	80	7
	Jun	5	91	4

cont'd . . .

		United	Divided	DK
	Jul	13	83	4
	Aug	22	73	5
	Sep	24	69	7
	Sep	14	79	6
	Nov	13	80	6
	Dec	15	79	5
1998	Jan	18	76	7
	Feb	24	69	6
	Mar	27	63	10
	Apr	32	59	9
	Apr	26	64	10
	May	28	64	8
	Jun	25	64	11
	Aug	30	59	11
	Sep	27	63	11
	Sep	21	68	10
	Oct	24	68	8
	Nov	24	64	12
1999	Jan	27	61	11
	Feb	21	66	12
	Mar	23	66	11
	Apr	25	65	11
	May	26	65	9
	May	21	69	10
	Jun	25	64	12
	Jul	25	63	12
	Aug	21	68	11
	Sep	25	66	9
	Oct	24	69	7
	Nov	19	71	9
2000	Jan	13	77	10
	Feb	19	70	10
	Mar	25	67	8
	Apr	34	58	9
	May	28	61	11
	Jun	28	56	15
	Jul	37	47	15
	Aug	34	57	10
	Sep	31	60	9
	Sep	42	47	11
	Nov	35	53	12
2000	Dec	29	61	10

A Prior to 1971 question read: 'Do you think the Conservative Party at the present time is a united party or still rather at loggerheads?'

TABLE 2.2:   LABOUR PARTY UNITY 1956–2000

Q. Do you think the Labour Party is united or divided at the present time? A

		United	Divided	DK
1956	May	53	25	22
1956	Oct	40	40	20
1961	Oct	33	45	22
1962	May	25	47	28
1963	Mar	41	34	25
	Dec	51	31	18
	May	38	51	11
1965	Oct	47	36	17
1966	Aug	31	57	12
	Sep	38	46	16
1967	Feb	42	46	12
	Mar	24	62	14
	Dec	27	59	14
1968	Jan	17	72	11
	Mar	15	76	9
	Apr	18	67	15
1969	Sep	31	55	14
1970	Sep	41	40	19
1971	Sep	30	53	17
	Oct	15	70	14
	Nov	13	74	13
	Nov	18	70	12
1972	May	15	72	13
	Sep	28	55	17
1973	Apr	19	60	21
	Jul	19	55	25
	Oct	37	46	17
1974	Apr	57	24	19
	Jun	37	42	21
1975	Feb	40	45	15
	Mar	32	54	14
	Apr	18	70	12
	May	12	73	15
	Jun	14	75	11
	Sep	24	66	10
	Oct	22	69	9

cont'd . . .

		United	Divided	DK
1976	Feb	29	58	14
	Apr	21	65	13
	Apr	29	60	11
	May	28	58	15
	Aug	28	59	13
	Sep	29	58	13
	Oct	18	73	10
1976	Nov	14	77	10
1977	Sep	24	63	13
	Sep	30	57	13
	Oct	32	56	12
1978	Sep	33	48	19
1979	Sep	10	77	13
1980	Jul	8	81	11
	Aug	12	75	12
	Oct	7	86	7
	Oct	7	88	5
	Nov	16	76	8
	Dec	16	78	6
1981	Jan	9	84	8
	Feb	5	90	5
	Feb	4	91	6
	Mar	5	91	4
	Mar	9	86	5
	Apr	7	87	6
	May	10	82	8
	Jun	5	88	7
	Jul	7	86	7
	Oct	8	86	7
	Oct	13	80	7
	Oct	10	85	5
1982	Mar	7	88	5
	Mar	10	84	6
	Apr	9	87	5
	May	9	86	6
	Jun	6	90	4
	Jul	7	88	6
	Aug	6	89	5
	Sep	8	88	4
	Oct	12	82	6
	Nov	12	82	6
	Dec	10	86	4
1983	Jan	12	82	6

cont'd . . .

		United	Divided	DK
	Feb	12	82	5
	Mar	10	85	5
	Apr	19	73	8
	May	15	76	8
	May	17	75	8
	May	21	72	8
	May	22	70	8
	May	19	75	6
	Jun	14	79	7
	Jun	10	84	6
	Jul	10	86	5
	Aug	6	90	4
	Sep	6	91	3
	Oct	33	60	7
	Nov	34	57	9
	Dec	36	55	9
1984	Jan	29	62	9
	Feb	34	60	7
	Mar	38	54	7
	Apr	33	60	7
	May	33	60	6
	Jun	31	62	6
	Jul	35	57	8
	Aug	26	66	8
	Sep	30	62	9
	Oct	19	74	6
	Nov	21	73	6
	Dec	15	79	5
1985	Jan	16	76	8
	Feb	15	78	7
	Mar	23	69	7
	Apr	23	71	7
	May	25	69	6
	Jun	25	67	8
	Jul	20	72	8
	Aug	21	70	9
	Sep	19	71	11
	Oct	22	71	7
	Nov	20	71	9
1985	Dec	16	77	8
1986	Jan	22	69	9
	Feb	33	58	9
	Mar	21	71	7

cont'd . . .

		United	Divided	DK
	Apr	21	72	7
	May	29	62	9
	Jun	27	65	7
	Jul	24	68	8
	Aug	26	64	10
	Sep	29	62	9
	Oct	37	55	8
	Nov	31	58	11
1986	Dec	24	67	9
1987	Jan	28	61	11
	Feb	27	63	10
	Mar	17	75	9
	Apr	15	77	8
	May	17	77	6
	Jun	24	72	4
	Jul	21	72	7
	Aug	23	70	8
	Sep	24	68	8
	Oct	19	75	6
	Nov	20	73	7
	Dec	19	74	7
1988	Jan	19	73	8
	Feb	20	72	7
	Mar	19	72	9
	Apr	14	79	7
	May	19	72	9
	Jun	15	77	8
	Jul	12	81	7
	Aug	13	78	9
	Sep	14	79	7
	Oct	14	79	7
	Nov	17	75	8
	Dec	12	82	6
1989	Jan	14	74	12
	Feb	16	76	8
	Mar	22	69	10
	Apr	22	69	9
	Apr	22	68	10
	May	22	68	10
	Jul	34	57	9
	Aug	33	57	10
	Sep	34	54	11
	Sep	30	61	9

cont'd . . .

		United	Divided	DK
	Oct	32	57	10
	Oct	47	46	8
	Dec	49	39	11
1990	Jan	46	43	11
	Jan	42	46	11
	Feb	47	42	11
	Apr	50	40	10
	Apr	41	47	12
	Jun	48	44	8
	Jul	47	45	9
	Jul	45	44	11
	Sep	45	42	12
	Sep	48	41	11
	Oct	43	46	11
	Dec	54	36	10
1991	Jan	47	39	13
	Feb	42	46	12
	Feb	40	49	11
	Mar	44	45	11
	May	47	44	9
	Jun	52	39	9
	Jun	45	45	10
	Aug	36	53	11
	Sep	39	50	11
	Sep	40	47	14
	Sep	35	54	10
	Nov	49	39	11
	Dec	46	44	10
1992	Jan	46	43	11
	Feb	42	47	11
	Mar	51	39	11
	May	22	70	7
	May	18	74	8
	Jul	20	70	9
	Aug	38	47	15
	Sep	37	50	13
	Oct	42	45	13
	Nov	53	37	10
	Nov	48	40	12
1993	Jan	37	50	13
	Jan	40	46	14
	Feb	40	46	14
	Apr	48	40	12

cont'd . . .

		United	Divided	DK
	May	42	45	13
	May	47	40	13
	Jul	42	45	12
	Aug	46	43	11
	Sep	35	52	13
	Sep	36	50	14
	Nov	43	44	13
	Dec	47	39	15
1994	Jan	47	37	16
	Jan	55	32	13
	Feb	52	32	16
	Apr	51	33	15
	May	55	30	15
	May	59	30	11
	Jun	51	38	11
	Jul	62	27	11
	Sep	55	32	13
	Sep	51	31	18
	Oct	54	32	14
	Dec	58	29	13
1995	Jan	57	32	11
	Jan	44	43	13
	Feb	49	37	14
	Mar	54	34	11
	May	53	35	12
	Jun	59	28	14
	Jul	63	26	11
	Jul	55	33	11
	Sep	44	45	11
	Sep	35	49	16
	Oct	37	49	15
	Oct	53	33	14
	Dec	54	33	13
1996	Jan	55	31	14
	Feb	44	45	11
	Mar	51	38	11
	Mar	47	38	15
	May	50	38	12
	Jun	44	43	13
	Jun	37	48	14
	Aug	37	51	13
	Sep	33	55	11
	Sep	29	58	14

cont'd . . .

		United	Divided	DK
	Sep	34	55	11
	Nov	48	39	12
	Nov	47	40	13
1997	Jan	60	35	5
	Feb	56	36	8
	Mar	61	34	4
	Apr	64	28	8
	Apr	56	32	12
	Jun	85	10	5
	Jul	84	11	5
	Aug	79	16	4
	Sep	74	22	4
	Sep	75	20	5
	Nov	75	20	6
	Dec	71	23	5
1998	Jan	54	41	4
	Feb	58	37	5
	Mar	56	37	7
	Apr	61	33	5
	Apr	68	25	7
	May	66	28	6
	Jun	62	31	7
	Aug	56	38	7
	Sep	58	34	8
	Sep	55	38	6
	Oct	60	33	6
	Nov	54	38	8
1999	Jan	40	50	10
	Feb	48	43	9
	Mar	50	41	9
	Apr	62	30	8
	Apr	59	34	7
	May	56	37	7
	Jun	50	42	7
	Jul	49	45	6
	Aug	51	42	7
	Sep	54	39	7
	Oct	54	41	6
	Nov	56	36	8
2000	Jan	55	36	10
	Feb	50	41	9
	Mar	37	57	6
	Apr	46	48	6

cont'd . . .

		United	Divided	DK
	May	45	46	8
	Jun	43	45	11
	Jul	31	62	7
	Aug	40	54	6
	Sep	38	55	6
	Sep	36	58	7
	Nov	42	49	9
2000	Dec	51	43	7

A Prior to 1971 question read: 'Do you think the Labour Party at the present time is a united party or still rather at loggerheads?'

TABLE 2.3: BEST PARTY TO HANDLE SPECIFIC PROBLEMS 1945–2000

GENERAL ISSUES

Q. *Which party do you think can best handle the problem, or isn't there much to choose between them on the issue of the differences between the well-to-do and ordinary people?*

		Cons	Lab	Lib	Nothing	DK
1959	Sep	24	17	2	34	25
1964	Oct	23	28	6	18	25
1966	Mar	22	29	4	18	27

Q. *Which party in this country do you think is doing the best job in getting its ideas across to the voters?*

		Cons	Lab	Lib	Other	DK
1951	Oct	35	41	3	4	17

Q. *Who do you think is putting their case across better to the voters – Conservative or Labour?*

		Cons	Lab	Lib	Other	DK
1963	Dec	27	44	4	0	25

Q. Which party do you think can do the best job in looking after people like yourself?

		Cons	Lab	Lib	Other	DK
1951	Dec	41	43.5	7	1	7.5
1952	Jan	38.5	44	6.5	2	9

Q. Which (political) party do you think is best for people like yourself?

		Cons	Lab	Lib	Other	DK
1952	Mar	36	43	10	2	9
	May	35.5	44.5	10	2	8
1952	Oct	36.5	45	8.5	1	9
1954	Aug	37	45	8	1	9
1955	Dec	40	43	7	1	9
1957	Sep	31	43	12	1	13
1959	Feb	33	41	10	1	15
	Apr	34	39	9	1	17
1959	Sep	41	39	7	0	13
1962	Jul	28	34	18	1	19
	Sep	28	37	20	1	14
1965	Jul	36	40	8	1	15
1968	Oct	44	29	11	3	13
1970	Dec	39	40	5	2	14

Q. Leaving on one side the question of which party you support, which party is best for people like yourself?

		Cons	Lab	Lib	Other	DK
1974	Feb	37	39	10	1	13
1974	Oct	32	40	11	1	16
1983	May	40	36	12	0	11
1983	Jun	36	30	20	1	13
1987	May	33	34	16	1	15
1987	Jun	36	37	14	1	11
1991	Oct	36	37	11	2	14
1991	Nov	35	37	11	2	15
1992	Jan	39	37	10	2	12

Q. Which party do you think can best handle the problem, or isn't there much to choose between them on the issue of choice of prime minister?

		Cons	Lab	Lib	Nothing	DK
1959	Sep	39	24	I	19	17
1964	Oct	31	33	4	14	18
1966	Mar	25	32	3	16	24

Q. Which party do you think can best handle the problem, or isn't there much to choose between them on the issue of having the best ministers and leaders?

		Cons	Lab	Lib	Nothing	DK
1959	Sep	42	24	2	16	16
1964	Oct	37	33	4	8	20
1966	Mar	28	35	3	14	20

Q. As of today, which political party – Conservative or Labour – do you think best serves the interests of …. ?

	Cons	Lab	No diff	DK
JANUARY 1965				
business and professional people	65	12	12	II
white collar workers	52	17	18	13
scientists and technologists	35	29	18	18
skilled workers	25	47	16	12
unskilled workers	15	59	14	12
people like yourself	32	43	15	10

Q. Which party do you think can be trusted most?

		Cons	Lab	Lib	Other	DK
1988	Aug	33	23	6	5	33
1988	Nov	28	24	10	2	36
1990	Jan	26	31	6	2	34
1991	Apr	29	24	12	3	33

Q. Which party do you think is most likely to keep its promises?

		Cons	Lab	Lib	Other	DK
1988	Aug	34	25	7	5	29
	Nov	26	26	12	1	35
1990	Jan	23	33	8	3	34
1991	Apr	26	26	12	2	34

Q. Which party do you think has most concern for the interests of people like yourself?

		Cons	Lab	Lib	Other	DK
1988	Aug	30	37	8	5	19
	Nov	28	40	13	1	16
1990	Jan	24	44	8	2	22
1991	Apr	26	40	13	2	18

Q. Which party do you think would do most to improve the standard of living of people like yourself?

		Cons	Lab	Lib	Other	DK
1988	Aug	36	33	8	4	19
1988	Nov	33	38	12	1	16
1990	Jan	28	42	5	2	22
1991	Apr	31	38	12	2	18

Q. Which party would be better able to handle problems here at home, the Conservatives or Labour, or wouldn't there be any difference between them on this?

		Cons	Lab	No diff	DK
1992	Feb	35	36	21	9

THE ECONOMY

Q. *Which party do you think can best handle the problem, or isn't there much to choose between them on the issue of maintaining the value of the £ sterling?*

	Cons	Lab	Lib	Nothing	DK
1959 Sep	49	17	1	12	21
1964 Oct	36	25	3	13	23
1966 Mar	34	28	3	14	21

Q. *Looking ahead for the next five years, which political party do you think will do the best job of keeping the country prosperous, Conservative, Labour or Liberal?*

	Cons	Lab	Lib	Other	DK
1957 Dec	34	34	9	2	21

Q. *Looking ahead for the next five years, which political party do you think will do the best job of keeping the country prosperous?*

	Cons	Lab	Lib	Other	DK
1962 Apr	30	23	23	1	23
1962 Jul	27	28	19	1	25

Q. *Which political party – the Conservative or Labour party – do you think would do the best job of keeping the country prosperous?*

	Cons	Lab	Lib	DK
1965 Apr	41	37	12	10
1965 Dec	35	40	11	14

Q. *Which party do you think can best handle the problem, or isn't there much to choose between them on the issue of increasing production, the country's prosperity?*

	Cons	Lab	Lib	Nothing	DK
1959 Sep	44	26	3	12	15
1964 Oct	39	32	4	9	16
1966 Mar	30	36	4	11	19

Q. *Which party do you think can best handle the problem, or isn't there much to choose between them on the issue of increasing export trade?*

		Cons	Lab	Lib	Nothing	DK
1959	Sep	43	23	3	14	17
1964	Oct	37	29	4	11	19
1966	Mar	33	32	3	12	20

Q. *Which party do you think can best handle the problem, or isn't there much to choose between them on the issue of nationalisation and private enterprise?*

		Cons	Lab	Lib	Nothing	DK
1959	Sep	37	33	4	7	19
1964	Oct	36	32	4	8	20
1966	Mar	29	35	3	10	23

Q. *Which party do you think is best for prosperity?*

		Cons	Lab	Lib	Other	DK
1962	Jun	35	27	14	0	24

Q. *Which of the political parties do you think has the most right to claim that it has forward looking plans for improving our standard of living and making the world a better place to live in?*

		Cons	Lab	Lib	None	DK
1961	Oct	29	27	12	14	18
1967	Oct	33	27	9	14	17

Q. *Which do you think would be better at maintaining prosperity, a Conservative government or a Labour government?*

		Cons	Lab	Same	DK
1964	Jan	37	38	8	17
1964	May	38.5	39.5	9	13
1970	Jul	36	39	5	20

Q. *Which government do you think should be better at maintaining prosperity – a Conservative government or a Labour government?*

	Cons	Lab	Same	DK
1964 Oct	47	34	4	15

Q. *Which party do you think has produced the best economic plan?*

	Cons	Lab	Lib	Other	DK
1965 Oct	26	42	3	1	28

Q. *Which party do you think can best handle the problem of maintaining prosperity?*

	Cons	Lab	Lib	Other	DK
1966 Mar	41	41	4	0	14
1968 Oct	50	25	3	2	20
1968 Nov	45	30	3	1	21

Q. *Which party do you think can best handle the problem, or isn't there much to choose between them, on the issue of the present economic situation?*

	Cons	Lab	Lib	Nothing	DK
1967 Oct	37	23	5	23	12

Q. *Which party do you think can best handle th problem, or isn't there much to choose between them, on the issue of getting the co-operation of big businesses and industry?*

	Cons	Lab	Lib	Nothing	DK
1968 Oct	62	16	1	10	11

Q. *Which party do you think can best handle the problem, or isn't there much to choose between them, on the issue of maintaining prosperity?*

	Cons	Lab	Lib	Nothing	DK
1969 Feb	41	19	3	24	13

Q. Which party do you think can best handle the problems of the present economic situation?

		Cons	Lab	Lib	Other	DK
1969	Oct	38	37	3	I	21
1970	Sep	44	29	I	I	25
1970	Oct	43	28	I	I	27
1971	Oct	36	35	3	I	25
1972	Oct	34	33	3	I	29
1973	Oct	24	29	16	I	30
1974	Feb	35	32	8	2	23
	Jul	31	29	10	3	27
	Oct	28	31	9	2	30
	Nov	29	29	6	2	24
1975	May	33	33	4	2	28
	May	37	27	3	2	31
1975	Oct	37	32	6	2	23

Q. Which party do you think would best handle each of the following four problems? (THE ECONOMY)

		Cons	Lab	Lib	Other	DK
1995	Oct	24	44	8	I	22

Q. I am going to read out a list of things that most people in Britain want. From this card would you tell me which party you think would be best at making Britain more prosperous?

		Cons	Lab	Lib	Other	No diff	DK
1979	May	46	29	7	I	7	10
1983	Jun	51	20	14	I	4	11
1987	Jun	51	25	11	I	5	8

Q. Irrespective of your own preferences, which party do you think would be most likely to improve your and your family's living standards?

		Cons	Lab	Lib	Other	DK
1987	Jun	40	32	15	I	13
	Jul	45	29	11	I	14
	Sep	44	30	11	I	14
	Dec	44	30	9	I	16
1988	Aug	43	33	7	I	16
1988	Dec	38	30	12	2	18

Q. I am going to read out a list of problems facing the country. Could you tell me for each of them which political party you personally think would handle the problem best? (HIGH INTEREST RATES)

		Cons	Lab	Lib	Green	Other	DK
1989	Dec	31	42	6	0	0	21
1990	Feb	23	45	6	0	0	25
	Apr	26	44	5	1	1	23
	Jul	30	41	4	0	0	25
	Sep	27	37	6	1	2	28
1990	Oct	31	37	8	0	0	23

Q. I am going to read out a list of problems facing the country. Could you tell me for each of them which political party you personally think would handle the problem best? (THE ECONOMY)

		Cons	Lab	Lib	Green	Other	DK
1989	Dec	40	36	6	0	0	18
1990	Feb	32	41	6	0	1	19
	Apr	33	40	7	1	1	19
	Jul	36	38	5	1	0	20
	Sep	35	33	7	1	1	23
1990	Oct	35	39	8	0	0	17

Q. Taking everything together, which party is presenting its case better, leaving on one side your own political preferences?

		Cons	Lab	Lib	Other	DK
1964	Jan	29	32	6	0	32
1970	Jul	23	38	11	1	27
1996	Feb	12	50	13	1	23
	Jul	16	47	10	1	26
	Sep	18	46	8	0	27
	Sep	14	47	17	1	21
	Nov	14	53	8	1	25
	Dec	16	55	7	1	22
1997	Jan	23	54	8	0	15
	Feb	20	52	7	1	21
1997	Mar	16	56	9	1	17

Q. Which party do you think can best handle the problem of high prices?

		Cons	Lab	Lib	Other	DK
1953	Sep	36	41	4	1	18
1954	Sep	36	43	6	1	14
1956	Sep	30	46	6	1	17
1957	Oct	26	37	10	0	27

Q. Which party do you think can best handle the problem of prices and cost of living?

		Cons	Lab	Lib	Other	DK
1959	Sep	43	37	5	0	15

Q. Which party is best for preventing the cost of living from rising?

		Cons	Lab	Lib	Other	DK
1965	Apr	30	33	7	1	29
1968	Oct	40	25	3	3	29

Q. Which party do you think can best handle the problem of prices and the cost of living?

		Cons	Lab	Lib	Other	DK
1970	Sep	40	29	2	0	29
	Oct	39	28	2	1	30
1971	Mar	30	37	3	2	28
	Apr	35	34	2	1	28
	Oct	26	43	3	2	26
1972	Oct	27	42	3	1	27
1973	Oct	16	35	16	1	32
1974	Feb	31	36	9	1	23
	Jul	27	36	11	3	23
	Oct	26	37	10	2	25
	Nov	26	41	6	2	25
1975	Mar	28	33	4	3	32
	May	37	28	4	2	29
1975	Oct	35	35	6	2	22

Q. Over the next two or three years, which party do you think will be best for keeping prices down?

	Cons	Lab	Lib	Other	DK
1964 Aug	32	39	5	0	23
1975 Jun	36	34	5	1	24

Q. Which party do you think is best for keeping prices down?

	Cons	Lab	Lib	Other	DK
1964 Aug	26	34	3	0	37
1970 Jul	32	19	3	1	45

Q. Which party do you think can best handle the problem, or isn't there much to choose between them, on the issue of preventing the cost of living from rising?

	Cons	Lab	Lib	Nothing	DK
1969 Feb	39	14	3	29	16

Q. Which party do you think can best handle the problem of controlling prices and incomes?

	Cons	Lab	Lib	Other	DK
1969 Apr	42	20	6	2	30

Q. Which party do you think can best handle the problem, or isn't there much to choose between them on the issue of prices and the cost of living?

	Cons	Lab	Lib	Nothing	DK
1959 Sep	41	38	4	9	8
1964 Oct	34	36	5	11	14
1966 Mar	32	35	3	15	15

Q. Which party do you think can best handle the problem of inflation?

		Cons	Lab	Lib	Other	DK
1973	Oct	19	27	13	1	40
1974	Feb	33	30	9	1	27
	Jul	29	27	9	3	32
	Oct	27	33	8	2	30
1974	Nov	27	39	5	2	27
1975	Mar	31	26	4	2	37
	May	37	24	4	2	33
1975	Oct	37	31	6	1	25

Q. I am going to read out a list of problems facing the country. Could you tell me for each of them which political party you personally think would handle the problem best? (INFLATION AND PRICES)

		Cons	Lab	Lib	Green	Other	DK
1991	May	44	32	10	0	0	14
	Jun	42	35	9	0	1	13
	Sep	44	30	8	0	0	16
	Sep	49	29	8	0	1	13
1991	Nov	42	35	7	0	1	15
1992	Jan	48	29	7	0	0	15
	Feb	46	31	6	0	1	15
	Mar	45	32	6	0	1	16
	Mar	42	28	9	0	0	20
	Mar	43	29	8	0	1	18
	Mar 31–Apr 1	45	27	9	0	1	18
	Apr 7/8	45	30	9	0	1	15
	Apr 10/11	54	25	6	0	0	15
	May	55	25	7	0	0	13
1993	Apr	42	38	5	0	0	14
	Nov	35	33	12	0	1	18
1994	Apr	32	42	9	0	1	16
	Aug	35	41	7	0	1	16
1995	Jan	30	45	4	0	1	20
	Sep	36	38	6	0	0	19
1996	Mar	37	39	6	0	0	17
	May	38	40	6	0	1	16
	Sep	40	36	5	0	1	18
1996	Dec	37	40	5	0	0	18
1997	Apr 4–4	42	36	5		0	16
	Apr 7–9	40	38	6		1	16
	Apr 10–13	43	34	6		1	16

cont'd . . .

		Cons	Lab	Lib	Green	Other	DK
	Apr 14–17	41	37	7		1	15
	Apr 18–21	43	34	6		1	15
	Apr 23–25	43	32	6		1	18
	Apr 29/30	39	36	7		1	17
	May 2/3	40	43	5		0	12
1998	Apr	33	50	4		0	12
2000	Jan	31	50	3		0	16
	May	36	45	4	0	1	13
2000	Sep	36	46	5	0	0	12

Q. Which parties do you think are particularly good at .....? Any others? (CONTROLLING INFLATION)

		Cons	Lab	Lib	Other	DK
1978	Jan	31	42	4	1	26
	Feb	30	44	3	1	27
	Mar	29	40	3	1	32
	Apr	28	42	3	1	30
	May	32	43	2	1	25
	Sep	32	37	2	1	30
	Nov	29	40	2	1	32
1979	Mar	36	30	3	2	31
	Apr	34	35	5	1	28
	Sep	28	41	3	2	30
1980	Feb	23	37	6	1	35
	May	30	36	4	1	32
1981	Jun	29	37	7	5	35
1981	Aug	28	25	13	1	36
1982	Feb	29	24	13	1	37
1982	Nov	54	19	8	0	20

Q. I am going to read out a list of things that most people in Britain want. From this card would you tell me which party you think would be best at keeping prices down?

		Cons	Lab	Lib	Other	No diff	DK
1979	May	30	38	6	1	15	10
1983	Jun	43	23	12	1	9	12

Q. Which party do you think has the best policies to deal with inflation and prices?

		Cons	Lab	Lib	Other	DK
1983	Apr	46	28	8	1	18
	May	52	23	8	0	17
1984	Mar	52	26	6	0	15
	Apr	55	23	6	1	16
	May	52	26	9	0	13
	Jun	49	24	10	0	16
	Jul	47	26	8	1	19
	Aug	47	26	8	0	19
	Sep	47	23	9	0	20
	Oct	52	21	8	1	18
	Nov	50	22	7	0	20
	Dec	48	22	12	0	18
1985	Jan	47	23	10	1	21
	Feb	43	23	13	1	21
	Mar	43	27	11	0	19
	Apr	44	26	11	1	18
	May	41	23	14	0	21
	Jun	41	25	13	0	21
	Jul	37	26	15	0	21
	Aug	34	29	14	0	23
	Sep	39	19	17	0	25
	Oct	41	25	13	1	21
	Nov	41	24	13	0	22
	Dec	45	22	14	0	20
1986	Jan	37	23	14	0	25
	Apr	41	27	11	1	19
	Jul	51	25	8	0	15
	Oct	55	19	8	0	18
1987	Jan	45	26	9	0	16
	Feb	50	20	12	0	18
	Mar	52	18	12	0	19
	Apr	51	17	13	0	19
	May	52	18	10	0	19
1989	May	40	25	5	0	29

Q. *Irrespective of your own preferences, which party do you think would be most likely to keep prices from rising too fast?*

		Cons	Lab	Lib	Other	DK
1987	Jun	49	24	13	o	13
	Jul	50	21	7	o	21
	Sep	49	25	9	I	16
1987	Dec	48	24	7	o	21
1988	Aug	47	26	6	o	20
1988	Dec	37	27	II	I	24

Q. *I am going to read out a list of problems facing the country. Could you tell me for each of them which political party you personally think would handle the problem best?* (INFLATION AND THE COST OF LIVING)

		Cons	Lab	Lib	Green	Other	DK
1989	Dec	38	41	6	o	I	15
1990	Feb	30	44	6	I	o	19
	Apr	33	41	7	I	I	17
	Jul	36	42	5	I	o	16
	Sep	31	35	9	I	I	23
1990	Oct	33	41	8	o	I	17

UNEMPLOYMENT

Q. *If unemployment should return, which party do you think could deal with the problem best?*

		Cons	Lab	Lib	Other	DK
1957	Oct	23	41	6	I	29

Q. *Which party do you think can best handle the problem of unemployment?*

		Cons	Lab	Lib	Other	DK
1959	Mar	30	40	2	1	27
1962	Jul	24	33	13	1	29
1971	Apr	31	40	2	1	26
	Oct	26	45	3	2	24
1972	Oct	28	43	3	1	25
1973	Oct	26	35	11	1	27
1974	Feb	33	38	7	1	21
	Jul	25	36	8	3	23
	Oct	24	43	8	2	23
	Nov	26	45	5	2	22
1975	Mar	31	36	4	2	27
	May	33	35	3	2	27
1975	Oct	35	36	6	1	22

Q. *Which party do you think can best handle the problem, or isn't there much to choose between them, on the issue of full employment, short-time working?*

		Cons	Lab	Lib	Nothing	DK
1959	Sep	36	39	2	14	9
1964	Oct	35	39	4	11	11
1966	Mar	29	41	3	13	14
1967	Oct	36	25	5	21	13
1968	Oct	34	27	3	28	8
1969	Feb	34	25	2	20	19

Q. *Over the next two or three years, which party do you think will be best for security of employment?*

		Cons	Lab	Lib	Other	DK
1964	Aug	34	43	4	0	19

Q. *I am going to read out a list of problems facing the country. Could you tell me for each of them which political party you personally think would handle the problem best?* (UNEMPLOYMENT)

		Cons	Lab	Lib	Green	Other	DK
1989	Dec	26	55	4	1	1	13
1990	Feb	24	56	6	1	1	13
	Apr	25	57	4	1	1	12

cont'd . . .

		Cons	Lab	Lib	Green	Other	DK
	Jul	23	56	4	1	0	15
	Sep	21	54	5	0	1	18
1990	Oct	21	55	8	0	1	16
1991	May	23	53	8	0	1	14
	Jun	20	57	7	0	1	14
	Sep	25	49	8	0	0	17
	Sep	26	49	7	0	1	15
	Nov	22	54	7	0	0	15
1992	Jan	24	53	7	0	0	15
	Feb	27	50	6	0	1	17
	Mar	23	52	7	0	1	17
	Mar	24	46	9	0	0	20
	Mar	25	49	8	0	1	17
	Mar 31– Apr 1	23	45	10	0	1	19
	Apr 7/8	26	48	11	0	1	15
	Apr 10/11	30	46	8	0	0	16
	May	29	52	7	0	1	12
1993	Apr	16	64	6	0	1	13
	Nov	13	61	10	0	1	16
1994	Apr	13	61	9	0	1	16
	Aug	13	67	6	0	1	13
1995	Jan	12	65	5	0	1	17
	Sep	15	61	4	0	0	18
1996	Mar	13	63	7	0	1	16
	May	15	66	5	0	1	13
	Sep	17	65	4	0	0	13
	Dec	15	63	4	0	0	17
1997	Apr 4–6	24	56	5	–	1	14
	Apr 7–9	24	53	5	–	1	17
	Apr 10–13	25	52	7	–	1	15
	Apr 14–17	26	53	6	–	1	15
	Apr 18–21	27	51	6	–	1	14
	Apr 23–25	25	49	7	–	1	18
	Apr 29/30	23	53	8	–	2	15
	May 2/3 1997	22	63	5	–	0	9
1998	Apr	18	66	5	–	0	10
2000	Jan	21	61	4	–	1	14
	May	21	61	5	0	1	12
2000	Sep	23	59	7	0	0	12

Q. *Which parties do you think are particularly good at .....? Any others?* (REDUCING UNEMPLOYMENT)

		Cons	Lab	Lib	Other	DK
1978	Jan	35	33	5	1	30
	Feb	34	35	4	1	31
	Mar	29	37	4	1	33
	Apr	31	36	4	2	32
	May	34	37	4	2	29
	Sep	41	30	3	2	28
1978	Nov	31	34	2	1	35
1979	Mar	39	28	4	2	31
	Apr	35	32	5	2	30
1979	Sep	24	43	3	1	32
1980	Feb	18	46	7	1	33
1980	May	22	44	5	2	32
1981	Jun	10	46	7	6	34
1981	Aug	14	43	14	1	33
1982	Feb	10	42	17	1	34
1982	Nov	18	41	11	1	32

Q. *I am going to read out a list of things that most people in Britain want. From this card would you tell me which party you think would be best at reducing unemployment?*

		Cons	Lab	Lib	Other	No diff	DK
1979	May	34	37	6	1	10	13
1983	Jun	28	33	16	1	12	10
1987	Jun	28	43	11	1	10	7

Q. *Which party do you think has the best policies to deal with unemployment?*

		Cons	Lab	Lib	Other	DK
1983	Apr	25	42	11	1	22
1983	May	28	42	10	0	21
1984	Mar	22	46	11	0	21
	Apr	23	42	9	1	26
	May	23	43	12	0	23
	Jun	22	45	12	0	21
	Jul	22	46	9	1	22
	Aug	20	45	10	0	24
	Sep	20	45	12	0	23
	Oct	23	39	13	1	25

		Cons	Lab	Lib	Other	DK
	Nov	26	41	11	0	22
	Dec	19	38	16	0	26
1985	Jan	19	40	16	1	24
	Feb	19	38	15	0	27
	Mar	17	47	13	0	22
	Apr	17	47	13	0	24
	May	16	42	18	0	24
	Jun	19	40	18	1	23
	Jul	15	45	17	0	21
	Aug	13	45	18	0	24
	Sep	16	34	24	0	26
	Oct	17	42	16	0	25
	Nov	18	40	15	0	26
	Dec	18	38	18	0	26
1986	Jan	14	42	18	1	25
	Apr	14	46	16	1	23
	Jul	15	48	13	0	24
	Oct	22	46	10	0	22
1987	Jan	21	46	12	1	21
	Feb	21	41	15	0	23
	Mar	24	38	17	0	21
	Apr	27	37	16	0	20
	May	25	38	15	1	21
1989	May	29	43	5	0	21

Q. Irrespective of your own preferences, which party do you think would be most likely to bring down unemployment?

		Cons	Lab	Lib	Other	DK
1987	Jun	28	42	16	0	14
	Jul	30	42	9	0	19
	Sep	30	40	12	1	18
	Dec	33	41	8	1	17
1988	Aug	35	40	6	0	18
1988	Dec	33	39	10	1	18

TAXATION

Q. Which party do you think can best handle the problem, or isn't there much to choose between them on the issue of income tax and other taxes?

		Cons	Lab	Lib	Other	DK
1959	Sep	40	32	3	13	12
1964	Oct	36	32	5	13	14
1966	Mar	30	31	4	17	18
1967	Oct	39	19	5	24	13

Q. Which party do you think can best handle the problem, or isn't there much to choose between them, on the issue of national insurance?

		Cons	Lab	Lib	Other	DK
1966	Mar	24	37	3	20	16

Q. I am going to read out a list of problems facing the country. Could you tell me for each of them which political party you personally think would handle the problem best? (TAXATION)

		Cons	Lab	Lib	Green	Other	DK
1991	May	42	33	10	0	1	13
	Jun	38	37	10	0	1	15
	Sep	40	33	8	0	0	19
	Sep	46	31	9	0	1	13
	Nov	39	35	9	0	0	16
1992	Jan	47	29	7	0	0	16
	Feb	44	31	7	0	1	17
	Mar	42	33	7	0	1	17
	Mar	42	32	9	0	0	16
	Mar	43	32	10	0	1	14
	Mar 31– Apr 1	41	30	12	0	1	16
	Apr 7/8	43	31	12	0	1	13
	Apr 10/11	49	29	9	0	0	12
1992	May	49	27	8	0	0	21
1993	Apr	33	42	7	1	0	17
	Nov	28	41	12	0	1	17
1994	Apr	21	46	11	0	1	21
	Aug	25	45	9	0	1	20
1995	Jan	24	45	7	0	1	23
	Sep	29	39	7	0	0	24

cont'd . . .

		Cons	Lab	Lib	Green	Other	DK
1996	Mar	27	45	8	0	0	19
	May	31	42	9	0	1	17
	Sep	33	39	7	0	1	20
	Dec	28	45	5	0	1	20
1997	Apr 4–6	34	39	10		1	17
	Apr 7–9	32	41	10		1	15
	Apr 10–13	31	40	12		1	16
	Apr 14–17	32	38	12		1	17
	Apr 18–21	33	37	13		1	16
	Apr 23–25	34	37	10		1	18
	Apr 29/30	32	39	12		1	16
1997	May 2/3	34	45	10		0	11
1998	Apr	32	49	7		1	12
2000	Jan	33	46	7		1	13
	May	38	40	6	0	1	14
2000	Sep	39	39	8	0	0	13

Q. Which parties do you think are particularly good at .....? Any others? (REDUCING TAXATION)

		Cons	Lab	Lib	Other	DK
1978	Jan	42	34	3	1	23
	Feb	36	33	3	1	30
	Mar	38	35	4	1	27
	Apr	36	38	5	1	25
	May	43	35	4	1	22
	Sep	47	29	3	1	23
	Nov	42	28	3	1	29
1979	Mar	47	22	4	2	29
	Apr	49	27	5	2	23
	Sep	50	25	3	1	25
1980	Feb	37	28	6	1	32
	May	44	29	5	1	26
1981	Jun	21	32	8	6	38
	Aug	23	30	12	1	37
	Feb	21	31	12	1	37
1982	Nov	35	30	8	0	29

Q. I am going to read out a list of things that most people in Britain want. From this card would you tell me which party you think would be best at cutting income tax?

		Cons	Lab	Lib	Green	Other	DK
1979	May	57	19	5	0	8	10
1983	Jun	37	23	10	1	11	19
1987	Jun	61	18	6	0	4	11

Q. Irrespective of your own preferences, which party do you think would be most likely to keep taxation as low as possible?

		Cons	Lab	Lib	Other	DK
1987	Jun	56	21	12	0	11
	Jul	56	20	7	0	17
	Sep	54	23	8	1	15
	Dec	57	21	6	0	16
1988	Aug	58	21	5	0	15
1988	Dec	52	23	9	1	16

Q. Could you tell me which political party you personally think would handle the problem of taxation best?

		Cons	Lab	Lib	Other	None	DK
2000	Dec	35	38	9	1	4	12

NATIONAL HEALTH SERVICE

Q. Which party do you think has the best policies to deal with the National Health Service?

		Cons	Lab	Lib	Other	DK
1983	Apr	24	45	9	1	21
	May	26	44	9	0	20
1984	Mar	20	52	11	0	17
	Apr	21	52	8	0	19
	May	23	51	11	0	15
	Jun	21	51	11	0	16
	Jul	20	52	11	0	17

cont'd . . .

		Cons	Lab	Lib	Other	DK
	Aug	19	53	11	0	16
	Sep	21	49	11	0	19
	Oct	25	47	10	0	18
	Nov	22	48	11	0	19
	Dec	20	49	14	0	16
1985	Jan	20	48	13	0	20
	Feb	17	48	15	0	19
	Mar	13	56	13	0	19
	Apr	14	54	11	1	20
	May	17	49	16	0	17
	Jun	17	48	16	0	18
	Jul	16	53	17	0	15
	Aug	12	52	18	0	19
	Sep	17	41	19	0	24
	Oct	16	48	14	0	21
	Nov	16	50	13	0	21
	Dec	17	46	17	0	21
1986	Jan	14	47	18	0	20
	Apr	13	54	13	1	19
	Jul	17	51	15	0	18
	Oct	19	51	11	0	20
1987	Jan	17	49	12	0	22
	Feb	19	48	14	1	19
	Mar	19	42	18	0	21
	Apr	20	42	16	0	21
	May	21	44	16	0	18
1989	May	17	52	8	1	23

Q. Which party do you think can best handle the problem, or isn't there much to choose between them, on the issue of the National Health Service?

		Cons	Lab	Lib	Other	DK
1959	Sep	28	44	4	16	8
1964	Oct	32	40	5	11	12
1966	Mar	25	45	4	13	13
1966	Mar	24	41	3	20	12

Q. Which party do you think can best handle the problem of the National Health Service?

		Cons	Lab	Lib	Other	DK
1970	Sep	36	42	2	0	20
	Oct	32	43	2	1	22
1971	Oct	28	48	3	1	20
1972	Oct	29	46	2	1	22
1973	Oct	23	42	11	0	24
1974	Feb	33	39	6	1	21
	Jul	31	36	8	2	23
	Oct	24	44	8	1	23
1974	Nov	29	47	5	1	18
1975	Mar	33	35	4	2	26
	May	34	39	4	1	22
1975	Oct	40	34	5	2	19

Q. I am going to read out a list of problems facing the country. Could you tell me for each of them which political party you personally think would handle the problem best? (THE NATIONAL HEALTH SERVICE)

		Cons	Lab	Lib	Green	Other	DK
1989	Dec	17	66	4	0	1	11
1990	Feb	12	67	6	1	0	14
	Apr	14	70	4	1	1	10
	Jul	14	68	4	0	0	13
	Sep	14	65	6	1	1	12
	Oct	14	65	9	0	0	12
1991	May	18	59	11	0	1	12
	Jun	18	58	10	0	1	12
	Sep	22	54	9	0	0	14
	Sep	23	52	10	0	1	13
	Nov	20	54	10	0	0	15
1992	Jan	25	53	7	0	0	14
	Feb	26	51	7	0	1	15
	Mar	24	53	8	0	1	14
	Mar	24	50	11	0	0	15
	Mar	25	52	10	1	1	11
	Mar 31–Apr 1	24	48	13	0	1	13
	Apr 7/8	26	51	11	0	0	11
	Apr 10/11	32	49	9	0	0	12
	May	27	54	9	0	1	10
1993	Apr	16	63	7	0	1	13
	Nov	13	62	12	0	1	12

cont'd . . .

		Cons	Lab	Lib	Green	Other	DK
1994	Apr	12	63	9	0	1	14
	Aug	12	67	8	0	1	13
1995	Jan	8	66	6	1	1	18
	Sep	11	64	6	1	0	18
1996	Mar	11	63	9	1	1	15
	May	10	67	8	1	1	13
	Sep	10	66	7	0	1	16
	Dec	13	65	6	0	0	15
1997	Apr 4–6	15	62	9	–	1	14
	Apr 7–9	18	58	8	–	1	15
	Apr 10–13	16	58	13	–	1	13
	Apr 14–17	16	60	10	–	1	13
	Apr 18–21	19	58	10	–	1	13
	Apr 23–25	18	55	11	–	2	14
	Apr 29/30	15	57	13	–	1	14
	May 2/3	14	68	10	–	1	8
1998	Apr	16	65	8	–	0	11
2000	Jan	23	50	9	–	0	18
	May	23	53	8	0	0	15
2000	Sep	27	52	9	0	0	12

Q. I am going to read out a list of things that most people in Britain want. From this card would you tell me which party you think would be best at providing properly for the Health Service?

		Cons	Lab	Lib	Other	No diff	DK
1983	Jun	25	42	17	1	5	11
1987	Jun	24	47	15	1	6	8

Q. Irrespective of your own preferences, which party do you think would be most likely to improve the quality of the Health Service?

		Cons	Lab	Lib	Other	DK
1987	Jun	24	44	20	0	12
	Jul	23	49	12	1	15
	Sep	23	49	13	1	14
	Dec	22	50	10	0	18
1988	Aug	17	53	9	1	20
1988	Dec	19	52	12	0	16

EDUCATION

Q. Which party do you think can best handle the following problems or isn't there much to choose between them on the issue of a satisfactory education system?

		Cons	Lab	Lib	Other	DK
1964	Oct	34	34	5	12	15
1966	Mar	29	33	4	15	19

Q. I am going to read out a list of problems facing the country. Could you tell me for each of them which political party you personally think would handle the problem best? (EDUCATIONAL STANDARDS)

		Cons	Lab	Lib	Green	Other	DK
1993	Nov	26	42	16	0	1	15

Q. Which party do you think has the best policies to deal with education and schools?

		Cons	Lab	Lib	Other	DK
1983	Apr	28	38	11	1	23
	May	35	36	10	0	20
1984	Mar	30	44	10	0	16
	Apr	31	39	9	0	20
	May	28	41	13	0	17
	Jun	30	41	12	0	17
	Jul	27	43	11	0	19
	Aug	26	44	12	0	17
	Sep	29	41	10	0	20
	Oct	35	35	10	1	19
	Nov	31	37	9	0	22
	Dec	28	37	15	0	20
1985	Jan	26	40	13	0	21
	Feb	23	41	17	0	20
	Mar	22	45	13	0	19
	Apr	21	45	14	1	19
	May	24	40	18	0	18
	Jun	23	41	18	0	18
	Jul	21	43	17	0	18
	Aug	18	42	21	0	20
	Sep	22	34	21	0	24
	Oct	22	39	16	0	22
	Nov	21	40	16	0	22
	Dec	22	38	18	0	22

cont'd . . .

		Cons	Lab	Lib	Other	DK
1986	Jan	17	40	19	1	23
	Apr	16	46	16	1	21
	Jul	23	42	16	0	17
	Oct	30	40	10	0	20
1987	Jan	25	40	13	0	22
	Feb	30	35	16	0	19
	Mar	25	34	19	0	21
	Apr	28	32	19	0	20
	May	30	32	18	0	19
1989	May	31	41	8	1	19

Q. Irrespective of your own preferences, which party do you think would be most likely to improve standards of education?

		Cons	Lab	Lib	Other	DK
1987	Jun	31	37	19	0	12
	Jul	35	31	14	0	21
	Sep	36	36	14	0	14
	Dec	37	36	10	0	17
1988	Aug	37	36	9	0	18
1988	Dec	35	35	13	1	17

Q. I am going to read out a list of problems facing the country. Could you tell me for each of them which political party you personally think would handle the problem best? (EDUCATION)

		Cons	Lab	Lib	Green	Other	DK
1989	Dec	29	48	7	1	0	14
1990	Feb	25	48	8	2	1	17
	Apr	25	51	8	1	1	13
	Jul	25	50	7	1	1	16
	Sep	26	45	9	1	1	18
1990	Oct	23	52	10	1	0	15

Q. Which party do you think can best handle the problem of education?

		Cons	Lab	Lib	Other	DK
1970	Sep	42	37	2	1	18
	Oct	38	40	2	0	20
1971	Oct	34	41	3	1	21
1972	Oct	33	37	3	1	26
1973	Oct	27	34	13	0	26
1974	Feb	38	31	6	1	24
	Jul	37	29	8	2	24
	Oct	35	33	8	1	23
	Nov	33	38	6	1	22
1975	Mar	40	31	3	1	25
	May	43	32	3	1	21
1975	Oct	44	33	4	1	18

Q. I am going to read out a list of problems facing the country. Could you tell me for each of them which political party you personally think would handle the problem best? (EDUCATION AND SCHOOLS)

		Cons	Lab	Lib	Green	Other	DK
1991	May	28	47	13	0	1	11
	Jun	25	49	11	0	1	13
	Sep	32	41	12	0	0	14
	Sep	31	42	12	0	1	14
	Nov	27	45	11	0	1	16
1992	Jan	33	44	8	0	0	14
	Feb	34	42	9	0	1	15
	Mar	30	43	11	0	1	15
	Mar	28	40	15	0	0	16
	Mar	27	41	19	1	1	12
	Mar 31–Apr 1	26	38	20	0	1	15
	Apr 7/8	27	41	20	0	1	11
	Apr 10/11	33	39	15	0	0	12
	May	31	43	14	0	0	12
1993	Apr	24	52	11	1	1	12
	Nov	19	49	17	0	1	15
1994	Apr	18	52	13	0	1	16
	Aug	17	56	11	0	1	15
1995	Jan	15	57	8	0	1	19
	Sep	18	51	11	1	0	19
1996	Mar	17	54	13	0	0	15
	May	18	57	12	0	1	12
	Sep	19	55	9	0	1	17
	Dec	18	59	9	0	0	14
1997	Apr 4–6	22	51	16	0	1	12

cont'd . . .

		Cons	Lab	Lib	Green	Other	DK
	Apr 7–9	22	48	17	–	1	12
	Apr 10–13	22	48	19	–	1	11
	Apr 14–17	21	47	20	–	1	12
	Apr 18–21	22	47	19	–	1	11
	Apr 23–25	22	44	20	–	1	14
	Apr 29/30	20	47	20	–	1	11
	May 2/3	15	59	18	–	0	7
1998	Apr	18	65	10	–	1	6
2000	Jan	25	53	9	–	1	12
	May	28	50	10	0	1	10
2000	Sep	29	50	11	0	0	10

Q. Which party do you think would best handle each of the following four problems? (EDUCATION)

		Cons	Lab	Lib	Other	DK
1995	Oct	18	50	13	2	17

Q. I am going to read out a list of things that most people in Britain want. From this card would you tell me which party you think would be best at providing children with a better education?

		Cons	Lab	Lib	Other	No diff	DK
1987	Jun	31	37	17	1	5	9

PENSIONS

Q. Which party do you think can best handle the problem of pensions and other social services?

		Cons	Lab	Lib	Other	DK
1957	Oct	20	52	8	0	20

Q. Which party do you think can deal best with the problem of pensions and retirement pay?

		Cons	Lab	Lib	Other	DK
1958	Nov	37	30	5	0	28

Q. *Which party do you think can best handle the problem of pensions?*

		Cons	Lab	Lib	Other	DK
1959	Sep	32	48	5	0	15

Q. *Which party do you think can best handle the problem, or isn't there much to choose between them, on the issue of pensions and the welfare of old people?*

		Cons	Lab	Lib	Nothing	DK
1959	Sep	26	48	5	12	9
1964	Oct	29	43	6	10	12
1966	Mar	24	46	5	12	13
1968	Oct	25	46	2	18	9
1969	Feb	30	35	4	19	11

Q. *Which party do you think is best for the welfare state?*

		Cons	Lab	Lib	Other	DK
1962	Jun	25	45	11	0	19

Q. *I am going to read out a list of problems facing the country. Could you tell me for each of them which political party you personally think would handle the problem best?* (PENSIONS)

		Cons	Lab	Lib	Green	Other	DK
1991	May	28	48	8	0	0	15
	Jun	25	52	8	0	1	14
	Sep	30	45	9	0	0	15
	Sep	33	43	8	0	1	15
	Nov	25	52	7	0	0	15
1992	Jan	30	46	5	0	0	18
	Feb	30	49	5	0	1	15
	Mar	27	48	6	0	1	18
	Mar	29	45	8	0	0	17
	Mar	28	46	7	0	1	18
	Mar 31–Apr 1	28	45	9	0	1	17
	Apr 7/8	29	47	8	0	0	15
	Apr 10/11	35	44	6	0	1	15
	May	31	48	6	0	0	15
1993	Apr	21	57	5	1	1	16

cont'd . . .

		Cons	Lab	Lib	Green	Other	DK
	Nov	14	59	10	0	1	16
1994	Apr	17	54	7	0	1	21
	Aug	16	58	7	0	1	18
1995	Jan	13	56	5	0	0	25
	Sep	19	52	5	0	0	24
1996	Sep	17	54	6	0	0	23
	Dec	16	59	5	0	1	19
1997	Apr 4–6	22	52	6	–	1	20
	Apr 7–9	22	48	7	–	1	21
	Apr 10–13	23	47	9	–	1	21
	Apr 14–17	22	50	9	–	1	19
	Apr 18–21	24	49	7	–	1	19
	Apr 23–25	25	47	8	–	1	19
	Apr 29/30	22	49	9	–	1	19
	May 2/3	19	61	7	–	0	13
1998	Apr	27	50	6	–	0	17
2000	Jan	26	49	6	–	0	19
	May	29	44	8	1	1	18
2000	Sep	31	44	10	0	0	15

Q. I am going to read out a list of problems facing the country. Could you tell me for each of them which political party you personally think would handle the problem best? (PENSIONS AND OTHER BENEFITS)

		Cons	Lab	Lib	Green	Other	DK
1989	Dec	17	64	5	0	0	13
1990	Feb	17	64	6	0	1	13
	Apr	18	65	4	1	0	11
	Jul	18	63	4	1	0	14
	Sep	17	62	7	0	1	14
1990	Oct	16	64	8	1	0	12

Q. Which party do you think would best handle each of the following four problems? (PENSIONS AND OTHER BENEFITS)

		Cons	Lab	Lib	Other	DK
1995	Oct	15	57	8	1	18

Q. Which parties do you think are particularly good at .....? Any others? (INCREASING PENSIONS)

		Cons	Lab	Lib	Other	DK
1978	Jan	33	51	6	1	20
	Feb	30	50	5	2	24
	Mar	30	49	4	1	25
	Apr	28	50	6	1	24
	May	31	51	5	3	20
	Sep	36	46	3	1	22
	Nov	30	49	4	1	23
1979	Mar	32	45	6	2	24
	Apr	34	48	6	1	21
	Sep	33	51	4	1	21
1980	Feb	25	52	8	1	24
	May	36	54	8	2	18
1981	Jun	16	50	9	6	28
	Aug	19	48	14	1	26
1982	Feb	19	46	17	1	27
1982	Nov	24	51	10	0	20

Q. I am going to read out a list of things that most people in Britain want. From this card would you tell me which party you think would be best at raising pensions?

		Cons	Lab	Lib	Other	No diff	DK
1979	May	26	47	5	1	13	10

Q. Irrespective of your own preferences, which party do you think would be most likely to look after Britain's pensioners?

		Cons	Lab	Lib	Other	DK
1987	Jun	23	47	18	1	11
	Jul	20	53	11	0	16
	Sep	22	52	12	1	13
	Dec	22	55	9	0	14
1988	Aug	19	55	8	1	17
1988	Dec	16	55	12	1	16

HOUSING

Q. Which do you think would handle the housing problem better, a Conservative, a Liberal or a Labour Government?

	Cons	Lab	Lib	Same	DK
1945 Jun	25	42	13	11	9

Q. Which party is best for handling the problem of housing?

	Cons	Lab	Lib	Other	DK
1965 Apr	32	41	5	0	22

Q. Which party do you think can best handle the problem of housing?

	Cons	Lab	Lib	Other	DK
1953 Sep	45	38	3	1	13
1954 Sep	46	38	4	1	11
1956 Sep	37	34	4	0	25
1957 Oct	33	37	6	1	23

Q. Which party do you think can best handle the problem, or isn't there much to choose between them, on the issue of housing and rents?

	Cons	Lab	Lib	Nothing	DK
1959 Sep	32	43	3	12	10
1964 Oct	31	41	4	9	15
1966 Mar	27	38	3	15	17
1969 Feb	34	28	2	21	14

Q. Over the next two or three years, which party do you think will be best for keeping rates/rents down?

	Cons	Lab	Lib	Other	DK
1964 Aug	25	46	3	0	26
1965 Jun	35	36	7	1	21

Q. *Which party do you think can best handle the problem of rates?*

		Cons	Lab	Lib	Other	DK
1966	Apr	35	34	5	1	25

Q. *Which parties do you think are particularly good at .....? Any others?* (BUILDING MORE HOUSES FOR OWNER-OCCUPIERS)

		Cons	Lab	Lib	Other	DK
1978	Jan	56	20	3	0	23
	Feb	55	19	3	1	26
	Mar	50	21	3	1	30
	Apr	51	22	4	1	26
	May	55	23	3	2	22
	Sep	52	24	3	1	24
	Nov	52	21	3	1	27
1979	Mar	52	20	4	1	26
	Apr	56	18	4	2	23
	Sep	52	23	3	1	25
1980	Feb	43	23	5	1	31
	May	52	24	5	1	24
1981	Jun	37	27	6	5	29
	Aug	35	26	11	1	30
1982	Feb	38	24	12	1	30
1982	Nov	42	25	7	0	28

LABOUR RELATIONS

Q. *Which party do you think can best handle the problem of strikes?*

		Cons	Lab	Lib	Other	DK
1956	Sep	27	43	4	2	24
1957	Oct	23	42	6	1	28

Q. *Which party do you think can best handle the problem, or isn't there much to choose between them, on the issue of strikes and trade disputes?*

		Cons	Lab	Lib	Nothing	DK
1959	Sep	28	40	3	15	14
1964	Oct	27	42	5	9	17
1966	Mar	22	39	2	16	21
1967	Oct	33	28	4	22	13
1968	Oct	30	33	2	25	10
1968	Nov	22	26	2	41	9

Q. *If there are threats of strikes on the part of postmen, electrical power workers and engineers, which party do you think could best handle the problem from the point of the country as a whole?*

		Cons	Lab	Lib	Other	DK
1964	May	29	39	2	1	29

Q. *Which party do you think has the best policies to deal with strikes and industrial disputes?*

		Cons	Lab	Lib	Other	DK
1983	Apr	43	29	7	0	20
	May	44	32	7	0	16
1984	Mar	43	33	7	0	16
	Apr	41	33	7	0	19
	May	40	33	9	0	17
	Jun	34	37	11	1	18
	Jul	33	40	7	0	20
	Aug	34	37	11	0	17
	Sep	33	37	9	0	21
	Oct	39	33	9	0	20
	Nov	41	31	8	0	21
	Dec	38	30	12	0	20
1985	Jan	35	32	11	1	21
	Feb	37	31	14	1	17
	Mar	39	37	10	0	14
	Apr	44	32	9	1	14
	May	41	30	14	0	15
	Jun	45	29	12	0	14
	Jul	39	30	13	0	18
	Aug	35	32	14	0	18
	Sep	38	27	15	0	20

cont'd . . .

		Cons	Lab	Lib	Other	DK
	Oct	40	28	12	0	19
	Nov	43	30	10	0	17
	Dec	44	30	11	0	15
1986	Jan	39	29	12	0	20
	Apr	40	34	10	1	15
	Jul	44	35	7	1	14
	Oct	45	31	7	0	17
1987	Jan	43	33	10	0	15
	Feb	42	27	11	0	19
	Mar	47	26	11	0	16
	Apr	46	26	11	0	16
	May	48	26	11	0	15
1989	May	46	28	6	1	19

Q. Which party do you think could best handle this kind of problem [workers setting up courts to punish people who go on working during unofficial strikes] – Conservative or Labour?

		Cons	Lab	Neither	DK
1966	Mar	28	36	15	21

Q. Which parties do you think are particularly good at .....? Any others? (IMPROVING LABOUR RELATIONS)

		Cons	Lab	Lib	Other	DK
1978	Jan	20	46	5	1	31
	Feb	19	49	5	1	31
	Mar	18	45	4	1	36
	Apr	17	50	4	1	32
	May	21	51	4	1	27
	Sep	25	44	4	1	30
	Nov	21	44	5	2	33
1979	Mar	26	36	5	2	35
	Apr	25	42	5	2	30
	Sep	20	47	4	1	31
1980	Feb	15	46	10	0	32
	May	20	49	9	1	27
1981	Jun	13	44	15	1	31
	Aug	13	45	15	1	31
1982	Feb	14	44	17	1	31
1982	Nov	19	45	14	1	27

Q. *Which party do you think can best handle the problem of trade unions?*

		Cons	Lab	Lib	Other	DK
1966	Mar	30	48	4	I	17

Q. *Which parties do you think are particularly good at .....? Any others?* (CONTROLLING THE UNIONS)

		Cons	Lab	Lib	Other	DK
1980	Feb	35	31	5	I	30
1980	May	48	32	5	I	19
1981	Jun	42	25	5	4	26
1981	Aug	38	24	9	I	29
1982	Feb	40	24	12	I	28
1982	Nov	51	22	7	I	22

Q. *Which party do you think can best handle the problem of strikes and industrial disputes?*

		Cons	Lab	Lib	Other	DK
1969	Apr	37	25	5	2	31
	May	33	23	4	2	38
	Jun	31	31	3	3	32
	Jul	32	26	4	2	36
	Oct	33	35	2	2	28
1970	Sep	37	32	I	I	29
	Oct	37	32	2	I	28
1971	Mar	38	35	2	2	23
	Apr	8	36	2	I	23
	Oct	34	41	3	2	20
1972	Oct	27	42	3	3	25
1973	Oct	20	37	12	0	31
1974	Feb	32	42	7	I	18
	Jul	25	46	7	3	19
	Oct	20	53	6	2	19
	Nov	24	50	4	2	20
1975	May	28	40	4	3	25
	May	32	35	3	3	27
1975	Oct	25	46	5	2	22

Q. Which party do you think can best handle the problem, or isn't there much to choose between them, on the issue of strikes and industrial disputes?

		Cons	Lab	Lib	Nothing	DK
1969	Feb	32	26	2	23	18

Q. Which party can best handle the problem of strikes and labour relations?

		Cons	Lab	Lib	Other	DK
1970	Jul	28	34	3	0	35

Q. Which party do you think can best handle the problem of industrial disputes?

		Cons	Lab	Lib	Other	DK
1966	Mar	30	48	3	1	18

Q. Which party do you think can best handle the problems of strikes and industrial disputes?

		Cons	Lab	Lib	Other	DK
1969	Jan	33	25	4	3	35

Q. I am going to read out a list of problems facing the country. Could you tell me for each of them which political party you personally think would handle the problem best? (STRIKES AND INDUSTRIAL DISPUTES)

		Cons	Lab	Lib	Green	Other	DK
1991	May	48	32	7	0	0	13
	Jun	45	34	7	0	0	13
	Sep	45	33	8	0	0	13
	Sep	49	31	7	0	1	12
	Nov	41	37	6	0	0	15
1992	Jan	49	33	5	0	0	12
	Feb	49	32	5	0	0	13
	Mar	46	30	6	0	1	16
	Mar	46	29	6	0	0	18
	Mar	45	32	7	0	1	15
	Mar 31– Apr 1	48	29	9	0	1	14

cont'd . . .

		Cons	Lab	Lib	Green	Other	DK
	Apr 7/8	48	30	8	0	0	14
	Apr 10/11	54	27	7	0	0	12
	May	56	27	6	0	0	11
1993	Apr	37	42	7	1	1	13
	Nov	32	44	9	0	1	15
1994	Apr	32	42	8	0	1	17
	Aug	27	46	8	0	1	18
1995	Jan	30	43	6	0	1	20
	Sep	32	40	5	0	0	23
1996	Mar	30	45	7	0	0	18
	May	32	44	6	0	1	17
	Sep	35	42	6	0	1	17
	Dec	31	45	4	0	1	18
1997	Apr 4–6	40	41	6	–	0	13
	Apr 7–9	36	40	6	–	1	17
	Apr 10–13	40	39	7	–	0	13
	Apr 14–17	39	39	8	–	0	14
	Apr 18–21	40	39	7	–	1	13
	Apr 23–25	41	35	7	–	1	17
	Apr 29/30	37	38	6	–	1	18
	May 2/3	37	46	6	–	0	10
1998	Apr	30	55	4	–	1	9
2000	Jan	31	51	3	–	0	14
	May	36	44	4	0	1	13
2000	Sep	36	45	6	0	0	12

Q. I am going to read out a list of things that most people in Britain want. From this card would you tell me which party you think would be best at cutting down strikes?

		Cons	Lab	Lib	Other	No diff	DK
1979	May	35	33	6	2	11	14
1983	Jun	51	20	11	1	7	11
1987	Jun	59	18	8	0	6	8

LAW AND ORDER

Q. Which party do you think can best handle the problem, or isn't there much to choose between them, on the issue of hanging and capital punishment?

		Cons	Lab	Lib	Nothing	DK
1959	Sep	24	18	3	31	24
1964	Oct	21	18	3	26	32
1966	Mar	26	21	2	24	27

Q. Which party do you think can best handle the problem of crime?

		Cons	Lab	Lib	Other	DK
1966	Mar	33	26	3	1	37

Q. Which party do you think has the best policies to deal with law and order?

		Cons	Lab	Lib	Other	DK
1983	Apr	46	22	6	0	25
	May	46	21	8	0	25
1984	Mar	52	22	6	0	20
	Apr	53	21	7	0	19
	May	50	21	9	0	20
	Jun	52	21	9	0	18
	Jul	50	23	7	0	20
	Aug	48	24	8	0	18
	Sep	48	23	8	0	22
	Oct	56	21	8	0	15
	Nov	56	19	7	0	19
	Dec	53	18	10	0	19
1985	Jan	52	20	8	1	19
	Feb	48	20	10	0	21
	Mar	49	24	8	0	19
	Apr	45	25	9	1	20
	May	46	21	11	0	22
	Jun	45	22	11	0	21
	Jul	42	23	11	0	23
	Aug	42	23	13	0	22
	Sep	42	17	14	0	26
	Oct	42	24	10	0	24
	Nov	47	22	11	0	20

cont'd . . .

		Cons	Lab	Lib	Other	DK
	Dec	46	18	12	0	24
1986	Jan	42	21	12	0	25
	Apr	40	27	10	1	22
	Jul	46	24	9	0	21
	Oct	48	22	8	0	21
1987	Jan	42	27	10	0	21
	Feb	45	21	12	0	22
	Mar	42	21	13	0	24
	Apr	45	19	14	0	22
	May	45	20	12	0	23
1989	May	47	24	6	0	27

Q. I am going to read out a list of problems facing the country. Could you tell me for each of them which political party you personally think would handle the problem best? (LAW AND ORDER)

		Cons	Lab	Lib	Green	Other	DK
1989	Dec	52	26	5	0	0	17
1990	Feb	50	30	4	0	1	16
	Apr	47	30	4	1	1	18
	Jul	44	30	5	0	1	20
	Sep	45	25	5	0	1	24
	Oct	45	27	7	0	0	21
1991	May	47	26	9	0	0	18
	Jun	41	29	9	0	1	20
	Sep	47	22	8	0	1	22
	Sep	45	25	8	0	1	21
	Nov	41	30	8	0	1	21
1992	Jan	46	24	7	1	1	22
	Feb	44	25	6	0	1	23
	Mar	44	23	7	0	1	25
	Mar	42	26	7	0	0	25
	Mar	42	27	8	0	1	21
	Mar 31–Apr 1	39	27	11	0	1	23
	Apr 7/8	41	29	10	0	1	20
	Apr 10/11	47	25	7	0	1	21
	May	46	23	7	0	1	23
1993	Apr	36	35	8	0	0	19
	Nov	29	34	12	0	1	25
1994	Apr	30	35	10	0	1	24
	Aug	27	40	9	0	1	23
1995	Jan	22	44	7	0	1	26

cont'd . . .

		Cons	Lab	Lib	Green	Other	DK
	Sep	29	36	6	I	0	28
1996	Mar	27	41	9	0	0	22
	May	32	39	8	0	I	20
	Sep	30	39	6	0	I	24
	Dec	29	43	5	0	0	22
1997	Apr 4–6	33	43	7	–	0	17
	Apr 7–9	31	42	7	–	I	20
	Apr 10–13	33	40	10	–	I	17
	Apr 14–17	32	41	7	–	I	19
	Apr 18–21	32	41	9	–	I	17
	Apr 23–25	31	39	9	–	I	20
	Apr 29/30	29	42	9	–	I	18
	May 2/3	26	53	8	–	0	12
1998	Apr	27	55	5	–	0	12
2000	Jan	34	44	5	–	I	16
	May	41	38	5	0	I	15
2000	Sep	43	40	6	0	0	II

Q. I am going to read out a list of problems facing the country. Could you tell me for each of them which political party you personally think would handle the problem best? (CREATING A MORE MORAL SOCIETY)

		Cons	Lab	Lib	Other	DK
1997	Apr 4–6	21	41	14	I	23
	Apr 7–9	18	42	15	2	25
	Apr 10–13	21	37	15	I	25
	Apr 14–17	20	39	15	I	25
	Apr 18–21	20	40	1	2	24
	Apr 23–25	21	37	16	1	25
1998	Apr	18	53	9	I	18
2000	Jan	23	45	10	I	21

Q. I am going to read out a list of problems facing the country. Could you tell me for each of them which political party you personally think would handle the problem best? (HONESTY AND HIGH STANDARDS IN PUBLIC LIFE)

		Cons	Lab	Lib	Green	Other	DK
1997	Apr 4–6	16	42	14	–	1	27
	Apr 7–9	16	40	14	–	1	28
	Apr 10–13	18	35	19	–	2	25
	Apr 14–17	16	36	18	–	1	30
	Apr 18–21	18	38	16	–	1	26
	Apr 23–25	19	36	14	–	1	29
1998	Apr	14	53	11	–	1	22
2000	Jan	18	41	11	–	1	29

Q. I am going to read out a list of problems facing the country. Could you tell me for each of them which political party you personally think would handle the problem best? (LAW AND ORDER AND CRIME)

		Cons	Lab	Lib	Green	Other	DK
1993	Nov	32	37	11	0	1	19

Q. Which party do you think would best handle each of the following four problems? (LAW AND ORDER)

		Cons	Lab	Lib	Other	DK
1995	Oct	29	39	8	1	22

Q. Which parties do you think are particularly good at .....? Any others? (MAINTAINING LAW AND ORDER)

		Cons	Lab	Lib	Other	DK
1978	Jan	42	28	5	1	33
	Feb	42	30	5	1	33
	Mar	42	29	6	1	34
	Apr	39	32	6	3	33
	May	46	30	6	3	28
	Sep	46	28	5	2	30
	Nov	44	27	5	2	30
1979	Mar	48	20	5	3	33
	Apr	49	27	7	3	23

cont'd . . .

		Cons	Lab	Lib	Other	DK
1979	Sep	53	23	4	2	26
1980	Feb	43	30	9	1	29
	May	54	28	8	2	23
1981	Jun	41	24	8	6	32
	Aug	39	23	15	1	31
1982	Feb	43	24	18	2	29
1982	Nov	39	23	15	1	31

Q. I am going to read out a list of things that most people in Britain want. From this card would you tell me which party you think would be best at reducing crime and vandalism?

		Cons	Lab	Lib	Other	No diff	DK
1979	May	48	17	4	2	14	15
1983	Jun	38	17	11	2	15	18
1987	Jun	31	25	11	1	18	13

Q. Irrespective of your own preferences, which party do you think would be most likely to reduce crime?

		Cons	Lab	Lib	Other	DK
1987	Jun	36	27	14	1	23
	Jul	38	21	7	0	34
	Sep	41	23	9	1	26
	Dec	41	20	5	1	33
1988	Aug	39	23	6	0	32
	Dec	41	21	8	1	29

Q. Could you tell me which political party you personally think would handle the problem of law and order best?

		Cons	Lab	Lib	Other	None	DK
2000	Dec	36 ·	34	6	0	9	15

IMMIGRATION

Q. Which party has the best policy for dealing with the problem of coloured immigrants?

		Cons	Lab	Lib	Other	DK
1964	May	22	19	1	0	57

Q. Which party do you think can best handle the following problems, or isn't there much to choose between them, on the issue of immigration of coloured people?

		Cons	Lab	Lib	Nothing	DK
1964	Oct	30	20	3	19	28
1966	Mar	26	26	3	20	25
1969	Feb	44	16	2	20	18

Q. Which party do you think can best handle the problem of coloured people or isn't there much to choose between them on this issue?

		Cons	Lab	Lib	Nothing	DK
1968	May	18	8	2	60	12
1969	Feb	40	15	2	21	22

Q. Which party do you think can best handle the problem of immigration?

		Cons	Lab	Lib	Other	DK
1966	Mar	34	33	4	0	29
1972	Oct	33	25	3	2	37
1973	Oct	29	27	13	1	30
1974	Feb	35	24	6	2	33
	Jul	33	22	8	3	34
	Oct	31	25	8	3	33
	Nov	30	29	5	3	33
1975	Mar	33	24	4	3	36
	May	34	24	5	4	33
1975	Oct	39	24	7	2	28

Q. *Which parties do you think are particularly good at .....? Any others?* (IMPROVING RACE RELATIONS)

		Cons	Lab	Lib	Other	DK
1978	Jan	23	34	7	2	41
	Feb	27	35	8	2	34
	Mar	29	33	6	2	37
	Apr	26	38	7	1	34
	May	28	37	6	2	33
	Sep	27	35	6	1	37
	Nov	24	34	7	3	39
1979	Mar	25	29	7	2	41
	Apr	27	38	8	3	32
	Sep	25	37	7	2	38
1980	Feb	18	40	10	1	38
	May	24	37	13	2	36
1981	Jun	15	30	12	8	41
	Aug	16	29	20	1	42
1982	Feb	18	30	21	1	40
1982	Nov	21	34	13	1	37

Q. *Which parties do you think are particularly good at .....? Any others?* (CONTROLLING IMMIGRATION

		Cons	Lab	Lib	Other	DK
1978	Feb	53	22	3	4	23
	Mar	53	22	3	2	25
	Apr	52	22	3	4	24
	May	52	25	4	3	22
	Sep	53	24	4	3	22
	Nov	49	22	4	3	26
1979	Mar	51	17	3	3	29
	Apr	51	22	5	3	23
	Sep	54	22	4	3	24
1980	Feb	47	23	6	3	26
	May	54	20	5	3	23
1981	Jun	45	18	7	5	29
	Aug	41	19	10	3	32
1982	Feb	42	18	11	3	32
1982	Nov	42	20	8	3	30

DEMOCRACY

Q. *Which party do you think can best handle the problem, or isn't there much to choose between them on the issue of personal freedom from restrictions and controls?*

		Cons	Lab	Lib	Nothing	DK
1959	Sep	41	23	6	13	17
1964	Oct	34	25	6	14	21
1966	Mar	31	26	4	17	22

Q. *Which parties do you think are particularly good at .....? Any others?* (PROTECTING PEOPLE'S PRIVACY)

		Cons	Lab	Lib	Other	DK
1978	Feb	44	23	5	1	34
	Mar	38	23	4	2	39
	Apr	38	27	6	2	36
	May	46	26	6	2	29
	Sep	45	24	6	1	33
	Nov	39	23	5	1	39
1979	Mar	43	19	7	2	37
	Apr	43	22	8	3	34
	Sep	39	26	8	1	35
1980	Feb	29	27	11	2	42
	May	40	26	10	2	36
1981	Jun	29	23	10	7	40
1981	Aug	29	22	17	1	41
1982	Feb	31	23	21	1	40
1982	Nov	35	23	10	1	38

Q. *Which parties do you think are particularly good at .....? Any others?* (PROTECTING FREEDOM OF SPEECH)

		Cons	Lab	Lib	Other	DK
1978	Feb	40	33	8	2	31
	Mar	38	31	7	3	34
	Apr	37	32	9	3	34
	May	44	32	10	3	26
	Sep	41	31	7	2	31
	Nov	39	31	8	3	34
1979	Mar	41	24	10	4	33
	Apr	42	29	11	4	31

cont'd . . .

		Cons	Lab	Lib	Other	DK
	Sep	41	34	11	3	31
1980	Feb	30	34	15	2	35
	May	42	36	16	3	28
1981	Jun	30	31	13	9	33
	Aug	31	29	24	2	35
1982	Feb	32	35	29	3	29
1982 .	Nov	38	32	19	2	28

Q. I am going to read out a list of things that most people in Britain want. From this card would you tell me which party you think would be best at: (A: MAKING GOVERNMENT MORE DEMOCRATIC; B: PROTECTING INDIVIDUAL FREEDOM AND RIGHTS)

		Cons	Lab	Lib	Other	No diff	DK
A	1987 Jun	29	25	27	1	6	13
B	1987 Jun	35	30	17	2	6	9

Q. Irrespective of your own preferences, which party do you think would be most likely to make Britain more democratic?

		Cons	Lab	Lib	Other	DK
1987	Jun	33	28	24	1	15
	Jul	30	25	21	0	23
	Sep	34	25	22	1	18
	Dec	33	28	16	0	22
1988	Aug	30	28	17	1	24
1988	Dec	28	27	20	1	23

EUROPE

Q. Which party can best handle Britain's negotiations about going into the Common Market?

		Cons	Lab	Lib	Other	DK
1962	Aug	32	22	11	3	32

Q. Which party do you think can best handle the problem of Europe and the Common Market?

		Cons	Lab	Lib	Other	DK
1966	Mar	42	29	5	0	24

Q. Which party do you think can best handle the problems of Britain and the European Common Market?

		Cons	Lab	Lib	Other	All equal	DK
1966	Dec	36	30	5	1	14	14
1967	Feb	29	39	4	0	14	14
1967	May	33	31	4	1	17	14

Q. Which party do you think can best handle the problems of Britain and the Common Market?

		Cons	Lab	Lib	Other	DK
1969	Oct	36	24	2	1	37
1971	May	30	31	3	1	35

Q. If we are to join the Common Market which party do you think can best handle the problem of entry?

		Cons	Lab	Lib	Other	DK
1971	Jun	35	30	1	2	32

Q. Which party do you think can best handle the problem of the Common Market?

		Cons	Lab	Lib	Other	DK
1970	Sep	41	23	1	1	29
	Oct	36	19	2	0	43
1971	Oct	37	32	3	1	27
1972	Oct	41	27	2	1	29
1973	Oct	26	28	12	0	34
1974	Jul	37	28	7	2	26
	Oct	34	31	9	1	25
	Nov	34	34	5	1	26
1975	Mar	35	35	3	1	26

cont'd . . .

		Cons	Lab	Lib	Other	DK
	May	42	26	3	2	27
1975	Oct	41	28	5	I	25

Q. I am going to read out a list of problems facing the country. Could you tell me for each of them which political party you personally think would handle the problem best? (THE CHANGES TAKING PLACE IN EASTERN EUROPE)

		Cons	Lab	Lib	Green	Other	DK
1990	Feb	32	34	6	I	I	26
	Apr	37	29	5	2	0	26
	Jul	37	31	4	I	I	26
	Sep	46	24	4	I	I	25
1990	Oct	35	28	6	0	I	30

Q. I am going to read out a list of problems facing the country. Could you tell me for each of them which political party you personally think would handle the problem best? (EUROPE)

		Cons	Lab	Lib	Green	Other	DK
1992	May	53	19	7	0	0	20
1993	Apr	38	28	11	0	I	22
	Nov	37	26	12	I	I	24
1994	Apr	30	32	12	0	I	24
	Aug	27	39	10	0	I	22
1995	Jan	25	36	8	I	I	29
	Sep	31	31	8	I	0	29
1996	Mar	29	37	9	0	I	24
	May	29	37	10	0	I	23
	Sep	32	35	8	0	I	24
	Dec	24	41	5	I	2	27
2000	May	37	39	7	0	I	17
2000	Sep	42	36	8	0	0	13

Q. I am going to read out a list of things that most people in Britain want. From this card would you tell me which party you think would be best at standing up for Britain's interests in the EEC?

		Cons	Lab	Lib	Other	No diff	DK
1979	May	37	34	5	2	7	15
1983	Jun	60	15	12	I	4	11

Q. Which party do you think has the best policies to deal with the Common Market?

		Cons	Lab	Lib	Other	DK
1983	Apr	40	29	7	1	24
	May	42	29	8	0	20
1984	Mar	44	27	8	1	21
	Apr	42	26	7	1	25
	May	41	25	11	0	23
	Jun	41	26	12	1	20
	Jul	42	26	10	1	22
	Aug	40	27	10	1	23
	Sep	43	25	11	0	21
	Oct	46	22	8	1	23
	Nov	44	24	8	0	24
	Dec	47	21	11	0	21
1985	Jan	40	23	10	1	25
	Feb	38	23	13	1	25
	Mar	40	24	9	0	28
	Apr	38	26	11	0	25
	May	40	23	12	0	25
	Jun	37	25	13	0	24
	Jul	35	23	13	0	28
	Aug	33	25	13	0	29
	Sep	34	20	14	0	31
	Oct	35	24	10	0	31
	Nov	39	21	11	1	28
	Dec	39	18	12	0	31
1986	Jan	29	24	14	0	32
	Apr	32	26	12	0	29
	Jul	37	25	10	0	28
	Oct	37	20	8	0	36
1987	Jan	33	22	10	0	34
	Feb	34	21	12	0	32
	Mar	35	20	13	0	33
	Apr	38	19	12	0	31
	May	42	18	11	0	28
1989	May	39	21	6	2	32

Q. I am going to read out a list of problems facing the country. Could you tell me for each of them which political party you personally think would handle the problem best? (BRITAIN'S RELATIONS WITH EUROPE)

		Cons	Lab	Lib	Green	Other	DK
1989	Feb	39	34	8	I	I	17
1990	Feb	31	38	7	2	I	22
	Apr	38	33	8	2	0	19
	Jul	38	36	6	I	0	19
	Sep	46	27	7	I	I	18
	Oct	39	31	9	I	0	21
1991	May	52	23	8	I	I	14
	Jun	50	24	9	I	I	16
	Sep	54	22	7	I	0	15
	Sep	53	21	9	I	I	15
	Nov	42	27	10	I	I	19
1992	Jan	50	23	9	I	0	18
	Feb	53	23	7	I	I	17
	Mar	47	23	8	0	I	21
	Mar	49	22	10	I	0	18
	Mar	47	25	10	0	I	17
	Mar 31–Apr I	45	22	15	I	I	17
	Apr 7/8	46	26	12	0	0	15
	Apr 10/11	55	21	8	I	0	15
1997	Apr 4–6	33	41	6	–	I	19
	Apr 7–9	33	36	9	–	2	20
	Apr 10–13	35	34	9	–	I	21
	Apr 14–17	31	36	11	–	2	20
	Apr 18–21	33	36	5	–	2	21
	Apr 23–25	35	33	9	–	2	22
	Apr 29/30	33	36	9	–	2	19
	May 2/3	30	47	8	–	I	14
1998	Apr	22	62	6	–	0	10
2000	Jan	30	49	6	–	I	14

DEFENCE

Q. I am going to read out a list of problems facing the country. Could you tell me for each of them which political party you personally think would handle the problem best? (DEFENCE)

		Cons	Lab	Lib	Other	No diff	DK
1989	Dec	50	27	6	1	0	15
1990	Feb	44	31	6	2	1	17
	Apr	44	28	6	2	1	19
	Jul	43	30	5	2	0	20
	Sep	55	23	5	2	1	16
1990	Oct	46	28	8	2	0	16

Q. Which party do you think can best handle the problem of the H-bomb?

		Cons	Lab	Lib	Other	DK
1956	Sep	35	24	4	2	35
1957	Oct	27	27	8	2	36
1964	Mar	34	26	4	1	35

Q. Which party do you think can best handle the problem, or isn't there much to choose between them, on the issue of the H-bomb?

		Cons	Lab	Lib	Nothing	DK
1959	Sep	32	25	3	20	20
1964	Oct	37	21	3	12	27
1966	Mar	22	22	3	21	32

Q. Who do you think is getting the best of the arguments on defence – the Conservatives or Labour?

		Cons	Lab	Neither	DK
1964	May	25	23	22	30

Q. *Which party do you think can best handle the problem of defence?*

		Cons	Lab	Lib	Other	DK
1970	Sep	43	27	1	1	28
	Oct	39	26	1	1	33
1971	Oct	35	28	2	1	34
1972	Oct	33	26	2	1	38
1973	Oct	29	26	9	0	36
1974	Feb	36	24	4	1	35
	Jul	32	22	6	2	38
	Oct	34	25	6	1	34
	Nov	33	31	3	1	32
1975	Mar	34	25	3	1	37
	May	39	25	2	1	33
1975	Oct	39	26	4	1	30

Q. *Which party do you think can best handle the problem, or isn't there much to choose between them, on the issue of armaments and national defence?*

		Cons	Lab	Lib	Nothing	DK
1959	Sep	35	21	2	20	22
1964	Oct	37	26	4	11	22
1966	Mar	27	26	2	18	27

Q. *I am going to read out a list of problems facing the country. Could you tell me for each of them which political party you personally think would handle the problem best?* (BRITAIN'S DEFENCE)

		Cons	Lab	Lib	Green	Other	DK
1991	May	61	18	6	1	0	13
	Jun	55	21	8	1	1	16
	Sep	54	19	7	1	0	18
	Sep	56	20	7	1	1	16
	Nov	48	26	8	1	0	18
1992	Jan	56	18	8	1	0	17
	Feb	57	20	5	0	0	18
	Mar	56	19	5	0	1	19
	Mar	53	18	8	1	0	20
	Mar	52	24	7	1	1	20
	Mar 31–Apr 1	51	21	9	0	1	18
	Apr 7/8	52	22	8	1	0	17
	Apr 10/11	59	18	5	1	0	16

cont'd . . .

		Cons	Lab	Lib	Green	Other	DK
1992	May	59	18	6	0	0	16
1993	Apr	42	31	8	1	0	18
	Nov	32	33	14	1	1	20
1994	Apr	34	31	12	0	1	23
	Aug	27	37	10	1	2	24
1995	Jan	32	32	8	1	1	26
	Sep	38	26	8	1	0	26
1996	Mar	33	31	9	1	0	26
	May	38	29	9	0	1	24
	Sep	43	28	7	0	0	22
	Dec	39	30	5	0	0	25
1997	Apr 4–6	45	29	6	–	1	19
	Apr 7–9	42	30	6	–	1	21
	Apr 10–13	46	30	7	–	1	17
	Apr 14–17	45	29	6	–	1	19
	Apr 18–21	44	28	6	–	1	21
	Apr 23–25	43	27	7	–	1	22
	Apr 29/30	39	30	7	–	1	23
	May 2/3	39	37	7	–	1	16
1998	Apr	38	42	4	–	0	15
2000	Jan	38	39	4	–	1	18
	May	45	32	4	0	1	17
2000	Sep	46	35	4	0	0	14

Q. I am going to read out a list of things that most people in Britain want. From this card would you tell me which party you think would be best at ensuring that Britain is safely defended?

		Cons	Lab	Lib	Other	No diff	DK
1983	Jun	61	15	12	1	4	9
1987	Jun	60	19	11	0	4	7

Q. I am going to read out a list of things that most people in Britain want. From this card would you tell me which party you think would be best at help to bring about disarmament?

		Cons	Lab	Lib	Other	No diff	DK
1987	Jun	20	54	10	1	4	11

Q. *Irrespective of your own preferences, which party do you think would be most likely to give Britain an effective defence?*

		Cons	Lab	Lib	Other	DK
1987	Jun	57	17	14	0	11
	Jul	67	13	8	0	11
	Sep	63	17	8	1	12
	Dec	63	18	5	0	14
1988	Aug	63	18	4	1	14
1988	Dec	63	16	6	1	15

Q. *Which party do you think has the best policies to deal with Britain's defence?*

		Cons	Lab	Lib	Other	DK
1983	Apr	48	22	8	1	21
	May	51	23	9	0	18
1984	Mar	54	22	7	0	16
	Apr	50	23	8	0	19
	May	50	24	10	0	15
	Jun	. 49	23	11	0	16
	Jul	52	23	8	0	16
	Aug	48	24	10	0	24
	Sep	51	23	8	0	17
	Oct	56	18	10	0	16
	Nov	55	21	9	0	15
	Dec	49	21	15	0	15
1985	Jan	50	21	11	1	17
	Feb	49	21	12	0	17
	Mar	46	25	11	0	18
	Apr	46	23	11	0	20
	May	44	24	12	0	19
	Jun	48	22	12	0	18
	Jul	44	20	15	0	22
	Aug	43	24	15	0	18
	Sep	43	19	16	0	23
	Oct	44	22	12	0	21
	Nov	47	21	11	0	21
	Dec	48	20	13	0	19
1986	Jan	40	23	14	0	23
	Apr	39	27	14	0	19
	Jul	47	26	11	0	17
	Oct	48	22	11	0	19
1987	Jan	46	26	11	0	17

cont'd . . .

		Cons	Lab	Lib	Other	DK
	Feb	46	23	15	0	16
	Mar	46	21	16	0	16
	Apr	49	20	15	0	15
	May	51	17	13	1	18
1989	May	51	22	7	1	19

INTERNATIONAL AFFAIRS

Q. Which party do you think can best handle the problem of representing Britain at summit talks?

		Cons	Lab	Lib		DK
1959	Sep	52	23	2	0	23

Q. Which party do you think can best handle the problem, or isn't there much to choose between them, on the issue of Britain's reputation abroad?

		Cons	Lab	Lib	Nothing	DK
1959	Sep	45	21	3	16	15
1964	Oct	41	23	4	15	17
1966	Mar	36	27	3	14	20

Q. Which party do you think can best handle the problem, or isn't there much to choose between them, on the issue of colonial policy?

		Cons	Lab	Lib	Nothing	DK
1959	Sep	28	21	2	14	35

Q. Which party do you think can best handle the problem, or isn't there much to choose between them, on the issue of foreign affairs?

		Cons	Lab	Lib	Nothing	DK
1959	Sep	43	21	3	14	19
1964	Oct	40	23	4	12	21
1966	Mar	33	26	2	14	25

Q. *Irrespective of your own preferences, which party do you think would be most likely to contrtibute most to world peace?*

		Cons	Lab	Lib	Other	DK
1987	Jun	41	29	15	1	15
	Jul	42	26	11	1	20
	Sep	38	30	13	1	18
	Dec	44	29	9	1	17
1988	Aug	42	28	7	2	21
1988	Dec	40	28	10	3	20

Q. *Which party do you think is best for keeping peace?*

		Cons	Lab	Lib	Other	DK
1962	Jun	32	28	13	0	27
1968	Oct	33	29	4	1	33

Q. *Which party do you think is best for maintaining Britain's position in the world?*

		Cons	Lab	Lib	Other	DK
1962	Jun	37	25	12	0	26

Q. *And which do you think would be better at keeping the peace – a Conservative government or a Labour government?*

		Cons	Lab	Same	DK
1964	Oct	38	30	13	19

Q. *Which party can best handle our relations with Russia?*

		Cons	Lab	Lib	Other	DK
1964	Jan	27	37	5	1	30

Q. *Which party do you think can best handle the problem of foreign policy?*

		Cons	Lab	Lib	Other	DK
1953	Sep	47	26	4	1	22
1954	Sep	45	27	4	3	21
1956	Sep	45	27	6	2	20

Q. *Which party do you think can best handle the problem of foreign affairs?*

		Cons	Lab	Lib	Other	DK
1957	Oct	39	26	8	2	25

Q. *I am going to read out a list of problems facing the country. Could you tell me for each of them which political party you personally think would handle the problem best?* (THE GULF CRISIS)

		Cons	Lab	Lib	Green	Other	DK
1990	Sep	54	19	3	1	1	23
1990	Oct	45	24	5	0	0	25

Q. *Which party would be better able to handle foreign affairs, the Conservatives or Labour, or wouldn't there be any difference between them on this?*

		Cons	Lab	No diff	DK
1992	Feb	52	12	25	10

MISCELLANEOUS ISSUES

Q. *Which party do you think can best handle the rail and transport problem?*

		Cons	Lab	Lib	Other	DK
1963	Apr	23	32	7	2	36

Q. Which party can best handle the modernisation of Britain?

		Cons	Lab	Lib	Other	DK
1964	Feb	31	37	6	1	25
1965	Sep	31	34	3	0	31

Q. Over the next two or three years, which party do you think will be best for keeping fares down?

		Cons	Lab	Lib	Other	DK
1964	Aug	24	38	4	1	33

Q. I am going to read out a list of problems facing the country. Could you tell me for each of them which political party you personally think would handle the problem best? (HOMELESSNESS)

		Cons	Lab	Lib	Green	Other	DK
1989	Dec	13	67	6	1	1	12
1990	Feb	9	70	6	0	1	13
	Apr	9	69	6	1	1	13
	Jul	11	68	6	1	0	14
	Sep	11	62	6	1	1	19
	Oct	12	66	6	0	1	15
1991	May	15	54	10	1	1	18
	Jun	13	59	10	0	1	18
	Sep	19	49	10	1	1	20
	Sep	19	50	10	1	1	20
	Nov	16	54	9	0	1	20
1992	Jan	16	55	7	1	1	20
	Feb	19	50	7	0	1	23
	Mar	16	53	9	0	1	21
	Mar	19	47	10	1	0	23
	Mar	18	49	10	1	1	22
	Mar 31–Apr 1	17	46	11	1	1	24
	Apr 7/8	20	48	11	1	1	20
	Apr 10/11	23	48	9	1	1	19
	May	19	51	10	0	0	20
1993	Apr	12	61	9	1	1	17
	Nov	8	59	12	0	1	20
1994	Apr	9	60	11	1	1	19
	Aug	9	63	9	1	1	18
1995	Jan	7	63	7	1	1	22
	Sep	8	61	7	1	0	23

cont'd . . .

		Cons	Lab	Lib	Green	Other	DK
1996	Mar	8	62	10	1	0	19
	May	8	64	9	1	1	17
	Sep	8	63	5	1	1	21
	Dec	9	63	5	1	1	22
2000	May	14	56	10	0	1	19
2000	Sep	17	57	9	0	0	17

Q. I am going to read out a list of problems facing the country. Could you tell me for each of them which political party you personally think would handle the problem best? (THE ENVIRONMENT)

		Cons	Lab	Lib	Green	Other	DK
1989	Dec	21	28	9	31	0	11
1990	Feb	16	28	8	33	1	13
	Apr	17	28	8	34	1	12
	Jul	20	27	7	30	0	16
	Sep	18	22	13	31	1	15
	Oct	15	24	15	31	0	16
1991	May	23	23	15	26	0	14
	Jun	22	26	19	17	1	15
	Sep	24	24	16	19	0	17
	Sep	26	22	14	20	1	16
	Nov	20	26	15	21	1	16
1992	Jan	24	24	16	20	0	17
	Feb	27	25	13	17	1	19
	Mar	24	24	13	17	1	21
	Mar	26	21	19	16	0	18
	Mar	22	23	17	21	1	15
	Mar 31–Apr 1	20	19	20	23	1	17
	Apr 7/8	21	25	18	21	1	15
	Apr 10/11	26	21	14	22	1	15
	May	25	19	18	18	1	20
1993	Apr	20	29	16	19	0	15
	Nov	16	25	22	18	1	19
1994	Apr	16	30	18	15	1	20
	Aug	14	34	15	16	2	18
1995	Jan	14	33	12	16	1	23
	Sep	14	31	15	17	0	23
1996	Mar	13	34	17	15	1	22
	May	13	34	15	18	1	19
	Sep	16	32	12	18	1	22
	Dec	14	38	13	14	0	20

cont'd . . .

		Cons	Lab	Lib	Green	Other	DK
1997	Apr 4–6	18	35	22	–	6	19
	Apr 7–9	18	33	22	–	8	20
	Apr 10–13	19	31	23	–	7	20
	Apr 14–17	20	32	22	–	7	19
	Apr 18–21	19	31	22	–	9	19
	Apr 23–25	19	29	24	–	8	20
	May 2/3	15	42	23	–	4	16
1998	Apr	17	51	14	–	4	13
2000	Jan	19	45	14	–	6	16
	May	20	37	16	10	1	16
2000	Sep	22	37	19	5	0	15

Q. I am going to read out a list of problems facing the country. Could you tell me for each of them which political party you personally think would handle the problem best? (PUBLIC TRANSPORT – THE RAILWAYS, BUSES, ETC.)

		Cons	Lab	Lib	Green	Other	DK
1990	Feb	17	56	6	1	1	20
	Apr	17	55	5	2	1	21
	Jul	16	56	4	2	0	21
	Sep	15	55	6	1	1	22
	Oct	16	51	9	1	0	22
1991	May	21	49	7	2	1	20
	Jun	22	50	9	1	0	17
	Sep	24	45	9	1	1	19
	Sep	24	46	8	1	1	19
	Nov	20	51	7	1	1	20
1992	Jan	24	50	5	1	0	20
	Feb	26	45	7	1	1	20
	Mar	23	48	7	0	1	21
	Mar	24	44	10	1	0	22
	Mar	23	47	9	1	1	19
	Mar 31–Apr 1	24	44	11	1	1	20
	Apr 7/8	25	46	10	1	1	18
	Apr 10/11	29	42	7	1	0	20
	May	27	45	7	0	0	21
1993	Apr	17	58	6	2	0	17
	Nov	10	62	9	1	0	19
	Apr	14	56	9	1	1	19
	Aug	12	61	6	1	1	18
1995	Jan	10	63	5	1	1	22

cont'd . . .

		Cons	Lab	Lib	Green	Other	DK
	Sep	12	55	7	2	0	24
1996	Mar	11	59	9	2	0	19
	May	12	62	8	1	0	16
	Sep	13	59	5	1	1	21
	Dec	13	60	5	1	0	20
2000	May	22	49	8	1	1	18
2000	Sep	24	49	11	1	0	15

Q. I am going to read out a list of problems facing the country. Could you tell me for each of them which political party you personally think would handle the problem best? (THE STATUS OF WOMEN)

		Cons	Lab	Lib	Green	Other	DK
1990	Feb	24	38	6	2	1	29
	Apr	22	41	7	3	1	26
	Jul	26	36	5	2	1	30
	Sep	25	33	9	2	1	29
	Oct	22	37	9	2	1	30
1991	May	23	38	11	1	1	26
	Jun	20	40	11	0	1	27
	Sep	27	34	11	2	0	26
	Sep	26	35	11	1	1	25
	Nov	25	37	10	1	1	26
1992	Jan	25	34	9	1	1	29
	Feb	26	35	8	1	1	30
	Mar	22	36	10	1	1	30
	Mar	25	33	11	1	0	29
	Mar	24	36	11	1	1	27
	Mar 31–Apr 1	22	34	12	1	2	29
	Apr 7/8	23	38	11	1	1	27
	Apr 10/11	28	35	9	1	1	26
	May	26	33	10	1	1	30
1993	Apr	20	42	10	1	1	27
	Nov	16	39	15	1	1	29
1994	Apr	15	44	11	0	1	29
	Aug	13	46	10	0	2	30
1995	Jan	11	46	8	1	1	33
	Sep	14	45	8	1	1	32
1996	Mar	10	48	10	1	1	30
	May	15	45	10	1	1	29
	Sep	14	47	8	1	1	29
1996	Dec	11	55	5	1	1	28

Q. I am going to read out a list of problems facing the country. Could you tell me for each of them which political party you personally think would handle the problem best? (UNITY OF THE UNITED KINGDOM)

		Cons	Lab	Lib	Green	Other	DK
1997	Apr 4–6	38	34	7	–	2	20
	Apr 7–9	34	36	6	–	1	23
	Apr 10–13	38	30	10	–	1	21
	Apr 14–17	34	36	8	–	1	21
	Apr 18–21	35	33	8	–	2	21
	Apr 23–25	36	32	7	–	2	23
	Apr 29/30	38	31	9	–	1	21
	May 2/3	32	46	7	–	1	14
1998	Apr	29	53	6	–	0	12
2000	Jan	34	44	4	–	1	17

Q. I am going to read out a list of problems facing the country. Could you tell me for each of them which political party you personally think would handle the problem best? (ISSUES RELATING TO THE FAMILY)

		Cons	Lab	Lib	Green	Other	DK
1993	Nov	17	45	14	0	1	23

Q. I am going to read out a list of problems facing the country. Could you tell me for each of them which political party you personally think would handle the problem best? (NORTHERN IRELAND)

		Cons	Lab	Lib	Green	Other	DK
1998	Apr	13	72	2	0	1	13
2000	Jan	19	58	3		1	20

Q. I am going to read out a list of problems facing the country. Could you tell me for each of them which political party you personally think would handle the problem best? (THE COUNTRYSIDE)

	Cons	Lab	Lib	Green	Other	DK
2000 May	30	30	15	8	1	17

Q. I am going to read out a list of problems facing the country. Could you tell me for each of them which political party you personally think would handle the problem best? (ASYLUM SEEKERS)

		Cons	Lab	Lib	Green	Other	DK
2000	May	44	31	6	1	1	17
2000	Sep	43	33	8	0	0	17

Q. Which parties do you think are particularly good at .....? Any others? (IMPROVING NATIONAL UNITY)

		Cons	Lab	Lib	Other	DK
1978	Jan	29	31	7	1	38
	Feb	27	32	8	2	39
	Mar	27	29	4	2	42
	Apr	26	31	6	2	41
	May	31	32	4	2	36
	Sep	29	31	4	2	38
	Nov	27	28	5	1	41
1979	Mar	28	22	7	2	44
	Apr	32	28	7	3	35
	Sep	26	30	7	3	40
1980	Feb	20	28	12	1	45
	May	27	30	10	2	36
1981	Jun	16	26	11	9	32
	Aug	17	24	24	1	40
1982	Feb	16	23	26	1	39
1982	Nov	27	22	15	1	38

Q. Which parties do you think are particularly good at .....? Any others? (CREATING A FAIR SOCIETY)

		Cons	Lab	Lib	Other	DK
1978	Feb	31	30	9	2	37
	Mar	28	31	5	2	40
	Apr	28	32	8	2	39
	May	30	34	6	2	34
	Sep	32	31	6	2	36
	Nov	28	30	6	2	41
1979	Mar	32	24	8	2	39
	Apr	34	31	11	3	32
	Sep	28	35	9	2	35
1980	Feb	20	35	12	2	39
	May	27	36	12	2	33

cont'd . . .

		Cons	Lab	Lib	Other	DK
1981	Jun	16	30	14	10	37
1981	Aug	15	29	22	1	41
1982	Feb	18	29	26	1	36
1982	Nov	23	32	17	1	32

Q. Which party do you think can best handle the problem, or isn't there much to choose between them, on the issue of young people?

		Cons	Lab	Lib	Nothing	DK
1959	Sep	24	25	4	27	20
1969	Feb	31	15	5	24	25

TABLE 2.4:   BEST PARTY TO HANDLE ECONOMY 1964–2000

Q. With Britain in economic difficulties, which party do you think could handle the problem best – the Conservative Party or the Labour Party?

		Cons	Lab	Neither	DK	
1964	Jan	44	32	5	19	A
	Oct	45	34	5	16	
	Oct	44	34	5	17	
	Nov	49	30	10	11	
1989	Sep	57	23	9	11	
	Nov	47	37	10	6	
1990	Mar	35	46	10	8	
	Oct	42	38	13	7	
1991	Jan	50	34	7	9	
	Mar	53	29	9	8	
	Mar	49	32	12	7	
	Apr	49.0	27.8	13.2	9.9	
	May	44.9	30.8	14.8	9.4	
	Jun	43.9	31.3	15.7	9.1	
	Jul	45.0	29.4	16.0	9.6	
	Aug	45.3	28.6	16.5	9.7	
	Sep	47.0	28.5	15.3	9.1	

cont'd . . .

		Cons	Lab	Neither	DK
	Oct	45.1	31.0	14.9	9.0
	Nov	45.1	30.8	15.3	8.6
	Dec	44.4	29.3	17.4	8.8
1992	Jan	43.5	30.4	17.4	8.6
	Feb	43.2	31.0	17.2	8.6
	Mar	39.7	32.5	17.1	10.7
	Apr	47.5	31.6	12.9	8.1
	May	48.8	30.3	11.3	9.0
	Dec	28.3	38.7	19.6	13.4
1993	Jan	31.8	39.6	18.5	10.1
	Feb	30.1	39.9	20.3	9.7
	Mar	26.9	40.5	22.2	10.4
	Apr	28.1	40.8	21.2	9.8
	May	27.1	40.5	22.3	10.1
	Jun	23.4	40.6	26.1	9.9
	Jul	25.7	40.0	23.5	10.8
	Aug	25.8	37.8	25.5	10.9
	Sep	24.7	41.5	23.2	10.5
	Oct	26.7	41.1	22.5	9.8
	Nov	24.8	40.6	23.7	10.9
	Dec	26.6	41.4	21.5	10.6
1994	Jan	24.6	43.3	21.4	10.7
	Feb	25.2	43.1	21.1	10.6
	Mar	24.2	42.5	21.2	12.0
	Apr	23.6	42.8	22.0	11.7
	May	22.5	43.4	18.7	15.4
	Jun	22.4	46.8	20.8	10.1
	Jul	21.5	47.2	20.6	10.7
	Aug	21.0	49.1	17.7	12.2
	Sep	22.0	48.0	18.6	11.3
	Oct	21.4	48.2	18.1	12.4
	Nov	20.8	48.1	18.8	12.3
	Dec	18.8	51.3	17.2	12.6
1995	Jan	20.5	49.5	18.4	11.6
	Feb	19.9	49.2	18.7	12.2
	Mar	20.3	46.9	19.5	13.3
	Apr	21.2	47.9	18.7	12.3
	May	20.1	50.4	17.7	11.9
	Jun	20.3	50.1	17.3	12.3
	Jul	23.9	46.8	17.2	12.0
	Aug	24.0	45.0	18.4	12.7
	Sep	25.0	44.9	18.1	12.0
	Oct	23.7	48.8	16.3	11.3

cont'd . . .

		Cons	Lab	Neither	DK
	Nov	23.8	47.1	17.8	11.4
	Dec	23.5	47.0	17.8	11.8
1996	Jan	22.8	45.4	19.0	12.8
	Feb	24.1	44.6	19.3	12.0
	Mar	22.8	46.9	18.4	11.9
	Apr	23.0	46.5	18.4	12.1
	May	24.5	45.6	18.4	11.5
	Jun	25.3	45.4	18.0	11.3
	Jul	25.7	42.4	19.5	12.4
	Aug	26.4	42.2	19.8	11.6
	Sep	26.8	43.2	17.8	12.1
	Oct	25.6	43.5	17.8	13.1
	Nov	26.7	44.1	17.2	12.1
	Dec	26.3	43.8	18.2	11.7
1997	Jan	36.3	44.6	9.1	10.0
	Feb	38.2	47.1	6.2	8.5
	Mar	35.3	49.0	5.8	9.9
	May	27.5	58.2	4.8	9.6
	Jun	33.6	54.2	4.6	7.6
	Jul	30.3	57.8	3.9	8.0
	Aug	32.7	54.7	4.8	7.8
	Sep	26.9	60.7	4.0	8.4
	Oct	27.0	60.9	4.2	7.9
	Nov	27.9	57.5	6.3	8.4
	Dec	29.2	54.9	7.7	8.2
1998	Jan	33.0	52.3	7.9	6.8
	Feb	33.3	52.8	5.8	8.1
	Mar	32.5	49.8	8.3	9.3
	Apr	31.6	52.3	7.2	8.9
	May	30.9	54.8	6.7	7.7
	Jun	32.2	53.2	6.6	8.1
	Jul	33.8	52.6	6.2	7.5
	Aug	34.1	51.7	6.9	7.3
	Sep	32.2	51.6	9.2	7.0
	Oct	30.5	55.1	7.7	6.7
	Nov	31.6	54.1	7.9	6.5
	Dec	31.0	52.8	8.8	7.4
1999	Jan	31.2	52.3	9.3	7.2
	Feb	30.1	52.0	9.9	8.0
	Mar	30.6	50.6	9.6	9.2
	Apr	30.0	56.0	7.5	6.5
	May	31.3	55.7	7.7	5.3
	Jun	32.6	50.5	8.8	8.1
	Jul	32.3	53.3	8.2	6.2

cont'd . . .

		Cons	Lab	Neither	DK
	Aug	31.9	53.1	8.8	6.3
	Sep	32.4	53.5	8.3	5.8
	Oct	31.4	54.1	7.9	6.6
	Nov	32.0	52.8	8.5	6.7
	Dec	28.8	53.4	9.4	8.3
2000	Jan	28.9	52.1	10.1	8.9
	Feb	31.7	51.4	9.3	7.5
	Mar	32.6	50.0	9.6	7.8
	Apr	33.9	48.0	9.5	8.5
	May	36.8	43.6	9.7	9.7
	Jun	35.3	42.6	12.4	9.6
	Jul	36.7	46.7	8.6	8.0
	Aug	35.2	49.6	7.9	7.4
	Sep	42.1	41.1	9.2	7.6
	Oct	39.4	44.4	8.1	8.1
	Nov	36.2	45.9	10.2	7.8
2000	Dec	36.7	47.9	8.0	7.4

A Question in 1964 through to May 1997 read 'If Britain ran into economic difficulties who do you think could handle the problem best – the Conservatives under Sir Alec Douglas-Home or Labour under Mr Wilson?' with relevant changes being made to the leaders.

TABLE 2.5: PARTY WITH THE BEST LEADERS 1955–96

Q. Taking everything into account, which party has the best set of leaders?

		Cons	Lab	Lib	Other	DK
1955	Apr	53	25	1	1	20
1959	Mar	42	31	1	1	25
1962	Jul	38	25	13	1	23
1963	May	33	33	6	1	27
	Dec	41	37	4	0	18
1965	Mar	33	44	7	0	16
1967	Oct	32	34	5	4	25
1968	Sep	41	36	1	0	22
	Oct	35	32	4	1	28

cont'd . . .

		Cons	Lab	Lib	Other	DK
1969	May	40	23	6	1	30
	Oct	35	40	4	1	21
1970	Oct	41	36	1	0	22
	Dec	40	36	3	1	20
1971	Oct	36	38	3	1	23
1974	Feb	36	31	12	1	20
	Oct	26	36	15	1	22
1975	Feb	24	41	7	1	27
	Feb	32	38	6	1	23
	Mar	37	35	7	1	20
	Mar	34	41	7	1	17
	Mar	31	39	5	3	22
	May	34	35	8	1	22
	Jul	34	39	7	2	18
	Oct	36	41	7	1	14
1976	Feb	36	36	6	2	21
	Apr	30	39	2	1	28
	Apr	30	42	5	1	21
	May	29	34	6	1	30
	Aug	30	36	5	1	27
	Oct	35	29	6	1	29
	Nov	39	27	7	2	24
1977	Sep	37	34	6	2	21
	Oct	35	38	4	1	22
1978	Aug	27	43	3	1	27
	Sep	29	41	7	2	21
	Nov	27	46	4	1	21
1979	Feb	42	29	8	1	20
	Mar	41	31	6	0	21
	Apr	31	41	7	0	21
	May	32	37	15	1	15
	Oct	39	36	11	1	14
1980	Jan	36	34	12	0	18
	Oct	39	33	10	1	17
	Nov	39	33	10	1	18
	Nov	37	31	10	0	22
	Dec	36	33	10	1	20
1981	Jan	34	27	11	1	27
	Jan	31	27	20	1	21
	Feb	33	25	16	1	24

cont'd . . .

		Cons	Lab	Lib	Other	DK
	Apr	28	22	14	6	30
	Sep	32	25	14	7	22
	Oct	35	20	30	0	17
1982	Jan	29	19	31	1	21
	Oct	48	13	23	0	15
	Nov	46	19	19	0	16
	Dec	48	17	20	0	14
1983	Jan	53	13	18	0	16
	Feb	48	16	22	0	15
	Mar	48	13	25	0	15
	Apr	48	16	20	1	16
	Apr	50	15	21	0	15
	May	54	15	18	0	12
	May	53	17	16	0	14
	May	49	16	21	0	13
	Jun	52	15	22	0	10
	Jul	56	10	25	0	9
	Aug	55	7	25	0	12
	Sep	57	9	21	0	13
	Oct	50	23	14	0	12
	Nov	52	21	14	0	13
	Dec	48	23	18	1	11
1984	Jan	51	23	14	0	12
	Feb	49	22	16	0	12
	Mar	47	26	15	0	12
	Apr	49	23	16	0	12
	May	43	24	20	0	12
	Jun	42	24	22	0	11
	Jul	43	26	19	1	12
	Aug	43	23	20	0	14
	Sep	43	24	20	0	13
	Oct	53	18	18	0	11
	Nov	52	21	16	0	11
	Dec	45	18	23	0	14
1985	Jan	45	20	22	1	14
	Feb	43	18	25	0	14
	Mar	41	22	23	0	13
	Apr	44	23	20	0	12
	May	39	19	28	1	13
	Jun	41	22	25	0	12
	Jul	32	22	33	0	13
	Aug	33	23	31	0	13
	Sep	34	17	35	0	14

cont'd . . .

		Cons	Lab	Lib	Other	DK
	Oct	37	26	21	0	15
	Nov	39	26	23	0	12
	Dec	42	22	23	1	11
1986	Jan	31	26	28	0	15
	Feb	29	25	31	0	15
	Mar	36	21	30	0	12
	Apr	33	25	28	0	14
	May	31	29	25	1	14
	Jun	36	27	21	1	15
	Jul	39	25	22	1	12
	Aug	35	24	25	0	16
	Sep	37	26	23	0	13
	Oct	43	26	19	0	12
	Nov	41	26	17	0	15
	Dec	43	21	21	0	16
1987	Jan	39	25	21	0	14
	Feb	44	22	22	0	13
	Mar	42	18	28	0	12
	Apr	50	14	25	0	11
	May	51	15	22	0	10
	May	49	21	16	0	14
	May	48	25	13	0	14
	Jun	47	26	14	0	13
	Jun	46	27	14	0	12
	Jul	54	25	13	0	8
	Aug	54	23	10	0	12
	Sep	56	22	11	1	10
	Oct	62	20	8	1	10
	Nov	57	22	10	1	11
	Dec	62	19	7	1	11
1988	Jan	61	22	6	1	11
	Feb	60	21	7	1	12
	Mar	57	20	8	1	14
	Apr	54	23	10	1	13
	May	59	21	7	1	13
	Jun	54	26	6	1	13
	Jul	57	21	10	0	12
	Aug	62	18	8	1	11
	Sep	60	20	10	0	10
	Oct	61	17	8	1	13
	Nov	57	18	10	0	15
	Dec	56	17	9	1	16
1989	Jan	55	16	13	1	15

cont'd . . .

		Cons	Lab	Lib	Other	DK
	Feb	53	18	12	1	17
	Mar	53	19	12	1	15
	Apr	53	18	11	1	16
	Apr	48	20	12	1	18
	May	56	22	7	1	15
	Jul	48	30	6	1	14
	Aug	45	26	9	1	19
	Sep	49	26	8	2	16
	Sep	49	26	9	2	15
	Oct	45	31	8	2	14
	Dec	45	32	8	1	15
1990	Jan	46	31	7	1	14
	Jan	42	31	7	1	20
	Feb	40	32	9	1	17
	Mar	36	37	9	2	16
	Apr	41	29	9	1	20
	Jun	36	37	8	1	17
	Jun	45	33	5	1	16
	Jul	43	31	6	1	19
	Sep	46	31	5	2	16
	Sep	42	31	8	1	17
	Oct	39	33	10	1	17
	Dec	49	24	8	1	17
1991	Jan	47	28	8	1	16
	Feb	51	24	7	2	16
	Feb	55	22	9	1	13
	Mar	44	24	14	1	15
	May	44	26	15	1	14
	Jun	39	31	16	0	13
	Oct	47	25	12	1	15
	Nov	39	28	15	1	17
	Dec	41	24	16	1	18
1992	Mar	40	27	18	1	13
	Mar	38	30	16	0	15
	Mar	37	25	25	1	11
	Apr	36	26	25	2	11
	Apr	48	20	13	1	18
1993	Apr	28	36	14	1	20
1995	Mar	18	45	10	2	25
	Mar	18	44	9	3	25
	Jul	19	48	10	1	21
1996	Mar	17	50	11	1	21
1996	Dec	21	49	11	1	17

cont'd . . .

TABLE 2.6:   PARTY WITH THE BEST POLICIES 1963–96

Q. Taking everything into account, which party has the best policies?

		Cons	Lab	Lib	Other	DK
1963	Nov	32	41	9	0	18
	Dec	36	37	11	0	1

		Cons	Lab	Lib	Other	DK
1974	Feb	37	31	12	1	19
	Oct	30	34	14	1	21
1975	Feb	31	37	9	2	21
	Feb	35	35	8	2	20
	Mar	39	33	7	2	19
	Mar	35	39	8	2	17
	Mar	34	34	6	2	25
	May	40	34	9	2	15
	Jul	37	36	9	2	16
	Oct	39	36	10	2	14
1976	Feb	37	33	7	2	22
	Apr	33	38	5	2	23
	Apr	35	37	6	2	19
	May	35	29	9	1	26
	Aug	32	34	8	2	24
	Oct	39	27	7	2	25
	Nov	42	24	9	2	24
1977	Sep	39	34	5	3	19
	Oct	38	35	5	1	20
1978	Aug	33	37	6	2	23
	Sep	32	38	8	3	19
	Nov	36	41	5	1	16
1979	Feb	44	29	9	1	16
	Mar	45	30	6	1	18
	Apr	38	34	7	1	20
	May	37	32	14	3	14
	Oct	37	37	9	2	15
1980	Jan	37	36	11	0	16
	Oct	38	35	9	2	16
	Nov	38	35	9	2	17

cont'd . . .

		Cons	Lab	Lib	Other	DK
	Nov	33	38	11	1	17
	Dec	34	35	10	2	20
1981	Jan	32	32	11	2	23
	Jan	29	31	16	2	22
	Feb	29	29	14	2	26
	Apr	23	28	11	6	31
	Sep	30	30	10	8	23
	Oct	31	25	24	1	18
1982	Jan	29	26	23	1	21
	Oct	39	23	19	0	19
	Nov	39	28	14	0	19
	Dec	38	28	15	0	18
1983	Jan	42	22	16	0	20
	Feb	41	26	16	0	17
	Mar	39	23	22	0	16
	Apr	38	28	17	1	17
	Apr	42	23	16	0	18
	May	44	24	15	0	16
	May	40	26	17	0	18
	May	43	25	15	1	16
	Jun	42	21	20	2	17
	Jul	45	21	20	0	13
	Aug	44	18	24	0	14
	Sep	45	17	21	1	15
	Oct	41	28	17	0	13
	Nov	41	27	16	0	16
	Dec	39	27	18	1	16
1984	Jan	43	29	14	1	14
	Feb	42	27	15	0	15
	Mar	40	30	15	1	14
	Apr	39	28	17	1	15
	May	37	29	19	0	15
	Jun	36	30	19	0	14
	Jul	35	30	17	1	16
	Aug	35	31	17	2	14
	Sep	37	27	18	0	17
	Oct	42	23	17	1	16
	Nov	41	26	17	1	15
	Dec	37	23	22	1	18
1985	Jan	34	27	20	1	17
	Feb	36	25	22	1	17
	Mar	29	33	21	1	16

cont'd . . .

		Cons	Lab	Lib	Other	DK
	Apr	32	30	20	I	18
	May	30	27	27	I	16
	Jun	32	28	23	0	15
	Jul	27	31	23	I	19
	Aug	25	34	25	I	16
	Sep	28	23	29	0	20
	Oct	28	31	21	I	19
	Nov	32	28	19	I	20
	Dec	31	26	24	I	19
1986	Jan	27	28	26	I	20
	Feb	25	29	23	I	21
	Mar	28	27	27	0	18
	Apr	25	32	25	I	18
	May	26	31	24	I	18
	Jun	32	31	19	I	19
	Jul	32	32	20	0	16
	Aug	28	30	21	I	19
	Sep	29	31	18	I	20
	Oct	35	33	15	0	16
	Nov	34	32	15	I	18
	Dec	34	26	19	I	20
1987	Jan	31	31	19	I	19
	Feb	33	27	20	0	19
	Mar	34	26	25	0	15
	Apr	36	24	24	I	16
	May	38	23	23	I	15
	May	36	25	16	2	21
	May	40	27	12	2	19
	Jun	37	29	15	2	18
	Jun	37	27	18	2	17
	Jun	38	29	17	2	15
	Jul	47	28	14	0	10
	Aug	45	29	13	I	13
	Sep	47	27	15	I	10
	Oct	51	25	12	I	10
	Nov	46	27	14	I	13
	Dec	47	29	II	I	12
1988	Jan	48	29	9	I	13
	Feb	44	28	10	I	15
	Mar	41	28	II	I	18
	Apr	39	32	9	I	18
	May	46	29	8	2	15
	Jun	43	33	7	2	15

cont'd . . .

		Cons	Lab	Lib	Other	DK
	Jul	44	29	10	1	16
	Aug	47	28	10	2	14
	Sep	42	30	13	1	14
	Oct	46	26	9	2	17
	Nov	43	27	12	2	17
	Dec	41	26	12	3	19
1989	Jan	40	25	13	2	20
	Feb	39	28	13	2	20
	Mar	39	28	13	1	19
	Apr	39	29	12	2	19
	Apr	37	29	10	3	21
	May	40	35	8	2	16
	Jul	35	38	6	4	17
	Aug	33	36	6	6	20
	Sep	35	34	6	5	19
	Sep	34	36	8	6	17
	Oct	35	36	7	5	18
	Dec	35	37	7	4	17
1990	Jan	37	38	5	4	16
	Jan	32	38	6	5	19
	Feb	30	38	7	4	21
	Mar	31	41	7	4	16
	Apr	35	33	7	5	19
	Jun	29	43	6	4	17
	Jun	35	38	5	3	18
	Jul	32	37	7	5	20
	Sep	35	40	4	5	15
	Sep	30	39	9	4	18
	Oct	31	38	10	4	16
	Dec	41	32	7	3	18
1991	Jan	39	34	7	2	18
	Feb	40	31	7	4	18
	Feb	42	29	9	3	18
	Mar	37	29	15	4	16
	May	37	31	13	3	16
	Jun	33	36	13	1	16
	Oct	38	31	10	3	18
	Nov	33	32	12	3	21
	Dec	34	29	13	3	20
1992	Mar	33	35	13	3	16
	Mar	30	36	14	3	17
	Mar	32	32	18	3	15
	Apr	30	33	19	3	14

cont'd . . .

		Cons	Lab	Lib	Other	DK
1992	Apr	39	36	11	2	12
1993	Apr	28	38	12	3	19
1995	Mar	18	44	11	1	25
1996	Mar	17	50	11	1	21
1996	Dec	20	49	9	2	20

TABLE 2.7: CONFIDENCE IN THE PARTIES 1976–95

Q. On the whole, how much confidence do you have in Conservative/Labour/Liberal/Liberal Democrat/SDP politicians to deal wisely with Britain's problems – very great, considerable little or very little?

VG   Very Great
C   Considerable
L   Little
VL   Very Little
N   None at all (Volunteered)
DK   Don't know

		VG	C	L	VL	N	DK
CONSERVATIVE							
1974	Sep	8	21	22	22	18	9
	Nov	8	24	23	20	17	8
1975	Feb	9	29	24	18	12	8
	Jun	10	32	20	18	14	7
1978	Jul	7	31	22	17	14	9
1979	Feb	11	36	23	18	8	4
	Mar	8	33	23	20	11	6
1980	May	9	33	22	20	12	4
1981	Mar	4	23	21	25	24	3
	Oct	6	26	19	25	23	2
	Dec	5	24	21	28	20	2
1983	May	11	34	20	19	14	2
1985	Sep	5	25	20	24	24	3
	Oct	7	26	18	25	22	3
1986	Jun	3	26	22	29	18	2
	Dec	6	23	25	22	20	3
1987	Aug	7	36	20	20	15	3
1989	Nov	8	33	22	20	15	2

cont'd . . .

		VG	C	L	VL	N	DK
1990	Oct	3	30	20	25	19	2
1992	Jul	4	28	27	18	19	3
1993	Mar	3	18	20	26	32	2
1994	Sep	2	15	26	29	26	3
1995	Jul	1	15	25	29	27	2

LABOUR

		VG	C	L	VL	N	DK
1974	Sep	7	18	25	23	21	6
	Nov	8	26	26	17	15	8
1975	Feb	9	25	25	20	16	5
	Jun	6	20	27	22	21	5
1978	Jul	6	28	25	19	15	8
1979	Feb	5	21	27	23	21	3
	Mar	7	21	27	22	19	4
1980	May	9	27	27	20	12	4
1981	Mar	5	23	24	23	23	3
	Oct	4	20	27	20	26	2
	Dec	3	21	24	25	25	2
1983	May	5	20	21	23	27	3
1985	Sep	5	20	24	22	25	4
	Oct	8	24	23	20	21	4
1986	Jun	5	28	24	22	19	3
	Dec	6	18	24	21	26	5
1987	Aug	6	21	26	23	20	4
1989	Nov	8	31	23	18	17	3
1990	Oct	5	26	25	22	17	5
1992	Jul	3	25	25	22	21	4
1993	Mar	4	29	28	19	17	4
1994	Sep	7	34	25	16	12	7
1995	Jul	7	34	28	13	11	6

LIBERAL

		VG	C	L	VL	N	DK
1974	Nov	2	14	21	20	30	13
1975	Feb	2	11	22	23	26	16
	Jun	3	15	21	19	25	17
1978	Jul	1	10	20	21	35	13
1979	Feb	1	12	22	25	28	11
	Mar	1	8	19	25	32	14
1981	Mar	3	20	26	21	19	10
	Oct	2	27	27	17	17	10
	Dec	2	22	27	21	16	12
1983	May	4	21	27	20	17	11
1985	Sep	3	30	27	16	13	11

cont'd . . .

		VG	C	L	VL	N	DK
	Oct	2	25	29	18	16	9
1986	Jun	2	22	31	20	17	8
	Dec	2	24	28	18	18	10
1987	Aug	2	18	29	23	21	8

LIBERAL DEMOCRAT

		VG	C	L	VL	N	DK
1990	Oct	2	16	26	19	22	15
1992	Jul	1	19	31	18	22	9
1993	Mar	1	17	31	19	24	8
1994	Sep	1	20	26	22	17	13
1995	Jul	2	17	27	20	18	15

SDP

		VG	C	L	VL	N	DK
1981	Oct	4	27	20	13	19	17
	Dec	3	27	21	14	19	16
1983	May	2	12	23	20	28	15
1985	Sep	5	31	23	14	15	11
	Oct	2	25	27	16	18	11
1986	Jun	1	19	29	19	21	10
	Dec	2	19	26	22	20	11
1987	Aug	1	14	25	24	26	10

TABLE 2.8: COMPETENCE OF PARTIES 1987–95

Q. How competent do you think the Conservative/Labour Party/Liberal SDP Alliance/Social and Liberal Democrats/SDP/Liberal Democrats is to manage the country's affairs?

V   Very competent
F   Fairly competent
NV Not very competent
NA Not at all competent
DK Don't know

		V	F	NV	NA	DK
CONSERVATIVE					
1987	Nov	25	43	19	10	3
1988	Jan	26	44	16	11	3
	Aug	30	47	13	9	2
	Nov	26	44	16	11	4
1989	May	23	44	18	10	5

cont'd . . .

		V	F	NV	NA	DK
1990	Jan	13	36	25	23	4
	Jan	14	43	23	17	4
	Apr	15	37	27	20	1
	Jun	13	38	26	20	3
1991	Mar	12	44	21	21	3
1992	Jul	11	45	24	18	3
	Oct	5	29	32	32	2
1993	Jun	4	29	34	30	2
1995	Apr	5	25	32	35	3
1995	May	3	26	35	33	3

LABOUR

		V	F	NV	NA	DK
1987	Nov	10	27	30	29	5
1988	Jan	8	33	32	23	5
	Aug	10	31	34	21	4
	Nov	11	30	29	24	6
1989	May	10	36	29	19	6
1990	Jan	8	36	26	20	10
	Jan	12	43	24	14	6
	Apr	18	44	21	14	3
	Jun	17	42	25	11	5
1991	Mar	9	29	25	29	8
1992	Jul	9	36	30	18	7
	Oct	7	42	27	16	8
1993	Jun	6	40	28	17	8
1995	Apr	10	45	20	11	13
1995	May	12	48	19	10	11

LIBERAL/SDP ALLIANCE/SOCIAL AND LIBERAL DEMOCRATS/LIBERAL DEMOCRATS

		V	F	NV	NA	DK
1987	Nov	4	24	32	29	11
1988	Jan	2	19	27	41	12
	Aug	3	19	26	30	22
	Nov	2	21	24	31	22
1989	May	2	21	25	33	19
1990	Jan	1	13	24	41	21
	Jan	3	14	25	41	17
	Apr	1	22	27	35	15
	Jun	1	18	24	40	17
1991	Mar	4	26	25	28	17
1992	Jul	3	29	29	25	13
	Oct	3	30	28	23	15
1993	Jun	6	37	25	17	15
1995	Apr	4	31	27	23	16
	May	3	38	27	14	17

cont'd . . .

		V	F	NV	NA	DK
SDP						
1988	Aug	2	16	26	33	22
	Nov	3	17	23	36	22
1989	May	3	21	24	32	20
1990	Jan	1	12	22	44	21
1990	Jan	2	12	23	46	18

CHAPTER 3
The Conservative Party

One challenge confronting all the polling organizations is that of 'digging behind' the responses to the standard voting-intention questions to discover how solid the various parties' support actually is and also whether people's feelings about the parties may be developing in ways that are not yet reflected in their statements of voting intention.

The questions reported in Tables 3.1 and 3.2 represent two responses to this challenge. Table 3.3 reports the responses to a number of different questions that sought to explore people's reasons for disliking the Conservative Party or their reluctance to vote for it. Most of these questions were asked in the late 1980s or during the 1990s.

TABLE 3.1: CONSERVATIVE PARTY'S REPUTATION 1978–97

Q. Regardless of your personal opinion, do you think that most people in Britain are holding a favourable opinion of the Conservative Party or don't you think so?

		Are	Are not	DK
1978	Apr	38	33	29
	May	33	37	30
	Jun	32	41	27
	Jul	34	39	27
	Aug	31	37	32
	Sep	38	35	27
	Oct	32	37	31
	Nov	31	41	29
1979	Jan	36	38	26
	Jan	37	38	25
	Jan	39	37	24
	Feb	39	34	27
	Mar	45	31	25
	Apr	42	33	25
	Apr	44	31	24
	Apr	43	34	24
	Apr	37	33	29
	Apr	36	38	25
	Jun	49	30	21
	Jul	33	46	21

cont'd . . .

		Are	Are not	DK
	Sep	38	41	21
	Sep	30	49	21
	Sep	36	44	20
	Sep	32	49	19
	Oct	40	40	20
	Oct	36	45	19
	Dec	26	58	16
1980	Feb	19	61	21
	Mar	20	61	19
	Apr	21	58	20
	May	23	60	17
	Jun	17	66	17
	Jul	24	59	17
	Aug	20	63	16
	Sep	22	64	14
	Oct	18	69	13
	Oct	24	60	16
	Nov	19	66	15
	Dec	14	73	13
1981	Jan	17	68	15
	Feb	13	75	12
	Feb	16	70	14
	Mar	13	76	10
	Mar	12	77	11
	Apr	14	72	15
	May	13	72	15
	Jun	14	74	13
	Jul	13	76	11
	Oct	11	77	12
	Oct	12	79	9
1982	Jan	10	80	10
	Mar	20	65	14
	Apr	22	67	11
	May	40	47	13
	Jun	64	27	10
	Jul	59	30	11
	Aug	49	37	13
	Sep	47	42	10
	Oct	47	40	13
	Nov	46	41	13
	Dec	41	49	11
1983	Jan	49	37	14
	Feb	50	39	11

cont'd . . .

		Are	Are not	DK
	Mar	47	41	12
	Apr	47	39	15
	Apr	47	36	17
	May	48	37	16
	May	58	29	12
	May	54	32	14
	May	66	22	12
	Jun	62	26	12
	Jun	67	26	8
	Jun	67	25	9
	Jul	68	25	7
	Aug	62	29	8
	Sep	67	27	7
	Oct	59	31	10
	Nov	54	37	9
	Dec	50	38	12
1984	Jan	57	32	11
	Feb	53	36	12
	Mar	46	43	11
	Apr	47	41	12
	May	44	44	12
	Jun	39	51	10
	Jul	36	53	11
	Aug	37	48	15
	Sep	40	48	12
	Oct	52	36	13
	Nov	54	36	11
	Dec	44	44	12
1985	Jan	46	42	13
	Feb	41	46	13
	Mar	34	55	11
	Apr	34	56	10
	May	29	57	14
	Jun	30	60	10
	Jul	25	67	8
	Aug	20	70	10
	Sep	28	60	12
	Oct	29	60	11
	Nov	33	54	13
	Dec	32	56	12
1986	Jan	27	56	14
	Feb	25	66	9
	Mar	29	60	10

cont'd . . .

		Are	Are not	DK
1987	May	52	37	11
	Jun	63	30	7
	Jun	63	29	8
	Jun	58	33	9
	Jul	58	34	8
1991	Jun	27	59	15
	Oct	30	58	12
1992	May	56	35	9
	Jul	51	40	10
	Aug	48	40	13
	Sep	39	51	10
	Oct	28	65	8
	Oct	20	73	7
	Nov	18	74	7
1993	Jan	25	66	9
	Jan	22	70	8
	Feb	20	72	8
	Apr	20	71	9
	Apr	25	67	9
	May	13	81	6
	Jun	15	77	8
	Jul	13	80	7
	Sep	13	81	6
	Sep	14	80	6
	Oct	15	79	6
	Dec	15	77	6
1994	Jan	15	78	7
	Jan	14	80	6
	Feb	13	79	8
	Apr	17	77	6
	May	11	83	6
	May	12	81	7
	Jul	12	81	7
	Jul	12	80	7
	Sep	12	81	8
	Sep	13	79	8
	Oct	12	81	7
	Dec	11	82	8
1995	Jan	9	83	7
	Jan	10	83	7
	Feb	9	84	7
	Apr	11	83	7
	May	10	85	6

cont'd . . .

		Are	Are not	DK
	Jun	8	86	6
	Jul	12	82	7
	Jul	14	78	7
	Sep	12	79	10
	Sep	11	80	8
	Oct	10	79	11
	Nov	11	79	10
	Dec	10	82	8
1996	Jan	11	82	7
	Feb	11	81	8
	Mar	10	80	9
	Mar	13	79	8
	May	12	80	8
	Jun	11	81	7
	Jun	12	80	8
	Aug	15	78	8
	Sep	15	78	8
	Oct	16	77	7
	Nov	16	73	11
	Dec	16	73	12
1997	Jan	18	81	4
	Feb	16	79	5
	Mar	14	82	4
1997	Apr	13	81	6

TABLE 3.2: CONSERVATIVE PARTY'S CONCERN AND RESPONSIBILITY 1973–94

Q. Do you think the Conservative Party is becoming more concerned for the interests of people like yourself, less concerned or is there no change?

Q. Do you think the Conservative Party is becoming more responsible in its approach to the important issues facing the country, less responsible or is there no change?

		Concern				Responsibility			
		More	Less	NC	DK	More	Less	NC	DK
1973	Oct	21	33	39	7	22	22	45	10
	Oct	28	31	35	6	29	20	42	9
1974	Jun	26	22	42	10	26	16	45	13
1975	Jul	34	12	44	10	35	7	46	12
	Oct	37	17	41	5	41	9	44	6
1976	Feb	38	10	44	8	43	7	41	9

cont'd . . .

			Concern				Responsibility		
		More	Less	NC	DK	More	Less	NC	DK
	Oct	26	17	51	6	27	17	48	8
	Oct	36	17	41	6	41	10	40	9
1977	Sep	26	17	51	7	–	–	–	–
	Oct	27	19	48	6	–	–	–	–
1978	Oct	32	14	45	9	33	13	43	11
1981	Feb	15	43	40	3	23	30	41	5
	Oct	13	39	45	2	23	28	46	3
1983	Oct	13	42	42	3	23	27	42	3
1984	Sep	11	45	40	3	17	33	46	4
	Oct	15	41	40	4	25	25	45	5
1985	Mar	11	50	35	4	19	37	38	6
	Jun	12	51	35	2	19	36	41	3
	Sep	11	49	37	3	17	36	42	4
1986	Jan	7	57	32	3	14	49	30	7
	Sep	12	45	41	2	18	36	43	3
1987	Sep	18	41	39	2	27	23	46	4
1988	May	17	52	28	3	24	41	32	3
	Oct	13	50	35	3	22	34	42	3
1989	Sep	12	53	31	3	18	41	37	4
1992	Jul	17	31	47	4	27	20	48	5
1993	Mar	11	50	37	2	17	46	34	2
	Oct	7	61	30	2	12	51	32	4
1994	Aug	6	58	33	3	8	51	36	4

TABLE 3.3: REASONS FOR NOT VOTING CONSERVATIVE

Q. Here are some reasons people give for not wanting to vote Conservative at the next election. Which of these reasons do you yourself have most sympathy with? And which next?

	Sep 1991	Nov 1991	Feb 1992	Mar 1992	Apr 1992	Apr 1994	Oct 1994	Oct 1995
FIRST REASON								
Mr Major is indecisive and dithers	6	7	5	5	6	17	7	8
The Conservatives don't care what hardships their policies cause	14	14	12	11	13	16	15	12
The Conservatives are not interested in the problems of the ordinary people and their families	14	19	18	20	19	17	21	21

cont'd . . .

	Sep 1991	Nov 1991	Feb 1992	Mar 1992	Apr 1992	Apr 1994	Oct 1994	Oct 1995
Public services, like education and the National Health Service, have been cut too much under the Conservatives	32	27	33	28	25	24	32	39
The Conservatives have mismanaged the economy	–	–	8	9	8	11	9	7
Conservative policies cause unemployment to rise without defeating inflation	10	11	9	8	12	7	8	6
None of these/don't know	16	15	15	18	18	8	8	7

	Sep 1991	Nov 1991	Feb 1992	Mar 1992	Apr 1992	Apr 1994	Oct 1994	Oct 1995
FIRST AND SECOND REASONS								
Mr Major is indecisive and dithers	8	11	7	10	9	26	12	13
The Conservatives don't care what hardships their policies cause	25	24	23	24	22	30	29	24
The Conservatives are not interested in the problems of the ordinary people and their families	30	38	34	35	36	38	45	44
Public services, like education and the National Health Service, have been cut too much under the Conservatives	51	44	51	46	46	46	53	62
The Conservatives have mismanaged the economy	–	–	20	19	17	24	19	18
Conservative policies cause unemployment to rise without defeating inflation	23	24	23	20	24	16	19	18

Q. *Why do you think the Conservative Party lost the [1966] election?*

MAR 1966

Poor leadership – Heath	13
No policy, weak policy	12
Past record	12
Bad campaign	9
Poor leadership – general	8
Country wanted change	6
For the better off, not the working class	5
Broken promises	3
Common Market policy	1
Other	11
Don't know	20

Q. *You said a moment ago that you voted Conservative at the last election but are not inclined to vote Conservative next time. People give various reasons for no longer supporting the Conservatives and I am going to read out some of them. Could you tell me for each whether it is very important in influencing your own thinking, fairly important, not very important or not at all important?*

	Very	Fairly	Not very	Not at all	DK
(MARCH 1994. A SAMPLE OF PEOPLE WHO CLAIMED TO HAVE VOTED CONSERVATIVE IN THE 1992 ELECTION BUT ARE NOT CURRENTLY SUPPORTING THE PARTY.)					
The budget deficit and the Government borrowing is too large	32	34	17	8	10
Neil Kinnock wouldn't have made a good prime minister but John Smith might	18	29	21	22	10
The Conservatives said they would keep taxes down but instead they've increased them	59	19	8	5	9
The Conservatives are continuing to undermine the National Health Service	64	15	8	4	9
The Labour Party is more electable now	23	31	18	17	10
The Conservatives are a shambles; everything they do seems to go wrong	45	28	13	5	9
There is more and more crime under the Conservatives	26	21	26	17	10

cont'd . . .

	Very	Fairly	Not very	Not at all	DK
It's time for a change; we've had one party in power for too long	38	26	14	12	9
The Conservatives are making a mess of running the economy	42	32	12	5	10
John Major is not a good prime minister	34	27	19	10	9
The Conservatives said they would take us out of recession but I don't think they have	41	28	15	7	9
All the public services - not just the NHS - continue to decline under the Conservatives	50	24	12	5	3
The Liberal Democrats and Paddy Ashdown look very impressive	19	27	23	22	9

Q. You said a moment ago that you voted Conservative at the last election but are not inclined to vote Conservative next time. People give various reasons for no longer supporting the Conservatives and I am going to read out some of them. Could you tell me for each whether it is very important in influencing your own thinking, fairly important, not very important or not at all important?

	Very	Fairly	Not very	Not at all	DK
(APRIL 1996. A SAMPLE OF PEOPLE WHO CLAIMED TO HAVE VOTED CONSERVATIVE IN THE 1992 ELECTION BUT ARE NOT CURRENTLY SUPPORTING THE PARTY.)					
The budget deficit and the Government borrowing is too large	20	31	24	15	10
Neil Kinnock wouldn't have made a good prime minister but Tony Blair has the look of a leader	21	30	18	22	8
The Conservatives said they would keep taxes down but instead they've increased them	44	27	11	9	9
The Conservatives are continuing to undermine the National Health Service	66	16	6	3	9
The Labour Party is more electable now	33	35	12	11	9
The Conservatives are a shambles; everything they do seems to go wrong	36	30	18	7	9
There is more and more crime under the Conservatives	23	20	26	21	10

cont'd . . .

	Very	Fairly	Not very	Not at all	DK
It's time for a change; we've had one party in power for too long	43	24	12	11	9
The Conservatives are making a mess of running the economy	34	33	16	8	10
John Major is not a good prime minister	26	28	21	16	9
The Conservatives said they would take us out of recession but I don't think they have	38	32	13	8	9
All the public services – not just the NHS – continue to decline under the Conservatives	55	23	8	5	8
The Liberal Democrats and Paddy Ashdown look very impressive	13	23	26	28	9
The Conservatives have broken their promises too often, they can no longer be trusted	47	26	12	6	9

Q. Here are some reasons for liking and disliking the present government under Mrs Thatcher. Could you tell me if any of them apply to you?

MARCH 1987

They've let the public services, like education and the health service, run down	62
They're not interested in tackling the problem of unemployment	49
They've created 'two nations' dividing rich from poor, North from South	51
They're too ready to push people around. They're too arrogant	31
Mrs Thatcher is simply not likeable as a person	28
None of these	18

Q. Here are some things people give for not wanting to vote Conservative at the next election. Which of these reasons do you yourself have most sympathy with? And which next?

	Nov 1969	Apr 1990	Oct 1990
FIRST REASON			
Mrs Thatcher is too bossy and dictatorial	26	23	14
The Conservatives don't care what hardships their policies cause	11	16	15

cont'd . . .

	Nov 1969	Apr 1990	Oct 1990
The Conservatives are not interested in the problems of the ordinary people and their families	16	18	20
Public services, like education and the National Health Service, have been cut too much under the Conservatives	27	25	31
Despite the country's sacrifices under the Conservatives, nothing has really been gained	4	4	8
Conservative policies cause unemployment to rise without defeating inflation	5	4	5
None of these	10	10	8

	Nov 1969	Apr 1990	Oct 1990
FIRST AND SECOND REASONS			
Mrs Thatcher is too bossy and dictatorial	38	31	22
The Conservatives don't care what hardships their policies cause	25	33	29
The Conservatives are not interested in the problems of the ordinary people and their families	36	45	38
Public services, like education and the National Health Service, have been cut too much under the Conservatives	46	45	51
Despite the country's sacrifices under the Conservatives, nothing has really been gained	10	10	22
Conservative policies cause unemployment to rise without defeating inflation	12	9	16
None of these	10	10	8

Q. Here are some things people give for not wanting to vote Conservative at the next election. Which of these reasons do you yourself have most sympathy with? And which next?

	Sep 1991	Nov 1991
FIRST REASON		
Mr Major is indecisive and dithers	6	7
The Conservatives don't care what hardships their policies cause	14	14
The Conservatives are not interested in the problems of the ordinary people and their families	14	19
Public services, like education and the National Health Service, have been cut too much under the Conservatives	32	27
Despite the country's sacrifices under the Conservatives, nothing has really been gained	8	8
Conservative policies cause unemployment to rise without defeating inflation	10	11
None of these	16	15

	Sep 1991	Nov 1991
FIRST AND SECOND REASONS		
Mr Major is indecisive and dithers	8	11
The Conservatives don't care what hardships their policies cause	25	24
The Conservatives are not interested in the problems of the ordinary people and their families	30	38
Public services, like education and the National Health Service, have been cut too much under the Conservatives	51	44
Despite the country's sacrifices under the Conservatives, nothing has really been gained	18	21
Conservative policies cause unemployment to rise without defeating inflation	23	24
None of these	16	15

Q. Here are some things people give for not wanting to vote Conservative at the next election. Which of these reasons do you yourself have most sympathy with? And which next?

	Feb 1992	Mar 1992	Apr 1992
FIRST REASON			
Mr Major is indecisive and dithers	5	6	6
The Conservatives don't care what hardships their policies cause	12	11	13
The Conservatives are not interested in the problems of the ordinary people and their families	18	20	19
Public services, like education and the National Health Service, have been cut too much under the Conservatives	33	28	25
The Conservatives have mismanaged the economy	8	9	8
Conservative policies cause unemployment to rise without defeating inflation	9	8	12
None of these	15	18	18

	Feb 1992	Mar 1992	Apr 1992
FIRST AND SECOND REASONS			
Mr Major is indecisive and dithers	7	10	9
The Conservatives don't care what hardships their policies cause	23	24	22
The Conservatives are not interested in the problems of the ordinary people and their families	34	35	36
Public services, like education and the National Health Service, have been cut too much under the Conservatives	51	46	46
The Conservatives have mismanaged the economy	20	19	17
Conservative policies cause unemployment to rise without defeating inflation	23	20	24
None of these	15	18	18

Q. I am going to read a list of five reasons people give for not wanting to vote for the Conservative Party. Could you tell me which one of the five you personally have the most sympathy with?
Q. And which one next?

	Sep 1999		Sep 2000	
	Top	Top two	Top	Top two
The Conservatives are too weak and divided	20	36	10	22
William Hague would not make a good Prime Minister	17	33	22	33
The Conservatives would make trouble for Britain in Europe	8	23	26	29
The Conservatives did not do a good job when they were in power	24	39	26	40
The Conservatives are not really interested in public services like the health service and education	21	36	21	37
None of them	5		5	
All of them	3		1	
Don't know	2		3	

CHAPTER 4
The Labour Party

The questions reported in this chapter run along much the same lines as those reported in Chapter 3 and were asked for much the same reasons. The two questions reported in Tables 4.1 and 4.2 are identical in format to those asked in Tables 3.1 and 3.2.

The questions about the Labour Party reported in Table 4.3 differ substantially, however, from the corresponding questions asked about the Conservatives. The reason is the obvious one: that people's reasons for being reluctant to vote Labour differ, and are likely to differ substantially, from their reasons for being reluctant to vote Conservative. In addition, because the Labour Party was in opposition in the 1980s and early 1990s and because it was far from clear at that time whether Labour could win the next general election, most of the 'reluctant to vote Labour' questions were asked between 1987 and 1996.

TABLE 4.1:   LABOUR PARTY'S REPUTATION 1978–97

Q. Regardless of your personal opinion, do you think that most people in Britain are holding a favourable opinion of the Labour Party or don't you think so?

		Are	Are not	DK
1978	Apr	34	44	22
	May	39	38	23
	Jun	45	35	20
	Jul	35	42	22
	Aug	35	40	25
	Sep	35	47	18
	Oct	31	44	25
	Nov	39	40	22
1979	Jan	30	51	19
	Jan	22	61	17
	Jan	20	64	16
	Feb	24	60	16
	Mar	22	60	19
	Apr	27	54	19
	Apr	23	56	20
	Apr	28	52	20
	Apr	29	47	24
	Apr	32	47	21
	Jun	25	55	21

cont'd . . .

		Are	Are not	DK
	Jul	38	42	20
	Sep	34	45	22
	Sep	34	50	16
	Sep	33	47	20
	Sep	34	44	21
	Oct	33	48	19
	Oct	40	43	18
	Dec	37	42	22
1980	Feb	35	41	23
	Mar	43	34	23
	Apr	38	35	27
	May	43	38	19
	Jun	39	41	19
	Jul	37	43	20
	Aug	41	40	19
	Sep	41	42	8
	Oct	40	45	15
	Oct	42	42	16
	Nov	47	33	19
	Dec	53	33	14
1981	Jan	43	41	17
	Feb	32	51	16
	Feb	32	53	15
	Mar	34	53	13
	Mar	36	49	15
	Apr	32	50	18
	May	39	44	17
	Jun	37	46	17
	Jul	38	46	17
	Oct	34	50	15
	Oct	39	48	14
1982	Jan	24	64	12
	Mar	27	56	16
	Apr	25	63	11
	May	21	67	12
	Jun	16	74	9
	Jul	19	71	10
	Aug	18	71	11
	Sep	22	68	10
	Oct	23	65	12
	Nov	25	62	13
	Dec	27	62	11
1983	Jan	23	64	13

cont'd . . .

		Are	Are not	DK
	Feb	25	64	10
	Mar	18	72	11
	Apr	27	60	14
	Apr	21	62	17
	May	23	62	14
	May	25	62	12
	May	22	64	14
	May	17	70	14
	Jun	17	70	14
	Jun	16	76	8
	Jun	14	77	9
	Jul	16	78	6
	Aug	13	82	5
	Sep	14	81	6
	Oct	29	57	14
	Nov	28	61	11
	Dec	33	53	14
1984	Jan	28	60	12
	Feb	31	57	12
	Mar	37	52	11
	Apr	33	56	12
	May	34	54	12
	Jun	33	56	11
	Jul	36	52	12
	Aug	32	54	14
	Sep	30	58	12
	Oct	25	64	11
	Nov	23	66	11
	Dec	20	70	10
1985	Jan	23	65	11
	Feb	21	67	13
	Mar	32	58	10
	Apr	33	54	13
	May	29	59	13
	Jun	33	58	10
	Jul	30	57	12
	Aug	35	53	12
	Sep	28	60	12
	Oct	36	51	12
	Nov	33	52	15
	Dec	29	58	13
1986	Jan	31	54	15
	Feb	32	56	12

cont'd . . .

		Are	Are not	DK
	Mar	32	55	12
1987	May	19	66	15
	Jun	24	66	10
	Jun	23	66	10
	Jun	23	66	10
	Jul	25	66	10
1991	Jun	45	38	18
	Oct	44	41	15
1992	May	24	61	15
	Jul	19	65	16
	Aug	27	53	20
	Sep	29	54	17
	Oct	35	48	17
	Oct	43	40	17
	Nov	42	42	16
1993	Jan	30	54	16
	Jan	37	47	17
	Feb	39	47	14
	Apr	42	43	15
	Apr	38	46	16
	May	42	41	17
	Jun	38	44	17
	Jul	42	44	14
	Sep	37	52	11
	Sep	37	47	16
	Oct	41	42	17
	Dec	42	44	14
1994	Jan	40	44	16
	Jan	43	38	19
	Feb	46	38	16
	Apr	49	35	17
	May	46	38	16
	May	58	24	18
	Jul	62	26	12
	Jul	65	21	14
	Sep	62	22	17
	Sep	59	23	17
	Oct	61	21	18
	Dec	62	20	18
1995	Jan	66	20	14
	Jan	64	20	17
	Feb	62	21	16

cont'd . . .

		Are	Are not	DK
	Apr	65	22	13
	May	73	12	15
	Jun	73	15	12
	Jul	67	19	15
	Jul	63	22	15
	Sep	62	20	18
	Sep	60	26	14
	Oct	63	20	17
	Nov	71	16	13
	Dec	67	18	15
1996	Jan	64	22	14
	Feb	60	22	18
	Mar	64	20	16
	Mar	61	22	16
	May	65	21	14
	Jun	64	22	14
	Jun	62	23	15
	Aug	59	27	14
	Sep	56	29	15
	Oct	60	26	14
	Nov	61	22	17
	Dec	62	24	14
1997	Jan	62	32	5
	Feb	63	30	7
	Mar	72	22	6
1997	Apr	72	20	7

TABLE 4.2: LABOUR PARTY'S CONCERN AND RESPONSIBILITY 1973–94

Q. Do you think the Labour Party is becoming more concerned for the interests of people like yourself, less concerned or is there no change?
Q. Do you think the Labour Party is becoming more responsible in its approach to the important issues facing the country, less responsible or is there no change?

		Concern				Responsibility			
		More	Less	NC	DK	More	Less	NC	DK
1973	Sep	28	20	39	12	26	18	42	14
	Oct	35	17	39	9	30	14	44	12
1974	Apr	38	17	35	10	42	15	30	13
	Jun	34	21	34	11	35	18	35	12

cont'd . . .

		Concern				Responsibility			
		More	Less	NC	DK	More	Less	NC	DK
1975	Jul	25	25	41	9	33	17	40	10
	Sep	15	37	44	4	26	28	39	7
	Oct	28	30	37	5	28	24	42	6
1976	Feb	26	27	43	4	27	20	46	7
	Sep	18	37	41	4	26	29	38	7
	Oct	16	42	35	6	24	35	35	7
1977	Sep	21	32	43	4	31	26	37	5
1978	Sep	17	31	46	7	23	23	44	10
1981	Feb	32	24	38	6	25	28	40	7
	Oct	33	21	42	4	27	23	43	6
1982	Sep	19	32	44	5	20	33	40	7
1983	Sep	20	29	45	5	17	38	37	7
1984	Sep	24	22	48	6	26	25	42	7
	Oct	35	21	37	6	31	28	35	6
1985	Mar	30	25	39	6	26	28	39	7
	Jun	40	18	34	8	35	19	37	8
	Sep	23	22	49	6	25	25	43	7
1986	Jan	34	19	38	9	33	21	37	9
	Sep	29	18	48	4	33	17	46	4
1987	Sep	29	19	48	4	31	19	46	5
1988	Sep	29	15	51	5	29	21	45	5
1989	Apr	43	11	40	7	46	12	36	6
	Sep	48	10	37	5	49	9	35	7
1992	Jul	35	17	42	6	37	12	44	7
1993	Mar	44	10	40	5	44	9	40	6
	Oct	41	12	42	6	45	10	38	6
1994	Aug	52	8	32	8	55	6	31	9

TABLE 4.3: REASONS FOR NOT VOTING LABOUR 1983-96

Q. Here are some reasons people give for not wanting to vote Labour at the next election. Which of these reasons do you yourself have most sympathy with? And which next?

	Feb 1991	Feb 1992	Sep 1995	Sep 1996
FIRST REASON				
Mr Blair would not make a good prime minister	18	26	8	7
Labour is in the pockets of the trade unions	14	12	12	13

cont'd ...

	Feb 1991	Feb 1992	Sep 1995	Sep 1996
A Labour Government would not do a good job of managing the country's economy	16	8	10	12
If there were a Labour Government, the rest of the world would lose confidence in Britain	10	8	10	6
A Labour Government would not provide a strong enough national defence	8	7	8	5
I would pay a lot more taxes under Labour without there being anything much to show for them	8	13	12	11
Prices would rise even faster under a Labour Government than they do now	6	6	7	9
None of these; don't know	21	20	34	37

	Feb 1991	Feb 1992	Sep 1995	Sep 1996
FIRST AND SECOND REASON				
Mr Blair would not make a good prime minister	30	36	11	12
Labour is in the pockets of the trade unions	24	22	21	21
A Labour Government would not do a good job of managing the country's economy	26	20	18	19
If there were a Labour Government, the rest of the world would lose confidence in Britain	20	18	17	14
A Labour Government would not provide a strong enough national defence	15	15	14	1
I would pay a lot more taxes under Labour without there being anything much to show for them	17	26	23	20
Prices would rise even faster under a Labour Government than they do now	14	13	17	17

Q. *People who say they are NOT going to vote Labour say there are various things about the Labour Party that worry them. Could you tell me for each of the following whether it is something that worries you personally or not*

	'Loyal'		'New'	
	Yes, a worry	No, is not	Yes, a worry	No, is not
AUGUST 1996				A
That taxes might go up so much that people would be squeezed financially	29	70	38	60
That no one really knows what Labour stands for	22	76	32	66
That the adoption of the European Social Chapter might cost jobs and deter inward investment from other countries	28	69	32	64
That under a Labour Government there might be a lot more strikes and industrial disputes	18	81	29	69
That with the setting up of a Scottish Parliament and a Welsh assembly the United Kingdom would disintegrate	20	78	22	76
That inflation, which is more or less under control at the moment, might begin to rise sharply	31	66	43	54
That we might hand over a lot of control of our own affairs to the European Union and Brussels	39	59	48	50
That under a Labour Government there would be even more crime and lawlessness than there is now	10	87	14	84
That a Labour Government would not be able to deliver on its promises	24	74	36	61

A Labour voters only. 'Loyal': Labour now and in 1992, 'New': Labour now but not in 1992

Q. *Why do you think the Labour Party lost the election?*

	Jun 1963
Too divided	32
Mr Foot's leadership	26
Poor manifesto/policies	24

cont'd . . .

	Jun 1963
Too far left	15
Nuclear policy	13
Back-biting comments	5
Common Market	4
Loss of confidence in them	3
Alliance split votes	3
Other	6
Don't know	8

Q. Here are some reasons give for liking and disliking the Labour government under Mr Kinnock. Could you tell me if any of them apply to you?

	May 1987
There are too many extremists in the Labour party	51
They would get rid of Britain's nuclear weapons	41
If Labour were back in power, inflation would start to rise again	36
Labour is too closely tied to the trade unions	35
They pay too much atention to people like gays, lesbians and blacks	35
They had their chance under Wilson and Callaghan and they made a mess of it	20
None of these	20

Q. Why do you think the Labour Party lost the election?

	Jun 1987
Defence policy	45
Too far left	21
Poor manifesto/policies	11
Kinnock's leadership	9
Taxation	4
Divided	3
Trade unions	3
Apathy	3
Other	22
Don't know	11

Q. Here are some reasons for not voting for the Labour Party. Which, if any, of these apply to you?

	Oct 1987	Jun 1988	Oct 1988
Labour's defence policy is dangerous	39	34	31
Trade unions have too much control of the Labour Party	35	39	34
Labour has moved too far to the left	34	30	22
Labour's too divided	34	39	35
The Labour Party can't control the unions	32	30	26
I can't see Neil Kinnock as Prime Minister	31	37	34
Taxes would go up under a Labour government	27	22	20
Labour governments can't control inflation	26	22	16
Labour's in the hands of extremists	25	23	15
I will be personally worse off under Labour	21	19	17
I don't know what Labour stands for any more	20	23	16
Labour's too concerned about helping minorities	19	18	14
I disagree with Labour's stand on privatisation	18	19	16
The real interests of the workers aren't what Labour is about today	18	16	14
I've never voted Labour and see no reason for changing now	15	18	15
I don't know who's in charge of the Labour Party today	13	12	9
There's too much secrecy in the Labour Party today	11	12	6
None of these	20	21	22

Q. Here are some reasons people give for not wanting to vote Labour at the next election. Which of these reasons do you yourself have most sympathy with? And which next?

	Nov 1989	Apr 1990
FIRST REASON		
A Labour Government would put at risk all the gains we have made over the past few years	20	17
Labour is in the pockets of the trade unions	13	16
If there were a Labour Government, the rest of the world would lose confidence in Britain	12	13

cont'd . . .

	Nov 1989	Apr 1990
Labour's policies are too extreme	4	4
Mr Kinnock would not make a good Prime Minister	12	16
A Labour Government would not provide a strong enough national defence	15	11
None of these	24	24

	Nov 1989	Apr 1990

FIRST AND SECOND REASON

	Nov 1989	Apr 1990
A Labour Government would put at risk all the gains we have made over the past few years	28	26
Labour is in the pockets of the trade unions	26	31
If there were a Labour Government, the rest of the world would lose confidence in Britain	26	24
Labour's policies are too extreme	10	11
Mr Kinnock would not make a good Prime Minister	22	26
A Labour Government would not provide a strong enough national defence	26	22
None of these	24	24

Q. Here are some reasons people give for not wanting to vote Labour at the next election. Which of these reasons do you yourself have most sympathy with? And which next?

A Labour is in the pockets of the trade unions
B If there were a Labour Government, the rest of the world would lose confidence in Britain
C Mr Kinnock would not make a good Prime Minister
D A Labour Government would not provide a strong enough national defence
E A Labour Government would not do a good job of managing the country's economy
F I would pay a lot more taxes under Labour, without anything much to show for them
G Prices would rise even faster under a Labour government than they do now
H None of these

		A	B	C	D	E	F	G	H
FIRST REASON									
1990	Jun	15	11	15	7	14	8	7	23
	Sep	13	7	15	9	13	6	8	28
1991	Jun	15	11	17	11	14	7	6	20
	Aug	14	8	19	4	13	10	7	26
	Aug	12	9	19	9	12	10	6	23
	Sep	14	10	18	8	16	8	6	21
1992	Feb	12	8	26	7	8	13	6	20
1992	Apr	14	8	24	9	8	11	6	20

		A	B	C	D	E	F	G	H
FIRST AND SECOND REASON									
1990	Jun	26	22	24	14	23	15	14	23
	Sep	22	16	24	16	22	14	17	28
1991	Jun	27	23	28	21	22	14	15	20
	Aug	24	19	28	10	21	19	16	26
	Aug	24	17	30	16	19	19	14	23
	Sep	24	20	30	15	26	17	14	21
1992	Feb	22	18	36	15	20	26	13	20
1992	Apr	26	18	34	16	18	22	14	20

CHAPTER 5

The Liberals, the Liberal/SDP Alliance and the Liberal Democrats

The Liberal Party and its successor parties never held power in the last half of the twentieth century and, except for a brief period in 1982–3, at no stage seemed on the brink of power. For that reason, although a considerable number of specific questions were asked about the Liberal Party and the Liberal/SDP Alliance in the early and mid 1980s, there are few continuous time-series concerning the Liberals and the other 'centre' formations.

Tables 5.1–5.3 report the few that there are and take much the same form as those reported for the Conservative Party in Table 3.1 and the Labour Party in Table 4.1. Asking the questions was complicated by the fact that the Liberals at the beginning of the 1980s were a completely independent, free-standing party. However, they then allied themselves with the short-lived Social Democratic Party before merging with the Social Democrats to form the Liberal Democrat Party (initially the Social and Liberal Democrats) in 1987. A number of consequential changes of question wording are reported in the footnotes.

TABLE 5.1   LIBERAL PARTY'S REPUTATION 1983–6

Q. Regardless of your personal opinion, do you think that most people in Britain are holding a favourable opinion of the Liberal Party or don't you think so?

		Are	Are not	DK
1983	Jan	28	46	26
	Feb	27	52	21
	Mar	42	37	21
	Apr	31	46	23
	Apr	33	43	25

cont'd . . .

		Are	Are not	DK
	May	32	44	24
	May	30	46	23
	May	33	44	23
	May	27	49	24
	Jun	38	37	25
	Jun	39	45	16
	Jun	39	43	18
	Jul	44	38	18
	Aug	42	41	17
	Sep	38	44	18
	Oct	38	42	20
	Nov	34	48	18
	Dec	30	48	22
1984	Jan	29	48	22
	Feb	30	49	21
	Mar	34	48	18
	Apr	32	47	21
	May	38	42	20
	Jun	33	49	18
	Jul	33	48	18
	Aug	33	45	22
	Sep	30	49	21
	Oct	28	51	21
	Nov	28	54	18
	Dec	31	48	21
1985	Jan	36	44	20
	Feb	31	46	22
	Mar	32	48	19
	Apr	32	50	19
	May	46	35	19
	Jun	44	41	15
	Jul	48	35	17
	Aug	44	37	19
	Sep	43	36	21
	Oct	39	44	17
	Nov	37	40	23
	Dec	42	35	23
1986	Jan	39	38	23
	Feb	42	39	19
1986	Mar	38	41	21

TABLE 5.2: LIBERAL/SDP ALLIANCE'S REPUTATION 1981–87

Q. Regardless of your personal opinion, do you think that most people in Britain are holding a favourable opinion of the Social Democratic Party or don't you think so?

		Are	Are not	DK	
1981	Mar	31	34	35	A
1982	Jan	58	19	23	
	Mar	37	33	30	
	Mar	46	26	27	
	Apr	51	23	26	
	May	41	34	25	
	Jun	28	45	28	
	Jul	31	42	27	
	Aug	28	42	29	
	Sep	28	44	28	
	Oct	22	49	29	
	Nov	26	44	31	
	Dec	23	50	27	
1983	Jan	24	47	29	B
	Feb	19	57	24	
	Mar	44	33	23	
	Apr	25	47	28	
	Apr	23	47	30	
	May	22	50	28	
	May	20	54	26	
	May	23	51	26	
	May	20	53	27	
	Jun	36	37	26	
	Jun	30	51	19	
	Jun	32	47	21	
	Jul	34	43	23	
	Aug	38	43	19	
	Sep	38	42	20	
	Oct	32	46	22	
	Nov	25	53	21	
	Dec	27	50	24	
1984	Jan	23	53	24	
	Feb	24	54	22	
	Mar	30	51	19	
	Apr	26	51	23	
	May	34	45	21	
	Jun	31	47	21	
	Jul	35	45	20	
	Aug	31	45	23	

cont'd . . .

		Are	Are not	DK	
	Sep	29	48	23	
	Oct	30	46	24	
	Nov	29	51	19	
	Dec	31	47	22	
1985	Jan	36	42	22	
	Feb	34	42	25	
	Mar	31	48	21	
	Apr	31	46	23	
	May	49	31	19	
	Jun	44	39	16	
	Jul	49	32	19	
	Aug	47	34	19	
	Sep	47	34	19	
	Oct	41	40	20	
	Nov	39	39	24	
	Dec	45	32	23	
1986	Jan	44	33	23	
	Feb	47	33	19	
	Mar	43	36	21	
1987	May	44	34	22	C
	Jun	16	69	15	
	Jun	19	65	15	
1987	Jun	13	72	15	

A Question in 1981 referred to the 'Social Democrats'.
B Question in January 1983 referred to 'Liberals and Social Democrats'.
C Question in 1987 referred to 'Liberal/SDP Alliance'.

TABLE 5.3: LIBERAL DEMOCRAT PARTY'S REPUTATION 1991-97

Q. *Regardless of your personal opinion, do you think that most people in Britain are holding a favourable opinion of the Liberal Democrats or don't you think so?*

		Are	Are not	DK
1991	Jun	33	39	28
1992	May	35	41	24
	Jul	27	52	21
	Aug	24	50	26
	Sep	28	49	23
	Oct	22	53	24

cont'd . . .

		Are	Are not	DK
	Oct	26	50	24
	Nov	28	50	22
1993	Jan	26	49	25
	Jan	27	48	25
	Feb	28	50	22
	Apr	27	47	27
	Apr	31	45	24
	May	50	31	19
	Jun	47	32	21
	Jul	52	26	22
	Sep	50	32	18
	Sep	51	30	18
	Oct	45	34	21
	Dec	39	37	24
1994	Jan	38	37	26
	Jan	36	38	26
	Feb	38	37	24
	Apr	40	34	26
	May	50	30	21
	May	52	25	23
	Jul	41	38	20
	Jul	38	40	23
	Sep	34	40	25
	Sep	26	46	27
	Oct	30	42	28
	Dec	30	41	29
1995	Jan	27	44	30
	Jan	27	44	29
	Feb	31	40	29
	Apr	29	41	30
	May	40	32	28
	Jun	37	34	29
	Jul	30	43	27
	Jul	32	41	27
	Sep	31	39	31
	Sep	32	41	27
	Oct	32	38	30
	Nov	27	42	32
	Dec	28	41	32
1996	Jan	36	36	28
	Feb	33	38	29
	Mar	38	34	29
	Mar	35	36	29
	May	40	33	27

cont'd . . .

		Are	Are not	DK
	Jun	36	38	26
	Jun	37	39	24
	Aug	30	42	28
	Sep	30	44	26
	Oct	34	41	24
	Nov	32	38	30
	Dec	30	43	27
1997	Jan	39	56	6
1997	Feb	33	56	10

CHAPTER 6

Governments

One of Gallup's longest-running time-series is reported in Table 6.1. It is in response to the question, 'Do you approve or disapprove of the government's record to date?' As noted in the footnotes to the table, the precise wording of the question was altered occasionally between 1946 and 1953, but the alterations were never substantial and since 1954 the question spelt out above has remained unchanged. The responses to it have formed part of the Gallup Index since November 1990.

Table 6.2 is more complicated and reports the responses to a question dealing with the government of the day's handling of specific policy fields. The specific fields changed from time to time, of course, as circumstances and the foci of public interest changed. The question was asked on various occasions, and with minor changes of wording, between 1958 and 1990. In more recent years, it has been largely replaced by the principal 'best to handle' question reported in Table 2.2 above.

Table 6.3 represents a response to the politically related 'sleaze' of the 1990s and to the belief, widespread after 1997, that the success or failure of the new Blair government would partly depend on whether or not it was perceived to be honest and trustworthy. As often happens in opinion research, there are, alas, no strictly comparable data from earlier decades. The opinion polls, like everyone else, usually begin to ask questions only when something untoward has already happened. By that time, it is too late, of course, to establish a suitable tracking series.

TABLE 6.1: APPROVAL OF GOVERNMENT'S RECORD 1946–2000

Q. Do you approve or disapprove of the Government's record to date?

		Approve	Disapprove	DK	
1946	Jun	42	45	13	A
1946	Aug	46	41	13	B
1947	Mar	39	54	7	
	May	42	48	10	C
	Jul	38	52	10	
	Dec	41	49	10	
1948	Jan	44	47	9	
	Mar	35	53	12	
	Jul	36	54	10	

cont'd . . .

		Approve	Disapprove	DK
	Sep	37	51	12
	Nov	43	46	11
1949	Jan	44	47	9
	Mar	46	43	11
	May	37	53	10
	Jul	39	48	13
	Sep	36	53	11
	Dec	39	51	10
1950	May	41	49	10
	Aug	44	46	10
	Oct	45	45	10
	Dec	38	51	11
1951	Feb	31	60	9
	Apr	32	59	9
	May	35	56	9
	Jul	31	56	13
	Sep	35	54	11
	Dec	44	29	27
1952	May	40	48	12
	Aug	44	44	12
	Nov	47	33	20
1953	Jan	46	38	16
	Jul	49	35	16
	Oct	54	31	15
1954	Jan	50	32	18
	Jun	47	33	20
1955	Jan	53	32	15
	Dec	44	40	16
1956	Apr	34	43	23
	May	40	45	15
	Jul	36	46	18
1957	Oct	37	42	21
1958	Jan	38	42	20
	May	30	43	27
	Aug	41	35	24
	Oct	43	27	30
	Nov	48	33	19
	Dec	50	29	21
1959	Jan	48	34	18

D

cont'd . . .

		Approve	Disapprove	DK
	Feb	41	30	29
	Apr	46	35	19
	May	47	32	21
	Jun	49	29	22
	Jul	53	24	23
	Aug	56	28	16
1960	Oct	59	23	18
	Dec	56	23	21
1961	Jan	48	32	20
	Feb	48	32	20
	Mar	51	30	19
	Apr	50	30	20
	May	49	33	18
	Jun	52	29	19
	Jul	49	36	15
	Aug	38	44	18
	Sep	39	43	18
	Oct	47	36	17
	Nov	43	38	19
1962	Jan	43	39	18
	Feb	41	40	19
	Apr	37	47	16
	May	38	44	18
	Jul	41	44	15
	Aug	37	51	12
	Sep	38	46	16
	Oct	36	45	19
	Nov	41	40	19
	Dec	36	43	21
1963	Jan	34	50	16
	Mar	30	52	18
	Apr	33	50	17
	May	38	45	17
	Jun	31	51	18
	Jul	32	53	15
	Aug	39	45	16
	Sep	38	46	16
	Oct	36	44	20
	Nov	44	41	15
	Dec	46	37	17
1964	Jan	41	37	22
	Feb	42	37	21

cont'd . . .

		Approve	Disapprove	DK
	Mar	41	40	19
	May	41	41	18
	Jul	43	38	19
	Aug	46	35	19
	Sep	42	35	23
	Nov	49	31	20
	Dec	48	30	22
1965	Jan	39	35	26
	Feb	43	40	17
	Mar	47	38	15
	Apr	45	34	21
	May	39	45	16
	Jun	35	47	18
	Jul	36	41	23
	Aug	39	45	16
	Sep	42	43	15
	Oct	49	36	15
	Nov	50	30	20
	Dec	55	32	13
1966	Jan	51	29	20
	Feb	48	36	16
	Apr	53	32	15
	May	54	31	15
	Jun	44	36	20
	Jul	42	37	21
	Aug	35	50	15
	Sep	36	49	15
	Oct	32	52	16
	Nov	33	50	17
	Dec	40	48	12
1967	Jan	40	45	15
	Feb	44	44	12
	Mar	40	45	15
	Apr	44	41	15
	May	38	47	15
	Jun	36	46	18
	Jul	35	45	20
	Aug	33	50	17
	Sep	29	56	15
	Nov	28	59	13
	Dec	21	64	15
1968	Jan	23	55	22

cont'd . . .

		Approve	Disapprove	DK
	Feb	23	63	14
	Mar	18	66	16
	Apr	17	69	14
	May	19	69	12
	Jun	19	67	14
	Jul	18	63	19
	Aug	21	60	19
	Sep	24	58	18
	Oct	28	54	18
	Nov	20	60	20
	Dec	17	70	13
1969	Jan	23	60	17
	Feb	22	61	17
	Mar	22	59	19
	Apr	21	64	15
	May	19	65	16
	Jun	24	60	16
	Jul	22	61	17
	Aug	25	58	17
	Sep	28	56	16
	Oct	35	47	18
	Nov	35	48	17
	Dec	31	53	16
1970	Jan	32	49	19
	Feb	31	51	18
	Mar	35	48	17
	Apr	42	42	16
	Jun	40	45	15
	Aug	21	24	55
	Oct	29	26	45
	Nov	31	47	22
	Dec	37	43	20
1971	Jan	35	44	21
	Feb	31	50	19
	Mar	33	49	18
	Apr	40	41	19
	May	31	54	15
	Jun	22	58	20
	Jul	26	57	17
	Aug	35	49	16
	Sep	30	52	18
	Oct	32	50	18

cont'd . . .

		Approve	Disapprove	DK
	Nov	35	44	21
	Dec	34	48	18
1972	Jan	37	45	18
	Feb	32	55	13
	Mar	35	49	16
	Apr	43	39	18
	May	36	46	18
	Jun	36	44	20
	Jul	31	50	19
	Aug	32	51	17
	Sep	30	52	18
	Oct	33	49	18
	Nov	33	57	10
	Dec	36	43	21
1973	Jan	33	46	21
	Feb	33	50	17
	Mar	38	46	16
	Apr	32	47	21
	May	35	48	17
	Jun	37	43	20
	Jul	31	51	18
	Aug	29	55	16
	Sep	29	51	20
	Oct	30	51	19
	Nov	31	49	20
	Dec	34	53	13
1974	Jan	36	50	14
	Feb	32	53	15
	Apr	48	27	25
	May	40	38	22
	Jun	41	38	21
	Jul	32	47	21
	Aug	37	43	20
	Sep	28	48	24
	Oct	37	43	20
	Nov	40	40	20
	Dec	42	36	22
1975	Jan	37	38	25
	Feb	32	47	21
	Mar	37	41	22
	Apr	32	50	18
	May	26	55	19

cont'd . . .

		Approve	Disapprove	DK
	Jun	31	49	20
	Jul	27	53	20
	Aug	32	53	15
	Sep	30	51	19
	Oct	30	55	15
	Nov	31	51	18
	Dec	27	54	19
1976	Jan	29	53	18
	Feb	32	51	17
	Mar	30	53	17
	Apr	39	41	20
	May	27	50	23
	Jun	28	53	19
	Jul	32	47	21
	Aug	29	52	19
	Sep	29	52	19
	Oct	20	64	16
	Nov	19	64	17
	Dec	18	64	18
1977	Jan	21	60	19
	Feb	21	62	17
	Mar	22	63	15
	Apr	23	62	15
	May	23	59	18
	Jun	28	55	17
	Jul	24	58	18
	Aug	33	53	14
	Sep	32	49	19
	Oct	41	43	16
	Nov	41	43	16
	Dec	41	44	15
1978	Jan	43	40	17
	Feb	43	40	17
	Mar	41	44	15
	Apr	44	39	17
	May	41	40	19
	Jun	40	42	18
	Jul	40	44	16
	Aug	39	42	19
	Sep	39	47	14
	Oct	44	42	14
	Nov	44	41	15
	Dec	37	44	19

cont'd . . .

		Approve	Disapprove	DK
1979	Jan	34	52	14
	Feb	23	63	14
	Mar	27	56	17
	Apr	33	50	16
	May			
	Jun	34	41	25
	Jul	34	48	18
	Aug	38	44	18
	Sep	36	46	18
	Oct	34	48	18
	Nov	38	50	12
	Dec	34	53	13
1980	Jan	33	53	14
	Feb	30	55	15
	Mar	30	59	11
	Apr	36	52	12
	May	37	52	12
	Jun	35	52	13
	Jul	33	54	13
	Aug	35	53	13
	Sep	30	57	13
	Oct	34	54	12
	Nov	29	60	11
	Dec	29	59	12
1981	Jan	26	63	11
	Jan	28	58	14
	Feb	29	60	11
	Mar	23	67	10
	Mar	22	69	9
	Apr	24	67	9
	May	29	60	11
	Jun	26	63	11
	Jul	23	66	11
	Aug	23	66	11
	Sep	26	63	11
	Oct	24	62	14
	Nov	23	66	11
	Dec	18	70	12
1982	Jan	24	65	11
	Feb	24	66	10
	Mar	29	59	12
	Apr	32	56	12
	May	42	46	12

cont'd . . .

		Approve	Disapprove	DK
	Jun	48	40	12
	Jul	47	41	12
	Aug	42	44	14
	Sep	40	48	12
	Oct	40	49	11
	Nov	39	48	13
	Dec	37	50	13
1983	Jan	43	43	14
	Feb	39	49	12
	Mar	41	48	11
	Apr	38	49	13
	May	45	43	12
	Jun	44	45	11
	Jul	46	43	11
	Aug	44	45	11
	Sep	47	42	11
	Oct	41	47	12
	Nov	40	49	11
	Dec	38	50	12
1984	Jan	42	46	12
	Feb	41	45	14
	Mar	41	49	10
	Apr	42	45	13
	May	37	51	12
	Jun	36	53	11
	Jul	36	54	10
	Aug	34	54	12
	Sep	34	52	14
	Oct	43	43	14
	Nov	41	46	13
	Dec	34	52	14
1985	Jan	33	54	13
	Feb	31	55	13
	Mar	30	58	12
	Apr	32	57	11
	May	28	58	14
	Jun	31	59	9
	Jul	28	59	13
	Aug	23	65	12
	Sep	29	56	15
	Oct	29	59	13
	Nov	29	59	13
	Dec	34	54	12

cont'd . . .

		Approve	Disapprove	DK
1986	Jan	27	58	14
	Feb	25	65	10
	Mar	29	60	11
	Apr	23	64	12
	May	27	61	12
	Jun	27	60	13
	Jul	30	58	12
	Aug	25	62	13
	Sep	30	56	14
	Oct	33	56	11
	Nov	36	52	12
	Dec	34	51	16
1987	Jan	30	57	13
	Feb	32	53	15
	Mar	35	51	13
	Apr	41	47	12
	May	38	48	13
	Jun	36	52	11
	Jul	44	45	11
	Aug	44	46	10
	Sep	42	48	10
	Sep	43	45	12
	Oct	46	41	12
	Nov	43	45	12
	Dec	42	47	12
1988	Jan	42	46	11
	Feb	40	49	11
	Mar	40	47	13
	Apr	35	55	10
	May	40	48	12
	Jun	39	50	11
	Jul	39	48	14
	Aug	41	46	13
	Sep	42	47	12
	Oct	43	44	13
	Nov	38	49	13
	Dec	38	50	12
1989	Jan	36	49	15
	Feb	32	52	16
	Mar	36	51	14
	Apr	37	51	13
	May	33	54	13
	Jun	35	53	12

cont'd . . .

		Approve	Disapprove	DK
	Jul	28	59	13
	Aug	31	56	13
	Sep	31	58	11
	Oct	29	58	12
	Nov	28	60	13
	Dec	31	57	12
1990	Jan	30	58	12
	Feb	26	60	13
	Mar	21	71	8
	Apr	23	69	8
	May	25	64	11
	Jun	24	67	9
	Jul	28	61	10
	Aug	27	61	12
	Sep	30	61	9
	Oct	29	60	10
	Nov	29.8	58.5	11.7
	Dec	34.3	53.4	12.3
1991	Jan	36.6	50.0	13.5
	Feb	37.0	48.9	14.2
	Mar	33.0	54.0	13.0
	Apr	33.2	53.3	13.5
	May	29.7	56.8	13.5
	Jun	29.8	56.3	13.9
	Jul	30.4	55.5	14.1
	Aug	31.4	54.4	14.2
	Sep	33.9	51.9	14.1
	Oct	33.2	52.6	14.1
	Nov	32.3	54.2	13.5
	Dec	33.2	54.2	12.6
1992	Jan	30.1	56.4	13.5
	Feb	29.7	56.6	13.7
	Mar	29.4	57.0	13.5
	Apr	29	61	11
	May	40	48	12
	Jun	35	54	11
	Jul	30.4	55.5	14.1
	Aug	26.2	60.7	13.1
	Sep	22.4	64.5	13.1
	Oct	14.0	75.6	10.4
	Nov	13.9	77.4	8.7
	Dec	15.9	74.9	9.2

cont'd . . .

		Approve	Disapprove	DK
1993	Jan	17.4	72.1	10.5
	Feb	16.0	74.3	9.8
	Mar	14.4	76.0	9.6
	Apr	16.0	74.4	9.6
	May	13.8	77.4	8.8
	Jun	11.0	80.4	8.7
	Jul	12.2	79.0	8.8
	Aug	12.0	79.0	9.0
	Sep	11.9	79.5	8.6
	Oct	13.1	77.3	9.5
	Nov	12.3	78.9	8.8
	Dec	14.0	76.5	9.4
1994	Jan	13.8	77.2	9.0
	Feb	14.0	77.3	8.6
	Mar	13.9	76.6	9.5
	Apr	12.0	78.9	9.1
	May	11.1	79.5	9.4
	Jun	10.7	78.9	10.4
	Jul	11.3	78.3	10.5
	Aug	11.9	77.9	10.3
	Sep	12.4	77.1	10.5
	Oct	12.7	76.4	10.9
	Nov	11.1	78.1	10.8
	Dec	9.7	81.1	9.2
1995	Jan	10.5	80.0	9.5
	Feb	10.5	80.0	9.5
	Mar	11.2	78.6	10.1
	Apr	11.5	79.0	9.5
	May	10.4	79.3	10.3
	Jun	11.9	77.8	10.4
	Jul	13.9	74.4	11.7
	Aug	13.8	74.4	11.7
	Sep	13.2	75.6	11.2
	Oct	14.7	73.9	11.4
	Nov	13.5	74.2	12.3
	Dec	14.7	74.5	10.8
1996	Jan	13.8	74.7	11.5
	Feb	14.4	74.7	10.9
	Mar	13.3	75.3	11.5
	Apr	14.0	73.6	12.3
	May	13.8	73.6	12.6
	Jun	15.0	72.2	12.8
	Jul	16.5	69.7	13.8

cont'd . . .

		Approve	Disapprove	DK
	Aug	18.1	68.9	12.9
	Sep	19.3	67.3	13.3
	Oct	18.7	67.1	14.2
	Nov	20.3	65.4	14.2
	Dec	19.3	67.8	12.9
1997	Jan	24.0	65.2	10.8
	Feb	25.5	63.3	11.2
	Mar	25.5	64.0	10.5
	Apr	27.0	62.0	11.0
	May	76.0	13.1	10.9
	Jun	71.7	13.3	15.0
	Jul	67.6	21.8	10.6
	Aug	63.4	27.0	9.5
	Sep	71.1	17.5	11.5
	Oct	69.6	19.9	10.5
	Nov	61.0	27.4	11.6
	Dec	54.3	35.6	10.1
1998	Jan	52.5	37.6	9.9
	Feb	52.4	38.5	9.1
	Mar	46.8	40.9	12.3
	Apr	54.9	34.0	11.1
	May	61.2	29.0	9.8
	Jun	54.8	36.9	8.3
	Jul	55.0	36.9	8.1
	Aug	54.4	38.1	7.5
	Sep	53.3	35.8	10.9
	Oct	55.6	35.6	8.9
	Nov	54.7	36.2	9.0
	Dec	53.2	36.0	10.8
1999	Jan	51.8	39.0	9.2
	Feb	50.3	37.3	12.3
	Mar	50.3	37.1	12.6
	Apr	56.5	35.7	7.8
	May	56.5	36.3	7.2
	Jun	51.6	37.2	11.2
	Jul	52.9	38.5	8.6
	Aug	53.0	40.7	6.3
	Sep	51.8	42.4	5.8
	Oct	52.9	39.9	7.2
	Nov	51.3	41.5	7.2
	Dec	52.1	39.8	8.1
2000	Jan	49.1	42.4	8.5

cont'd . . .

		Approve	Disapprove	DK
	Feb	47.0	46.5	6.5
	Mar	44.8	47.6	7.6
	Apr	44.2	46.8	9.0
	May	39.4	47.9	12.7
	Jun	38.4	49.6	12.0
	Jul	42.2	51.8	6.1
	Aug	45.5	47.6	6.9
	Sep	34.5	60.9	4.6
	Oct	36.7	57.3	6.0
	Nov	39.2	53.3	7.6
2000	Dec	43.8	48.1	8.1

A Question in June 1946 began, 'In general, . . .?'

B Question in August 1946 to March 1947, April 1951 to July 1953, and January 1954 read, 'Are you satisfied or disatisfied with the Government's record to date?'

C Question in May 1947 to December 1950 read, 'On the whole, are you satisfied or dissatisfied with the Government's record to date?'

D Question in February 1951 and October 1953 read, 'Are you satisfied with the Government's record to date?'

TABLE 6.2: APPROVAL OF GOVERNMENT'S HANDLING OF SPECIFIC POLICY FIELDS

Q. In general, do you approve or disapprove of the way the Government is handling:

DEF	Defence and armaments?
COL	The cost of living and prices?
ECON	Economic and financial affairs?
LAB	Labour relations?
EMP	Employment problems?
EDU	Education?
HEA	Health services?
HOU	Housing?
CM	The Common Market?
PEN	Pensions?
IMM	Immigration of coloured people?
ROA	Roads and transport?
LAW	Law and order?
TAX	Taxation
ENV	The environment

A	Approve
D	Disapprove
DK	Don't Know

cont'd . . .

contd . .

Year	Month	DEF			COL			ECON			LAB			EMP			EDU			HEA			HOU			CM			PEN			IMM			ROA			LAW			TAX			ENV			Note
		A	D	DK	A	D	DK	A	D	DK	A	D	DK	A	D	DK	A	D	DK	A	D	DK	A	D	DK	A	D	DK	A	D	DK	A	D	DK	A	D	DK	A	D	DK	A	D	DK	A	D	DK	
1958	Dec	–	–	–	–	–	–	49	25	26	–	–	–	38	40	22	–	–	–	–	–	–	–	–	–	–	–	–	–	–	–	–	–	–	–	–	–	–	–	–	–	–	–	–	–	–	–	
1959	Jan	–	–	–	–	–	–	48	33	19	–	–	–	32	48	20	–	–	–	–	–	–	–	–	–	–	–	–	–	–	–	–	–	–	–	–	–	–	–	–	–	–	–	–	–	–	–	
	Feb	–	–	–	–	–	–	39	30	31	–	–	–	28	45	27	–	–	–	–	–	–	–	–	–	–	–	–	–	–	–	–	–	–	–	–	–	–	–	–	–	–	–	–	–	–	–	
	Mar	–	–	–	–	–	–	49	27	24	–	–	–	30	46	24	–	–	–	–	–	–	–	–	–	–	–	–	–	–	–	–	–	–	–	–	–	–	–	–	–	–	–	–	–	–	–	
	Apr	–	–	–	–	–	–	52	22	26	–	–	–	34	46	20	–	–	–	–	–	–	–	–	–	–	–	–	–	–	–	–	–	–	–	–	–	–	–	–	–	–	–	–	–	–	–	
	May	–	–	–	–	–	–	47	30	23	–	–	–	35	43	22	–	–	–	–	–	–	–	–	–	–	–	–	–	–	–	–	–	–	–	–	–	–	–	–	–	–	–	–	–	–	–	
	Jun	–	–	–	–	–	–	53	18	29	–	–	–	43	32	25	–	–	–	–	–	–	–	–	–	–	–	–	–	–	–	–	–	–	–	–	–	–	–	–	–	–	–	–	–	–	–	
	Jul	–	–	–	–	–	–	50	21	29	–	–	–	42	36	22	–	–	–	–	–	–	–	–	–	–	–	–	–	–	–	–	–	–	–	–	–	–	–	–	–	–	–	–	–	–	–	
	Aug	–	–	–	–	–	–	–	–	–	–	–	–	47	37	16	–	–	–	–	–	–	–	–	–	–	–	–	–	–	–	–	–	–	–	–	–	–	–	–	–	–	–	–	–	–	–	
	Dec	–	–	–	–	–	–	53	26	21	–	–	–	–	–	–	–	–	–	–	–	–	–	–	–	–	–	–	–	–	–	–	–	–	–	–	–	–	–	–	–	–	–	–	–	–	–	
1967	Mar	–	–	–	–	–	–	41	44	15	–	–	–	32	52	17	–	–	–	–	–	–	–	–	–	–	–	–	–	–	–	–	–	–	–	–	–	–	–	–	–	–	–	–	–	–	–	
	May	–	–	–	–	–	–	38	42	20	–	–	–	33	50	17	–	–	–	–	–	–	–	–	–	–	–	–	–	–	–	–	–	–	–	–	–	–	–	–	–	–	–	–	–	–	–	
1968	Jul	25	48	27	12	80	8	18	63	19	21	48	31	23	55	22	41	38	21	49	39	12	37	42	21	–	–	–	34	48	18	26	56	18	29	45	26	–	–	–	–	–	–	–	–	–	A
1969	Mar	24	45	31	11	84	5	18	62	20	21	52	27	28	50	22	44	36	20	56	32	12	36	45	19	–	–	–	38	49	13	23	56	21	29	43	28	–	–	–	–	–	–	–	–	–	
1970	May	33	37	30	12	81	7	38	44	18	–	–	–	40	39	21	54	29	17	65	25	10	39	43	18	17	58	25	39	49	12	22	61	17	47	35	18	–	–	–	–	–	–	–	–	–	B
	Oct	33	22	45	16	59	25	26	37	37	27	49	24	28	33	39	45	27	28	49	22	29	39	29	32	21	43	36	33	37	30	34	32	34	32	20	48	–	–	–	–	–	–	–	–	–	C
1971	Oct	28	26	46	14	80	6	28	50	22	29	60	11	14	70	6	46	30	24	48	37	15	40	39	21	27	51	22	36	52	12	28	46	26	41	25	34	–	–	–	–	–	–	–	–	–	D
1972	Oct	38	24	38	15	80	5	28	54	18	27	63	10	21	62	17	52	29	19	61	28	11	35	49	16	36	47	17	31	61	8	26	63	11	51	23	26	–	–	–	–	–	–	–	–	–	E
1973	Oct	38	26	36	15	78	7	27	56	17	29	59	12	48	33	19	49	31	20	58	30	12	25	59	16	31	53	16	42	48	10	23	61	16	45	29	26	–	–	–	–	–	–	–	–	–	
1974	May	30	27	43	36	53	11	33	42	25	36	52	12	47	25	28	41	39	20	60	24	16	33	48	19	35	45	20	72	21	7	23	47	30	40	24	36	–	–	–	–	–	–	–	–	–	
	Jul	33	29	38	13	80	7	18	63	19	17	75	8	20	60	20	38	39	23	48	38	14	30	51	19	54	27	19	59	30	11	25	51	24	43	23	34	–	–	–	–	–	–	–	–	–	
1975	Jun	21	48	31	35	57	7	36	46	18	35	54	12	47	25	28	34	54	17	38	56	7	41	40	19	32	51	17	60	32	9	28	59	13	38	39	24	33	57	11	–	–	–	–	–	–	
1978	Oct	23	48	29	35	58	7	36	46	18	24	61	14	30	50	20	38	48	14	42	50	8	43	38	20	32	49	20	56	34	10	26	59	15	34	40	26	31	59	10	–	–	–	–	–	–	
	Dec	26	44	30	31	61	8	30	49	21	25	64	11	32	52	15	38	47	15	43	48	9	45	37	18	30	50	20	53	35	12	25	57	18	37	41	22	35	52	14	–	–	–	–	–	–	
1979	Feb	23	43	33	24	69	7	27	55	17	14	79	7	23	60	16	39	48	13	36	57	7	42	38	20	27	55	19	52	36	12	22	60	18	32	47	21	39	52	9	–	–	–	–	–	–	
	Feb	24	46	30	20	76	4	21	64	15	11	84	5	20	68	13	35	53	12	32	60	8	38	40	22	25	54	21	48	42	10	24	60	16	37	43	19	30	59	11	–	–	–	–	–	–	
	Mar	27	43	30	21	72	7	23	61	16	16	78	6	21	66	14	38	47	16	34	57	8	42	42	16	30	49	21	50	41	10	26	54	20	33	45	22	34	55	12	–	–	–	–	–	–	
	Jun	38	23	39	24	63	13	33	41	27	26	38	37	30	34	36	48	29	22	45	34	21	45	30	25	34	44	22	65	22	13	40	37	23	22	32	46	54	25	21	–	–	–	–	–	–	
	Jul	39	26	35	22	67	11	34	44	22	31	48	21	29	46	25	37	46	17	39	44	17	46	36	18	33	44	23	54	31	15	37	46	17	22	34	43	52	32	16	40	48	12	–	–	–	

TABLE 6.2 cont'd

		DEF			COL			ECON			LAB			EMP			EDU			HEA			HOU			CM			PEN			IMM			ROA			LAW			TAX			ENV		
		A	D	DK	A	D	DK	A	D	DK	A	D	DK	A	D	DK	A	D	DK	A	D	DK	A	D	DK	A	D	DK	A	D	DK	A	D	DK	A	D	DK	A	D	DK	A	D	DK	A	D	DK
1979	Aug	43	26	31	22	67	11	34	46	20	31	47	22	31	50	19	37	48	15	38	52	10	44	37	20	34	46	20	53	33	14	35	52	14	24	43	33	54	33	13	42	46	12	—	—	—
	Sep	37	29	33	21	69	10	33	47	20	28	59	13	27	51	22	35	51	14	34	55	11	43	38	20	31	48	22	48	39	14	34	50	16	26	44	30	49	39	11	40	47	13	—	—	—
	Oct	37	26	37	23	69	8	33	46	20	35	49	16	33	47	20	29	55	17	28	58	14	42	34	25	31	42	27	54	29	17	44	36	20	26	36	38	58	25	17	47	41	12	—	—	—
	Oct	40	24	36	25	66	9	36	42	22	35	50	16	28	49	23	35	52	14	35	52	12	45	36	19	30	49	21	48	34	19	46	37	17	25	37	38	59	29	12	48	39	13	—	—	—
1980	Mar	39	32	29	19	75	6	28	58	13	32	59	9	23	61	16	25	62	13	29	64	8	32	50	18	33	49	18	40	45	15	40	41	18	25	46	28	58	28	13	36	52	11	—	—	—
	Jul	44	36	21	20	72	8	31	48	21	39	51	9	20	64	16	26	64	10	29	64	7	31	50	19	36	49	15	44	41	15	35	46	20	27	43	30	60	28	12	33	53	14	—	—	—
	Sep	43	29	28	19	75	5	31	48	21	32	57	12	23	62	15	23	62	15	27	63	11	30	48	22	32	46	22	31	57	12	31	44	25	23	45	32	48	39	13	32	51	17	—	—	—
	Dec	40	42	19	25	70	5	29	59	12	36	55	10	15	77	8	31	56	13	30	63	7	31	58	12	37	47	16	42	46	13	39	42	18	30	47	23	54	37	9	30	59	10	—	—	—
1981	Mar	34	47	19	15	80	5	22	63	14	33	58	10	11	81	8	26	63	11	31	59	10	25	58	18	35	49	16	39	49	12	30	46	24	22	54	24	54	34	12	22	70	8	—	—	—
	Jun	34	48	18	22	72	6	25	60	15	34	58	8	14	79	7	33	55	12	36	56	7	35	52	14	35	50	15	39	49	12	39	46	15	27	51	22	49	44	7	23	67	10	—	—	—
	Dec	37	46	17	18	78	4	20	68	12	35	56	9	12	81	7	27	62	11	28	64	8	32	55	13	35	50	15	34	55	11	32	51	17	27	51	22	48	41	10	19	72	9	—	—	—
1982	Aug	39	50	11	31	63	6	38	47	15	41	51	8	19	71	10	34	54	12	34	59	6	40	45	15	33	52	14	41	48	11	35	47	17	31	52	18	50	42	8	30	59	11	—	—	—
	Sep	39	52	9	36	60	4	37	48	15	37	56	7	14	76	10	30	61	9	23	72	5	41	44	15	39	44	17	42	47	11	35	47	18	27	51	22	46	45	9	29	60	11	—	—	—
1983	Jul	48	42	10	40	54	6	42	44	13	41	48	11	20	72	10	31	58	11	30	64	6	43	43	14	48	38	14	38	51	11	32	48	20	25	55	20	43	50	7	33	57	11	—	—	—
	Oct	53	36	11	40	53	7	44	43	13	50	40	10	19	70	11	28	63	10	19	75	6	41	42	16	51	34	15	34	55	11	34	45	21	26	51	22	49	44	7	30	57	13	—	—	—
	Dec	45	47	7	38	57	6	40	48	12	43	47	10	17	73	11	29	61	11	21	74	5	39	45	16	47	42	11	33	57	11	40	39	21	34	46	20	55	37	8	28	58	14	—	—	—
1984	Feb	44	49	7	39	56	4	39	48	13	42	50	7	16	74	10	30	61	9	26	70	4	40	45	15	42	47	11	35	56	10	36	46	18	33	50	17	54	40	6	28	63	9	—	—	—
	Oct	46	42	12	35	60	5	36	48	16	31	60	9	16	71	13	26	63	11	17	77	6	36	46	18	40	42	18	25	61	14	34	44	21	27	52	21	50	43	7	30	58	12	—	—	—
1985	Jun 43	46	11	34	60	6	37	53	11	45	48	7	14	76	10	27	63	10	21	72	7	31	57	12	46	37	16	27	62	12	38	46	16	26	54	20	47	45	8	32	56	12	—	—	—	—
1986	Sep	39	51	11	32	61	6	34	54	12	37	56	7	14	77	9	22	70	8	20	74	6	26	58	16	39	45	16	23	65	12	27	54	19	29	50	21	46	47	7	28	60	13	—	—	—
	Feb	34	52	13	30	63	7	27	59	14	38	54	8	11	80	9	16	75	10	17	75	7	28	56	16	33	47	20	22	66	12	24	58	18	25	60	15	41	50	9	24	66	10	—	—	—
	May	33	60	7	35	62	3	37	52	11	37	56	8	9	86	5	13	80	7	16	81	4	26	62	11	42	42	15	20	74	6	29	52	19	27	58	15	40	53	7	30	60	10	—	—	—
	Aug	34	56	10	38	57	4	38	50	12	38	54	8	7	86	6	18	74	8	16	80	4	25	61	14	35	46	19	16	75	9	29	55	16	27	56	18	42	51	7	32	55	13	—	—	—
	Nov	41	49	9	38	55	6	39	50	11	43	49	8	16	75	9	23	69	7	19	75	6	27	63	10	40	40	20	22	69	9	34	52	14	34	50	16	48	45	7	36	54	11	—	—	—
1987	Feb	41	52	7	42	54	4	42	45	13	42	51	8	15	76	9	28	64	8	20	74	6	26	62	12	42	37	21	22	72	7	38	46	17	30	54	16	45	47	8	37	53	10	—	—	—
	Nov	50	38	12	33	59	7	41	45	10	45	46	10	30	60	9	31	57	12	17	78	5	26	60	14	43	34	23	16	76	8	32	41	27	28	55	17	45	48	8	38	52	10	—	—	—
1989	Apr	51	39	10	29	65	6	39	48	14	45	47	10	39	54	8	31	60	9	16	80	3	27	64	10	43	38	19	17	76	7	31	47	21	26	59	15	46	46	8	42	50	8	—	—	—
	Oct	48	41	11	18	77	5	24	65	11	40	52	9	31	61	9	26	63	12	14	83	3	23	65	11	38	41	21	15	77	9	29	50	21	31	53	16	45	47	7	34	56	9	29	61	10
1990	Oct	49	40	11	15	80	5	22	68	10	41	49	10	23	68	9	21	71	8	14	82	3	20	71	10	38	41	21	16	77	7	28	54	18	28	61	11	37	53	10	29	62	9	29	60	11

A Question in 1968 dropped the introduction 'In general, ...?' and the first item ended with the word 'generally'.

B Question in May 1970 changed to 'educational facilities' as the seventh item, 'the Health Service' as the eighth, 'old age pensions' as the twelfth, 'roads' for item thirteen and 'immigration' for the fourteenth..

C Question in October 1970 changed first item to simply 'the economy', the third to 'full employment' and added 'strikes and' to 'labour relations'. The seventh item reverted to 'education'.

D Question in October 1971 reverted to 'economic and financial affairs generally' as first item and expanded to 'The National Health Service'.

E Question in 1972 reverted to 'The Health Service'.

TABLE 6.3: GOVERNMENT'S HONESTY AND TRUSTWORTHINESS 1998–2000

Q. Do you think that the Government has, on balance, been honest and trustworthy or not?

		Yes	No	DK
1998	Jan	56	39	5
	Mar	50	44	6
	Apr	55	41	3
	Apr	60	36	3
	Jun	57	39	4
	Jul	56	41	3
	Sep	57	39	4
	Sep	55	41	5
	Nov	54	41	5
	Dec	54	41	5
1999	Jan	48	45	7
	Feb	52	43	5
	Mar	47	48	5
	Apr	55	41	4
	Apr	54	42	3
	Jun	51	45	3
	Jun	49	45	5
	Aug	54	42	3
	Aug	50	47	3
	Sep	52	44	3
	Oct	50	47	3
	Dec	48.5	47.4	4.1
2000	Jan	45.3	49.7	5.0
	Feb	44.0	52.3	3.8
	Mar	42.6	53.3	4.1
	Apr	42.7	52.5	4.9
	May	41.4	52.8	5.8
	Jun	39.3	53.8	6.9

cont'd . . .

		Yes	No	DK
	Jul	41.3	54.7	4.0
	Aug	42.7	53.4	3.9
	Sep	35.8	61.2	3.0
	Oct	37.0	60.1	2.9
	Nov	38.9	57.6	3.4
2000	Dec	42.4	54.3	3.3

CHAPTER 7
Prime Ministers

Like the 'government approval 'question reported in Table 6.1 above, Gallup's 'prime ministerial satisfaction' question is one of the longest-running in its repertoire. It has been asked, with only minor variations of question wording, since the autumn of 1938, when Neville Chamberlain was Prime Minister. Between 1938 and 1952 the question was asked only occasionally, but since 1953 it has been asked frequently and since 1960 almost every month.

Beginning in 1974, Gallup has also asked respondents which of the main party leaders they think would make the best Prime Minister. The list of party leaders included in the question has always comprised the Conservative, Labour and Liberal/Liberal Democrat leaders. Between 1982 and 1988 it also comprised the names of the leaders of the Social Democratic Party (successively Roy Jenkins, David Owen and Robert Maclennan). Like many of the other questions reported in this book, the best Prime Minister question was at first asked only sporadically, but since 1985 it has been asked in most months. Since 1994 it has formed part of the Gallup Index.

TABLE 7.1:   SATISFACTION WITH PRIME MINISTERS 1938–2000

Q. Are you satisfied or dissatisfied with ..... as prime minister?

		Satisfied	Dissatisfied	DK	
NEVILLE CHAMBERLAIN					
1938	Oct	51	39	10	A
	Nov	50	40	11	
	Dec	51	40	9	
1939	Jan	54	40	6	
	Feb	48	37	15	
	Mar	52	38	10	
	Apr	55	38	7	
	May	53	43	4	
	Jun	52	43	5	
	Jul	55	38	7	
	Oct	65	29	6	
	Nov	68	27	5	
	Dec	64	30	6	B
1940	Jan	56	32	12	
	Feb	59	30	11	

cont'd . . .

		Satisfied	Dissatisfied	DK
	Mar	57	36	7
1940	May	33	60	7

WINSTON CHURCHILL

		Satisfied	Dissatisfied	DK
	Jul	88	7	5
	Oct	89	6	5
	Nov	88	7	5
1941	Jan	85	7	8
	Mar	88	7	5
	Jun	87	9	4
	Oct	84	11	5
	Dec	88	8	4
1942	Jan	89	7	4
	Feb	82	11	7
	Mar	81	13	6
	Apr	82	13	5
	May	87	8	5
	Jun	86	9	5
	Jul	78	15	7
	Aug	82	11	7
	Sep	82	10	8
	Oct	83	11	6
	Nov	91	7	2
	Dec	93	5	2
1943	Jan	91	7	2
	Apr	90	7	3
	Jun	93	4	3
	Aug	93	5	2
	Nov	91	6	3
1944	Jan	89	7	4
	Mar	86	10	4
	Apr	88	9	3
	Jun	91	7	2
	Aug	89	8	3
	Oct	91	7	2
1945	Jan	81	16	3
	Feb	85	11	4
	Mar	87	10	3
	Apr	91	7	2
	May	83	14	3

CLEMENT ATTLEE

		Satisfied	Dissatisfied	DK
1946	Oct	53	35	12
	Dec	52	30	18

cont'd . . .

		Satisfied	Dissatisfied	DK
1947	Mar	46	45	9
	May	51	36	13
	Jul	51	37	12
	Oct	41	46	13
	Dec	44	46	10
1948	Jan	45	43	12
	Mar	39	48	13
	Jul	40	49	11
	Sep	37	46	17
	Nov	45	40	15
1949	Jan	45	44	11
	Mar	47	38	15
	May	44	42	14
	Jul	46	42	12
	Sep	45	43	12
	Dec	43	45	12
1950	May	50	39	11
	Aug	49	43	8
	Oct	47	40	13
	Dec	49	38	13
1951	Feb	44	47	9
	Apr	49	40	11
	May	57	35	8
	Jul	43	43	14

WINSTON CHURCHILL

		Satisfied	Dissatisfied	DK
	Dec	55	37	8
1952	May	51	42	7
	Aug	48	44	8
	Nov	51	39	10
1953	Jan	51	40	9
	Oct	56	34	10
1955	Jan	52	40	8

SIR ANTHONY EDEN

		Satisfied	Dissatisfied	DK
1955	Apr	73	14	13
	Jul	68	17	15
	Oct	63	21	16
	Dec	61	26	13
1956	Jan	60	24	16
	Feb	50	34	16
	Apr	45	37	18
	Jul	50	33	17
	Sep	51	34	15

cont'd . . .

		Satisfied	Dissatisfied	DK	
	Oct	47	36	17	
	Nov	57	35	8	
	Dec	56	33	11	

HAROLD MACMILLAN

		Satisfied	Dissatisfied	DK	
1957	Jan	50	25	25	D
	Mar	45	23	32	
	Apr	44	34	22	
	Jun	54	27	19	
	Oct	44	34	22	
	Nov	39	39	22	
!958	Jan	47	37	16	
	Feb	35	41	24	
	May	37	40	23	
	Jul	50	32	18	
	Aug	53	27	20	
	Oct	55	24	21	
	Nov	55	28	17	
	Dec	55	26	19	
1959	Jan	53	32	15	
	Feb	54	26	20	
	Mar	57	26	17	
	Apr	60	28	12	
	May	62	24	14	
	Jun	58	24	18	
	Jul	62	21	17	
	Aug	67	23	10	
1960	Mar	64	19	17	
	Apr	57	27	16	
	May	79	16	5	
	Jun	70	22	8	
	Jul	69	18	13	
	Aug	65	22	13	
	Oct	74	16	10	
	Nov	72	14	14	
	Dec	69	19	12	
1961	Jan	65	23	12	
	Feb	64	26	10	
	Mar	63	27	10	
	Apr	64	23	13	
	May	58	28	14	
	Jun	58	29	13	
	Jul	54	33	13	
	Aug	45	42	13	

cont'd . . .

		Satisfied	Dissatisfied	DK
	Sep	43	44	13
	Oct	55	33	12
	Nov	54	34	12
1962	Jan	43	39	18
	Feb	50	37	13
	Apr	46	43	11
	May	47	43	10
	Jul	47	39	14
	Aug	42	48	10
	Sep	42	50	8
	Oct	43	43	14
	Nov	47	45	8
	Dec	41	45	14
1963	Jan	42	45	13
	Mar	35	53	12
	Apr	35	54	11
	May	41	49	10
	Jun	35	52	13
	Jul	37	52	11
	Aug	42	47	11
	Sep	40	48	12
	Oct	41	48	11

SIR ALEC DOUGLAS-HOME

		Satisfied	Dissatisfied	DK
	Nov	42	36	22
	Dec	48	26	26
1964	Jan	44	27	29
	Feb	40	32	28
	Mar	40	40	20
	May	40	43	17
	Jul	45	40	15
	Aug	45	38	17
	Sep	46	38	16

HAROLD WILSON

		Satisfied	Dissatisfied	DK
1964	Nov	60	26	14
	Dec	64	26	10
1965	Jan	56	26	18
	Feb	60	30	10
	Mar	58	32	10
	Apr	63	28	9
	May	56	34	10
	Jun	48	40	12
	Jul	51	35	14

cont'd . . .

		Satisfied	Dissatisfied	DK
	Aug	50	40	10
	Sep	54	35	11
	Oct	61	29	10
	Nov	65	24	11
	Dec	66	26	8
1966	Jan	65	25	10
	Feb	60	32	8
	Apr	63	29	8
	May	69	25	6
	Jun	58	31	11
	Jul	61	29	10
	Aug	52	42	6
	Sep	52	41	7
	Oct	47	45	8
	Nov	46	44	10
	Dec	51	42	7
1967	Jan	51	40	9
	Feb	57	36	7
	Mar	53	40	7
	Apr	52	37	11
	May	48	41	11
	Jun	43	43	14
	Jul	48	40	12
	Aug	45	48	7
	Sep	40	53	7
	Oct	34	54	12
	Nov	41	51	8
	Dec	34	57	9
1968	Jan	33	54	13
	Feb	36	55	9
	Mar	35	56	9
	Apr	31	60	9
	May	27	61	12
	Jun	28	61	11
	Jul	30	59	11
	Aug	30	58	12
	Sep	33	54	13
	Oct	38	52	10
	Nov	31	57	12
	Dec	28	61	11
1969	Jan	34	58	8
	Feb	32	57	11
	Mar	35	52	13

cont'd . . .

		Satisfied	Dissatisfied	DK
	Apr	30	59	11
	May	29	60	11
	Jul	30	60	10
	Aug	36	54	10
	Sep	39	52	9
	Oct	43	48	9
	Nov	41	49	10
	Dec	38	52	10
1970	Jan	42	48	10
	Feb	42	48	10
	Mar	41	49	10
	Apr	49	43	8
	Jun	51	43	6

EDWARD HEATH

		Satisfied	Dissatisfied	DK
1970	Aug	35	27	38
	Oct	42	27	31
	Nov	39	45	16
	Dec	45	42	13
1971	Jan	41	46	13
	Feb	37	49	14
	Mar	38	50	12
	Apr	43	43	14
	May	35	55	10
	Jun	31	57	12
	Jul	32	58	10
	Aug	37	52	11
	Sep	32	55	13
	Oct	35	54	11
	Nov	38	50	12
	Dec	39	51	10
1972	Jan	39	51	10
	Feb	37	55	8
	Mar	36	56	8
	Apr	41	49	10
	May	39	52	9
	Jun	40	51	9
	Jul	35	54	11
	Aug	45	43	12
	Sep	33	55	12
	Oct	34	56	10
	Nov	33	57	10
	Dec	39	50	11
1973	Jan	38	52	10

cont'd . . .

		Satisfied	Dissatisfied	DK
	Feb	37	52	11
	Mar	41	51	8
	Apr	37	53	10
	May	38	53	9
	Jun	43	47	10
	Jul	37	54	9
	Aug	34	57	9
	Sep	36	53	11
	Oct	36	54	10
	Nov	39	50	11
	Dec	36	54	10
1974	Jan	39	52	9
	Feb	38	55	7

HAROLD WILSON

		Satisfied	Dissatisfied	DK
	Apr	53	32	15
	May	50	40	10
	Jun	49	40	11
	Jul	41	48	11
	Aug	44	45	11
	Sep	41	47	12
	Oct	45	44	11
	Nov	50	40	10
	Dec	51	36	13
1975	Jan	49	38	13
	Feb	47	42	11
	Mar	51	39	10
	Apr	44	46	10
	May	40	49	11
	Jun	46	44	10
	Jul	46	46	8
	Aug	45	47	8
	Sep	45	48	7
	Oct	46	49	5
	Nov	45	45	10
	Dec	40	50	10
1976	Jan	42	48	10
	Feb	45	48	7
	Mar	46	47	7

JAMES CALLAGHAN

		Satisfied	Dissatisfied	DK
	Apr	57	16	27
	May	43	21	36
	Jun	38	27	35

cont'd . . .

		Satisfied	Dissatisfied	DK
	Jun	36	32	32
	Jul	46	28	26
	Aug	44	30	26
	Sep	46	34	20
	Oct	36	47	17
	Nov	33	50	17
	Dec	35	47	18
1977	Jan	37	48	15
	Feb	36	45	19
	Mar	37	43	20
	Apr	38	46	16
	May	43	44	13
	Jun	44	44	12
	Jul	43	44	13
	Aug	45	43	12
	Sep	49	39	12
	Oct	59	33	8
	Nov	55	35	10
	Dec	53	34	13
1978	Jan	57	34	9
	Feb	54	36	10
	Mar	51	40	9
	Apr	51	38	11
	May	54	35	11
	Jun	50	41	9
	Jul	52	39	9
	Aug	55	34	11
	Sep	51	41	8
	Oct	56	37	7
	Nov	54	36	10
	Dec	53	38	9
1979	Jan	48	44	8
	Feb	33	58	9
	Mar	39	52	9
	Apr	48	43	9

MARGARET THATCHER

		Satisfied	Dissatisfied	DK
	Jun	41	40	19
	Jul	41	47	12
	Aug	45	44	11
	Sep	45	45	10
	Oct	46	45	9
	Nov	44	48	8
	Dec	40	51	9

cont'd . . .

		Satisfied	Dissatisfied	DK
1980	Jan	39	54	7
	Feb	37	55	8
	Mar	38	56	7
	Apr	41	54	5
	May	44	51	5
	Jun	43	52	5
	Jul	41	51	8
	Aug	41	54	5
	Sep	37	58	5
	Oct	38	56	6
	Oct	38	56	6
	Nov	34	60	6
	Dec	35	59	6
1981	Jan	31	63	6
	Jan	34	61	5
	Feb	34	60	6
	Mar	30	64	6
	Mar	30	66	4
	Apr	30	65	5
	May	35	60	5
	Jun	33	61	6
	Jul	30	65	5
	Aug	28	66	6
	Sep	32	62	6
	Oct	33	62	5
	Nov	28	66	6
	Dec	25	70	5
1982	Jan	32	65	3
	Feb	29	66	5
	Mar	34	62	4
	Apr	35	60	5
	May	44	51	5
	Jun	51	44	5
	Jul	52	43	5
	Aug	49	47	4
	Sep	48	47	5
	Oct	46	50	4
	Nov	44	52	4
	Dec	44	53	3
1983	Jan	49	45	6
	Feb	45	50	5
	Mar	47	48	5
	Apr	44	50	6

cont'd . . .

		Satisfied	Dissatisfied	DK
	May	50	46	4
	Jun	48	48	4
	Jul	52	44	4
	Aug	51	46	3
	Sep	53	43	4
	Oct	48	47	5
	Nov	49	47	4
	Dec	47	48	5
1984	Jan	49	46	5
	Feb	48	48	4
	Mar	46	52	2
	Apr	46	50	4
	May	41	54	5
	Jun	41	54	5
	Jul	41	55	4
	Aug	39	56	5
	Sep	40	56	5
	Oct	50	44	6
	Nov	48	48	4
	Dec	43	52	5
1985	Jan	40	54	6
	Feb	37	57	6
	Mar	37	58	5
	Apr	38	57	5
	May	36	59	5
	Jun	38	56	6
	Jul	34	60	5
	Aug	30	65	5
	Sep	35	60	5
	Oct	33	62	5
	Nov	36	58	5
	Dec	39	56	5
1986	Jan	31	64	5
	Feb	29	67	3
	Mar	33	63	4
	Apr	28	67	5
	May	31	63	5
	Jun	30	66	4
	Jul	34	61	4
	Aug	28	66	7
	Sep	35	60	5
	Oct	36	59	5
	Nov	36	59	5

cont'd . . .

		Satisfied	Dissatisfied	DK
1986	Dec	38	57	6
1987	Jan	35	61	5
	Feb	35	58	6
	Mar	39	54	6
	Apr	43	50	6
	May	44	52	5
	Jun	41	56	3
	Jul	47	48	4
	Aug	46	50	4
	Sep	46	51	3
	Sep	48	49	3
	Oct	52	44	4
	Nov	47	48	4
	Dec	47	49	4
1988	Jan	48	48	4
	Feb	45	51	4
	Mar	42	53	5
	Apr	40	56	4
	May	43	52	5
	Jun	42	53	4
	Jul	42	54	4
	Aug	45	49	6
	Sep	45	50	5
	Oct	48	47	5
	Nov	45	50	5
	Dec	44	50	6
1989	Jan	43	51	6
	Feb	40	53	7
	Mar	41	54	5
	Apr	42	52	6
	May	40	54	5
	Jun	37	58	5
	Jul	34	60	6
	Aug	34	62	4
	Sep	36	59	5
	Oct	35	60	5
	Nov	29	66	5
	Dec	33	62	5
1990	Jan	33	61	6
	Feb	31	64	5
	Mar	26	71	4
	Apr	20	75	5
	May	27	69	4

cont'd . . .

		Satisfied	Dissatisfied	DK	
	Jun	23	73	4	
	Jul	30	64	5	
	Aug	32	63	6	
	Sep	31	64	5	
	Oct	35	57	8	
	Nov	29	66	5	

JOHN MAJOR

		Satisfied	Dissatisfied	DK	
	Dec	51	29	21	E
1991	Jan	41	24	35	
	Feb	58	21	22	
	Mar	59	23	18	
	Apr	53	28	19	
	May	53	32	15	
	Jun	51	32	17	
	Jul	51	35	14	
	Aug	46	38	16	
	Sep	55	32	13	
	Oct	49	38	12	
	Nov	47	41	12	
	Dec	52	37	10	
1992	Jan	46	43	11	
	Feb	50	41	9	
	Mar	43	48	9	
	Apr	42	50	8	
	May	53	37	9	
	Jun	52	41	7	
	Jul	53	38	9	
	Aug	45	46	9	
	Sep	47	44	9	
	Oct	28	65	7	
	Oct	22	69	9	
	Nov	24	68	7	
	Nov	23	71	6	
1993	Jan	33	62	5	
	Jan	33	60	7	
	Feb	29	64	7	
	Mar				
	Apr	26	69	5	
	May	28	66	6	
	May	21	73	6	
	Jun				
	Jul	19	76	5	
	Aug	20	73	7	

cont'd . . .

		Satisfied	Dissatisfied	DK
	Sep	18	75	7
	Sep	21	71	8
	Oct	22	70	8
	Nov			
	Dec	24	71	5
1994	Jan	22	72	6
	Jan	20	73	6
	Feb	22	73	5
	Mar			
	Apr	21	73	6
	May	20	75	5
	May	20	73	6
	Jun			
	Jul	23	71	6
	Jul	19	76	5
	Aug			
	Sep	19	76	5
	Sep	23	71	6
	Oct	18	74	8
	Oct	23	70	8
	Nov			
	Dec	19	75	6
1995	Jan	15	78	7
	Jan	17	76	7
	Feb			
	Mar	19	76	6
	Apr	21	72	7
	May	21	73	7
	Jun	20	74	7
	Jul	27	67	7
	Jul	28	65	7
	Aug			
	Sep	26	67	7
	Sep	25	67	8
	Oct	25	68	7
	Nov			
	Dec	27	66	7
1996	Jan	25	69	7
	Feb	23	69	7
	Mar	24	70	6
	Mar	23	70	7
	Apr			
	May	23	69	8

cont'd . . .

		Satisfied	Dissatisfied	DK
	Jun	23	69	9
	Jun	26	66	8
	Jul			
	Aug	25	69	6
	Sep	28	65	8
	Sep	27	66	7
	Oct			
	Nov	30	62	8
	Dec	25	67	8
1997	Jan	36	62	2
	Feb	36	59	5
	Mar	33	63	4
	Apr	33	60	6
	May			

TONY BLAIR

		Satisfied	Dissatisfied	DK
1997	Jun	82	10	7
	Jul	83	13	4
	Aug	83	13	4
	Sep	76	20	4
	Oct	83	12	4
	Nov	78	17	4
	Dec	74	22	4
1998	Jan	66	30	5
	Feb	66	31	4
	Mar	62	32	6
	Apr	69	27	4
	Apr	72	25	4
	May	70	26	4
	Jun	68	28	5
	Jul			
	Aug	67	30	4
	Sep	67	28	5
	Sep	68	27	5
	Oct	67	29	4
	Nov	65	30	5
	Dec	66	29	5
1999	Jan	65	30	5
	Feb	63	34	4
	Mar	67	28	5
	Apr	66	31	2
	May	65	31	4
	Jun	62	32	6
	Jul	66	32	2

cont'd . . .

		Satisfied	Dissatisfied	DK
	Aug	64	33	3
	Sep	65	32	3
	Oct	63	34	3
	Nov			
	Dec	61	33	6
2000	Jan	62	33	4
	Feb	55	42	3
	Mar	54	43	3
	Apr	54	42	3
	May	52	44	5
	Jun	55	40	5
	Jul	47	49	4
	Aug	52	45	3
	Sep	45	52	3
	Sep	38	59	3
	Nov	45	51	5
2000	Dec	49	48	3

A Question in October 1938 to November 1939 and April to July 1956 read, 'Are you satisfied with ..... as Prime Minister?'

B Question in December 1939 to May 1945 and May 1947 to January 1951 read, 'In general, do you approve or disapprove of ..... as Prime Minister?'

C Question in February 1951 to October 1955 read, 'Do you approve or disapprove of ..... as prime minister?'

D Question in January 1957 read, 'Do you approve or disapprove of the appointment of Mr Harold Macmillan as Prime Minister?'

E Question in December 1990 read, 'Do you think Mr Major will or will not prove a good Prime Minister?'

TABLE 7.2: WHO WOULD MAKE THE BEST PRIME MINISTER? 1974–2000

Q. Who would make the best Prime Minister [among major party leaders whose names form part of question]?

		Harold Wilson	Edward Heath	Jeremy Thorpe	DK
1974	Oct	37	25	22	16

		James Callaghan	Margaret Thatcher	David Steel	DK
1977	Sep	41	32	10	17
	Oct	46	29	10	16
1978	Nov	50	26	7	16

cont'd . . .

		James Callaghan	Margaret Thatcher	David Steel	DK	
1979	Feb	32	41	14	13	
	Mar	36	37	12	15	
	Apr	39	29	21	11	
	May	43	30	16	11	

		Margaret Thatcher	Michael Foot	David Steel	DK	
1981	Oct	32	20	34	14	
1982	Jan	30	19	36	15	
1982	Apr	32	16	38	13	

		Margaret Thatcher	Michael Foot	David Steel	Roy Jenkins	DK
1983	May	47	14	23	8	8
	May	48	13	25	7	7
	Jun	45	14	29	7	6
	Jun	44	11	31	6	9

		Margaret Thatcher	Neil Kinnock	David Steel	David Owen	DK
1984	Jun	34	25	18	15	9
	Jul	34	27	14	16	9
	Aug	35	25	16	14	10
	Sep	34	24	15	15	11
	Oct	43	19	11	19	8
	Nov	42	21	16	13	8
	Dec	38	20	14	19	8
1985	Jan	35	22	16	17	9
	Feb	33	20	17	19	10
	Mar	32	25	18	16	9
	Apr	34	23	15	19	9
	May	32	22	18	18	11
	Jun	34	22	21	15	8
	Jul	27	24	21	19	9
	Aug	25	25	22	16	11
	Sep	27	18	19	24	12
	Oct	30	29	16	14	11
	Nov	31	27	15	16	11
	Dec	33	24	17	15	11

cont'd . . .

		Margaret Thatcher	Neil Kinnock	David Steel	David Owen	DK
1986	Jan	26	25	19	18	12
	Feb	24	27	16	22	11
	Mar	27	23	19	22	9
	Apr	24	27	17	19	13
	May	27	29	16	17	11
	Jun	29	28	18	15	10
	Jul	31	26	17	18	9
	Aug	27	28	18	17	10
	Sep	30	29	13	20	8
	Oct	34	27	12	17	10
	Nov	35	27	12	14	11
	Dec	33	24	13	18	11
1987	Jan	31	29	13	15	12
	Feb	35	29	16	15	9
	Mar	35	20	18	17	9
	Apr	40	16	16	16	11
	May	41	19	15	16	8
	May	46	22	11	12	9
	May	46	27	8	11	8
	Jun	44	29	9	12	7
	Jun	42	28	8	15	7

		Margaret Thatcher	Neil Kinnock	David Steel	Robert Maclennan	DK
	Oct	54	23	11	2	11
	Nov	51	24	12	1	10
	Dec	53	24	11	2	12
1988	Jan	53	26	9	2	10
	Feb	53	24	10	2	11

		Margaret Thatcher	Neil Kinnock	David Steel	Robert Maclennan	David Owen	DK
	Mar	39	20	8	0	15	17
	Apr	34	21	9	1	16	20

		Margaret Thatcher	Neil Kinnock	Paddy Ashdown	David Owen	DK
	Sep	45	23	8	14	11
	Oct	46	22	5	14	13

cont'd . . .

		Margaret Thatcher	Neil Kinnock	David Steel	David Owen	DK
	Nov	48	20	7	13	12
	Dec	45	18	10	14	13
1989	Jan	45	19	7	18	12
	Feb	43	20	9	15	12
	Mar	42	20	7	18	12
	Apr	41	24	7	15	13
	May	44	25	5	12	13
	Jul	39	32	5	12	12
	Aug	39	29	5	13	14
	Sep	40	29	4	14	13
	Sep	39	28	7	14	12
	Oct	37	31	6	11	15
	Dec	35	33	7	11	13
1990	Jan	36	33	5	12	14
	Jan	33	34	6	11	16
	Feb	33	33	6	12	15
	Mar	28	38	7	14	14
	Apr	31	32	8	14	15
	Jun	28	39	7	10	16

		Margaret Thatcher	Neil Kinnock	Paddy Ashdown	DK
	Jun	38	37	11	14
	Jul	35	36	12	17
	Sep	41	35	9	15
	Sep	36	35	14	15
	Oct	33	38	15	14

		John Major	Neil Kinnock	Paddy Ashdown	DK
	Dec	52	24	11	13
1991	Jan	48	28	10	14
	Feb	51	24	11	14
	Feb	56	23	13	8
	Mar	45	25	18	12
	May	46	26	18	10
	May	40	30	22	9
	Jun	42	25	20	13
	Aug	42	28	17	14
	Aug	46	22	20	11

cont'd . . .

		John Major	Neil Kinnock	Paddy Ashdown	DK
	Sep	47	24	16	13
	Sep	48	24	17	11
	Oct	40	29	19	12
	Nov	42	25	21	12
1992	Jan	45	23	20	12
	Feb	48	22	18	12
	Feb	41	25	21	13
	Mar	42	24	17	17
	Mar	39	28	16	17
	Mar	36	28	19	17
	Apr	38	26	21	15
	Apr	39	28	18	15
	Apr	48	18	19	15

		John Major	Neil Kinnock	Paddy Ashdown	DK
	May	45	24	18	13
	May	51	18	19	12

		John Major	John Smith	Paddy Ashdown	DK
	Jul	43	27	17	13
	Aug	41	30	15	14
	Sep	40	29	16	14
	Oct	26	35	21	18
	Oct	23	38	18	20
	Nov	21	38	16	26
1993	Jan	29	32	16	23
	Jan	28	33	17	23
	Feb	25	32	18	24
	Apr	23	36	19	22
	Apr	24	31	20	25
	May	19	34	23	23
	Jul	17	30	26	27
	Jul	18	32	23	28
	Sep	16	30	24	30
	Sep	18	28	25	30
	Oct	16	32	23	29
	Dec	18	34	19	29
1994	Jan	19	32	21	28

cont'd . . .

		John Major	John Smith	Paddy Ashdown	DK
	Jan	17	35	21	27
	Feb	19	36	19	26
	Apr	15	36	19	29
	May	16	31	22	30

		John Major	Tony Blair	Paddy Ashdown	DK
1994	Jul	15.2	32.2	21.1	31.5
	Aug	15.6	41.5	14.5	28.4
	Sep	16.5	39.4	14.7	29.4
	Oct	17.2	40.8	13.7	28.3
	Nov	15.9	40.4	12.8	30.9
	Dec	13.8	43.9	13.2	29.2
1995	Jan	14.7	43.5	12.5	29.3
	Jan	14.8	43.4	12.9	28.9
	Feb	15.5	42.5	12.3	29.8
	Apr	15.3	42.0	13.8	28.9
	May	14.7	44.1	12.7	28.6
	Jun	15.7	46.0	11.5	26.8
	Jul	20.8	41.8	10.8	26.6
	Jul	18.5	39.4	13.0	29.1
	Sep	19.4	38.7	13.5	28.4
	Sep	18.8	42.6	12.9	25.7
	Oct	17.9	42.0	12.6	27.5
	Dec	18.5	42.2	12.0	27.3
1996	Jan	17.2	40.6	14.2	28.0
	Feb	18.3	38.2	14.9	28.6
	Mar	17.8	41.8	13.9	26.6
	Mar	17.2	42.1	13.8	26.9
	May	17.5	39.2	15.6	27.7
	Jun	18.9	38.4	14.7	28.1
	Jun	18.4	37.7	14.8	29.2
	Aug	19.4	36.1	14.6	29.9
	Sep	23.0	35.4	14.4	27.2
	Oct	23.3	35.6	14.1	27.0
	Nov	24.3	36.3	13.1	26.4
	Dec	23.7	36.0	13.8	26.5
1997	Jan	28.2	38.6	14.2	19.1
	Feb	28.1	38.9	13.3	19.7
	Mar	24.6	41.2	12.4	21.9
	Apr	25	41	12	21

cont'd . . .

		William Hague	Tony Blair	Paddy Ashdown	DK
1997	May	10.1	62.2	13.4	14.3
	Jul	10.5	60.7	14.9	13.9
	Aug	11.4	58.7	15.0	14.9
	Sep	12.2	63.4	13.1	11.3
	Oct	8.3	66.8	11.1	13.8
	Nov	8.2	60.1	15.4	16.2
	Dec	8.4	58.6	16.0	16.9
1998	Jan	10.7	55.7	19.4	14.2
	Feb	11.4	55.1	18.9	14.6
	Mar	12.9	50.9	20.0	16.2
	Apr	12.0	55.0	17.4	15.6
1999	Aug	15.3	55.5	16.2	13.0

		William Hague	Tony Blair	Charles Kennedy	DK
1999	Sep	14.7	57.3	13.8	14.3
	Oct	15.9	27.4	11.4	15.3
	Nov	16.5	56.5	11.5	15.5
	Dec	14.5	57.2	10.5	17.7
2000	Jan	14.2	54.2	11.6	20.0
	Feb	16.0	53.9	12.5	17.6
	Mar	18.0	52.8	12.1	17.0
	Apr	18.2	50.6	12.2	19.0
	May	17.5	46.6	12.2	23.7
	Jun	20.2	45.4	12.2	22.2
	Jul	21.7	48.5	12.7	17.1
	Aug	20.4	51.1	13.7	14.8
	Sep	24.1	39.1	18.7	18.0
	Oct	24.0	42.5	16.7	16.7
	Nov	23.7	43.4	14.6	18.2
2000	Dec	22.0	47.3	13.4	17.3

CHAPTER 8

Party Leaders

In addition to seeking voters' views about incumbent Prime Ministers and who would make the best Prime Minister, Gallup since the mid 1950s has also sought their opinions about successive Leaders of the Opposition and leaders of the Liberal, Social Democratic and Liberal Democrat parties. The relevant question has normally read, 'Do you think ——— is or is not proving a good leader of the ——— Party?', though sometimes it has read, more bluntly, 'Do you think ——— is or is not a good leader of the ——— Party?' In the first two or three months of a new leader's tenure, one or other of the above questions has usually been couched in the future tense ('Do you think ——— will prove . . .?'). As so often in these pages, there is no reason to think that these slight variations in question wording have had any substantial effect on the responses.

In addition, between 1980 and 1996 Gallup from time to time asked respondents to place one or other of the various party leaders on an eight-point left-right scale. The volunteered response 'middle of the road' was also included in the tabulations. The findings elicited by this set of questions can be found in Table 8.6.

TABLE 8.1: CONSERVATIVE LEADERS IN OPPOSITION 1964–2000

Q. Do you think ..... is or is not proving a good leader of the Conservative Party?

		Is	Is not	DK	
SIR ALEC DOUGLAS-HOME					
1964	Nov	39	47	14	
	Dec	41	39	20	
1965	Jan	38	42	20	
	Feb	37	48	15	
	Mar	38	43	20	
	Apr	34	48	18	
	May	36	48	16	
	Jun	36	48	16	
	Jul	32	46	22	
EDWARD HEATH					
1965	Aug	64	7	29	A

cont'd . . .

		Is	Is not	DK
	Aug	51	8	41
	Sep	49	7	44
	Oct	47	15	38
	Nov	48	18	34
	Dec	43	27	30
1966	Jan	48	21	31
	Feb	40	36	24
	Mar			
	Apr	39	39	22
	May	44	35	21
	Jun	33	41	26
	Jul	33	46	21
	Aug	32	46	22
	Sep	38	39	23
	Oct	46	35	19
	Nov	34	41	25
	Dec	35	47	18
1967	Jan	29	47	24
	Feb	24	55	21
	Mar	26	52	22
	Apr	32	45	23
	May	35	44	21
	Jun	37	40	23
	Jul	32	44	24
	Aug	28	50	22
	Sep	31	43	26
	Oct	43	34	23
	Nov	44	41	15
	Dec	37	42	21
1968	Jan	32	44	24
	Feb	31	49	20
	Mar	29	52	19
	Apr	28	47	25
	May	31	49	20
	Jun	28	51	21
	Jul	28	48	24
	Aug	27	50	23
	Sep	27	50	23
	Oct	27	50	23
	Nov	37	40	23
	Dec	30	49	21
1969	Jan	31	45	24
	Feb	34	42	24

cont'd . . .

		Is	Is not	DK	
	Mar	31	42	27	
	Apr	29	45	26	
	May	28	44	28	
	Jun	29	48	23	
	Jul	40	35	25	
	Aug	29	47	24	
	Sep	32	46	22	
	Oct	33	44	23	
	Nov	33	43	24	
	Dec	32	41	27	
1970	Jan	38	41	21	
	Feb	41	36	23	
	Mar	39	40	21	
	Apr	34	43	23	
	May	28	52	20	
	Jun	28	56	16	
1974	Apr	38	48	14	
	May	35	54	11	
	Jun	36	52	12	
	Jul	33	53	14	
	Aug	35	52	13	
	Sep	29	53	18	
	Oct	32	53	15	
	Nov	32	52	16	
	Dec	31	47	22	
1975	Jan	29	53	18	

MARGARET THATCHER

		Is	Is not	DK	
1975	Feb	64	15	21	B
	Mar	60	20	20	
	Apr	45	16	39	
	May	41	25	34	
	Jun	35	35	30	
	Jul	37	39	24	
	Aug	37	40	23	
	Sep	39	39	22	
	Oct	45	33	22	
	Nov	42	36	22	
	Dec	40	35	25	
1976	Jan	42	38	20	
	Feb	49	32	19	
	Mar	43	37	20	
	Apr	40	45	15	
	May	36	46	18	

cont'd . . .

		Is	Is not	DK	
	Jun	31	53	16	
	Jul	33	50	17	
	Aug	33	52	15	
	Sep	40	45	15	
	Oct	40	45	15	
	Nov	41	42	17	
	Dec	34	52	14	
1977	Jan	39	47	14	
	Feb	35	49	16	
	Mar	35	49	16	
	Apr	40	48	12	
	May	45	40	15	
	Jun	44	41	15	
	Jul	42	42	16	
	Aug	45	42	13	
	Sep	47	39	14	
	Oct	49	38	13	
	Nov	47	40	13	
	Dec	44	43	13	
1978	Jan	42	44	14	
	Feb	41	44	15	
	Mar	45	46	9	
	Apr	39	50	11	
	May	40	48	12	
	Jun	38	49	13	
	Jul	38	50	12	
	Aug	35	51	14	
	Sep	40	46	14	
	Oct	39	49	12	
	Nov	33	55	12	
	Dec	39	51	10	
1979	Jan	38	50	12	
	Feb	48	39	13	
	Mar	47	39	14	
	Apr	44	42	13	

WILLIAM HAGUE

		Is	Is not	DK	
1997	Jul	40	37	23	C
	Aug	40	40	20	
	Sep	39	41	20	
	Oct	20	60	19	
	Nov	25	58	17	
	Dec	24	60	16	
1998	Jan	28	55	17	

cont'd . . .

		Is	Is not	DK
	Feb	31	55	14
	Mar	31	50	19
	Apr	38	49	13
	Apr	29	56	15
	May	33	52	15
	Jun	29	58	12
	Aug	29	57	14
	Sep	29	57	14
	Sep	28	55	16
	Oct	32	56	13
	Nov	33	54	13
	Dec	33	56	11
1999	Jan	31	56	13
	Feb	28	60	13
	Mar	32	56	12
	Apr	32	58	10
	May	26	62	11
	Jun	32	54	14
	Jul	32	55	12
	Aug	27	62	11
	Sep	29	60	12
	Nov	36	57	7
	Dec	32	54	14
2000	Jan	25	62	12
	Feb	30	60	10
	Mar	30	60	9
	Apr	38	53	9
	May	33	54	13
	Jun	36	53	11
	Jul	38	48	14
	Aug	37	51	12
	Sep	34	55	11
	Sep	34	56	10
	Nov	37	52	10
2000	Dec	37	56	7

A Question in first survey in August 1965 read, 'Do you think Mr Heath will or will not be a good leader of the Conservative Party?'

B Question in January and February 1975 read, 'Do you think Mrs Thatcher will or will not be a good leader of the Conservative party?'

C Question in July 1997 read, 'Do you think Mr Hague will or will not prove a good leader of the Conservative Party?'

TABLE 8.2:   LABOUR LEADERS IN OPPOSITION 1956-97

Q. Do you think Mr. ..... is or is not proving a good leader of the Labour Party?

		Is	Is not	DK
HUGH GAITSKELL				
1956	May	42	24	34
	Jul	46	18	36
	Sep	53	17	30
	Nov	44	30	26
1957	May	41	27	32
	Sep	39	23	38
1958	Jan	40	23	37
	Aug	37	25	38
	Sep	32	25	43
	Oct	41	25	34
	Nov	42	21	37
	Dec	45	21	34
1959	Jan	47	24	29
	Feb	43	24	33
	Mar	46	22	32
	Apr	48	28	24
	May	47	25	28
	Jun	44	24	32
	Jul	42	30	28
	Aug	46	24	30
1960	Feb	43	23	34
	Mar	40	36	24
	Apr	46	31	23
	May	47	29	24
	Jun	56	25	19
	Jul	43	34	23
	Aug			
	Sep	43	33	24
	Oct	48	27	25
	Nov	44	32	24
1961	Jan	45	31	24
	Feb	45	32	23
	Mar	45	37	18
	Apr	43	34	23
	May	45	31	24
	Jun	45	33	22
	Jul	51	30	19
	Aug	47	28	25
	Sep	46	27	27

cont'd . . .

		Is	Is not	DK
	Oct	57	26	17
1961	Nov	52	30	18
1962	Jan	50	27	23
	Feb	45	35	20
	Mar	50	27	23
	Apr	48	30	22
	May	48	29	23
	Jun	48	29	23
	Jul	47	30	23
	Aug	47	33	20
	Sep	51	30	19
	Oct	54	26	20
	Nov	51	30	19
	Dec	52	27	21
1963	Jan	48	30	21

HAROLD WILSON

		Is	Is not	DK
1963	Mar	44	13	43
	Apr	52	15	33
	May	53	13	34
	Jun	54	13	33
	Jul	57	16	27
	Aug	59	12	29
	Sep	56	15	29
	Oct	60	11	29
	Nov	67	14	19
	Dec	65	14	21
1964	Jan	60	13	27
	Feb	62	17	21
	Mar	67	18	15
	Apr	61	19	20
	May	66	18	16
	Jun	65	19	16
	Jul	58	22	20
	Aug	57	22	21
	Sep	59	24	17
1970	Sep	59	24	17
	Oct	62	22	16
	Nov	66	21	13
	Dec	59	28	13
1971	Jan	61	24	15
	Feb	61	26	13
	Mar	59	28	13
	Apr	57	27	16

cont'd . . .

		Is	Is not	DK
	May	61	26	13
	Jun	58	24	18
	Jul	58	30	12
	Aug	51	35	14
	Sep	57	31	13
	Oct	54	34	12
	Nov	52	36	12
	Dec	54	32	14
1972	Jan	54	29	17
	Feb	53	34	13
	Mar	51	37	12
	Apr	39	47	14
	May	45	40	15
	Jun	44	39	17
	Jul	45	40	15
	Aug	47	38	15
	Sep	43	42	15
	Oct	53	32	15
	Nov	50	36	14
	Dec	44	40	16
1973	Jan	40	44	16
	Feb	45	42	13
	Mar	41	45	14
	Apr	41	40	19
	May	40	44	16
	Jun	41	42	17
	Jul	45	38	17
	Aug	39	43	18
	Sep	42	39	19
	Oct	46	38	16
	Nov	37	44	19
	Dec	37	47	16
1974	Jan	38	47	15
	Feb	38	49	13

JAMES CALLAGHAN

		Is	Is not	DK
1979	Jun	63	26	11
	Jul	61	28	11
	Aug	57	30	12
	Sep	53	34	13
	Oct	57	31	12
	Nov	55	34	11
	Dec	53	33	14
1980	Jan	53	35	12

cont'd . . .

		Is	Is not	DK	
	Feb	50	36	14	
	Mar	53	35	13	
	Apr	55	33	12	
	May	51	36	13	
	Jun	48	37	15	
	Jul	46	41	13	
	Aug	53	34	14	
	Sep	48	39	13	
	Oct	48	39	13	
	Oct	51	35	14	
MICHAEL FOOT					
	Nov	38	38	24	A
	Dec	30	35	35	
1981	Jan	26	42	32	
	Jan	23	43	34	
	Feb	22	49	29	
	Mar	23	52	25	
	Mar	20	55	25	
	Apr	21	54	25	
	May	26	52	22	
	Jun	28	48	24	
	Jul	25	52	23	
	Aug	23	57	20	
	Sep	28	54	18	
	Oct	27	54	19	
	Nov	16	67	17	
	Dec	19	67	14	
1982	Jan	18	67	15	
	Feb	19	66	15	
	Mar	21	65	14	
	Apr	23	61	16	
	May	18	71	11	
	Jun	14	75	11	
	Jul	16	72	12	
	Aug	15	74	10	
	Sep	16	74	10	
	Oct	20	69	11	
	Nov	22	67	11	
	Dec	20	69	11	
1983	Jan	17	69	14	
	Feb	17	72	11	
	Mar	19	71	10	
	Apr	21	64	15	

cont'd . . .

		Is	Is not	DK	
	May	18	70	12	
	Jun	17	77	6	
	Jul	11	82	7	
	Aug	10	84	6	
	Sep	9	84	7	

NEIL KINNOCK

		Is	Is not	DK	
	Oct	58	17	25	B
	Nov	48	14	38	
	Dec	40	20	40	
1984	Jan	43	23	34	
	Feb	45	24	31	
	Mar	47	27	26	
	Apr	42	34	24	
	May	42	33	25	
	Jun	43	36	21	
	Jul	43	37	20	
	Aug	37	44	19	
	Sep	43	37	20	
	Oct	35	48	17	
	Nov	39	44	17	
	Dec	36	49	15	
1985	Jan	36	49	15	
	Feb	31	54	15	
	Mar	37	47	16	
	Apr	36	48	16	
	May	38	45	17	
	Jun	37	51	12	
	Jul	38	47	15	
	Aug	34	48	18	
	Sep	29	52	19	
	Oct	50	35	15	
	Nov	46	39	16	
	Dec	47	39	14	
1986	Jan	44	39	17	
	Feb	40	44	16	
	Mar	39	47	14	
	Apr	40	44	16	
	May	47	39	14	
	Jun	41	43	15	
	Jul	43	45	12	
	Aug	38	46	16	
	Sep	46	40	15	
	Oct	47	41	12	

cont'd . . .

		Is	Is not	DK
	Nov	44	41	15
	Dec	36	53	12
1987	Jan	39	44	17
	Feb	37	48	15
	Mar	34	52	14
	Apr	26	63	12
	May	30	60	10
	Jun	45	45	10
	Jul	41	51	8
	Aug	35	54	11
	Sep	36	54	10
	Sep	40	49	11
	Oct	39	50	12
	Nov	39	52	9
	Dec	40	49	11
1988	Jan	35	53	11
	Feb	36	53	11
	Mar	32	56	12
	Apr	39	50	10
	May	39	47	13
	Jun	38	51	11
	Jul	32	56	12
	Aug	27	62	12
	Sep	30	59	11
	Oct	33	56	11
	Nov	29	58	13
	Dec	26	62	12
1989	Jan	29	58	13
	Feb	27	59	15
	Mar	31	59	10
	Apr	33	56	11
	May	33	55	12
	Jun	37	52	11
	Jul	38	49	14
	Aug	37	48	14
	Sep	36	52	12
	Oct	50	38	12
	Nov	39	46	15
	Dec	45	43	12
1990	Jan	41	47	12
	Feb	39	45	16
	Mar	38	48	15
	Apr	41	44	16

cont'd . . .

		Is	Is not	DK
	May	34	52	14
	Jun	43	45	12
	Jul	39	49	12
	Aug	38	49	12
	Sep	44	43	13
	Oct	47	40	12
	Nov	37	48	15
	Dec	33	59	8
1991	Jan	37	54	9
	Feb	41	50	9
	Mar	38	52	10
	Apr	34	55	11
	May	36	54	10
	Jun	40	52	8
	Jul	36	55	9
	Aug	36	54	10
	Sep	34	56	11
	Oct	41	47	12
	Nov	42	48	10
	Dec	34	57	10
1992	Jan	33	57	10
	Feb	35	55	10
	Mar	34	56	9
	Apr	42	47	11
	May	51	22	27

JOHN SMITH

		Is	Is not	DK
	Jun	49	23	27
	Jul	46	24	30
	Aug	52	15	32
	Sep	33	20	47
	Oct	44	18	38
	Oct	44	18	39
	Nov	44	21	35
	Nov	49	25	26
	Dec	49	23	27
1993	Jan	41	32	28
	Jan	45	28	27
	Feb	44	31	25
	Mar	50	28	22
	Apr	50	28	22
	May	47	29	24
	May	46	31	23
	Jun	42	35	23

cont'd . . .

		Is	Is not	DK
	Jul	43	38	19
	Aug	49	33	18
	Sep	40	38	22
	Sep	45	35	20
	Oct	54	27	19
	Nov	53	28	19
	Dec	52	30	18
1994	Jan	46	35	19
	Jan	54	28	18
	Feb	51	30	18
	Mar	52	30	18
	Apr	53	28	18
	May	49	32	19

TONY BLAIR

		Is	Is not	DK	
	Aug	58	23	19	D
	Sep	52	11	37	
	Sep	47	15	38	
	Oct	45	14	41	
	Oct	52	15	33	
	Nov	48	14	38	
	Dec	54	17	28	
1995	Jan	56	17	27	
	Jan	56	19	24	
	Feb	59	18	23	
	Mar	59	20	21	
	Apr	63	18	19	
	May	65	16	19	
	Jun	68	15	17	
	Jul	65	18	17	
	Jul	62	19	19	
	Aug	62	17	20	
	Sep	54	23	23	
	Sep	56	25	19	
	Oct	65	17	17	
	Nov	61	22	16	
	Dec	67	18	16	
1996	Jan	63	19	18	
	Feb	55	23	21	
	Mar	62	22	17	
	Apr	64	21	15	
	May	62	21	17	
	Jun	58	23	19	
	Jul	56	26	18	

cont'd . . .

		Is	Is not	DK
	Aug	55	27	18
	Sep	55	28	18
	Sep	55	28	17
	Oct	66	18	16
	Nov	61	22	16
	Dec	62	24	14
1997	Jan	67	26	6
	Feb	67	24	9
	Mar	67	24	10
1997	Apr	70	19	12

A Question in November 1980 read, 'Do you think Mr Foot will or will not prove a good leader of the Labour Party?'

B Question in October 1983 read, 'Do you think Mr Kinnock will or will not prove a good leader of the Labour Party?'

C Question in June–August 1992 read, 'Do you think Mr Smith will/would or will/would not prove a good leader of the Labour Party?'

D Question in August 1994 read, 'Do you think Mr Blair will or will not prove a good leader of the Labour Party?'

TABLE 8.3:   LIBERAL LEADERS 1957–88

Q. Do you think that Mr ..... is or is not doing a good job as leader of the Liberal Party?

		Is	Is not	DK
JO GRIMOND				
1957	Sep	19	7	74
1962	Jul	65	5	30
1964	Nov	69	10	21
	Dec	74	7	19
1965	Jan	58	10	32
	Feb	64	12	24
	Mar	66	12	22
	Apr	66	10	24
	May	65	11	24
	Jun	65	11	24
	Sep	57	12	31
1966	Feb	53	17	30

cont'd . . .

		Is	Is not	DK	

JEREMY THORPE

1967	Feb	51	7	42	A
	Dec	46	16	38	
1968	Sep	43	13	44	
1974	Apr	60	19	21	
	May	57	21	22	
	Jun	59	20	21	
	Jul	59	21	20	
	Aug	63	19	18	
	Sep	55	21	24	
	Oct	57	25	18	
	Nov	45	28	27	
	Dec	45	27	28	
1975	Jan	47	25	28	
	Feb	43	31	26	
	Mar	41	32	27	
	Apr	39	34	27	
	May	40	33	27	
	Jun	47	28	25	
	Jul	44	34	22	
	Aug	48	32	20	
	Sep	49	30	21	
	Oct	48	30	22	
	Nov	44	35	21	
	Dec	47	30	23	
1976	Jan	45	32	23	
	Feb	41	36	23	
	Mar	32	45	23	
	Apr	36	44	20	

JO GRIMOND

	Jun	42	15	43	
	Jun	42	21	37	

DAVID STEEL

1976	Jul	45	11	44	B
	Aug	40	12	48	
	Sep	34	18	48	
	Oct	35	19	46	
	Nov	40	17	43	
	Dec	40	18	42	
1977	Jan	43	19	38	
	Feb	36	21	43	

cont'd . . .

		Is	Is not	DK
	Mar	41	18	41
	Apr	37	37	26
	May	33	35	32
	Jun	35	36	29
	Jul	44	31	25
	Aug	42	32	26
	Sep	37	35	28
	Oct	43	34	23
	Nov	44	32	24
	Dec	39	33	28
1978	Jan	38	34	28
	Feb	42	33	25
	Mar	40	37	23
	Apr	42	36	22
	May	37	36	27
	Jun	36	38	26
	Jul	40	37	23
	Aug	34	39	27
	Sep	34	42	24
	Oct	44	33	23
	Nov	37	36	27
	Dec	38	34	28
1979	Jan	34	35	31
	Feb	44	30	26
	Mar	42	30	28
	Apr	63	19	18
	May			
	Jun	64	18	18
	Jul	61	21	18
	Aug	53	25	22
	Sep	50	23	27
	Oct	58	19	23
	Nov	57	20	23
	Dec	57	19	24
1980	Jan	62	19	19
	Feb	60	18	22
	Mar	60	19	22
	Apr	60	19	21
	May	61	19	20
	Jun	57	18	25
	Jul	53	24	23
	Aug	58	18	24
	Sep	59	19	22

cont'd . . .

		Is	Is not	DK
	Oct	56	20	24
	Oct	57	20	23
	Nov	54	22	24
	Dec	59	17	24
1981	Jan	63	19	18
	Jan	57	19	24
	Feb	64	16	20
	Mar	63	15	22
	Mar	61	19	20
	Apr	60	20	20
	May	63	17	20
	Jun	61	18	21
	Jul	56	20	24
	Aug	61	18	21
	Sep	56	21	23
	Oct	60	20	20
	Nov	64	17	19
	Dec	63	18	19
1982	Jan	59	22	19
	Feb	59	23	18
	Mar	58	22	20
	Apr	63	18	19
	May	64	20	16
	Jun	62	21	18
	Jul	61	20	19
	Aug	62	19	18
	Sep	59	21	20
	Oct	60	22	18
	Nov	59	22	19
	Dec	60	23	17
1983	Jan	62	19	19
	Feb	62	21	17
	Mar	69	14	17
	Apr	64	17	19
	May	61	21	18
	Jun	74	15	11
	Jul	72	14	14
	Aug	71	15	14
	Sep	65	22	13
	Oct	60	23	17
	Nov	63	21	16
	Dec	64	21	15
1984	Jan	59	23	18

cont'd . . .

		Is	Is not	DK
	Feb	61	22	17
	Mar	67	18	15
	Apr	61	22	17
	May	67	19	14
	Jun	63	23	14
	Jul	61	22	17
	Aug	55	23	22
	Sep	59	23	17
	Oct	57	26	17
	Nov	56	27	17
1984	Dec	57	27	16
1985	Jan	57	26	17
	Feb	57	24	18
	Mar	60	23	17
	Apr	60	24	17
	May	64	19	16
	Jun	63	22	15
	Jul	65	20	15
	Aug	63	21	17
	Sep	56	25	19
	Oct	53	29	18
	Nov	55	27	18
	Dec	59	24	18
1986	an	59	21	20
	Feb	59	25	16
	Mar	58	27	16
	Apr	55	27	18
	May	55	25	20
	Jun	51	32	17
	Jul	55	30	15
	Aug	55	26	19
	Sep	51	29	20
	Oct	47	35	18
	Nov	49	32	18
	Dec	46	35	19
1987	Jan	55	25	21
	Feb	55	29	17
	Mar	62	24	14
	Apr	56	28	16
	May	60	27	14
	Jun	51	34	14
	Jul	42	43	15
	Aug	38	46	16

cont'd . . .

		Is	Is not	DK
	Sep	41	44	15
	Sep	40	42	19
	Oct	40	46	14
	Nov	39	46	15
	Dec	39	42	19
1988	Jan	27	57	17
	Feb	32	52	16

A Question in February 1967 read, 'Do you think Mr Thorpe is or is not a good choice as leader of the Liberals?'
B Question in July/August 1976 read, 'Do you think Mr Steel will or will not prove a good leader of the Liberal Party?'

TABLE 8.4:   SOCIAL DEMOCRAT LEADERS 1982–90

Q. Do you think Mr ..... is or is not proving a good leader of the Social Democratic Party?

		Is	Is not	DK	
ROY JENKINS					
1982	Jul	50	22	28	A
	Aug	42	31	27	
	Sep	37	32	31	
	Oct	35	34	31	
	Nov	37	33	30	
	Dec	34	34	32	
1983	Jan	30	31	39	
	Feb	33	39	28	
	Mar	39	35	26	
	Apr	31	41	28	
	May	30	45	25	
	Jun	30	49	21	
DAVID OWEN					
	Jul	55	19	26	
	Aug	54	19	27	
	Sep	54	20	26	
	Oct	48	25	27	
	Nov	47	24	29	
	Dec	51	23	26	
1984	Jan	45	25	30	
	Feb	45	24	31	

cont'd . . .

		Is	Is not	DK
	Mar	48	23	29
	Apr	48	25	27
	May	51	25	24
	Jun	52	22	26
	Jul	52	23	25
	Aug	50	23	27
	Sep	53	20	27
	Oct	59	20	21
	Nov	54	23	23
	Dec	55	25	20
1985	Jan	52	27	21
	Feb	55	21	24
	Mar	53	21	25
	Apr	52	26	22
	May	56	21	23
	Jun	56	23	21
	Jul	54	24	22
	Aug	54	24	23
	Sep	59	21	20
	Oct	47	30	23
	Nov	52	26	22
	Dec	56	23	21
1986	Jan	55	21	24
	Feb	57	21	22
	Mar	54	25	21
	Apr	52	29	19
	May	52	25	23
	Jun	47	33	20
	Jul	51	30	20
	Aug	51	25	24
	Sep	49	28	23
	Oct	52	29	19
	Nov	49	32	19
	Dec	49	32	19
1987	Jan	48	26	26
	Feb	53	29	18
	Mar	54	26	20
	Apr	56	25	19
	May	55	29	16
	Jun	48	36	16
1987	Jul	40	46	14

cont'd . . .

	Is	Is not	DK
ROBERT MACLENNAN			
1987 Sep	15	11	74
Sep	11	22	67
Oct	12	26	61
Nov	11	27	62
Dec	12	24	64
1988 Jan	12	36	51
1998 Feb	11	46	43
DAVID OWEN			
1988 Apr	42	40	18
May	37	43	20
Jun	39	41	20
Jul	40	43	18
Aug	37	39	23
Sep	39	40	21
Oct	39	40	21
Nov	38	38	24
Dec	37	41	22
1989 Jan	41	37	22
Feb	41	36	23
Mar	47	35	18
Apr	43	36	21
May	32	47	21
Jun	32	47	21
Jul	30	47	22
Aug	31	47	22
Sep	33	46	20
Oct	30	52	18
Nov	26	49	24
Dec	32	46	22
1990 Jan	31	46	23
Feb	30	46	24
Mar	24	54	21
Apr	30	47	23
May	31	45	24
Jun	25	51	25

A Question in July/August 1982 read, 'Do you think Mr Jenkins will or will not prove a good leader of the Social Democrat Party?'

TABLE 8.5: LIBERAL DEMOCRAT LEADERS 1988–2000

Q. Do you think Mr ..... is or is not proving a good leader of the Social and Liberal Democratic Party?

		Is	Is not	DK	
DAVID STEEL AND ROBERT MACLENNAN					
1988	Apr	22	39	38	
	May	19	56	25	
	Jun	18	51	31	
	Jul	25	54	21	
PADDY ASHDOWN					
	Aug	22	16	63	
	Sep	19	23	57	
	Oct	24	22	54	
	Nov	24	24	53	
	Dec	25	25	50	
1989	Jan	23	28	49	
	Feb	27	24	49	
	Mar	28	33	39	
	Apr	30	29	42	
	May	26	36	38	
	Jun	25	36	38	
	Jul	30	47	22	
	Aug	22	41	37	
	Sep	23	43	35	
	Oct	23	47	30	
	Nov	22	43	35	
	Dec	26	43	31	A
1990	Jan	27	41	33	
	Feb	24	41	35	
	Mar	26	39	35	
	Apr	29	39	32	
	May	37	32	31	
	Jun	30	39	31	
	Jul	28	37	35	
	Aug	33	35	32	
	Sep	28	41	32	
	Oct	39	30	31	
	Nov	45	28	27	
	Dec	42	32	26	
1991	Jan	41	33	27	
	Feb	44	30	27	
	Mar	58	22	20	
	Apr	52	22	26	

cont'd . . .

		Is	Is not	DK
	May	55	23	22
	Jun	62	18	20
	Jul	62	20	18
	Aug	52	25	23
	Sep	57	23	20
	Oct	57	21	22
	Nov	56	22	22
	Dec	56	25	18
1992	Jan	53	22	24
	Feb	62	23	15
	Mar	59	26	15
	Apr	64	22	14
	May	66	21	13
	May	71	17	12
	Jun	66	21	13
	Jul	60	24	15
	Aug	54	24	21
	Sep	54	29	17
	Oct	57	23	20
	Oct	54	25	21
	Nov	53	28	19
	Nov	55	28	17
1993	Jan	56	26	18
	Jan	58	25	17
	Feb	59	25	17
	Apr	57	24	19
	May	59	24	17
	May	64	19	17
	Jul	64	22	15
	Aug	63	20	17
	Sep	64	19	17
	Sep	66	20	14
	Oct	64	20	17
	Dec	56	23	21
1994	Jan	54	27	19
	Jan	58	24	18
	Feb	55	23	22
	Apr	57	24	19
	May	59	22	19
	May	57	22	21
	Jul	62	21	18
	Jul	58	23	19
	Sep	61	20	19

cont'd . . .

		Is	Is not	DK
	Sep	47	33	20
	Oct	51	29	20
	Oct	52	29	20
	Dec	52	27	21
1995	Jan	50	29	21
	Jan	51	26	23
	Feb	52	27	21
	Apr	55	24	21
	May	58	23	19
	Jun	56	24	20
	Jul	52	26	22
	Jul	53	25	22
	Sep	52	25	24
	Sep	52	26	22
	Oct	54	24	21
	Dec	55	23	22
1996	Jan	56	21	22
	Feb	55	21	24
	Mar	58	20	22
	Mar	57	24	19
	May	62	18	20
	Jun	57	22	21
	Jun	62	20	18
	Aug	55	24	21
	Sep	53	26	22
	Sep	61	21	18
	Nov	56	22	22
	Dec	57	24	19
1997	Jan	70	23	8
	Feb	63	23	14
	Mar	66	21	13
	Apr	67	18	15
	Jun	73	14	13
	Jul	76	16	8
	Aug	74	18	8
	Sep	68	23	8
	Oct	76	15	8
	Nov	73	17	10
	Dec	79	13	7

CHARLES KENNEDY

		Is	Is not	DK	
1999	Sep	51	15	34	B
	Oct	54	15	31	
	Nov	58	18	23	

cont'd . . .

	Is	Is not	DK
2000 Feb	43	24	34
Mar	45	26	30
Apr	45	24	31
May	47	20	33
Jun	42	22	36
Jul	41	21	38
Aug	47	24	29
Sep	47	22	31
Sep	55	20	25
Nov	46	23	31
2000 Dec	51	21	28

A Question in December 1989 onwards related to the 'Liberal Democrats.'

B Question in September–November 1999 read, 'Do you think Mr Kennedy will or will not prove a good leader of the Liberal Democrats?'

TABLE 8.6:   LEFT/RIGHT SCALE, 1980–96

Q. *Whereabouts on this scale would you place .....?*

FL   Far left
SuL Substantially left
ML   Moderately left
SL   Slightly left
AL   All left (sum of FL–SL)
SR   Slightly right
MR   Moderately right
SuR Substantially right
FR   Far right
AR   All right (sum of SR–FR)
MoR Middle of the road (volunteered)
DK   Don't know

	FL	SuL	ML	SL	AL	SR	MR	SuR	FR	AR	MoR	DK
JAMES CALLAGHAN												
1980 Jan	4	6	25	18	53	8	11	2	2	23	3	20
MARGARET THATCHER												
1980 Jan	4	2	2	2	10	5	12	27	24	68	2	20
1986 Jul	4	2	1	1	8	2	10	25	37	24	0	18

cont'd . . .

		FL	SuL	ML	SL	AL	SR	MR	SuR	FR	AR	MoR	DK
1990	Mar	4	2	I	I	7	3	6	20	45	74	I	17
	Nov	3	I	I	I	6	3	9	23	39	74	2	19

DAVID STEEL

		FL	SuL	ML	SL	AL	SR	MR	SuR	FR	AR	MoR	DK
1980	Jan	I	I	5	12	19	17	15	3	I	36	II	34
1986	Jul	I	2	9	16	28	17	II	2	I	31	10	30

NEIL KINNOCK

		FL	SuL	ML	SL	AL	SR	MR	SuR	FR	AR	MoR	DK
1986	Jan	10	17	27	12	66	4	5	I	2	12	2	19
1990	Mar	10	14	31	12	68	5	4	2	2	13	3	16
1990	Nov	10	13	29	13	65	5	4	I	2	12	3	20
1991	Jan	10	15	30	13	68	4	3	2	I	10	3	20
1991	Nov	9	16	29	12	66	5	3	I	2	II	I	21

DAVID OWEN

		FL	SuL	ML	SL	AL	SR	MR	SuR	FR	AR	MoR	DK
1986	Jul	2	2	7	14	25	18	12	3	I	34	8	33
1990	Mar	2	0	5	14	21	17	8	2	I	28	8	43

PADDY ASHDOWN

		FL	SuL	ML	SL	AL	SR	MR	SuR	FR	AR	MoR	DK
1990	Mar	I	2	8	17	28	12	5	I	I	19	9	44
1990	Nov	I	I	7	16	25	16	7	I	I	25	13	38
1991	Jan	2	I	7	16	26	16	7	0	I	24	12	37
1991	Nov	I	2	6	18	27	17	8	I	I	27	13	32
1992	Mar	I	I	6	20	28	19	7	I	I	28	15	29
1992	Aug	I	I	7	22	31	16	5	I	0	22	12	35
1993	Mar	I	I	7	17	26	21	8	I	I	31	14	29
1993	Oct	3	2	10	17	32	16	8	I	I	26	13	29
1994	Aug	I	I	9	19	30	14	6	I	I	22	13	34
1996	Jan	I	I	6	19	27	14	5	I	I	21	13	39

JOHN MAJOR

		FL	SuL	ML	SL	AL	SR	MR	SuR	FR	AR	MoR	DK
1991	Jan	2	I	I	I	5	9	30	17	9	65	3	26
1991	Nov	2	I	2	2	7	12	32	16	8	68	3	21
1992	Mar	2	I	I	2	6	10	31	22	II	73	I	20
1992	Aug	I	I	I	2	5	10	31	18	8	67	3	24
1993	Mar	3	2	I	2	8	9	26	20	13	68	3	20
1993	Oct	3	I	2	2	8	II	26	19	10	66	3	23
1994	Aug	2	I	I	2	6	9	24	19	12	64	3	28
1996	Jan	2	I	I	3	7	12	24	15	10	61	4	29

JOHN SMITH

		FL	SuL	ML	SL	AL	SR	MR	SuR	FR	AR	MoR	DK
1992	Aug	5	10	26	15	56	5	3	I	I	10	2	33
1993	Mar	7	II	31	16	65	5	3	2	I	II	3	21
1993	Oct	6	10	29	17	62	5	4	2	2	13	3	21

cont'd . . .

	FL	SuL	ML	SL	AL	SR	MR	SuR	FR	AR	MoR	DK

TONY BLAIR

		FL	SuL	ML	SL	AL	SR	MR	SuR	FR	AR	MoR	DK
1994	Aug	3	7	27	16	53	8	4	1	1	14	5	29
1996	Jan	4	6	20	19	49	11	5	2	1	19	5	28

CHAPTER 9

Chancellors of the Exchequer and their Budgets

Beginning in 1946, Gallup has asked voters to rate every Chancellor of the Exchequer, usually at the time of the Chancellor's spring or autumn Budget but sometimes, in addition, at other times of the year. If for some reason the relevant question was not asked at the time of an annual Budget, the corresponding row in Table 9.1 has been left blank.

The same procedure has also been adopted in connection with Table 9.2, which reports the answers since 1952 to the question 'Do you think the Budget is a fair one or not?' A question containing the word 'fair' may seem to be inviting the respondent to reply largely or exclusively in terms of his or her theory of distributive justice; and some respondents may be doing precisely that. But it seems more probable that the great bulk of respondents interpret the question as simply inviting them record their overall approval or disapproval of the Budget in question.

TABLE 9.1:   CHANCELLORS OF THE EXCHEQUER 1946–2000

Q. Do you think that .... is doing a good job or a bad job as Chancellor of the Exchequer?

		Good job	Bad job	DK	
HUGH DALTON					
1946	May	55	14	31	A
SIR STAFFORD CRIPPS					
1949	Apr	57	24	19	
	Oct	45	34	21	
R. A. BUTLER					
1952	Apr	49	25	26	
	Dec	55	21	24	
1953	Jan	53	17	30	

cont'd . . .

		Good job	Bad job	DK
	Apr	63	31	6
1954	Feb	61	13	26
	Apr	53	31	16
1955	Feb	61	21	18
	Mar	62	21	17
	Apr	62	14	24
	Dec	35	47	18

HAROLD MACMILLAN

1956	Apr	42	33	25
	Jul	40	35	25

PETER THORNEYCROFT

1957	Mar	25	19	56
	Apr	50	23	27
	Nov	29	33	38

DERICK HEATHCOAT AMORY

1959	Apr	46	11	43
1960	Apr	43	28	29
1961	Mar	32	22	46

SELWYN LLOYD

	Apr	36	31	33
1961	Aug	31	49	20
1962	Apr	42	30	28

REGINALD MAUDLING

1963	Apr	59	19	22
1964	Apr	47	33	20

JAMES CALLAGHAN

	Nov	43	23	34
1965	Mar	46	17	37
	Apr	48	24	28
	May	56	27	17
	Jul	41	34	25
	Aug	39	35	26
	May	61	18	21
	Aug	43	29	28
1967	Apr	51	26	23

ROY JENKINS

1968	Apr	41	28	31

cont'd . . .

		Good job	Bad job	DK
1969	Apr	49	32	19
1970	Apr	61	19	20

ANTHONY BARBER

		Good job	Bad job	DK
1971	Mar	56	18	26
1972	Mar	49	19	32
1973	Apr	57	17	26
	Jul	44	27	29
	Mar	57	23	20

DENIS HEALEY

		Good job	Bad job	DK
1974	Mar	43	22	35
	Aug	43	27	30
	Nov	53	23	24
1975	Apr	44	36	20
	Jul	54	24	22
1976	Apr	60	23	17
	Nov	25	54	21
1977	Apr	38	46	16
	Nov	58	23	19
1978	Apr	57	27	16

SIR GEOFFREY HOWE

		Good job	Bad job	DK
1979	Jun	38	30	32
1980	Mar	51	29	19
1981	Mar	24	61	15
1982	Mar	49	39	13
1983	Mar	51	36	13

NIGEL LAWSON

		Good job	Bad job	DK
	Nov	22	36	41
1984	Mar	57	26	17
1985	Mar	33	51	16
1986	Mar	43	42	15
1987	Mar	49	37	14
1988	Mar	47	42	12
	Nov	37	45	18
1989	Jan	24	61	15
	Mar	36	46	17

JOHN MAJOR

		Good job	Bad job	DK
1990	Mar	33	22	45

cont'd . . .

	Good job	Bad job	DK
NORMAN LAMONT			
1991 Mar	33	31	36
1992 Feb	29	46	25
Mar	43	43	14
1993 Mar	18	70	13
KENNETH CLARKE			
1993 Dec	36	40	24
1994 Dec	24	59	17
1995 Dec	33	49	18
1996 Nov	38	46	16
GORDON BROWN			
1997 Jul	70	12	18
1998 Mar	71	21	8
1999 Mar			
2000 Mar	63	24	13

A The 1946 question began with 'On the whole, do you ....?'

TABLE 9.2:   FAIRNESS OF BUDGETS 1952–2000

Q. Do you think the Budget is a fair one or not?

	Fair	Not fair	DK
R. A. BUTLER			
1952 Apr	60	32	8
1953 Apr	50	37	13
1955 Apr	50	32	18
HAROLD MACMILLAN			
1956 Apr	43	43	14
PETER THORNEYCROFT			
1957 Apr	42	40	18
DERICK HEATHCOAT AMORY		
1958 Apr	62	23	15
1959 Apr	56	34	10
1960 Apr	41	47	12

cont'd . . .

	Fair	Not fair	DK
SELWYN LLOYD			
1961 Apr	33	51	16
1962 Apr	48	34	18
REGINALD MAUDLING			
1963 Apr	59	24	17
1964 Apr	41	48	11
JAMES CALLAGHAN			
1964 Nov	56	33	11
1965 Apr	51	34	15
1966 May	60	24	16
1967 Apr	56	23	21
1968 Apr	42	47	10
ROY JENKINS			
1969 Apr	59	32	9
1970 Apr	66	24	10
ANTHONY BARBER			
1971 Mar	61	29	10
1972 Apr	64	27	9
1973 Mar	55	34	11
DENIS HEALEY			
1974 Mar	56	32	12
1974 Nov	59	27	14
1975 Apr	51	37	12
1976 Apr	63	23	14
1977 Apr	36	54	10
1978 Apr	68	24	8
SIR GEOFFREY HOWE			
1979 Jun	44	49	7
1980 Mar	57	36	7
1981 Mar	22	73	5
1982 Mar	56	38	6
1983 Mar	53	39	8
NIGEL LAWSON			
1984 Mar	60	36	4
1985 Mar	41	51	8
1986 Mar	49	44	7

cont'd . . .

		Fair	Not fair	DK
1987	Mar	50	44	6
1988	Mar	28	67	5
1989	Mar	45	42	13
JOHN MAJOR				
1990	Mar	49	39	13
NORMAN LAMONT				
1991	Mar	42	46	12
1992	Mar	45	44	11
1993	Mar	19	75	6
KENNETH CLARKE				
1993	Dec	35	56	9
1994	Dec	23	65	13
1995	Dec	31	57	12
1996	Dec	30	57	13
GORDON BROWN				
1997	Jul	82	12	5
1998	Mar	65	31	3
2000	Mar	55	38	7

CHAPTER 10

Taxation and Government Expenditure

Table 2.2 in Chapter 2 reported the responses to questions asking voters to say which party they thought would best handle the issue of taxation and also various matters involving large-scale public expenditures, such as education and the National Health Service. However, Gallup has also asked questions about people's preferred balance between taxation and public expenditure and about whether they believed enough money was, or was not, being spent on certain items of expenditure. Table 10.1 reports the results of a question, devised in the late 1970s by Professor Ivor Crewe of the University of Essex, which asks people whether they would like to see taxes cut even if it meant some reduction in government services or whether, in order to expand government services, they would be prepared to envisage some tax increases. The question is still asked by the Gallup Poll at least once in most years. Table 10.2 reports the results of a question that lists specific policy areas and asks whether respondents believe the right amount of money is being spent in that area, too little or too much. The question was asked quite frequently between the early 1960s and the mid 1990s.

TABLE 10.1: TAX CUTS OR SERVICE EXPANSION 1979–2000

Q. People have different views about whether it is more important to reduce taxes or keep up government spending. How about you? Which of these statements comes closest to your own view?

TC   Taxes being cut, even if it means some reduction in government services, such as health, education and welfare
SQ   Things should be left as they are
SE   Government services such as health, education and welfare should be extended, even if it means some increases in taxes
DK   Don't know

		TC	SQ	SE	DK
1979	Mar	20	26	44	10
	Dec	25	23	44	9
1980	Feb	22	20	52	6
	Mar	21	24	48	7
1983	Feb	23	22	49	6
1984	May	14	25	54	7
	Nov	12	24	58	7
1985	Feb	16	18	59	6
1986	Feb	16	19	60	5
	Jun	17	14	64	5
	Sep	9	18	68	5
1987	May	12	21	61	5
	Sep	11	19	66	5
1988	Oct	10	15	71	4
1989	Apr	10	14	73	3
	Oct	9	15	70	5
	Dec	13	18	64	5
1990	Feb	11	16	66	7
	Aug	13	14	69	4
	Dec	10	16	69	5
1991	May	11	13	72	4
	Aug	10	20	64	6
	Sep	9	21	64	6
1992	Mar	10	20	66	4
1993	Apr	10	13	69	8
	Jul	8	15	75	3
1995	Feb	8	16	69	7
1996	Mar	9	13	71	7
	Sep	9	16	70	6
1997	Apr	7	18	72	3
1998	Apr	10	26	62	2
1999	Sep	12	22	64	3
2000	Nov	14	23	60	3
2000	Dec	14	26	57	3

TABLE 10.2: TOO MUCH EXPENDITURE, ENOUGH OR TOO LITTLE? 1961–95

Q. Do you think the government is spending too much, too little or about the right amount on:

EDU Education and schools
ROA Roads
NHS National Health Service
DEF Armaments and defence
PEN Old age pensions

A   Too much
B   Too little
C   About right
D   Don't know

		EDU				ROA				NHS				DEF				PEN			
		A	B	C	D	A	B	C	D	A	B	C	D	A	B	C	D	A	B	C	D
1961	Mar	14	34	43	9	4	52	31	13	23	30	39	8	46	10	28	16	1	81	14	4
	Nov	13	47	32	8	4	62	23	11	15	34	41	10	26	18	27	27	2	81	13	4
1965	Apr	17	40	33	10	7	52	29	12	17	23	46	14	43	8	28	21	2	67	25	6
1967	Mar	15	39	36	10	6	57	26	11	19	24	47	10	58	5	20	17	2	71	22	5
1968	Sep	18	36	38	8	8	48	32	12	21	24	43	12	37	16	24	23	2	73	19	6
1975	Dec	17	44	27	12	27	29	31	13	10	54	27	9	36	19	27	18	3	61	32	4
1976	Mar	17	45	28	10	24	28	37	11	13	42	35	10	24	33	23	20	3	59	32	7
	Aug	15	43	33	9	23	24	43	11	12	43	39	7	21	34	27	18	3	56	37	5
1977	Feb	13	55	22	10	20	39	29	12	12	53	26	9	24	31	25	20	3	62	31	4
	Oct	10	58	23	10	15	38	35	12	8	59	25	7	23	36	25	17	2	61	32	5
1978	Jun	8	52	29	11	9	35	39	16	4	66	22	7	17	37	23	24	1	44	48	7
1979	Nov	11	59	22	8	8	48	30	14	6	60	26	7	28	25	29	19	2	52	38	7
1980	Mar	5	65	22	8	6	45	29	20	4	68	22	6	19	29	31	21	1	59	31	9
1982	Jun	6	70	18	5	6	63	22	8	4	70	21	5	27	40	25	8	1	66	27	5
1983	Feb	5	72	17	5	6	62	23	9	5	71	19	5	49	13	31	8	1	64	29	5
	Jul	5	67	20	8	5	61	24	10	4	70	23	3	46	12	34	8	2	64	30	4
1985	Jul	4	74	15	7	5	63	24	9	2	77	17	5	53	9	27	11	1	70	24	5
	Sep	1	78	17	4	4	50	34	14	1	80	16	3	53	10	29	8	2	71	20	7
1986	Jun	3	81	11	5	5	63	25	7	2	82	13	4	60	8	24	9	1	77	18	4
	Nov	3	74	16	6	7	56	28	9	1	82	14	3	54	10	27	8	1	79	17	4
1988	May	2	71	18	9	4	58	27	11	1	84	13	2	50	7	30	12	1	80	15	4
	Nov	2	69	23	6	5	57	27	12	1	84	14	2	45	8	36	11	1	81	14	4
1990	Jan	2	81	12	6	7	64	21	8	1	88	10	2	56	8	26	11	0	85	11	3
	Oct	2	84	10	4	12	55	24	8	1	87	10	3	45	10	36	10	1	84	11	4
1991	Apr	3	81	13	4	10	55	29	6	1	84	12	2	44	9	36	11	1	79	15	5
1992	Dec	3	78	15	5	11	56	27	6	1	80	16	2	42	14	34	10	1	81	14	4
1993	Feb	2	75	17	6	13	44	33	10	1	86	10	3	42	15	30	12	1	83	12	4
	May	3	78	15	4	13	43	36	7	1	86	11	2	37	20	32	11	1	81	15	4
1995	Oct	1	80	13	6	19	42	29	11	1	82	13	3	32	20	29	18	0	78	14	8

CHAPTER 11

Foreign Secretaries and Other Ministers

The Chancellor of the Exchequer is the only minister other than the Prime Minister whose standing with the public is monitored regularly. However, Gallup frequently asks members of the public about other ministers, usually ones who are in the public eye at any given moment.

Table 11.1 sets out the responses to a question that usually takes the form, 'Do you think that ——— is doing a good job or a bad job as ———?'. The question has, however, occasionally been varied. One variation, for example, asks either, 'On the whole, do you approve of ——— as ———?' or 'Do you approve or disapprove of ——— as ——— ? Another variation asks, 'On the whole are you satisfied or dissatisfied with ——— as ———?' Reference letters and footnotes are used in Table 1.1 to indicate when the question wording has been varied from the basic 'good job/bad job' formulation. In practice, the responses have probably been little affected by these slight variations in wording. The questions and the responses to them have been grouped by the offices in question rather than chronologically.

The remaining tables in this chapter report the responses to a variety of questions asked since the early 1970s about a number of individual ministers. Tables 11.3–11.5 violate our general rule against reporting data that do not form part of time-series, but in these cases it can be argued that the findings, and other similar opinion poll findings, were of continuing political importance.

TABLE 11.1: SATISFACTION WITH MINISTERS 1941–98

Q. Do you think that Bevin is doing a good job or a bad job as Minister of Labour?

	Apr 1941	Mar 1943
Good job	63	64
Bad job	14	16
Don't know	23	20

Q. Do you think that Lord Woolton is or is not doing a good job as Minister of Food?

	Apr 1941	May 1942
Is	57	79
Is not	31	12
Don't know	12	9

Q. Do you approve or disapprove of Sir Stafford Cripps as Leader of the House of Commons?

	May 1942
Approve	76
Disapprove	5
Don't know	19

Q. Do you think Mr Herbert Morrison is or is not doing a good job as Minister of Home Affairs and Security?

	Apr 1942
Is	50
Is not	20
Don't know	30

Q. Do you think that Mr Morrison is or is not doing a good job as Home Secretary?

	Dec 1943
Is	49
Is not	31
Don't know	20

Q. Do you think that Ernest Bevin is or is not doing a good job as Foreign Secretary?

	Dec 1945	Feb 1946	Nov 1946	Dec 1946	Feb 1947	Oct 1947	Dec 1950
Is	47	73	58	54	58	55	43
Is not	18	12	19	20	21	20	28
Don't know	35	15	23	26	21	25	29

Q. On the whole, are you satisfied or dissatisfied with the job Mr Shinwell is doing as Minister of Fuel and Power?

	Jan 1947
Satisfied	45
Dissatisfied	36
Don't know	19

Q. Do you think that Mr Strachey is doing a good job or a bad job as Minister of Food?

	Apr 1947	Sep 1949	A
Good job	38	43	
Bad job	49	45	
Don't know	13	12	

A Question in 1949 began with 'On the whole, ...?'

Q. On the whole, do you approve or disapprove of Mr Bevin as Foreign Minister?

	Feb 1949
Approve	50
Disapprove	27
Don't know	23

Q. On the whole, do you approve or disapprove of Mr Bevan as Health Minister?

	Jul 1949
Approve	46
Disapprove	38
Don't know	16

Q. Do you approve or disapprove of Mr Maurice Webb as Food Minister?

	Jun 1950
Approve	57
Disapprove	17
Don't know	26

Q. Do you think that Mr Maurice Webb is doing a good job or a bad job as Minister of Food?

	Jan 1951
Good job	44
Bad job	47
Don't know	9

Q. Do you think that Morrison is doing a good job or bad job as Foreign Secretary?

	May 1951
Good job	29
Bad job	22
Don't know	49

Q. Do you think that Mr Eden is doing a good job or a bad job as Foreign Secretary?

	Dec 1951	Mar 1953	Apr 1954	Feb 1955	A
Good job	66	68	59	82	
Bad job	5	9	19	6	
Don't know	29	23	22	12	

A Question in 1955 spoke of Sir Anthony Eden.

Q. Do you think that Sir Oliver Lyttelton is doing a good job or a bad job as Colonial Secretary?

	Jan 1954
Good job	38
Bad job	27
Don't know	35

Q. Do you think that Sir Walter Monckton is doing a good job or a bad job as Minister of Labour?

	Jan 1954
Good job	39
Bad job	14
Don't know	47

Q. *Do you think Mr Macleod is doing a good job or a bad job as Minister of Labour?*

	Aug 1956
Good job	37
Bad job	11
Don't know	52

Q. *Do you think that Mr Selwyn Lloyd is doing a good job or a bad job as Foreign Secretary?*

	Jun 1958	Feb 1958
Good job	37	34
Bad job	22	36
Don't know	41	30

Q. *Do you think Mr Selwyn Lloyd is or is not doing a good job as Foreign Secretary?*

	Jun 1959
Is	51
Is not	16
Don't know	33

Q. *Taking everything into account, do you think that Dr Beeching of British Railways is doing a good job or a bad job?*

	Oct 1962	Apr 1963	Aug 1964
Good job	23	47	39
Bad job	57	30	38
Don't know	20	23	23

Q. *Do you think that Mr Marples is doing a good job or bad job as Minister of Transport?*

	Oct 1962	Aug 1964
Good job	46	55
Bad job	33	25
Don't know	21	20

Q. *Do you think that Mr R. A. Butler is doing a good job or a bad job as Foreign Secretary?*

	Dec 1963
Good job	49
Bad job	9
Don't know	42

Q. *Do you think that Mr Bevins is doing a good job or a bad job as Postmaster General?*

	Aug 1964
Good job	33
Bad job	33
Don't know	34

Q. *Do you think that George Brown will do a good job or a bad job as First Secretary of State and Minister for Economic Affairs?*

	Nov 1964
Good job	44
Bad job	21
Don't know	35

Q. *And how about Mr James Callaghan as Chancellor of the Exchequer?*

	Nov 1964
Good job	50
Bad job	12
Don't know	38

Q. *And how about Mrs Barbara Castle as Minister of Overseas Development?*

	Nov 1964
Good job	41
Bad job	18
Don't know	41

Q. And Mr Patrick Gordon Walker as Foreign Secretary?

	Nov 1964
Good job	52
Bad job	13
Don't know	35

Q. And Mr Richard Crossman as Minister of Housing and Local Government?

	Nov 1964
Good job	48
Bad job	11
Don't know	41

Q. And how about Mr Frank Cousins as Minister of Technology?

	Nov 1964
Good job	41
Bad job	22
Don't know	37

Q. Do you think that Mr Ray Gunter will do a good job or a bad job as Minister of Labour?

	Nov 1964
Good job	42
Bad job	8
Don't know	50

Q. Do you think that Mr Brown is doing a good job or a bad job as First Secretary of State and Minister for Economic Affairs?

	Dec 1964
Good job	48
Bad job	21
Don't know	30

Q. *Do you think Mr Crossman is or is not doing a good job as Minister of Housing and Local Government?*

	Apr 1965
Is	39
Is not	19
Don't know	42

Q. *Do you think that Mr Kenneth Robinson is doing a good job or a bad job as Minister of Health?*

	Dec 1964
Is	42
Is not	12
Don't know	46

Q. *Do you think that Mr Peart is or is not doing a good job as Minister of Agriculture, Fisheries and Food?*

	Apr 1965
Is	28
Is not	22
Don't know	50

Q. *Do you think that Mr George Brown is doing a good job or a bad job as Minister for Economic Affairs?*

	Jun 1965	Oct 1965
Good job	35	52
Bad job	41	23
Don't know	24	25

Q. *Do you think Mrs Barbara Castle will do a good job or a bad job as Minister of Transport?*

	Jun 1966
Good job	31
Bad job	24
Don't know	45

Q. *Do you think Mr Ray Gunter is doing a good job or a bad job as Minister of Labour?*

	Jul 1966
Good job	54
Bad job	23
Don't know	23

Q. *Do you think Mr Michael Stewart is or is not doing a good job as Foreign Secretary?*

	Jul 1966
Good job	33
Bad job	38
Don't know	29

Q. *Of people in Mr Wilson's Government, has or has not a success been made of the job handled by:*

	Has	Has not	Don't know
OCTOBER 1966			
Mrs Castle, the present Minister of Transport?	49	30	21
Mr Callaghan, the present Chancellor of the Exchequer?	45	36	19
Mr Robinson, the present Minister of Health?	43	23	34
Mr Gunter, the present Minister of Labour?	39	34	27
Mr Crossman, the present Leader of the House?	35	21	44
Mr Bowden, the present Secretary of State for Commonwealth Affairs?	32	24	44
Mr Stewart, the present Secretary of State for Economic Affairs?	27	28	45
Mr Brown, the present Foreign Secretary?	27	49	24

Q. *Do you think that Mr Roy Jenkins is doing a good job or a bad job as Foreign Secretary?*

	Nov 1966
Good job	35
Bad job	27
Don't know	38

Q. *Of people in Mr Wilson's Government, has or has not a success been made of the job handled by:*

	Has	Has not	Don't know
MARCH 1967			
Mrs Castle, the present Minister of Transport?	50	33	17
Mr Callaghan, the present Chancellor of the Exchequer?	54	28	18
Mr Robinson, the present Minister of Health?	48	17	35
Mr Gunter, the present Minister of Labour?	38	32	30
Mr Crossman, the present Leader of the House?	33	20	47
Mr Healey, the present Minister of Defence?	33	31	36
Mr Stewart, the present Secretary of State for Economic Affairs?	29	24	47
Mr Brown, the present Foreign Secretary?	38	44	18

Q. *Do you think that Mr Brown is doing a good job or a bad job as Foreign Secretary?*

	Jul 1967	Oct 1967	Nov 1967
Good job	37	42	39
Bad job	42	40	42
Don't know	21	18	19

Q. Do you think that Mr Callaghan is doing a good job or a bad job as Home Secretary?

	Apr 1968
Good job	31
Bad job	27
Don't know	42

Q. Of people in this Labour Government, do you think a success has been made of the job handled by:

	Has	Has not	Don't know
OCTOBER 1968			
Mr Wilson, the Prime Minister?	40	52	8
Mrs Castle, the present Secretary of State for Employment and Productivity?	46	41	13
Mr Jenkins, the present Chancellor of the Exchequer?	39	34	27
Mr Robinson, the present Minister of Health?	37	28	35
Mr Gunter, the former Minister of Labour and Power?	47	27	26
Mr Crossman, in charge of cordinating social services?	31	35	34
Mr Healey, the present Minister of Defence?			
Mr Stewart, the present Foreign Secretary?	36	29	35
Mr Brown, the former Foreign Secretary?	35	48	17
Mr Callaghan, the present Home Secretary?	38	35	27
Mr March, the present Minister of Transport?	28	30	42

cont'd . . .

	Has	Has not	Don't know
Mr Wedgwood-Benn, the present Minister of Technology?	32	24	44
Mr Crosland, the present President of the Board of Trade?	36	29	35

Q. *Do you think that Mrs Barbara Castle is doing a good job or a bad job as Secretary of State for Employment and Productivity?*

	Jan 1969	May 1969	Jan 1970
Good job	40	54	46
Bad job	38	33	30
Don't know	22	13	24

Q. *Do you think that Sir Alec Douglas-Home is doing a good job or a bad job as Foreign Secretary?*

	Oct 1971	Dec 1971	Feb 1972	Jun 1972
Good job	47	60	50	52
Bad job	15	16	26	18
Don't know	38	24	24	30

Q. *Here is a list of Conservative politicians. Which, if any, of them would you say are an asset to the Conservative Party?*

	Oct 1972	Apr 1973	Jul 1973	Oct 1973	Feb 1974
Sir Alec Douglas-Home	42	36	35	36	33
Enoch Powell	41	41	38	36	31
Anthony Barber	39	37	35	31	23
Robert Carr	39	28	28	24	22
Edward Heath	36	34	35	31	30
William Whitelaw	29	25	27	24	46
Reginald Maudling	26	22	20	18	13
Peter Walker	25	18	19	15	14
Mrs Margaret Thatcher	24	19	18	21	13
Sir Keith Joseph	23	18	19	17	15
Lord Carrington	22	14	12	11	15
Maurice Macmillan	20	16	12	12	7
None of these	19	19	21	24	19

Q. And which, if any, of them would you say are not an asset to the Conservative Party?

	Oct 1972	Apr 1973	Jul 1973	Oct 1973
Enoch Powell	26	25	26	26
Edward Heath	24	23	18	17
Mrs Margaret Thatcher	21	15	17	16
Reginald Maudling	20	11	12	8
Sir Alec Douglas-Home	16	12	12	12
William Whitelaw	15	10	7	7
Maurice Macmillan	15	10	10	7
Sir Keith Joseph	12	7	12	5
Lord Carrington	12	7	8	7
Anthony Barber	11	6	6	9
Robert Carr	11	7	7	6
Peter Walker	11	6	5	5
None of these	38	42	44	41

Q. Here is a list of Labour politicians. Which, if any, of them would you say are an asset to the Labour Party?

A Harold Wilson
B Denis Healey
C Roy Jenkins
D James Callaghan
E Mrs Shirley Williams
F Mrs Barbara Castle
G Michael Foot
H Anthony Wedgwood-Benn (Tony Benn)
I Anthony Crosland
J Edward Short
K Reg Prentice
L Peter Shore
M Eric Varley
N David Ennals
O Bruce Millan
P Albert Booth
Q Edmund Dell
R Dr David Owen
S Mrs Judith Hart
T Roy Mason
U Roy Hattersley
V Merlyn Rees
W John Silkin
X William Rodgers
Y None of these

cont'd . . .

		A	B	C	D	E	F	G	H	I	J	K	L	M	N	O	P	Q	R	S	T	U	V	W	X	Y
1974	Apr	45	40	39	39	35	33	30	24	23	18	17	15	–	–	–	–	–	–	–	–	–	–	–	–	24
	Jul	37	32	43	38	39	35	27	20	21	17	14	13	–	–	–	–	–	–	–	–	–	–	–	–	25
	Sep	36	29	38	37	35	30	26	19	20	14	12	10	–	–	–	–	–	–	–	–	–	–	–	–	29
	Nov	47	30	43	38	46	35	22	18	18	14	14	10	–	–	–	–	–	–	–	–	–	–	–	–	28
1975	Jan	45	33	39	42	38	33	21	18	20	15	15	15	–	–	–	–	–	–	–	–	–	–	–	–	25
	Feb	52	36	40	42	45	34	18	17	15	14	13	10	–	–	–	–	–	–	–	–	–	–	–	–	19
	Apr	49	26	31	35	34	23	13	13	12	9	11	7	–	–	–	–	–	–	–	–	–	–	–	–	25
	May	47	32	36	38	34	27	15	14	14	13	11	9	–	–	–	–	–	–	–	–	–	–	–	–	26
	Jun	49	28	35	33	33	24	15	12	12	10	12	10	–	–	–	–	–	–	–	–	–	–	–	–	25
	Sep	38	28	32	33	25	23	15	15	13	8	14	11	–	–	–	–	–	–	–	–	–	–	–	–	14
	Oct	48	32	35	38	32	22	20	17	13	10	20	10	–	–	–	–	–	–	–	–	–	–	–	–	21
1976	Feb	47	32	38	32	40	19	16	13	11	8	14	9	–	–	–	–	–	–	–	–	–	–	–	–	18
	Apr	52	33	44	59	31	19	29	19	15	13	12	9	–	–	–	–	–	–	–	–	–	–	–	–	15
	May	45	32	39	52	31	–	24	16	18	–	12	7	9	3	3	2	1	–	–	–	–	–	–	–	18
	Aug	31	26	33	43	30	–	22	14	13	–	12	8	7	4	2	2	2	–	–	–	–	–	–	–	27
	Sep	28	25	28	31	28	–	18	12	12	–	6	6	5	3	2	1	1	–	–	–	–	–	–	–	28
	Oct	35	18	31	35	44	–	20	14	15	–	12	7	9	4	2	2	2	–	–	–	–	–	–	–	24
1977	Mar	25	20	–	24	35	–	18	14	–	–	12	8	10	7	1	2	3	23	7	7	6	–	–	–	26
1977	Sep	22	22	–	32	31	–	14	10	–	–	–	9	5	7	1	2	1	19	6	7	6	8	4	2	26

Q. And which, if any, of them would you say are not an asset to the Labour Party?

A Anthony Wedgwood-Benn (Tony Benn)
B Mrs Barbara Castle
C Harold Wilson
D Michael Foot
E Denis Healey
F Peter Shore
G Edward Short
H Mrs Shirley Williams
I Anthony Crosland
J Reg Prentice
K Roy Jenkins
L James Callaghan
M David Ennals
N Eric Varley
O Albert Booth
P Edmund Dell
Q Bruce Millan
R Dr David Owen
S Mrs Judith Hart
T Roy Mason

cont'd . . .

U Roy Hattersley
V Merlyn Rees
W John Silkin
X William Rodgers
Y None of these

		A	B	C	D	E	F	G	H	I	J	K	L	M	N	O	P	Q	R	S	T	U	V	W	X	Y
1974	Apr	20	18	16	15	9	9	9	8	8	8	6	6	–	–	–	–	–	–	–	–	–	–	–	–	57
	Jul	30	19	17	18	13	11	15	10	8	12	8	9	–	–	–	–	–	–	–	–	–	–	–	–	47
	Sep	30	20	16	19	10	11	12	10	10	10	9	8	–	–	–	–	–	–	–	–	–	–	–	–	48
	Nov	26	14	9	21	10	9	9	6	6	7	6	7	–	–	–	–	–	–	–	–	–	–	–	–	53
1975	Jan	28	20	9	20	10	7	8	9	6	7	7	6	–	–	–	–	–	–	–	–	–	–	–	–	48
	Feb	32	17	8	23	7	8	9	6	6	6	5	4	–	–	–	–	–	–	–	–	–	–	–	–	46
	Apr	34	21	9	29	11	10	10	7	7	10	8	5	–	–	–	–	–	–	–	–	–	–	–	–	42
	May	40	21	12	28	11	13	9	11	9	10	8	6	–	–	–	–	–	–	–	–	–	–	–	–	41
	Jun	39	23	10	27	8	14	9	9	6	10	7	6	–	–	–	–	–	–	–	–	–	–	–	–	39
	Sep	40	23	16	27	12	12	11	12	9	14	13	7	–	–	–	–	–	–	–	–	–	–	–	–	24
	Oct	31	29	11	22	7	11	8	8	8	9	8	5	–	–	–	–	–	–	–	–	–	–	–	–	38
1976	Feb	37	34	13	28	12	11	7	11	8	8	8	6	–	–	–	–	–	–	–	–	–	–	–	–	34
	Apr	35	26	6	25	8	9	6	9	6	11	5	2	–	–	–	–	–	–	–	–	–	–	–	–	26
	May	34	–	7	27	9	8	–	10	6	7	7	2	4	4	3	3	3	–	–	–	–	–	–	–	41
	Aug	35	–	14	25	13	9	–	10	7	10	9	6	7	8	3	4	4	–	–	–	–	–	–	–	41
	Sep	36	–	9	26	9	6	–	9	6	9	9	5	5	5	4	3	4	–	–	–	–	–	–	–	43
	Oct	33	–	11	27	18	9	–	6	9	8	7	6	4	4	4	3	3	–	–	–	–	–	–	–	40
1977	Mar	32	–	13	30	15	6	–	12	–	8	–	9	4	4	3	3	3	2	9	3	5	–	–	–	39
1977	Sep	33	–	11	30	17	9	–	10	–	–	–	7	5	5	4	4	5	6	10	6	6	8	6	4	38

Q. You have probably heard that Mr John Major, the Prime Minister, is shortly to reshuffle his Cabinet. Could you tell me for each of the following whether you think that, from the Government's own point of view, it would be a good or bad idea for Mr Major to sack him?

	Good idea	Bad idea	Don't know
JUNE 1994			
Douglas Hurd, Foreign Secretary	22	53	25
John Patten, Education Secretary	60	19	21
Michael Portillo, Chief Secretary to the Treasury	37	29	33
Virginia Bottomley, Health Secretary	59	26	15
Kenneth Clarke, Chancellor of the Exchequer	41	38	21
Peter Lilley, Social Services Secretary	42	26	32

cont'd . . .

	Good Idea	Bad Idea	Don't know
Michael Heseltine, President of the Board of Trade	31	49	20
William Waldegrave, Minister for the Citizen's Charter	34	22	44
Michael Howard, Home Secretary	32	33	35
John MacGregor, Transport Secretary	39	30	31

Q. Please tell me whether you think each of the following Cabinet Ministers is doing a good job or a bad job?

	Good Job	Bad Job	Don't know
APRIL 1998			
Mo Mowlam, Northern Ireland Secretary	86	9	6
Jack Straw, Home Secretary	70	18	12
Gordon Brown, Chancellor	71	21	8
Robin Cook, Foreign Secretary	51	40	9
John Prescott, Deputy Prime Minister	70	20	10
David Blunkett, Education Secretary	67	25	8
Harriet Harman, Social Security Secretary	37	49	15
Clare Short, Secretary of State for International Development	51	24	24
Frank Dobson, Secretary of State for Health	50	36	14
Peter Mandelson, Minister without Portfolio	34	36	30
Margaret Beckett, President of the Board of Trade	54	22	24

Q. Here is a list of people in the Government. For each of them tell me whether you think they are an asset or a liability to the Conservative Party?

	Asset	Liablility	Don't know
OCTOBER 1995			
Michael Portillo	27	33	40

	Asset	Liablility	Don't know
Gillian Shephard	34	21	44
George Young	12	17	71
Stephen Dorrell	11	16	73
Brian Mawhinney	17	20	63
Peter Lilley	18	26	56
MIchael Heseltine	50	28	23
Kenneth Clarke	36	36	28
John Major	37	44	19
Malcolm Rifkind	26	25	49
Michael Howard	20	26	54
Virginia Bottomley	21	52	27

Q. Here is a list of people in the Government. For each of them tell me whether you think they are an asset or a liability to the Conservative Party?

	Asset	Liablility	Don't know
OCTOBER 1996			
Michael Portillo	24	37	39
Gillian Shephard	36	23	41
John Redwood	21	38	41
Stephen Dorrell	14	19	67
Brian Mawhinney	21	28	51
Peter Lilley	24	27	49
Michael Heseltine	48	27	24
Kenneth Clarke	41	32	27
John Major	37	43	20
Malcolm Rifkind	30	25	45
Michael Howard	25	32	42
Virginia Bottomley	26	45	29
William Hague	11	15	74

Q. Is the name 'Peter Mandelson' familiar to you or not?

	Sep 1997
Yes, familiar	49
No	51

Q. *Please tell me what Peter Mandelson's job in the Government is.*

	Sep 1997
Minister without Portfolio	22
Chief PR man	2
Tony Blair's right-hand man	3
Tony Blair's fixer	1
Spokesperson	1
Media man	2
Other	3
Don't know	15
All aware	49

Q. *Do you think he is doing a good job or a bad job in that position?*

	Sep 1997
Good job	16
Bad job	9
Don't know	23
All aware	49

Q. *Do you think John Prescott is doing a good job or a bad job as Deputy Prime Minister?*

	Sep 1997
Good job	72
Bad job	15
Don't know	13

Q. *Do you think the following people are an asset or a liability to the Labour Party at the moment?*

	Asset	Liability	Don't know
SEPTEMBER 1997			
Gordon Brown	64	15	21
Jack Straw	55	18	27
Peter Mandelson	33	23	44
Tony Blair	90	7	3
Robin Cook	60	25	14
John Prescott	74	15	10

Q. For each of the following people, please tell me whether you think the person is doing a good job or a bad job in their position. How about ..... ? (Asked of people correctly identifying the person's position)

	Good job	Bad job	Don't know	All correct
SEPTEMBER 1997				
Gordon Brown	26	7	5	38
John Prescott	32	8	7	47
Jack Straw	10	2	3	15
Tony Blair	77	6	8	92
David Blunkett	30	5	7	43
Robin Cook	29	5	8	42
Chris Smith	5	2	2	9
Mo Mowlam	34	5	6	44

Q. Do you think that Mr ..... is doing a good job or a bad job as .....?

	Good job	Bad job	Don't know
SEPTEMBER 1991			
Mr Lamont, Chancellor of the Exchequer	38	37	25
Mr Mellor, Chief Secretary to the Treasury	24	27	49
Mr Baker, Home Secretary	40	34	26
Mr Waldegrave, Health Secretary	21	57	22
Mr Lilley, Trade and Industry Secretary	18	35	47
Mr Heseltine, Environment Secretary	48	29	22
Mr Clarke, Secretary of Education and Science	24	58	18
Mr Major, Prime Minister	62	26	12
Mr Hurd, Foreign Secretary	69	17	14
Mr Howard, Employment Secretary	13	56	31
Mr Patten, Conservative Party Chairman	34	26	40

Q. Here is a list of people who are prominent in the Conservative Party at the moment. Could you tell me for each whether you think they are an asset or a liability to the Conservative Party?

	Mar 1992				Apr 1992		
	Asset	Liablility	DK		Asset	Liability	DK
Chris Patten	28	29	43		32	35	33
Douglas Hurd	49	24	27		52	25	23
John Major	60	24	16		65	25	10
Norman Lamont	23	43	34		29	48	23
Michael Heseltine	49	30	22		55	29	16
Tom King	37	24	39		39	25	36
Kenneth Clarke	19	48	33		26	45	29
William Waldegrave	18	34	48		21	37	42

CHAPTER 12

Most Urgent Problems Facing the Country

The tables in this chapter, like those in Chapters 1, 2, 6, 7 and 9, report the responses to questions that have been asked over a considerable period of time. Gallup began in the early 1960s by frequently asking a question of the form, 'Which of these is the most important problem facing the country today?' The word 'important' was used, and the question, like most of Gallup's questions, was closed-ended, in the sense that respondents were given a specific range of options to choose from. The results, dating from 1960 to 1964, are reported in Table 12.1.

No similar question was asked between 1964 and 1968. In that year, however, Gallup introduced a revised wording: 'What would you say is the most urgent problem facing the country at the present time?' The reasons for substituting the word 'urgent' for the word 'important' are not clear; but, as usual, it is doubtful whether the change made much practical difference. What did make a difference was the fact that the new question was not closed-ended but instead was open-ended, inviting the respondent to say in his or her own words which the most urgent problem was. The consequence was, of course, a much wider scattering of responses, with a larger proportion of responses having to be coded as 'Other'. The data in both Tables 12.1 and 12.2 provide striking evidence of voters' changing political preoccupations over the past four decades of the last century.

It should be added, in connection with the post-1968 question, that Gallup's interviewers, having ascertained what problem the respondent regarded as the most urgent facing the country, then asked, 'And what would you say is the next most urgent problem?' For reasons of space – Table 12.2, which is already large, would otherwise be enormous – the responses to this follow-up question have not been reported here. They seldom have much effect on the initial rank-ordering.

Table 12.3 reports the results of another follow-up question, which was asked between 1959 and 1997. Having learned what problem the respondent believed to be the most urgent facing the country, Gallup's interviewers then asked, 'Which party do you think can best handle that problem?' The question was dropped following the 1997 general election partly because there appeared to be only a loose connection, if any, between the problem identified by the majority as being the most urgent facing the country and the success, or lack of it, of any particular political party.

TABLE 12.1: MOST IMPORTANT PROBLEM 1960-64

Q. Which of these is the most important problem facing the country today?

EC Economic affairs
HO Housing
P   Pensions
L   Labour relations
ED Education
R   Roads
HE Health
I   International affairs
D   Defence
C   Colonial affairs
O   Other
DK None/don't know

		EC	HO	P	L	ED	R	HE	I	D	C	O	DK
1960	Jan	18	9	11	8	4	4	4	17	13	4	2	6
	Feb	16	7	10	5	4	7	3	17	14	6	4	7
	Mar	13	6	10	5	4	9	3	14	17	6	6	7
	Apr	13	8	10	5	5	6	3	11	21	9	2	7
	May	13	6	11	3	5	7	2	12	22	11	2	6
	Jun	11	5	10	2	4	7	3	23	23	7	1	4
	Jul	9	6	9	2	3	5	3	28	25	4	2	4
	Aug	11	7	9	2	3	4	3	25	23	4	3	6
	Sep	11	8	8	4	3	3	2	26	18	6	2	8
	Oct	11	9	7	5	3	3	2	25	21	5	2	7
	Nov	12	8	8	3	3	3	1	24	25	2	4	7
	Dec	19	7	9	3	3	4	2	16	23	2	5	7
1961	Jan	22	7	10	3	3	3	4	18	3	18	3	6
	Feb	24	7	8	4	3	3	4	16	4	18	3	6
	Mar	22	7	8	2	3	2	5	17	4	19	5	6
	Apr	14	8	9	2	5	3	4	20	3	18	7	7
	May	16	8	9	4	6	4	5	14	20	4	3	7
	Jun	16	9	8	5	4	4	5	15	20	3	5	6
	Jul	23	8	7	5	3	3	4	19	15	4	4	5
	Aug	32	6	6	6	3	2	2	19	10	4	3	7
	Sep	25	5	4	4	3	1	2	28	17	3	2	6
	Oct	16	5	3	6	3	1	2	29	25	3	2	5
	Nov	16	6	5	7	3	1	2	17	33	3	2	5
1962	Jan	24	7	6	5	2	0	3	18	20	3	6	6
	Mar	25	7	7	9	2	1	3	12	22	3	4	5
	Apr	24	8	8	4	3	1	4	11	23	3	5	6

cont'd . . .

		EC	HO	P	L	ED	R	HE	I	D	C	O	DK
	Jun	28	9	7	5	3	2	4	11	20	2	5	3
	Sep	29	10	8	7	3	2	3	11	16	3	5	3
	Aug	30	11	7	2	2	2	3	12	17	3	6	5
	Sep	40	8	6	2	1	2	2	14	13	3	3	6
	Oct	42	7	6	4	1	2	2	16	10	2	2	6
	Nov	34	9	7	6	2	2	3	17	12	2	2	4
	Dec	38	7	7	6	2	1	3	14	13	3	2	4
1963	Feb	52	6	6	4	2	1	2	10	10	2	2	3
	Mar	54	9	5	4	3	1	1	7	6	2	4	4
	Apr	49	12	6	3	4	2	1	7	7	1	4	4
	May	43	10	8	5	3	4	2	5	9	1	4	6
	Jun	54	9	5	4	3	1	1	7	6	2	4	4
	Jul	23	13	6	2	4	3	2	7	14	2	17	7
	Aug	21	15	5	2	5	3	3	7	15	2	13	9
	Sep	26	18	6	3	5	3	3	7	11	2	9	7
	Oct	24	19	10	4	6	3	3	7	7	1	10	6
	Nov	22	18	11	3	6	3	4	7	7	1	12	6
	Dec	24	16	9	3	6	5	3	8	9	2	8	7
1964	Jan	24	13	7	4	6	8	3	12	8	3	5	7
	Feb	22	14	8	4	5	6	2	14	8	4	7	6
	Mar	22	15	8	3	6	4	4	12	8	4	8	6
	May	22	17	11	3	7	4	3	9	6	3	8	7
	Jul	16	16	12	2	8	5	8	8	6	3	9	7
	Aug	14	16	10	3	7	3	3	17	7	3	8	9
1964	Oct	15	14	11	6	5	4	2	17	7	4	6	9

TABLE 12.2.1: MOST URGENT PROBLEM 1966–2000

Q. What would you say is the most urgent problem facing the country at the present time?

EC Economic affairs
C   Cost of living
UN Unemployment
OE Other economic
ED Education
HE Health
HO Housing, rates
IM Immigrants
S   Strikes
P   Pensions

cont'd . . .

D   Defence
IN   International affairs
CM   Common Market
IR   Ireland
L   Law and order
F   Fuel shortage
O   Other
DK   Don't know

		EC	C	UN	OE	ED	HE	HO	IM	S	P	D	IN	CM	IR	L	F	O	DK
1966	Mar	48	–	–	–	6	–	16	5	8	13	7	25	–	–	–	–	7	11
1968	Feb	59	–	–	–	3	3	5	6	6	5	3	17	–	–	–	–	9	8
	Jun	52	–	–	–	3	2	5	27	7	1	3	14	–	–	–	–	8	7
1970	May	–	35	9	11	3	2	10	10	13	10	2	8	–	–	–	–	9	7
	Dec	–	31	3	6	1	1	3	3	48	4	0	3	4	–	–	–	6	2
1971	Mar	–	32	16	7	0	1	2	5	35	5	1	2	5	–	–	–	5	3
	Apr	–	31	15	9	1	1	3	4	26	3	0	1	4	–	–	–	5	4
	May	–	31	23	6	1	1	4	5	12	4	0	1	11	–	–	–	5	4
	Jun	–	41	18	4	1	0	4	4	9	3	0	1	19	–	–	–	4	3
	Aug	–	24	28	5	0	0	3	3	8	3	0	1	13	15	–	–	4	3
	Sep	–	27	28	2	1	0	2	6	8	4	0	1	10	17	–	–	4	5
	Oct	–	22	36	4	1	1	4	2	4	3	0	0	13	12	–	–	5	4
	Nov	–	20	32	2	0	1	3	3	5	4	0	1	13	20	–	–	5	2
	Dec	–	21	43	2	1	1	3	3	4	6	0	1	7	12	–	–	3	2
1972	Jan	–	18	37	4	1	1	4	3	13	2	1	2	5	12	–	–	5	3
	Feb	–	14	27	2	0	1	2	2	33	3	0	0	2	14	–	–	5	1
	Mar	–	25	28	3	1	1	5	2	11	3	0	1	7	17	–	–	5	2
	Apr	–	21	27	2	1	1	7	1	13	3	0	0	7	16	–	–	4	4
	May	–	18	30	2	2	0	6	1	20	5	0	2	6	8	–	–	4	4
	Jun	–	33	24	2	1	1	7	2	16	4	0	0	6	8	–	–	4	1
	Jul	–	36	16	4	0	0	5	3	9	4	0	0	5	19	–	–	4	2
	Aug	–	24	14	3	0	0	4	6	41	4	0	0	3	13	–	–	4	1
	Sep	–	33	14	3	1	0	6	23	12	3	0	1	3	8	–	–	3	2
	Oct	–	39	14	3	0	1	5	12	10	4	0	0	10	13	–	–	3	3
	Nov	–	50	12	3	1	0	6	8	12	5	0	0	5	6	–	–	4	3
	Dec	–	39	11	3	1	0	6	10	7	5	0	0	6	13	–	–	5	4
1973	Jan	–	57	9	3	1	1	6	4	9	4	0	0	5	7	–	–	4	2
	Feb	–	52	7	4	1	0	6	5	11	3	0	0	3	11	–	–	4	2
	Mar	–	42	6	3	1	1	4	3	24	4	0	0	2	10	–	–	4	3
	Apr	–	50	5	3	1	1	13	6	10	4	0	0	2	7	–	–	6	2
	May	–	52	6	4	1	0	10	4	9	5	0	1	2	4	–	–	5	3
	Jun	–	45	5	3	1	1	11	4	10	4	0	1	3	7	3	–	5	3
	Jul	–	58	3	3	1	1	10	4	6	4	0	1	5	6	2	–	2	2
	Aug	–	64	2	3	0	0	7	4	3	5	0	0	3	5	2	–	5	3
	Sep	–	59	3	4	0	0	8	2	2	3	1	1	2	8	0	–	5	3

cont'd . . .

		EC	C	UN	OE	ED	HE	HO	IM	S	P	D	IN	CM	IR	L	F	O	DK	
	Oct	−	58	0	6	0	0	7	1	5	2	0	6	2	7	1	−	5	3	
	Nov	−	51	1	6	0	0	5	1	16	3	0	1	1	1	0	9	3	2	
	Dec	−	27	1	5	0	0	0	1	26	0	0	0	0	0	0	30	5	2	
1974	Jan	−	29	2	8	0	0	1	1	35	1	0	0	0	0	1	16	5	1	
	Feb	−	44	8	11	0	0	2	0	26	2	0	0	3	0	0	5	7	2	
	Mar	−	33	14	6	0	0	1	0	38	1	0	0	2	0	0	1	6	2	
	Apr	−	49	2	7	1	0	15	1	5	4	0	0	3	3	1	1	4	6	
	May	−	48	2	9	1	1	8	1	18	1	0	0	3	2	2	0	7	2	
	Jun	−	57	1	7	1	1	5	1	8	1	0	0	2	9	2	0	5	2	
	Jul	−	58	1	9	0	2	6	1	8	1	0	0	2	1	1	0	7	3	
	Aug	−	65	2	5	0	1	6	1	5	1	0	0	1	2	0	0	7	3	
	Sep	−	72	3	6	1	0	5	1	5	2	0	0	2	1	3	1	5	3	A
	Oct	−	70	3	6	0	0	4	0	4	1	0	0	3	0	0	0	10	4	
	Nov	−	64	3	9	1	2	4	1	8	1	0	0	1	2	1	2	6	9	
	Dec	−	62	1	7	0	0	2	1	9	1	0	0	2	6	1	1	4	3	
1975	Apr	−	61	5	6	0	0	3	0	7	0	0	0	10	0	0	0	9	1	
	May	−	61	6	5	0	0	0	0	9	0	0	0	7	0	0	0	10	2	
	Jun	−	70	5	6	0	0	0	0	8	0	0	0	0	0	0	0	8	3	
	Jul	−	75	5	5	0	0	0	0	6	0	0	0	0	0	0	0	7	2	
	Aug	−	64	14	4	0	0	0	0	4	0	0	0	0	0	0	0	12	2	
	Sep	−	60	19	4	0	0	0	0	7	0	0	0	0	0	0	0	9	1	
	Oct	−	62	15	7	0	0	0	0	4	0	0	0	0	0	0	0	11	1	
	Nov	−	56	16	6	0	0	0	0	5	0	0	0	0	0	0	0	16	1	
	Dec	−	50	18	5	0	0	0	0	6	0	0	0	0	4	3	0	12	2	
1976	Jan	−	50	28	7	1	0	2	1	4	1	0	0	0	3	1	0	6	3	
	Feb	−	46	28	7	1	0	2	1	4	1	0	0	0	3	1	0	6	3	
	Mar	−	54	20	7	1	0	1	1	4	1	0	0	1	2	1	0	5	1	
	Apr	−	57	19	6	0	1	1	1	5	0	1	1	0	2	1	0	5	2	
	May	−	54	13	7	1	0	2	5	4	1	0	0	0	1	2	0	7	2	
	Jun	−	49	14	10	1	1	1	10	2	1	0	0	0	2	2	0	6	3	
	Jul	−	44	18	10	1	0	2	8	3	1	0	0	1	1	2	0	6	3	
	Aug	−	41	21	10	1	1	3	6	2	1	1	0	0	2	1	0	7	2	
	Sep	−	45	25	8	1	0	2	4	3	1	0	0	0	1	2	0	6	3	
	Oct	−	56	15	13	1	0	1	2	3	1	0	0	0	0	1	0	6	1	
	Nov	−	56	17	15	1	0	1	1	3	−	0	0	0	0	1	0	4	1	
	Dec	−	48	14	17	1	0	1	2	3	1	0	1	0	1	1	0	7	3	
1977	Jan	−	45	16	14	1	1	2	2	5	1	0	0	0	0	1	0	9	1	
	Feb	−	49	17	11	1	1	2	3	4	1	0	0	0	1	1	0	8	1	
	Mar	−	53	17	7	2	0	1	2	7	1	0	0	0	1	1	0	7	2	
	Apr	−	58	13	8	0	0	1	2	7	1	0	1	0	0	1	0	6	2	
	May	−	56	17	6	1	0	1	2	4	1	0	0	0	1	1	0	7	3	
	Jun	−	51	16	10	1	0	1	1	3	2	0	0	2	1	3	0	5	2	
	Jul	−	57	15	7	0	1	1	2	5	1	0	0	2	0	2	0	4	2	

cont'd . . .

	EC	C	UN	OE	ED	HE	HO	IM	S	P	D	IN	CM	IR	L	F	O	DK
Aug	–	43	23	9	2	0	1	2	5	1	1	0	1	3	3	0	5	2
Sep	–	41	28	6	1	0	0	3	10	1	0	0	0	0	4	0	4	2
Oct	–	34	27	7	2	1	1	2	9	1	0	0	0	0	5	0	7	2
Nov	–	30	23	6	1	0	2	2	24	1	0	0	0	0	1	0	7	2
1977 Dec	–	32	23	6	0	1	1	3	19	1	0	0	0	0	3	0	8	2

A Question in September 1974 related to most urgent problem 'to be discussed at the General Election?'

TABLE 12.2.2: MOST URGENT PROBLEM 1966–2000

Q. What would you say is the most urgent problem facing the country at the present time?

A Cost of living
B Unemployment
C Other economic
D Education
E Health
F Housing
G Immigrants
H Strikes
I Pensions
J Roads
K Poll tax
L Law and order
M Fuel shortage
N Social security benefits
O Increase productivity
P Commonwealth
Q Defence
R International affairs
S Common Market
T Ireland
U Environment
V Middle East
W Other
X Don't know

	A	B	C	D	E	F	G	H	I	J	K	L	M	N	O	P	Q	R	S	T	U	V	W	X
1978 Jan	28	27	7	1	1	1	4	14	1	0	–	3	1	1	2	0	0	0	1	0	–	–	4	3
Feb	35	22	5	1	1	1	9	10	1	0	–	2	1	1	3	0	0	0	1	0	–	–	4	2
Mar	23	34	8	1	1	1	9	5	1	0	–	6	0	1	2	0	0	1	1	1	–	–	6	3

cont'd . . .

		A	B	C	D	E	F	G	H	I	J	K	L	M	N	O	P	Q	R	S	T	U	V	W	X
	Apr	25	36	8	2	1	2	7	4	1	0	—	3	0	2	3	0	0	0	0	0	—	—	2	3
	May	28	34	7	1	1	2	4	3	1	0	—	5	0	1	2	0	1	0	1	0	—	—	4	4
	Jun	27	30	9	1	2	3	6	4	1	0	—	5	0	1	2	0	1	0	1	1	—	—	3	3
	Jul	29	28	7	1	2	2	5	3	1	0	—	6	0	1	2	0	0	0	1	1	—	—	4	4
	Aug	25	33	6	2	1	1	5	5	2	0	—	6	0	1	2	0	0	0	0	1	—	—	5	4
	Sep	24	43	6	1	1	1	2	5	2	0	—	4	0	1	2	0	0	1	0	0	—	—	4	3
	Oct	29	27	6	1	2	1	3	13	1	0	—	7	0	1	2	0	1	0	0	0	—	—	3	4
	Nov	30	26	7	1	1	2	2	17	1	0	—	4	0	1	1	0	0	0	0	0	—	—	3	3
	Dec	34	24	7	1	2	1	2	11	1	0	—	5	0	1	2	0	1	0	1	0	—	—	3	4
1979	Jan	20	11	4	0	0	1	0	53	1	0	—	1	0	1	2	0	0	0	0	0	—	—	3	1
	Feb	20	7	7	0	1	0	1	51	1	0	—	1	0	1	3	0	0	0	0	0	—	—	4	2
	Mar	26	18	7	0	2	1	1	28	1	0	—	3	0	0	2	0	0	0	0	0	—	—	6	4
	Jun	45	19	8	1	0	1	3	6	1	0	—	2	4	0	2	0	0	0	1	0	—	—	3	3
	Jul	40	14	4	2	1	2	3	9	2	0	—	4	8	1	3	0	0	0	0	0	—	—	3	3
	Aug	32	22	7	1	1	2	5	7	0	0	—	3	5	1	2	0	0	1	1	1	—	—	5	4
	Sep	25	18	6	2	2	1	3	20	1	0	—	3	3	1	1	0	0	1	1	6	—	—	4	4
	Oct	28	19	4	1	3	1	4	19	1	0	—	4	1	1	3	0	0	0	1	1	—	—	5	4
	Nov	31	16	5	4	3	2	3	11	1	0	—	4	1	2	4	0	1	1	1	1	—	—	5	4
	Dec	34	12	10	3	2	3	2	11	1	0	—	2	1	0	3	0	0	0	5	1	—	—	4	4
1980	Jan	30	15	6	2	1	1	2	24	0	0	—	1	1	0	3	0	1	4	1	1	—	—	4	2
	Feb	28	13	5	1	1	1	1	31	1	0	—	2	1	1	2	0	1	4	2	0	—	—	3	2
	Mar	36	18	7	2	2	1	2	17	1	0	—	1	1	1	3	0	1	1	1	0	—	—	2	3
	Apr	34	19	6	2	1	1	2	11	1	0	—	5	1	0	2	0	1	4	2	0	—	—	3	4
	May	41	23	5	1	2	1	2	7	1	0	—	3	0	0	2	0	1	4	2	1	—	—	2	2
	Jun	38	29	6	2	1	1	1	4	1	0	—	2	1	0	2	0	3	2	3	0	—	—	2	3
	Jun	27	49	3	2	1	2	2	4	0	0	—	1	0	0	2	0	1	1	1	0	—	—	2	3
	Aug	25	53	4	1	0	1	1	2	0	0	—	2	0	0	1	0	1	1	1	0	—	—	4	1
	Sep	18	64	5	1	1	0	1	2	1	0	—	1	0	0	1	0	1	0	0	0	—	—	4	1
	Oct	16	68	4	1	0	0	1	2	1	0	—	1	0	0	2	0	1	0	0	0	—	—	2	2
	Nov	20	60	6	1	0	1	1	3	0	0	—	1	0	0	1	0	2	0	0	0	—	—	3	1
	Dec	13	68	6	0	0	0	0	2	1	0	—	1	0	0	2	0	1	1	0	0	—	—	3	1
1981	Jan	13	69	7	0	0	1	0	2	0	0	—	0	0	0	1	0	1	0	0	0	—	—	2	1
	Feb	13	71	4	1	0	1	0	2	0	0	—	1	0	0	2	0	1	0	0	0	—	—	2	1
	Mar	15	66	5	0	0	0	1	2	1	0	—	0	0	0	2	0	1	0	0	0	—	—	4	1
	Apr	11	72	4	0	0	0	1	1	0	0	—	1	0	0	1	0	2	1	1	0	—	—	2	1
	May	9	71	4	0	0	1	2	1	0	0	—	2	0	0	1	0	1	0	0	1	—	—	4	2
	Jun	11	73	2	0	0	0	1	3	0	0	—	3	0	0	1	0	0	0	0	1	—	—	2	1
	Jul	5	69	3	1	0	0	2	1	0	0	—	10	0	0	1	0	1	0	0	0	—	—	4	1
	Aug	9	72	3	0	0	0	2	1	0	0	—	3	0	0	2	0	2	0	0	0	—	—	4	1
	Sep	8	77	3	1	0	1	1	1	0	0	—	2	0	0	1	0	1	0	0	0	—	—	2	1
	Oct	10	77	3	1	0	1	0	1	0	0	—	0	0	0	1	0	1	0	0	0	—	—	2	0
	Nov	10	71	4	0	0	0	0	2	1	0	—	1	0	0	1	0	3	1	0	1	—	—	2	1
	Dec	10	74	5	1	0	0	1	1	1	0	—	1	0	0	1	0	1	0	0	0	—	—	3	1

cont'd . . .

	A	B	C	D	E	F	G	H	I	J	K	L	M	N	O	P	Q	R	S	T	U	V	W	X
1982 Jan	11	72	4	1	0	0	0	3	1	0	-	0	0	0	1	0	1	0	1	0	-	-	4	2
Feb	7	78	3	1	0	0	1	2	1	0	-	1	0	0	1	0	1	0	1	0	-	-	3	1
Mar	8	74	3	1	1	1	1	1	0	0	-	3	0	0	1	0	1	0	0	0	-	-	3	2
Apr	8	47	2	1	0	0	0	0	0	0	-	3	0	0	1	0	3	27	0	0	-	-	3	2
May	4	45	1	0	0	0	0	0	1	0	-	1	0	0	0	0	2	42	0	0	-	-	2	1
Jun	7	50	3	0	0	1	1	0	1	0	-	1	0	0	0	0	2	30	0	0	-	-	3	1
Jul	9	70	3	1	0	0	0	5	1	0	-	2	0	0	1	0	1	2	0	0	-	-	2	2
Aug	6	74	4	0	1	0	1	2	1	0	-	2	0	0	1	0	1	0	0	0	-	-	3	2
Sep	5	79	2	0	2	0	0	3	1	0	-	2	0	0	1	0	0	0	0	0	-	-	2	1
Oct	5	79	2	0	2	1	1	2	1	0	-	1	0	0	1	0	0	1	0	0	-	-	2	2
Nov	5	82	2	0	2	0	0	1	1	0	-	1	0	0	1	0	2	1	0	0	-	-	1	1
Dec	4	80	3	1	0	0	0	1	0	0	-	2	0	0	1	0	2	0	0	2	-	-	2	1
1983 Jan	6	79	3	0	0	0	0	0	0	0	-	1	0	0	1	0	3	0	0	0	-	-	2	2
Feb	5	77	3	1	0	0	1	4	0	0	-	1	0	0	0	0	4	1	0	0	-	-	2	1
Mar	4	81	3	1	1	0	1	1	1	0	-	2	0	0	1	0	2	0	0	0	-	-	3	1
Apr	4	79	2	0	0	1	1	1	1	0	-	2	0	0	1	0	4	0	0	0	-	-	2	1
May	3	82	2	0	0	0	1	1	1	0	-	1	0	0	0	0	4	0	0	0	-	-	2	1
Jul	4	80	2	0	0	0	0	1	1	0	-	3	-	0	0	-	4	0	0	0	-	-	2	2
Aug	6	76	3	0	1	0	1	0	1	0	-	3	-	0	1	-	3	0	0	0	-	-	2	1
Sep	3	73	3	1	2	0	0	1	1	0	-	3	-	0	0	-	4	0	0	0	-	-	3	2
Oct	6	70	3	1	5	0	1	1	1	0	-	2	-	0	0	-	5	0	0	0	-	-	2	2
Nov	4	68	2	0	4	0	0	0	1	0	-	2	-	0	0	-	13	0	0	0	-	-	2	2
Dec	4	66	2	1	4	0	0	1	1	0	-	2	-	0	1	-	12	1	0	0	-	-	1	1
1984 Jan	4	74	3	1	1	0	0	1	1	0	-	1	-	0	1	-	8	0	0	0	-	-	2	2
Feb	3	72	3	1	2	1	1	1	1	0	-	2	-	0	0	-	5	1	0	0	-	-	2	3
Mar	4	77	1	0	1	1	0	2	1	0	-	3	-	0	1	-	4	0	0	0	-	-	1	2
Apr	3	72	1	1	1	1	0	9	1	0	-	2	-	0	0	-	4	0	0	0	-	-	2	2
May	3	71	2	1	1	0	0	11	1	0	-	2	-	0	0	-	3	0	0	0	-	-	2	1
Jun	2	65	1	1	0	0	1	17	0	0	-	3	-	0	0	-	4	0	0	0	-	-	2	1
Jul	4	60	3	0	1	1	1	23	0	0	-	2	-	0	0	-	1	0	0	0	-	-	2	2
Aug	3	61	2	0	1	0	0	22	1	0	-	2	-	0	0	-	2	0	0	0	-	-	3	1
Sep	3	53	2	0	1	0	0	32	1	0	-	2	-	0	0	-	2	0	0	0	-	-	2	1
Oct	2	57	2	0	0	0	0	27	0	0	-	3	-	0	0	-	3	1	0	0	-	-	2	2
Nov	2	69	2	0	0	0	0	15	1	0	-	1	-	0	0	-	3	0	0	0	-	-	3	1
Dec	2	69	2	1	1	0	0	16	1	0	-	2	-	0	0	-	2	0	0	0	-	-	2	2
1985 Jan	2	75	2	1	0	0	0	10	1	0	-	1	-	0	1	-	3	0	0	0	-	-	3	1
Feb	5	70	3	1	1	0	0	13	1	0	-	1	-	0	0	-	1	0	0	0	-	-	2	2
Mar	3	83	2	0	1	1	0	1	1	0	-	2	-	0	0	-	1	0	0	0	-	-	2	1
Apr	2	80	1	1	2	1	0	1	1	0	-	3	-	1	1	-	2	0	0	0	-	-	3	2
May	4	80	2	1	2	1	0	0	1	0	-	2	-	0	0	-	2	0	0	0	-	-	2	2
Jun	5	77	1	1	2	1	1	1	1	0	-	5	-	0	0	-	2	0	0	0	-	-	3	1
Jul	4	79	1	1	2	1	1	0	1	0	-	2	-	1	0	-	1	1	0	0	-	-	3	2
Aug	2	81	1	1	1	1	1	1	1	0	-	2	-	1	1	-	1	0	0	0	-	-	3	2

cont'd . . .

		A	B	C	D	E	F	G	H	I	J	K	L	M	N	O	P	Q	R	S	T	U	V	W	X
	Sep	2	78	1	1	1	0	3	1	1	0	—	5	—	0	0	—	1	0	0	0	—	—	4	1
	Oct	2	76	1	1	1	0	3	0	1	0	—	9	—	0	0	—	1	0	0	0	—	—	2	2
	Nov	2	77	1	1	1	1	2	0	0	0	—	9	—	0	0	—	1	0	0	0	—	—	3	1
	Dec	2	77	2	1	1	1	1	1	0	0	—	8	—	0	1	—	1	0	0	0	—	—	3	1
1986	Jan	4	75	2	1	1	1	1	0	1	0	—	6	—	0	1	—	1	1	0	0	—	—	3	3
	Feb	2	79	3	1	2	1	1	1	1	0	—	3	—	0	1	—	0	0	0	0	—	—	4	1
	Mar	2	81	2	1	1	0	1	0	2	0	—	3	—	0	1	—	1	0	0	0	—	—	2	2
	Apr	2	77	2	2	2	1	1	0	1	0	—	4	—	0	0	—	2	1	0	0	—	—	3	1
	May	2	71	2	3	1	1	0	0	1	0	—	5	—	0	0	—	3	2	0	0	—	—	6	2
	Jun	2	78	1	2	3	1	1	0	0	0	—	4	—	0	0	—	2	1	0	0	—	—	4	1
	Jul	2	75	1	2	2	2	1	0	1	0	—	3	—	0	1	—	2	2	0	1	—	—	4	1
	Aug	2	72	1	1	2	0	2	0	2	0	—	3	—	0	0	—	2	4	0	1	—	—	4	2
	Sep	2	77	1	1	3	1	2	0	1	0	—	3	—	0	0	—	2	0	0	0	—	—	3	1
	Oct	2	77	2	1	3	2	2	0	2	0	—	2	—	0	0	—	3	0	0	0	—	—	3	1
	Nov	2	74	1	2	3	1	1	1	1	0	—	5	—	0	0	—	3	0	0	0	—	—	3	2
	Dec	2	70	1	2	4	1	1	0	1	0	—	3	—	1	1	—	7	0	0	0	—	—	4	2
1987	Jan	3	73	3	1	4	1	0	0	4	0	—	2	—	0	0	—	4	0	0	0	—	—	3	1
	Feb	2	73	1	2	4	1	0	0	1	0	—	4	—	0	0	—	2	1	0	0	—	—	5	2
	Mar	2	74	2	2	3	2	2	0	1	0	—	5	—	0	1	—	1	0	0	0	—	—	3	1
	Apr	1	69	1	3	5	2	1	0	2	0	—	6	—	1	1	—	2	0	0	0	—	—	3	2
	May	1	77	1	2	3	1	1	0	1	0	—	5	—	0	0	—	3	0	0	0	—	—	3	1
	Jul	3	67	2	3	4	2	1	0	2	0	—	7	—	0	0	—	2	0	0	0	—	—	4	2
	Aug	3	64	1	2	3	3	1	0	1	0	—	6	—	0	0	—	3	3	0	0	—	—	7	2
	Sep	4	60	1	2	4	2	2	1	2	—	—	8	—	—	—	—	4	3	—	—	—	—	5	3
	Oct	3	57	2	2	5	4	2	0	1	—	—	10	—	—	—	—	2	2	—	—	—	—	7	3
	Nov	5	57	4	3	6	2	1	0	2	—	—	6	—	—	—	—	3	1	—	—	—	—	7	2
	Dec	2	46	3	4	22	3	1	0	2	—	—	4	—	—	—	—	3	0	—	—	—	—	6	3
1988	Jan	1	36	3	3	39	3	0	0	1	—	—	4	—	—	—	—	2	0	—	—	—	—	5	3
	Feb	1	31	2	2	46	2	0	1	1	—	—	5	—	—	—	—	2	0	—	—	—	—	4	2
	Mar	2	33	2	2	41	2	1	1	2	—	—	5	—	—	—	—	1	0	—	—	—	—	7	3
	Apr	4	40	2	2	26	6	1	0	3	—	—	4	—	—	—	—	1	0	—	—	—	—	9	2
	May	3	41	2	2	16	7	2	2	2	—	—	5	—	—	—	—	2	1	—	—	—	—	11	5
	Jun	3	40	3	1	20	5	1	0	3	—	—	10	—	—	—	—	2	1	—	—	—	—	10	3
	Jul	4	41	3	2	16	6	1	0	3	—	—	11	—	—	—	—	2	1	—	—	—	—	6	4
	Aug	4	36	3	2	18	5	2	1	2	—	—	12	—	—	—	—	2	1	—	—	—	—	9	4
	Sep	8	45	5	3	14	4	1	3	1	—	—	6	—	—	—	—	2	1	—	—	—	—	6	2
	Oct	7	35	6	3	14	4	0	0	4	—	—	9	—	—	—	—	2	0	—	—	—	—	11	5
	Nov	8	29	4	2	18	5	1	0	7	—	—	7	—	—	—	—	1	1	—	—	—	—	11	5
	Dec	12	35	6	1	11	4	1	0	5	—	—	6	—	—	—	—	1	0	—	—	—	—	13	4
1989	Jan	16	29	5	2	13	8	1	0	3	—	—	8	—	—	—	—	2	0	—	—	—	—	9	4

TABLE 12.2.3: MOST URGENT PROBLEM 1966–2000

Q. What would you say is the most urgent problem facing the country at the present time?

A   Cost of living
B   Unemployment
C   Other economic
D   Education
E   Health
F   Housing
G   Immigrants
H   Strikes
I   Pensions
J   Poll tax
K   Law and order
L   Defence
M   International affairs
N   Europe
O   Ireland
P   Environment
Q   Middle East
R   Petrol prices
S   Mad cow
T   Other
U   Don't know

		A	B	C	D	E	F	G	H	I	J	K	L	M	N	O	P	Q	R	S	T	U
1989	Feb	10	26	4	1	20	8	1	1	4	–	6	1	0	–	–	–	–	–	–	13	5
	Mar	14	25	3	1	17	8	1	0	4	–	5	1	0	–	–	6	–	–	–	10	5
	Apr	15	25	5	1	13	7	2	0	4	–	6	2	1	–	–	5	–	–	–	8	6
	May	12	23	5	2	18	7	1	1	4	–	3	3	0	–	–	5	–	–	–	9	6
	Jun	18	18	5	2	12	7	1	3	3	–	3	2	1	–	–	8	–	–	–	13	4
	Aug	14	21	4	2	14	7	1	2	3	–	4	2	1	–	–	10	–	–	–	12	5
	Sep	16	20	6	2	17	7	1	0	3	–	3	1	0	–	–	9	–	–	–	9	6
	Sep	20	16	8	2	15	7	1	0	2	–	4	1	0	–	–	9	–	–	–	12	5
	Oct	33	9	14	1	11	10	1	1	2	–	3	0	0	–	–	4	–	–	–	8	4
	Dec	22	16	2	1	14	11	1	3	3	–	1	1	1	–	–	3	–	–	–	10	5
1990	Jan	17	13	8	2	14	14	1	8	3	–	2	0	1	–	–	5	–	–	–	8	4
	Jan	21	13	9	2	11	14	1	7	3	–	3	0	1	–	–	5	–	–	–	7	3
	Feb	25	11	6	2	8	24	1	2	2	–	2	0	1	–	–	3	–	–	–	7	5
	Mar	17	9	8	2	7	36	0	1	1	–	2	0	0	–	–	5	–	–	–	8	2
	Mar	17	7	6	1	7	5	0	0	2	38	2	0	1	–	–	4	–	–	–	7	3
	Apr	17	7	7	2	6	5	1	0	1	35	4	0	0	–	–	4	–	–	–	6	3
	Jun	19	12	6	2	7	6	1	0	2	21	2	0	1	–	–	8	–	–	–	8	5

cont'd . . .

		A	B	C	D	E	F	G	H	I	J	K	L	M	N	O	P	Q	R	S	T	U
	Jun	19	13	5	3	9	5	0	0	1	18	5	0	1	–	–	6	–	–	–	9	5
	Jul	24	12	3	4	11	5	1	0	2	17	4	1	1	–	–	6	–	–	–	6	4
	Sep	23	11	4	3	9	3	1	0	1	9	3	1	12	–	–	2	10	–	–	4	3
	Sep	31	11	6	5	6	4	1	0	2	7	2	0	1	–	–	3	17	–	–	4	2
	Oct	23	14	5	7	11	3	0	0	2	9	2	0	0	–	–	2	10	–	–	6	5
	Dec	14	8	4	4	10	4	0	0	1	29	1	0	1	–	–	1	16	–	–	4	2
	Jan	20	14	5	2	7	4	0	0	1	13	1	0	0	–	–	1	27	–	–	3	3
1991	Feb	19	13	6	1	5	3	0	0	1	8	1	0	0	–	–	1	37	–	–	3	1
	Feb	22	18	10	3	6	4	1	0	2	14	1	0	0	–	–	1	13	–	–	3	1
	Mar	20	21	8	3	6	3	0	0	2	22	2	0	0	–	–	2	1	–	–	5	4
	May	19	29	8	4	13	5	0	0	2	9	1	0	1	–	–	1	–	–	–	5	3
	May	14	33	5	5	22	3	1	0	2	4	2	0	0	–	–	1	–	–	–	4	3
	Jun	18	35	9	2	10	4	1	0	1	3	2	0	2	4	–	2	–	–	–	5	2
	Aug	19	38	9	2	9	4	2	0	2	4	1	1	1	–	–	1	–	–	–	5	3
	Aug	20	40	8	2	8	4	1	0	1	3	2	1	1	–	–	2	–	–	–	3	3
	Sep	13	37	8	6	13	2	1	0	2	2	5	1	1	–	–	1	–	–	–	5	4
	Nov	12	36	7	3	18	3	1	0	2	4	2	0	1	–	–	2	–	–	–	3	6
	Nov	13	33	6	4	14	4	2	0	2	4	4	0	0	9	–	1	–	–	–	3	2
1992	Jan	16	40	12	5	9	4	1	0	1	1	2	0	1	1	–	1	–	–	–	3	3
	Jan	15	38	11	3	10	4	1	0	2	4	3	0	1	0	–	0	–	–	–	4	3
	Feb	13	44	12	3	9	3	0	0	1	3	3	0	0	1	–	1	–	–	–	5	2
	Mar	15	40	14	3	12	4	0	0	2	2	2	0	0	0	–	1	–	–	–	3	2
	Mar	15	41	13	5	9	3	0	0	1	2	1	0	0	1	–	1	–	–	–	5	2
	Mar	15	36	11	5	17	3	1	0	1	2	2	0	0	0	–	1	–	–	–	4	3
	Apr	16	34	16	4	14	4	1	0	1	3	2	0	0	1	–	1	–	–	–	2	2
	May	10	45	10	5	9	4	1	0	1	2	4	0	0	1	–	1	–	–	–	4	3
	May	9	45	10	4	6	5	1	0	1	3	2	0	1	1	–	5	–	–	–	4	3
	Jul	11	48	6	3	7	3	1	0	1	1	3	1	0	4	–	3	–	–	–	5	3
	Aug	12	48	14	3	4	5	1	0	1	1	2	0	0	1	–	1	–	–	–	3	3
	Sep	16	46	13	2	3	5	1	0	1	1	1	0	1	1	–	1	–	–	–	4	3
	Oct	16	48	19	1	1	2	0	0	0	0	1	0	1	4	–	0	–	–	–	4	3
	Oct	14	56	13	1	3	1	0	0	1	0	1	0	0	2	–	1	–	–	–	6	2
	Nov	13	56	14	0	3	3	1	0	1	0	1	0	0	2	–	1	–	–	–	4	2
1993	Jan	10	61	10	1	3	3	1	0	0	0	3	0	1	1	–	1	–	–	–	3	1
	Jan	10	64	6	2	4	2	1	0	0	0	3	1	2	0	–	1	–	–	–	3	2
	Feb	5	73	5	1	3	1	0	0	0	0	6	0	0	1	–	0	–	–	–	3	1
	Apr	6	65	8	1	3	2	1	0	1	1	4	0	0	1	–	0	–	–	–	4	2
	Apr	8	57	8	3	4	3	1	0	1	0	3	1	2	0	–	1	–	–	–	5	2
	May	9	55	11	2	8	1	1	0	1	0	3	0	0	1	–	0	–	–	–	4	2
	Jul	8	54	10	3	8	2	1	0	1	0	5	0	1	0	–	1	–	–	–	6	1
	Jul	10	55	7	2	5	2	0	0	1	0	6	0	0	2	–	0	–	–	–	6	3
	Sep	8	50	8	2	8	3	1	0	2	0	9	0	0	0	–	0	–	–	–	4	2
	Sep	6	56	7	2	6	3	1	0	1	0	8	0	0	1	–	0	–	–	–	5	3

cont'd . . .

		A	B	C	D	E	F	G	H	I	J	K	L	M	N	O	P	Q	R	S	T	U
	Oct	9	47	8	1	6	2	1	0	2	0	9	0	1	1	—	0	—	—	—	8	4
	Dec	9	54	7	2	8	2	1	0	2	0	4	0	0	0	—	0	—	—	—	6	3
1994	Jan	7	51	6	4	7	2	1	0	2	0	10	1	1	0	—	1	—	—	—	6	2
	Jan	7	49	9	1	7	3	1	0	1	0	10	0	0	1	—	1	—	—	—	7	3
	Feb	10	45	9	3	11	2	1	0	2	0	7	0	0	0	—	0	—	—	—	7	2
	Apr	7	47	7	3	8	3	0	0	1	1	8	0	0	4	—	1	—	—	—	7	3
	May	8	45	7	3	9	3	1	0	1	2	8	1	0	1	—	0	—	—	—	9	3
	May	5	57	4	2	9	3	1	0	2	0	9	0	0	1	—	0	—	—	—	5	3
	Jul	5	53	5	1	7	3	0	0	1	0	10	0	0	2	—	0	—	—	—	8	2
	Jul	6	57	4	4	6	3	1	0	1	0	6	1	0	1	—	0	—	—	—	6	3
	Sep	6	48	4	3	8	3	1	0	1	0	13	1	0	1	—	1	—	—	—	8	3
	Sep	8	52	3	2	9	2	0	0	1	0	12	0	0	0	—	1	—	—	—	8	3
	Oct	6	52	4	2	9	2	1	0	2	0	10	1	0	1	—	1	—	—	—	6	2
	Dec	8	47	5	2	9	3	1	0	3	1	6	0	0	3	—	0	—	—	—	9	5
1995	Jan	5	45	5	2	11	3	0	0	3	1	9	0	0	2	—	1	—	—	—	10	4
	Jan	7	46	5	3	11	3	0	0	1	0	7	0	0	4	—	1	—	—	—	9	3
	Feb	7	39	4	4	14	3	2	0	1	0	6	0	1	6	—	1	—	—	—	8	4
	Apr	6	38	5	5	16	3	1	0	2	1	8	0	0	3	—	0	—	—	—	8	4
	May	6	38	5	8	17	3	1	0	1	1	8	0	0	2	—	1	—	—	—	6	2
	Jun	8	39	4	6	12	4	1	0	1	0	8	0	1	3	—	1	—	—	—	10	2
	Jul	6	39	4	4	14	6	0	0	1	1	8	0	0	5	—	0	—	—	—	8	4
	Jul	5	39	5	5	13	6	1	0	2	0	8	0	0	2	—	1	—	—	—	8	3
	Sep	8	42	5	3	13	3	0	0	1	0	7	1	0	1	—	1	—	—	—	11	3
	Sep	6	40	5	4	17	2	2	0	1	0	7	0	0	2	—	0	—	—	—	10	4
	Oct	5	41	4	6	13	4	2	0	2	0	9	0	0	1	—	1	—	—	—	10	2
	Dec	7	43	6	6	13	4	1	0	2	0	6	0	0	1	—	0	—	—	—	7	3
1986	Jan	6	40	4	6	13	4	1	0	1	0	8	0	0	4	—	0	—	—	—	10	4
	Feb	5	34	4	10	18	3	1	0	2	0	6	0	0	2	—	0	—	—	—	10	4
	Mar	4	40	4	8	15	3	1	0	1	0	8	1	1	1	—	1	—	—	—	12	3
	Mar	4	31	3	5	10	2	1	0	2	0	6	0	0	2	—	0	—	—	21	9	4
	May	3	36	3	5	13	4	1	0	1	0	8	0	0	19	0	0	—	—	4	6	4
	Jun	5	28	2	7	15	2	1	0	1	0	10	0	0	9	0	1	—	—	8	7	4
	Jul	4	40	4	7	13	3	1	0	1	0	7	0	0	6	0	0	—	—	2	7	3
	Aug	4	40	3	6	12	2	1	0	1	0	8	0	0	5	0	1	—	—	2	10	3
	Sep	4	36	2	7	13	4	1	0	2	0	10	0	0	3	0	1	—	—	1	9	6
	Sep	4	36	4	6	15	2	1	0	1	0	8	0	0	6	0	0	—	—	1	11	4
	Nov	4	27	2	16	10	3	1	0	1	0	16	0	0	7	0	0	—	—	0	9	3
	Dec	6	29	4	11	17	2	1	0	1	0	7	0	0	8	0	0	—	—	0	10	4
1997	Jan	3	25	3	9	24	2	0	0	2	0	7	0	0	11	0	0	—	—	1	10	3
	Feb	1	20	3	11	24	2	1	0	2	0	6	0	0	15	0	0	—	—	0	12	5
	Mar	2	25	1	13	20	3	1	0	1	0	6	0	0	12	0	0	—	—	1	12	4
	Apr	2	23	2	13	22	1	0	0	2	0	6	0	0	9	0	0	—	—	0	13	7
	Jun	1	25	1	11	19	1	1	0	2	0	11	0	0	10	0	0	—	—	0	13	4

cont'd . . .

		A	B	C	D	E	F	G	H	I	J	K	L	M	N	O	P	Q	R	S	T	U
	Jul	1	29	1	11	24	2	1	0	2	0	5	0	0	4	0	2	—	—	0	11	6
	Aug	2	25	1	12	18	2	1	0	1	0	7	0	0	4	0	1	—	—	0	18	5
	Sep	3	24	2	12	20	4	1	0	1	0	5	0	0	2	0	1	—	—	0	21	6
	Oct	1	20	1	12	22	2	1	0	2	0	7	0	0	3	0	1	—	—	0	21	6
	Nov	1	16	1	8	17	2	2	0	2	0	6	0	0	13	0	0	—	—	0	21	9
	Dec	1	19	2	9	22	2	1	0	2	0	4	0	0	8	0	2	—	—	0	19	7
1998	Jan	1	22	1	8	18	3	1	0	2	0	4	0	0	8	0	1	—	—	0	25	9
	Feb	1	16	2	8	20	2	1	0	2	0	3	0	0	4	0	1	—	—	0	28	9
	Mar	2	18	1	9	22	1	0	0	1	0	3	0	0	4	0	1	—	—	0	25	9
	Apr	3	21	3	7	21	2	2	0	2	0	3	0	0	5	0	0	—	—	0	22	7
	Apr	2	19	1	10	19	1	1	0	2	0	4	0	0	4	0	1	—	—	0	28	8
	Jun	1	17	2	10	27	1	1	0	1	0	5	0	0	4	0	1	—	—	0	18	9
	Jul	3	17	3	7	25	1	1	0	1	0	4	0	0	10	0	1	—	—	0	17	9
	Aug	4	15	5	7	25	2	1	0	3	0	3	0	0	3	0	1	—	—	0	22	8
	Sep	6	15	7	6	15	1	1	0	1	0	4	0	0	2	0	1	—	—	0	27	9
	Sep	4	21	8	7	18	1	1	0	1	0	3	0	0	5	0	1	—	—	0	20	8
	Nov	5	23	7	5	18	2	1	0	1	0	4	0	0	5	0	1	—	—	0	19	6
1999	Jan	2	17	5	8	26	2	2	0	1	0	1	0	4	14	0	0	—	—	0	12	6
	Feb	3	16	3	7	29	2	2	0	2	0	3	0	1	9	0	1	—	—	0	15	5
	Mar	2	15	3	6	25	1	2	0	4	0	3	0	1	13	0	1	—	—	0	15	8
	Apr	2	13	3	5	14	2	1	0	1	0	2	0	8	3	0	0	—	—	0	33	7
	Apr	1	13	1	5	10	1	1	0	1	0	3	0	5	1	0	0	—	—	0	40	5
	Jun	1	11	1	6	16	2	1	0	1	0	3	0	26	8	0	0	—	—	0	14	6
	Jun	2	14	2	7	14	3	1	0	2	0	3	0	5	12	5	1	—	—	0	18	10
	Aug	1	12	1	7	26	2	1	0	2	0	4	0	1	10	4	1	—	—	0	16	8
	Sep	3	11	2	5	24	2	4	0	1	0	5	0	0	4	5	0	—	—	0	24	8
	Sep	2	13	2	8	23	2	4	0	2	0	5	0	0	5	1	1	—	—	0	24	9
	Nov	1	11	1	8	18	2	1	0	3	0	4	0	1	13	1	1	—	—	3	24	7
	Dec	3	11	2	9	24	2	1	0	2	1	4	0	1	8	2	1	—	—	2	20	9
2000	Jan	2	11	2	6	41	1	1	0	2	0	3	0	0	5	0	0	—	—	0	12	7
	Feb	1	6	1	33	51	0	3	0	1	1	2	0	0	5	0	0	—	—	0	13	7
	Mar	0	9	1	5	45	1	4	0	2	1	4	0	0	3	0	0	—	—	0	17	8
	Apr	1	7	2	4	40	1	5	0	3	0	4	0	0	3	0	0	—	—	0	18	6
	May	2	10	1	6	26	1	5	0	3	1	9	0	0	3	0	0	—	—	0	22	8
	Jun	2	7	2	7	48	1	3	0	3	1	5	0	0	3	0	0	—	—	0	14	4
	Jul	3	5	2	6	31	1	4	0	2	1	3	0	0	10	0	0	—	0	0	18	5
	Aug	2	5	2	5	34	1	4	0	4	1	4	0	0	7	0	0	—	0	0	19	7
	Sep	3	3	2	4	26	1	2	0	2	1	1	0	0	6	0	1	—	26	0	14	5
	Sep	1	3	4	4	18	0	2	0	7	1	0	0	0	4	0	1	—	35	0	8	7
	Nov	3	3	2	3	16	1	2	0	3	3	2	0	0	4	0	4	—	18	0	24	3
2000	Dec	2	4	2	5	29	1	2	0	1	1	8	0	0	8	0	1	—	4	0	24	7

TABLE 12.3:BEST PARTY TO HANDLE 1959–97

Q. Which party do you think can best handle that problem (the most urgent problem facing the country)?

		Cons	Lab	Lib	Other	DK
1959	Mar	35	33	4	1	27
	Sep	41	36	4	0	19
	Oct	38.5	35.5	5	0	21
1970	May	36	36	3	2	23
	Dec	40	32	2	2	24
1971	Mar	33	35	2	2	28
	Apr	38	31	3	1	27
	May	28	38	3	2	29
	Jun	27	38	3	2	30
	Aug	31	34	2	1	32
	Sep	28	35	3	2	32
	Oct	29	37	3	2	29
	Nov	30	33	2	2	33
	Dec	31	33	2	2	32
1972	Jan	27	31	3	2	37
	Feb	27	34	3	2	34
	Mar	31	35	4	2	28
	Apr	33	28	3	2	34
	May	29	33	3	1	34
	Jun	32	34	3	1	30
	Jul	27	31	4	2	36
	Aug	30	34	3	4	29
	Sep	29	33	3	2	33
	Oct	32	31	3	2	32
	Nov	29	36	7	2	26
	Dec	27	30	4	3	36
1973	Jan	29	28	6	2	35
	Feb	29	30	4	2	35
	Mar	29	31	5	2	33
	Apr	30	27	6	3	34
	May	30	31	6	3	30
	Jun	31	28	6	2	33
	Jul	28	32	6	2	32
	Aug	24	26	12	3	35
	Sep	25	30	9	2	34
	Oct	28	28	7	2	35
	Nov	30	29	9	2	30

cont'd . . .

		Cons	Lab	Lib	Other	DK
	Dec	30	28	5	3	34
1974	Jan	35	26	6	3	30
	Feb	37	36	8	1	18
	Feb	33	29	13	1	24
	Mar					
	Apr	24	41	6	2	27
	May	25	39	8	2	26
	Jun					
	Jul	28	29	10	3	30
	Aug	29	30	8	4	29
	Sep					
	Oct	30	35	10	2	23
	Oct	27	32	10	3	28
	Nov	27	39	6	3	25
	Dec	24	36	5	3	32
1975	Jan					
	Feb					
	Mar					
	Apr	34	30	4	2	30
	May	34	25	4	3	34
	Jun	34	27	4	3	32
	Jul	33	29	5	3	30
	Aug					
	Sep	30	26	7	4	33
	Oct	36	29	7	3	25
	Nov	30	31	5	3	31
	Dec	31	26	7	4	32
1976	Jan	30	27	5	3	35
	Feb	35	29	4	2	30
	Mar	34	30	3	3	30
	Apr	31	35	3	2	29
	May	32	31	4	3	30
	Jun	32	27	4	3	35
	Jul	32	28	4	4	31
	Aug	31	29	4	3	33
	Sep	32	31	3	3	31
	Oct	39	21	4	5	31
	Nov	43	21	5	4	27
	Dec	38	22	5	4	31
1977	Jan	38	21	6	4	31

cont'd . . .

		Cons	Lab	Lib	Other	DK
	Feb	33	21	5	7	35
	Mar	37	22	4	4	33
	Apr	35	24	4	4	33
	May	41	21	3	2	33
	Jun	37	25	3	3	32
	Jul	34	26	4	4	32
	Aug	32	27	3	5	32
	Sep	35	31	3	4	28
	Oct	36	33	4	2	25
	Nov	34	33	3	2	28
	Dec	34	34	3	3	26
1978	Jan	34	35	3	2	26
	Feb	39	31	2	2	26
	Mar	38	32	2	2	26
	Apr	35	33	2	3	26
	May	32	32	4	3	29
	Jun	35	33	3	2	26
	Jul	34	33	3	2	27
	Aug	31	33	2	2	33
	Sep	38	33	2	2	25
	Oct	32	35	2	2	29
	Nov	31	35	1	2	30
	Dec	36	32	2	2	28
1979	Jan	35	31	2	2	30
	Feb	37	25	3	4	31
	Mar	38	25	3	2	31
	Apr	41	33	4	1	21
	May					
	Jun	36	33	3	2	26
	Jul	34	36	4	2	24
	Aug	34	34	5	2	25
	Sep	33	32	3	2	30
	Oct	34	35	5	1	26
	Nov	33	30	4	2	30
	Dec	30	34	6	2	29
1980	Jan	31	34	5	3	28
	Feb	30	33	6	2	29
	Mar	30	38	4	2	26
	Apr	32	34	6	3	25
	May	33	33	5	2	27
	Jun	33	35	4	2	25
	Jul	30	37	5	2	25
	Aug	30	35	6	3	26

cont'd . . .

		Cons	Lab	Lib	Other	DK
	Sep	26	37	7	4	26
	Oct	31	37	5	2	24
	Nov	28	39	5	1	27
	Dec	26	37	5	3	29
1981	Jan	26	37	5	3	29
	Feb	27	30	7	7	29
	Mar	20	33	6	8	33
	Apr	23	29	15	1	33
	May					
	Jun	21	32	13	1	32
	Jul	20	34	10	2	33
	Aug	20	34	16	1	29
	Sep	21	31	14	2	33
	Oct	23	25	19	1	31
	Nov	20	28	23	2	29
	Dec	15	23	25	1	36
1982	Jan	21	25	20	2	32
	Feb	20	31	17	1	31
	Mar	24	30	15	1	30
	Apr	26	23	17	2	32
	May	38	24	10	1	25
	Jun	44	20	11	0	24
	Jul	34	25	13	1	26
	Aug	31	25	15	1	28
	Sep	31	27	12	1	29
	Oct	29	27	13	2	29
	Nov	29	31	10	1	29
	Dec	29	30	12	0	28
1983	Jan	30	26	11	1	32
	Feb	31	31	12	1	24
	Mar	29	26	20	1	26
	Apr	31	32	12	1	24
	May	37	29	10	0	24
	Jun					
	Jul	38	23	14	1	23
	Aug	36	21	16	1	26
	Sep	36	20	17	0	26
	Oct	31	34	11	1	22
	Nov	34	29	12	0	24
	Dec	30	31	10	1	28
1984	Jan	33	31	9	1	26
	Feb	30	30	12	1	28

cont'd . . .

		Cons	Lab	Lib	Other	DK
	Mar	29	35	10	1	27
	Apr	33	34	9	1	24
	May	30	32	12	1	25
	Jun	27	33	14	1	27
	Jul	28	35	11	1	26
	Aug	27	35	11	2	25
	Sep	30	32	12	1	26
	Oct	32	27	11	1	29
	Nov	34	29	11	1	25
	Dec	26	29	13	1	30
1985	Jan	26	28	16	1	29
	Feb	24	27	15	1	33
	Mar	22	36	15	1	27
	Apr	22	33	13	1	30
	May	20	33	17	1	29
	Jun	25	32	17	1	25
	Jul	19	35	19	1	27
	Aug	15	36	18	1	30
	Sep	19	25	22	1	33
	Oct	23	31	15	1	30
	Nov	24	30	15	1	29
	Dec	23	30	17	1	30
1986	Jan	19	31	20	1	29
	Feb	19	34	16	1	29
	Mar	20	31	17	1	31
	Apr	17	36	14	1	32
	May	20	35	15	1	29
	Jun	22	34	13	1	30
	Jul	21	36	13	1	30
	Aug	20	35	14	1	30
	Sep	20	35	12	1	31
	Oct	26	34	10	1	29
	Nov	27	34	10	2	28
	Dec	27	31	11	1	31
1987	Jan	24	36	10	1	28
	Feb	23	32	14	1	30
	Mar	27	30	16	0	26
	Apr	29	29	16	1	25
	May	32	29	14	1	24
	May	33	35	15	1	17
	May	35	37	11	1	16
	Jun	33	37	13	0	16
	Jun	34	36	16	1	14

cont'd . . .

		Cons	Lab	Lib	Other	DK
	Jul	37	32	8	0	23
	Aug	35	31	9	1	24
	Sep	34	30	10	1	26
	Oct	40	28	7	1	25
	Nov	36	30	8	1	25
	Dec	35	31	8	2	24
1988	Jan	33	34	7	1	25
	Feb	32	34	6	1	26
	Mar	29	36	8	2	26
	Apr	29	38	7	1	24
	May	32	34	5	2	27
	Jun	30	36	4	1	28
	Jul	32	35	7	2	24
	Aug	34	30	7	2	27
	Sep	34	34	8	1	23
	Oct	34	28	9	1	27
	Nov	31	32	8	2	26
	Dec	34	27	9	3	26
1989	Jan	32	31	8	2	27
	Feb	28	33	7	1	31
	Mar	30	33	8	2	27
	Apr	30	33	7	3	27
	May	29	37	7	2	25
	Jun	28	40	4	7	22
	Jul	26	37	4	5	27
	Aug	27	37	4	5	27
	Sep	27	34	5	5	28
	Oct	29	33	6	5	27
	Nov	28	39	5	2	25
	Dec					
1990	Jan	26	39	3	3	28
	Jan	26	37	4	4	28
	Feb	24	40	4	3	28
	Mar	22	42	6	5	25
	Apr	27	35	6	4	27
	May					
	Jun	25	42	4	5	24
	Jul	28	39	5	2	26
	Jul	25	38	4	4	28
	Aug					
	Sep	33	36	3	4	25
	Sep	27	37	6	2	28
	Oct	29	38	6	3	25

cont'd . . .

		Cons	Lab	Lib	Other	DK
	Nov					
	Dec	42	30	5	2	21
1991	Jan	38	30	4	0	27
	Feb	42	25	4	2	27
	Mar	39	28	7	2	25
	Mar	30	30	10	3	27
	Apr					
	May	30	34	10	2	24
	Jun	26	39	10	2	23
	Jun	31	32	8	2	26
	Jul					
	Aug	30	33	8	2	27
	Sep	32	30	8	2	27
	Sep	31	32	9	3	25
	Oct					
	Nov	27	39	8	2	25
	Dec	32	33	8	2	25
1992	Jan	31	33	8	2	26
	Feb	33	31	6	1	28
	Mar	30	33	8	1	27
	Mar	33	39	7	3	19
	Mar	29	40	9	3	20
	Mar	33	36	11	2	17
	Apr	30	39	11	2	18
	May	35	34	8	2	21
	Jun	36	31	9	3	23
	Jul	33	31	7	3	25
	Aug	30	36	6	1	27
	Sep	29	32	7	2	30
	Oct	25	35	6	2	31
	Nov	22	39	6	4	30
	Dec	20	44	8	2	27
1993	Jan	25	40	8	3	25
	Jan	23	39	9	2	27
	Feb	20	41	8	2	28
	Mar					
	Apr	21	44	7	1	27
	May	22	40	10	2	25
	May	19	41	11	0	27
	Jun					
	Jul	17	38	14	1	29
	Aug	17	38	15	2	28

cont'd . . .

		Cons	Lab	Lib	Other	DK
	Sep	18	39	14	1	28
	Sep	16	37	16	2	29
	Oct					
	Nov	16	38	13	3	31
	Dec	20	41	11	2	26
1994	Jan	19	39	11	2	29
	Jan	17	39	12	3	30
	Feb	18	42	12	1	26
	Mar					
	Apr	15	45	9	1	29
	May	17	37	15	2	29
	May	15	48	11	1	24
	Jun					
	Jul	14	47	9	2	28
	Jul	13	50	8	0	28
	Aug					
	Sep	15	49	11	2	22
	Sep	13	51	7	1	28
	Oct	14	48	9	0	28
	Nov					
	Dec	14	50	7	3	27
1995	Jan	12	51	6	2	29
	Jan	13	51	5	3	28
	Feb	12	52	7	3	26
	Mar					
	Apr	15	48	7	1	28
	May	15	48	8	1	28
	Jun	13	51	7	3	26
	Jul	16	48	7	1	28
	Jul	15	48	7	1	28
	Aug					
	Sep	17	44	7	2	30
	Sep	17	45	8	4	28
	Oct	16	48	7	1	27
	Nov					
	Dec	15	49	6	1	29
1996	Jan	13	48	8	0	30
	Feb	15	45	8	1	31
	Mar	17	46	7	0	28
	Mar	16	44	8	2	31
	Apr					
	May	15	46	9	2	29
	Jun	16	45	8	0	30

cont'd . . .

		Cons	Lab	Lib	Other	DK
	Jun	18	41	9	2	30
	Jul					
	Aug	17	45	7	3	29
	Sep	16	45	7	2	30
	Sep	18	42	10	2	28
	Oct					
	Nov	19	44	6	2	28
	Dec	17	48	7	3	27
1997	Jan	26	48	7	3	17
	Feb	23	44	7	2	24
	Mar	23	46	9	1	20
1997	Apr	22	44	8	2	24

CHAPTER 13
Electoral Reform

We have until now repeatedly made the point that minor variations of question wording are unlikely to have made much difference to the pattern of responses. If people are asked what they think of the incumbent Prime Minister, they are unlikely, except in rare instances, to be swayed by whether they are asked whether they are satisfied with him or her or whether they approve of him or her. Most such questions are clearly understood by most respondents in a simple dichotomous fashion: yes/no, good/bad, thumbs up/thumbs down.

However, there are many other issues that are more complicated and, more important, are not ones that most people have either thought about very much or have settled views about. In cases like these, question wording can, and does, have a considerable impact on the responses that interviewers get. It is far from clear in these cases whether what is being tapped can reasonably be called 'opinion' at all. Respondents in large numbers of cases are either responding randomly or responding to verbal cues implicit in the question wording. For example, in the 1980s the responses to questions about the siting of American cruise missiles – about which most voters did not have strong opinions – depended crucially on whether the word 'British' was included in the question, somehow implying that the missiles were British, or whether it was not. If it was included, people tended to be (or sound as though they were) in favour. If not, not.

Electoral reform is another such case. The vast majority of people have no fixed opinions on the subject, if they have any opinions at all. As a result, if the issue is presented as one of fairness, the response tends to be favourable. If it is presented as one likely to lead to unstable government, the response tends to be unfavourable. Partly for this reason, Gallup has never settled on a single question in regard to proportional representation but has asked a variety of questions over the years, some of them in response to the ways in which the issue was being framed by politicians at the time. A few of the questions are concerned as much with tactical voting as with electoral reform as such. The questions and the responses to them are set out in Table 13 partly to illustrate the general point about the importance of question wording, but mainly because, at the turn of the twenty-first century, electoral reform is still a live issue.

TABLE 13:   ELECTORAL REFORM

Q. Would you approve or disapprove if the arrangements for the general election were changed by:

	Approve	Disapprove	Don't know
OCTOBER 1964			
Having two consecutive days for voting?	36	50	14
Having voting at weekends instead of weekdays?	29	57	14
Making it compulsory for everyone to vote?	51	41	8
Making polling day a public bank holiday?	36	52	12
Allowing anyone to apply for a postal vote who wanted one?	58	28	14
Closing down television, cinemas and other entertainment on polling day?	7	86	7
Putting the party labels against the candidates' names on the voting form?	64	22	14

Q. Would you approve or disapprove if the arrangements for the general election were changed by:

	Approve	Disapprove	Don't know
JUNE 1967			
Not publishing opinion poll results in the three days before polling ends?	34	37	29
Not publishing betting odds on the election in the three days before polling ends?	36	36	28
Putting the party labels against the candidates' names on the voting form?	70	15	15

Q. *Do you think that the present parliamentary system is satisfactory as it is or not? How strongly do you feel that?*

OCTOBER 1968

Is, very strongly	10
Is, strongly	13
Is, not strongly	18
Is not, not strongly	11
Is not, strongly	14
Is not, very strongly	19
Don't know	15

Q. *These are some of the changes which some people would like to see made to our system of government. Tell me for each, do you think it would be a good idea or a bad idea to:*

	Good idea	Bad idea	Don't know
OCTOBER 1968			
Reduce the numbers of Members of Parliament?	48	33	19
Appoint industrialists and others from outside Parliament to ministerial and other jobs?	61	19	20
Provide Members of Parliament with good office space and secretarial help?	51	29	20
Increase salaries of Members of Parliament?	13	77	10
Run government departments under committees which include some members drawn from parties in opposition?	56	24	20
Set a definite period for the government to stay in office and don't leave it to the discretion of the Prime Minister?	63	22	15
Abolish the House of Lords?	35	41	24
Set up regional parliaments for Wales, Scotland and other large areas?	47	33	20

Q. Do you think that the present parliamentary system is satisfactory as it is or not? How strongly do you feel this?

	Sep 1968	Aug 1976
Satisfactory – very strongly	10	6
Strongly	13	14
Not strongly	18	20
All satisfactory	41	40
Not satisfactory – not strongly	11	10
Strongly	14	15
Very strongly	19	17
All not satisfactory	44	42
Don't know	15	17

Q. At present, voting forms for parliamentary elections simply list the names of the candidates in alphabetical order. Would you approve or disapprove if the voting forms also showed the political party for which each candidate was standing?

	Dec 1968
Approve	72
Disapprove	13
Don't know	15

Q. Do you agree or disagree that the voting age should be reduced to eighteen?

	Dec 1968
Agree	43
Disagree	49
Don't know	8

Q. It has been suggested that parents of children under voting age should be given one additional vote at general elections to enable them to vote for their children's future. Do you think this is a good idea or a bad idea?

	Apr 1972
Good idea	18
Bad idea	67
Don't know	15

Q. It has been suggested that during general elections a fixed amount of public money should be given to political parties to finance election campaigns. Do you think this is a good idea or a bad idea?

	Aug 1975	May 1980
Good idea	33	27
Bad idea	57	61
Don't know	10	12

Q. It has been suggested that all private contributions from other sources, such as trade unions and big business, should be prohibited. Do you think this is a good idea or a bad idea?

	Aug 1975	May 1980
Good idea	50	48
Bad idea	34	34
Don't know	16	18

Q. Do you think there should or should not be a set limit to the amount of money political parties can spend on election campaigns?

	Aug 1975	May 1980
Should	82	81
Should not	10	11
Don't know	7	9

Q. These are some of the changes which some people would like to see made to our system of government. Tell me for each, do you think it would be a good idea or a bad idea to:

	Good idea	Bad idea	Don't know
AUGUST 1976			
Reduce the numbers of Members of Parliament?	54	30	16
Appoint industrialists and others from outside Parliament to ministerial and other jobs?	61	21	18
Provide Members of Parliament with better office space and secretarial help?	19	61	20
Increase salaries of Members of Parliament?	8	84	8

cont'd . . .

	Good idea	Bad idea	Don't know
Run government departments under committees which include some members drawn from parties in opposition?	57	21	22
Set a definite period for the government to stay in office and don't leave it to the discretion of the Prime Minister?	52	30	18
Abolish the House of Lords?	31	47	22
Set up regional parliaments for Wales, Scotland and other large areas?	37	42	21

Q. At present, the candidate who wins the most votes in an election becomes the MP. How satisfied are you with this system of choosing MPs? Are you:

	Jun 1963	Apr 1985	Nov 1985
Very satisfied	24	19	17
Quite satisfied	35	42	41
Not very satisfied	25	21	19
Not at all satisfied	14	12	12
Don't know	2	6	10

Q. How important do you think it is for us to change the system of choosing MPs?

	Jun 1963	Apr 1985	Nov 1985
Very important	29	23	22
Quite important	19	24	21
Not very important	16	22	25
Not at all important	26	21	21
Don't know	9	10	12

Q. Would you be in favour of a system where the number of seats in the House of Commons was proportional to the number votes it won nationally?

	Jun 1963	Apr 1985	Nov 1985
Yes	62	61	59
No	26	20	20
Don't know	12	19	21

Q. Under the present voting system, only one political party forms the Government while the alternative system might mean that the Government was made up of more than one political party. Would this make you more or less favourable to a change in the present voting system?

	Jun 1963	Apr 1985	Nov 1985
More favourable	45	48	43
Less favourable	43	31	32
Don't know	12	21	25

Q. In order to achieve a new system of electing MPs it might be necessary to merge several existing constituencies into a much larger constituency which would have more than one MP. Some people think that this would weaken the relationship between an individual constituency and its MP, while others say it wouldn't really make much difference. Would you be more or less favourable to a change in the present voting system if it meant that there were larger constituencies with more than one MP?

	Jun 1983	Apr 1983
More favourable	34	31
Less favourable	52	43
Don't know	14	26

Q. At present, both the Labour and Conservative parties are officially opposed to changing the present voting system. The Alliance is in favour of the proposed change. Do you think the decision on changing the electoral system should be left to Parliament or put to voters in the form of a referendum?

	Jun 1983
Left to Parliament	18
A referendum	77
Don't know	5

Q. Would you be in favour of a voting system which kept the present constituencies but where voters could list candidates in order of preference?

	Jun 1983	Apr 1983
Yes	59	61
No	29	25
Don't know	12	14

Q. *If the opinion polls in a general election said that a party you disliked most was going to win, with your party in third place, but that the party in second place stood a chance of winning, would you stick to voting for your own party, seriously think of voting for the party in second place, or decide not to vote?*

	Apr 1983	Sep 1983
Stick to own party	77	70
Think of voting for other party	14	16
Decide not to vote	4	6
Don't know	5	7

Q. *There's a lot of talk about how the parties choose their parliamentary candidates to fight each constituency at an election. How interested are you in this topic:*

	Jan 1985
Very interested	10
Fairly interested	29
Not very interested	34
Not at all interested	25
Don't know	2

Q. *Do you think this is:*

	Jan 1985
Very important	32
Fairly important	44
Not very important	14
Not at all important	6
Don't know	5

Q. *Do you think a sitting Member of Parliament should automatically be re-adopted as a constituency's candidate, or should he have to go before the local party for approval again?*

	Jan 1985
Automatically re-adopted	10
Seek re-approval	76
Don't know	14

Q. In the case of a sitting MP, should there be: (All saying seek re-approval)

	Jan 1985
Several other people on the short-list in competition with the MP	76
Should the party simply be asked whether or not it wants to re-nominate the MP, without considering others	20
Don't know	4

Q. When a party has to choose a new parliamentary candidate, how do you think this ought to be done?

	Jan 1985
The national party headquarters	4
A committee of constituency party leaders	11
All members of the constituency party having a vote	41
All the people who normally vote for the party	37
Don't know	10

Q. Which of these do you think important in choosing a parliamentary candidate?

	Jan 1985
Views on major political issues	56
Attitude toward the party leader	19
Knowing and being known in the constituency	56
Personality of wife/husband	7
Experience of local council problems	63
Ability to have an impact in Westminster	58
Pleasing personality and manners	24
None of these; don't know	4

Q. Which two of these characteristics is most important?

	Jan 1985
Views on major political issues	44
Attitude toward the party leader	7
Knowing and being known in the constituency	35
Personality of wife/husband	1
Experience of local council problems	46
Ability to have an impact in Westminster	43
Pleasing personality and manners	5
None of these; don't know	5

Q. All in all, which is more important in an MP?

	Jan 1985
Devotes himself to looking after constituency concerns, or	51
Makes a real contribution nationally in Parliament	35
Both	5
Don't know	9

Q. If you thought the party you most disliked was likely to win the election for an MP in your constituency and the party you favoured most hadn't a chance of winning, would you stick to voting for your own party, or seriously think of voting for the party in second place?

	Jan 1985
Stick to own party	75
Think of voting for other party	21
Don't know	5

Q. Some people say that we should change the voting system to allow smaller political parties to get a fairer share of MPs. Others say that we should keep the voting as it is to produce effective government. Which view comes closest to your own?

	Dec 1985	May 1987	Jan 1988	Jun 1993
Change	45	35	38	41
Keep as it is	47	56	51	50
Don't know	8	9	11	8

Q. Some people say that we should change the voting system to allow smaller political parties to get a fairer share of MPs. Others say that we should keep the voting system as it is to produce effective government. Which view comes closest to your own?

	Dec 1985	May 1987	Jan 1988
Change the system	45	35	38
Keep as it is	47	56	51
Don't know	8	9	11

Q. I'm going to read two opposite views about coalition governments. Which one of these comes closest to your own point of view? A government formed by two or more political parties:

	Sep 1986	Jan 1988	Jun 1988	Sep 1988
Which agreed to work together would provide the stability required for Britain's economy to grow and the unity needed to deal with our social problems	49	31	40	31
Would not last long in Britain because it could not provide strong leadership and would get little done	40	54	49	57
Don't know	11	15	11	11

Q. Let's say at the next general election you thought the party you favoured most was going to do badly; the party you disliked was going to win; but that the party in second place stood a chance of defeating the party you disliked. In such circumstances would you stick to voting for your initial choice, or vote for the party in second place?

	Dec 1986	Mar 1987	Mar 1987	Apr 1987	Apr 1987	May 1987	May 1987	Mar 1992
Stick to own party	62	58	59	63	65	65	64	60
Second place party	26	29	31	28	24	24	26	29
Decide not to vote	4	4	3	3	3	4	3	3
Don't know	8	9	7	6	7	7	7	9

Q. I'm going to read two opposite views about coalition governments. Which one of these comes closest to your own point of view? A government formed by two or more political parties:

	Sep 1986	Jan 1988	Jun 1993
Which agreed to work together would provide the stability required for Britain's economy to grow and the unity needed to deal with our social problems	49	31	48
Would not last long in Britain because it could not provide strong leadership and would get little done	40	54	42
Don't know	11	15	10

Q. A proposal is being put forward at the moment that the House of Lords should continue to exist for the time being but that hereditary peers — those who have inherited the title — should no longer have the right to vote in the House of Lords. From what you know, do you approve of the proposal or not?

	Mar 1997
Approve	53
Disapprove	38
Don't know	9

Q. Another proposal being put forward is that during the lifetime of the next Parliament there should be a national referendum on whether or not we should change our electoral system to one of proportional representation, which would mean the parties having seats in the House of Commons roughly proportional to their share of votes in the country. From what you know, do you think there should be such a referendum or not?

	Mar 1997
Yes, should	68
No, should not	25
Don't know	7

Q. If there were such a referendum, how do you think you would vote: in favour of proportional representation or against it?

	Mar 1997
In favour	66
Against	26
Wouldn't vote	2
Don't know	6

Q. Which one of these following statements comes closest to your own view?

	Sep 1996
Our electoral system should be changed so political parties are represented in proportion to the number of votes cast for them	50
The present electoral system has, on the whole, served the country well and should be left as it is	47
Don't know	2

CHAPTER 14

The Monarchy and the Royal Family

Before the 1990s, survey questions were seldom asked about the Monarchy as an institution and about the Royal Family as part of that institution. Both seemed too stable and secure to warrant detailed enquiry. The only question about the Monarchy as an institution that Gallup asked prior to 1991 concerned the possibility that Queen Elizabeth might abdicate at some stage in favour of her son Prince Charles.

The 1990s, however, saw a new interest both in the personalities of the members of the Royal Family and in the future of the Monarchy: whether it would actually have a future and, if so, what form that future should take. This chapter reports the findings of a number of questions, not about the personalities and behaviour of individual members of the Royal Family, but about the institution of the Monarchy and how, if at all, it should develop. In some cases, the specific wordings of the questions vary in keeping with changing circumstances.

TABLE 14.1: WHETHER THE MONARCHY WILL CONTINUE TO EXIST 1991–2000

Q. *Do you think the Monarchy and the Royal Family will still exist in the next century?*

		Yes	No	Don't know	
1991	Jul	78	14	8	A
1992	Mar	74	20	7	B
	Dec	74	20	7	
1993	Feb	69	19	11	
	Jun	71	17	12	
1997	Sep	71	23	6	
2000	Jun	72	21	7	C

A In July 1991 the question read, 'Do you think the Royal Family will still exist in the next century?'

B In March 1992 the question read, 'Do you think the Monarchy will still exist in the next century?'

C In June 2000 the question read, 'Do you think the Monarchy and Royal Family will still exist when Prince William is due to come to the throne in perhaps thirty or forty years time?'

TABLE 14.2: PREFERENCES FOR FUTURE OF MONARCHY 1992–2000

Q. Which of these statements comes closest to your own view?

A The Monarchy and the Royal Family should stay pretty much as they are now

B The Monarchy and the Royal Family should continue to exist but should become more 'democratic and approachable', rather like the Monarchy and Royal Family in the Netherlands

C The Monarchy should be abolished and replaced by a non-executive figurehead president like the ones they have in some continental countries

D Don't know

		A	B	C	D
1992	Dec	26	59	13	2
1993	Feb	24	65	9	2
	Jun	35	50	11	4
	Nov	30	56	10	4
1994	Sep	36	49	12	3
1995	Oct	32	50	13	6
	Nov	26	54	15	5
1996	Mar	28	51	17	4
	Nov	31	50	16	3
1997	Sep	15	72	11	2
1998	Nov	25	62	12	0
2000	Jun	27	60	11	3

TABLE 14.3: POSSIBLE ABDICATION OF QUEEN ELIZABETH 1976–98

Q. Which would you prefer – for the Queen to continue as Head of State for as long as she can or for her to abdicate after her Silver Jubilee in a few years' time to let Prince Charles become King?

		Queen continue	Queen abdicate	Don't know
1976	Jan	52	36	12
	May	64	25	11
1977	Jan	70	18	12

Q. *Do you think it would be a good idea or not for the Queen to 'retire' early, so as to give Prince Charles the chance to become King before he is much older?*

		Good idea	Not good idea	Don't know
1988	Dec	59	29	12
1989	Sep	57	30	13

Q. *Do you think the Queen should or should not abdicate in favour of Prince Charles?*

		Should	Should not	Don't know
1989	Dec	53	36	11

Q. *Do you think the Queen should or should not abdicate in favour of Prince Charles some time within the next few years?*

		Should	Should not	Don't know
1992	Dec	24	68	7
1993	Feb	21	72	7
	Jun	26	66	8
1993	Nov	29	56	15
1994	May	28	59	13
1994	Jul	29	63	8
1995	Oct	27	63	11
1995	Nov	20	69	11
1996	Mar	16	73	12
1996	Sep	19	73	8
1997	Dec	30	65	5
1998	Nov	33	63	4

TABLE 14.4: 'SKIPPING A GENERATION' 1992–97

Q. *It is sometimes said that Prince Charles may be too old when he becomes King and that his marital problems may have undermined his own sense of fitness for the role. In your view, should the Royal Family 'skip a generation', with Prince William becoming King in Prince Charles's stead or not?*

		Should	Should not	Don't know
1992	Dec	36	52	11
1993	Feb	38	50	12

cont'd . . .

		Should	Should not	Don't know
1993	Jun	33	54	14
1994	Jul	24	66	10
1995	Oct	36	51	13
1995	Nov	40	47	13
1996	Mar	39	46	15
1996	Sep	45	44	11

Q. In your view, should the Royal Family 'skip a generation' with Prince William becoming King instead of Prince Charles, or not?

		Should	Should not	Don't know
1997	Sep	51	41	8

Q. It is sometimes said that Prince Charles may be too old when he becomes King. In your view, should the Royal Family 'skip a generation', with Prince William becoming King in Prince Charles's stead or not?

		Should	Should not	Don't know
1997	Dec	41	54	4

Chapter 15
Europe

No issue in recent decades has aroused more vehement controversy among the political classes in Britain than the issue of whether the United Kingdom should or should not belong to the European Union and its predecessor organizations and the closely associated issue of how the European Union and the United Kingdom's relationship with it should develop in the future.

Gallup began as early as the autumn of 1972 to ask a broad-brush question seeking to find out from respondents, in the most general terms, whether they thought British membership of (initially) the Common Market was a good thing, a bad thing, or neither good nor bad. As indicated in the notes to Table 15.1, the question varied slightly until 1976 when it settled down in the form shown in the table. Only the name of the principal European entity mentioned in the question has changed as the name of the entity itself has changed: from Common Market to European Community and from European Community to European Union. Most respondents have almost certainly understood the question, whatever its precise wording, to refer to 'Europe' and Britain's involvement with it.

Tables 15.2 and 15.3 explore in more detail people's preferences concerning the European Community/Union's future shape and Britain's place in it, ranging from full integration, with a central European government, to complete British withdrawal. As can be seen, the list of options offered to respondents in the question was changed in 1995 to reflect changes in the European Union and the changing options apparently available to the United Kingdom and its people.

Tables 15.4 and 15.5 report Gallup's findings about people's beliefs about the political parties' stances on Europe and about which of the major parties they believe more accurately represents their own views. Tables 15.6 and 15.7 deal not with Europe in general but with the single European currency, the euro. In particular, Gallup has wanted to know both whether people think the euro has been a success and also how people would cast their ballots if a referendum were held on possible British membership of the euro.

TABLE 15.1: BRITAIN'S MEMBERSHIP – A GOOD THING OR BAD THING? 1972–2000

Q. Generally speaking, do you think that Britain's membership of the Common Market is a good thing, a bad thing or neither good nor bad?

		Good	Bad	Neither	DK	
1972	Oct	40	21	23	16	A
1976	Jan	50	24	17	9	
	Feb	48	26	17	8	
	Aug	40	31	21	9	
	Sep	33	37	19	11	B
1977	Jun	33	42	18	7	
	Oct	37	33	22	8	
1978	Jul	25	48	20	7	
1979	May	34	36	22	7	
	May	37	34	22	7	
	Jun	37	34	19	10	
	Oct	24	54	17	5	
	Nov	21	55	15	9	
1980	Apr	22	57	13	8	
	May	26	52	17	6	
	Jun	22	54	17	7	
	Oct	24	46	24	5	
1981	Mar	24	52	21	4	
1982	Mar	23	48	23	7	
	May	17	45	21	7	
	Nov	15	45	22	7	
1983	May	43	30	22	5	
	Aug	34	37	21	8	
1984	Mar	25	48	20	7	
	Apr	32	38	24	5	
	May	33	32	29	6	
	Jun	32	36	28	4	
	Jun	34	36	26	4	
	Jul	25	43	23	9	
1985	Jan	32	39	21	7	
1987	Jul	28	39	25	8	
	Oct	36	35	21	9	
1988	Sep	36	36	18	9	
1989	Mar	36	30	27	7	
	Jun	51	19	23	8	
1990	Nov	56	13	21	10	
1991	Nov	49	22	20	9	
1992	Jun	49	22	20	10	

cont'd . . .

		Good	Bad	Neither	DK
	Jul	42	27	22	9
	Sep	49	27	22	9
	Oct	42	27	20	13
	Dec	42	26	19	13
1993	Jan	41	29	19	10
	Oct	35	21	32	12
1994	Mar	40	23	28	8
	Apr	42	21	26	11
	Jun	49	19	22	10
	Oct	38	23	29	10
1995	Feb	36	29	22	13
	Jul	39	27	22	12
	Oct	39	25	28	9
1996	Jun	34	34	22	9
	Oct	35	33	19	12
	Nov	31	30	23	16
	Dec	34	34	22	11
1998	Dec	36	31	27	6
1999	Jun	43	24	29	4
	Nov	36	27	32	5
2000	Mar	38	28	31	3
2000	Jul	38	27	29	6

A Question in 1972 read, 'Generally speaking, do you think that membership is a good thing for Britain, a bad thing or neither good nor bad?'

B Since 1976 the question has remained as shown except for using the term 'European Community' or 'European Union'.

TABLE 15.2: DESIRED FUTURE FOR EUROPE 1989–95

Q. People hold different views about how they would like to see the European Community develop. Which of these statements comes closest to your own view?

	Jun 1989	Nov 1990	Nov 1991	Jan 1993	Jun 1994	Feb 1995
A fully integrated Europe with most major decisions taken by a European Government	13	13	11	9	10	10
A Europe more integrated than now, but with decisions that mainly affect Britain staying in British hands	48	56	48	44	46	42

cont'd . . .

	Jun 1989	Nov 1990	Nov 1991	Jan 1993	Jun 1994	Feb 1995
The situation as it is now, with Britain retaining a veto over major policy changes it does not like	21	19	23	23	24	23
Complete British withdrawal from the European Union	12	8	12	17	13	16
Don't know	7	4	6	7	6	9

TABLE 15.3: DESIRED FUTURE FOR EUROPE 1995–2000

Q. People hold different views about how they would like to see the European Union develop. Which of these statements comes closest to your own view?

	Jul 1995	Jun 1996	Oct 1996	Dec 1996	Mar 2000
A fully integrated Europe with all major decisions taken by a European Government	10	11	9	10	7
No European Government, but a more integrated European Union than now, with a single currency and no frontier controls	22	18	19	17	22
The situation more or less as it is now	22	19	17	18	27
A less integrated Europe than now, with the European Union amounting to little more than a free trade area	24	25	26	22	21
Complete British withdrawal from the European Union	12	19	15	23	18
Don't know	10	8	14	11	5

TABLE 15.4: WHICH PARTY MORE PRO-EUROPEAN 1995-2000

Q. Politicians and political parties are often described as 'pro-European' or 'anti-European'. Which of the two major parties – Conservative or Labour – do you regard as more pro-European at the moment?

	Jul 1995	Jun 1996	Oct 1996	Dec 1996	Mar 2000
Conservative	29	28	30	31	21
Labour	34	37	33	53	68
Neither, both equal	18	17	18	7	3
Don't know	18	19	19	8	8

TABLE 15.5: WHICH PARTY MORE REPRESENTATIVE 1995-2000

Q. Which of the two major parties – the Conservative or Labour – most closely represents your own views about Britain's future in Europe?

	Jul 1995	Jun 1996	Sep 1996	Mar 1997	Apr 1997	Mar 2000
Conservative	21	18	22	35	37	34
Labour	40	37	32	47	40	50
Neither, both equal	17	19	21	9	10	8
Don't know	22	25	25	9	13	7

TABLE 15.6: EURO: SUCCESS OR NOT? 1999-2000

Q. From what you know, do you think the single currency has or has not been a success so far?

	Jun 1999	Mar 2000
Yes, success	21	16
No, not success	59	75
Don't know	20	8

EUROPE // 305

TABLE 15.7: EURO: REFERENDUM VOTING 1996–2000

Q. If a popular referendum on the question of a single European currency were held during the next few months, how would you vote – in favour or against Britain joining the single currency and the abolition of the pound?

		In favour	Against	Would not vote	DK	
1996	Dec	26	56	5	14	A
	Dec	33	61	2	5	
1999	Jun	29	66	1	4	
	Jun	30	66	1	3	
	Nov	31	64	1	4	
2000	Mar	27	69	1	2	

A Question in December 1996 read, 'If such a referendum [a popular referendum on the question of a single European currency] were held during the next few months, how would you vote, in favour or against the creation of a single European currency and the abolition of the pound?'

Chapter 16
Economic Expectations

Few features of British electoral politics figured more prominently in the discussions of the 1980s and 1990s than what became known as the 'feel-good factor'. The view was widely held that the feel-good factor was of great political significance and that when the feel-good factor was positive the government of the day prospered electorally and that when it was negative the government suffered electorally. Whatever the feel-good factor's precise signifi-cance at the time of the 1997 general election, there can be little doubt that it still has a bearing on many individuals' vote decisions.

The Gallup Poll made discussions of the feel-good factor possible by initiating in the early 1980s a series of questions that read, without any subsequent variation in question wording, 'How do you think the financial situation of your household will change over the next twelve months? Will it get a lot better, a little better, a little worse, a lot worse, or will it stay the same?' The feel-good factor is obtained simply by subtracting the total proportion of people who think their financial situation will get a little or a lot worse over the next twelve months from the total proportion thinking it will get a little or a lot better. Table 16.1 reports Gallup's findings, including a calculation of the feel-good factor, between 1981 and 2000. Since 1991 the feel-good factor and the question from which it is calculated have formed part of the Gallup Index.

Between 1974 and 1996 Gallup also asked a question, not about respondents' personal economic expectations, but about their expectations concerning the economy as a whole. The results are reported in Table 16.2, together with the results of a calculation identical to the one performed to arrive at the feel-good factor. We have dubbed these results the 'optimism factor'.

TABLE 16.1: PERSONAL EXPECTATIONS – THE 'FEEL-GOOD FACTOR' 1981–2000

Q. How do you think the financial situation of your household will change over the next twelve months? Will it get?

		A lot better	A little better	Stay the same	A little worse	A lot worse	Feel-good factor	DK
1981	Nov	2	14	45	22	11	-17	7
	Dec	2	13	39	25	15	-25	5

cont'd . . .

		A lot better	A little better	Stay the same	A little worse	A lot worse	Feel-good factor	DK
1982	Jan	2	15	41	23	13	-19	6
	Feb	3	15	42	23	12	-17	5
	Mar	2	16	43	24	10	-16	5
	Apr	2	15	44	24	9	-16	6
	May	3	19	43	21	9	-8	6
	Jun	3	19	47	18	7	-3	6
	Jul	3	19	45	19	8	-5	6
	Aug	3	19	46	19	7	-4	6
	Sep	3	19	46	20	7	-5	6
	Oct	3	19	48	16	8	-2	7
	Nov	4	20	47	15	8	1	6
	Dec	2	18	47	19	8	-7	5
1983	Jan	3	18	50	18	6	-3	5
	Feb	3	18	48	18	6	-3	7
	Mar	3	21	49	16	6	2	7
	Apr	4	19	48	17	5	1	7
	May	3	22	48	14	5	6	7
	Jun	4	22	43	14	7	5	11
	Jul	3	18	47	19	7	-5	6
	Aug	4	20	47	17	6	1	6
	Sep	3	19	50	18	6	-2	5
	Oct	3	19	47	20	6	-4	5
	Nov	3	20	47	19	6	-2	6
	Dec	3	19	48	19	6	-3	5
1984	Jan	4	20	47	17	6	1	5
	Feb	3	19	47	18	6	-2	6
	Mar	4	19	46	20	6	-3	6
	Apr	3	20	47	19	6	-2	5
	May	4	19	46	19	6	-2	5
	Jun	3	20	46	18	7	-2	5
	Jul	4	19	47	18	7	-2	5
	Aug	3	18	46	19	7	-5	7
	Sep	4	19	49	19	6	-2	4
	Oct	4	18	49	18	6	-2	5
	Nov	4	19	47	17	7	-1	5
	Dec	5	22	45	16	5	6	6
1985	Jan	4	19	50	16	7	0	5
	Feb	3	17	46	19	9	-8	5
	Mar	3	18	46	20	8	-7	5
	Apr	3	17	43	22	8	-10	7
	May	3	18	43	22	9	-10	4
	Jun	3	18	47	19	8	-6	5

cont'd . . .

		A lot better	A little better	Stay the same	A little worse	A lot worse	Feel-good factor	DK
	Jul	3	18	49	19	7	-5	5
	Aug	3	17	47	20	8	-8	5
	Sep	3	18	47	18	8	-5	5
	Oct	4	20	47	17	7	0	5
	Nov	3	19	49	16	8	-2	5
	Dec	4	19	49	16	7	0	5
1986	Jan							
	Feb	3	16	47	19	8	-8	5
	Mar	3	19	44	21	8	-7	5
	Apr	4	19	43	20	8	-5	6
	May	4	18	47	16	8	-2	7
	Jun	5	19	48	17	7	0	5
	Jul	5	19	49	16	6	2	5
	Aug	4	19	48	18	6	-1	6
	Sep	3	19	50	15	7	0	6
	Oct	4	19	49	16	6	1	5
	Nov	4	20	49	16	6	2	6
	Dec	3	20	50	17	5	1	5
1987	Jan	4	20	50	16	6	2	5
	Feb	4	22	49	14	5	7	6
	Mar	5	23	48	13	5	10	6
	Apr	5	25	45	13	5	12	7
	May	6	23	45	12	5	12	8
	Jun	7	25	42	11	6	15	9
	Jul	6	22	46	15	6	7	6
	Aug	6	24	47	14	5	11	4
	Sep	6	20	49	16	5	5	5
	Oct	6	22	47	15	5	8	5
	Nov	5	22	44	19	5	3	5
	Dec	6	21	45	17	7	3	5
1988	Jan	6	23	46	14	7	8	4
	Feb	5	22	44	17	7	3	5
	Mar	6	22	43	16	7	5	6
	Apr	6	21	42	18	9	0	4
	May	6	23	42	15	8	6	5
	Jun	6	23	44	16	6	7	4
	Jul	6	22	46	16	6	6	5
	Aug	6	22	44	17	6	5	5
	Sep	6	20	46	19	6	1	3
	Oct	5	20	44	19	7	-1	5
	Nov	7	23	42	18	6	6	4
	Dec	6	17	43	18	9	-4	6

cont'd . . .

	A lot better	A little better	Stay the same	A little worse	A lot worse	Feel-good factor	DK
1989 Jan	5	18	42	22	8	-7	6
Feb	4	16	43	22	9	-11	6
Mar	4	17	43	21	10	-10	5
April	4	18	40	22	12	-12	5
May	5	20	42	20	9	-4	5
Jun	4	18	39	22	11	-11	5
Jul	3	18	42	22	10	-11	6
Aug	5	18	41	23	9	-9	4
Sep	4	18	42	21	8	-7	6
Oct	4	14	37	27	15	-24	4
Nov	3	16	40	24	12	-17	5
Dec	4	15	39	24	13	-18	5
1990 Jan	4	19	38	22	12	-11	5
Feb	4	16	39	22	14	-16	5
Mar	3	14	30	26	22	-31	5
Apr	3	13	38	28	14	-26	4
May	3	16	40	22	13	-16	5
Jun	4	16	42	21	12	-13	5
Jul	3	16	42	22	11	-14	6
Aug	4	16	43	23	10	-13	5
Sep	3	16	41	23	11	-15	5
Oct	4	21	39	20	12	-7	5
Nov	3	18	42	20	11	-10	5
Dec	4	22	44	17	8	1	5
1991 Jan	3	18	42	22	10	-11	5
Feb	4	16	44	21	10	-11	5
Mar	4	21	44	18	8	-1	6
Apr	4.6	22.2	41.4	18.4	8.9	-0.5	4.5
May	4.2	20.8	42.4	19.3	8.7	-3.0	4.5
Jun	4.0	20.4	43.1	19.7	8.9	-4.2	3.9
Jul	3.6	20.0	43.6	20.0	8.5	-4.9	4.3
Aug	3.7	20.3	44.9	19.2	6.9	-2.1	4.9
Sep	4.0	22.6	45.0	16.6	6.6	3.4	5.2
Oct	4.0	21.8	45.4	16.4	7.3	2.1	5.2
Nov	3.5	20.4	44.7	18.8	7.8	-2.7	5.0
Dec	3.5	19.3	45.7	19.0	7.5	-3.7	5.1
1992 Jan	3.3	19.8	46.9	17.8	6.7	-1.4	5.4
Feb	3.8	18.2	45.9	18.5	7.8	-4.3	5.8
Mar	3.3	18.9	44.2	16.6	8.2	-2.6	8.7
Apr							
May	3.7	22.9	47.4	14.9	7.0	4.7	4.0
Jun	3.3	19.9	48.0	17.3	7.4	-1.5	4.1

cont'd . . .

		A lot better	A little better	Stay the same	A little worse	A lot worse	Feel-good factor	DK
	Jul	3.8	16.7	46.3	20.1	9.6	−9.2	3.5
	Aug	2.9	14.6	45.5	22.8	10.3	−15.6	3.9
	Sep	2.8	12.9	45.3	23.6	11.4	−19.3	4.0
	Oct	2.1	12.4	42.3	25.9	13.2	−24.6	4.1
	Nov	2.2	12.2	42.7	25.6	13.2	−24.4	4.1
	Dec	2.7	12.9	42.2	24.5	13.6	−22.5	4.1
1993	Jan	3.0	17.4	46.2	19.9	9.8	−9.3	3.7
	Feb	2.7	14.9	43.9	23.8	11.4	−17.6	3.4
	Mar	2.7	13.6	38.4	26.9	14.6	−25.2	3.7
	Apr	2.9	16.1	42.6	24.1	11.2	−16.3	3.2
	May	3.0	16.9	42.9	23.3	10.8	−14.2	3.1
	Jun	2.8	14.8	42.9	24.1	11.4	−17.9	4.0
	Jul	2.8	15.4	42.5	23.3	12.2	−17.3	3.8
	Aug	2.9	16.5	43.7	23.0	10.0	−13.6	4.0
	Sep	2.8	14.2	42.4	24.9	12.8	−20.7	2.9
	Oct	2.9	12.7	38.9	27.8	14.8	−27.0	3.0
	Nov	2.6	13.2	36.8	28.6	15.3	−28.1	3.6
	Dec	2.2	11.4	34.0	31.8	17.3	−35.5	3.3
1994	Jan	2.8	13.3	35.0	29.7	16.0	−29.6	3.2
	Feb	2.6	11.7	34.5	29.8	18.5	−34.0	2.9
	Mar	3.5	11.2	29.7	32.6	20.0	−37.9	3.0
	Apr	2.3	10.8	30.6	34.2	18.5	−39.6	3.7
	May	2.8	12.7	38.2	28.5	14.1	−27.1	3.6
	Jun	2.5	13.6	41.2	26.9	11.5	−22.3	4.2
	Jul	3.0	14.1	42.4	26.6	10.2	−19.7	3.7
	Aug	3.2	14.6	44.5	24.5	9.0	−15.7	4.2
	Sep	3.1	14.2	42.7	25.4	10.9	−19.0	3.7
	Oct	2.6	15.1	43.3	24.9	9.3	−16.5	4.8
	Nov	2.5	13.9	42.7	26.2	11.2	−21.0	3.6
	Dec	2.3	11.4	37.4	31.2	13.7	−31.2	4.0
1995	Jan	3.0	13.5	43.5	26.6	9.7	−19.8	3.7
	Feb	2.5	13.3	41.7	27.8	10.8	−22.8	4.0
	Mar	3.0	14.3	41.4	26.4	11.0	−20.1	3.9
	Apr	3.4	14.3	40.9	27.1	10.2	−19.6	4.2
	May	3.2	14.5	44.5	24.9	8.8	−16.0	4.1
	Jun	3.1	14.7	47.2	22.3	8.2	−12.7	4.4
	Jul	3.1	14.6	48.1	22.2	7.8	−12.3	4.3
	Aug	3.2	15.4	47.6	21.9	7.3	−10.6	4.5
	Sep	3.5	14.7	47.5	21.8	8.3	−11.9	4.2
	Oct	3.2	15.3	47.7	21.9	7.8	−11.2	4.1
	Nov	2.9	15.5	47.2	22.2	6.8	−10.6	5.4
	Dec	3.0	15.1	47.4	23.4	6.8	−12.1	4.3
1996	Jan	3.1	17.4	49.0	20.0	6.3	−5.8	4.2

cont'd . . .

		A lot better	A little better	Stay the same	A little worse	A lot worse	Feel-good factor	DK
	Feb	3.4	16.3	47.1	21.7	7.0	-9.0	4.4
	Mar	3.2	16.3	46.7	22.2	7.2	-9.9	4.5
	Apr	3.2	17.2	47.6	20.0	7.1	-6.7	4.9
	May	3.2	17.8	49.9	18.7	5.6	-3.3	4.7
	Jun	3.8	17.2	50.5	17.5	5.9	-2.4	5.1
	Jul	3.5	18.7	49.2	17.5	6.1	-1.4	5.0
	Aug	3.3	18.4	48.9	18.2	5.6	-2.1	5.7
	Sep	3.6	17.6	51.4	17.3	5.3	-1.4	4.8
	Oct	3.4	18.3	51.1	16.2	5.1	0.4	5.8
	Nov	3.1	17.0	49.3	19.0	5.4	-4.3	6.1
	Dec	2.6	15.1	48.2	22.1	6.4	-10.8	5.6
1997	Jan	4.0	18.9	49.3	18.4	5.0	-0.5	4.4
	Feb	5.8	16.8	47.6	20.3	4.4	-2.1	5.1
	Mar	4.9	20.9	46.2	14.7	6.1	5.0	7.3
	Apr	6.0	21.0	49.0	12.0	4.0	11.0	7.0
	May	5.6	24.2	42.8	16.8	3.8	9.2	6.7
	Jun	5.0	21.0	41.7	20.7	6.3	-1.0	5.2
	Jul	3.3	17.7	40.4	26.1	7.8	-12.9	4.6
	Aug	3.9	17.2	39.5	25.4	9.8	-14.1	4.2
	Sep	4.4	19.7	42.9	21.0	6.7	-3.6	5.4
	Oct	4.1	18.4	46.3	19.3	6.6	-3.4	5.3
	Nov	3.4	17.9	45.0	22.3	7.1	-8.1	4.3
	Dec	3.9	15.7	39.5	24.4	12.0	-16.8	4.5
1998	Jan	4.0	15.6	41.7	24.6	9.9	-14.9	4.3
	Feb	4.0	17.2	41.3	24.6	9.7	-13.1	3.2
	Mar	3.7	15.3	39.4	26.5	10.4	-17.9	4.7
	Apr	3.6	16.4	42.9	24.0	9.2	-13.2	3.8
	May	4.2	19.7	44.1	20.7	7.6	-4.4	3.7
	Jun	4.0	16.4	43.9	25.1	8.9	-13.6	1.8
	Jul	4.2	17.8	42.6	23.6	9.1	-10.7	2.9
	Aug	3.5	17.2	43.0	24.2	9.8	-13.3	2.3
	Sep	3.8	17.1	45.1	23.4	7.9	-10.4	2.7
	Oct	3.5	16.9	44.6	24.5	7.8	-11.9	2.7
	Nov	3.3	17.5	45.3	22.9	8.5	-10.6	2.5
	Dec	3.8	17.4	44.4	21.9	9.6	-10.3	2.8
1999	Jan	3.8	21.3	44.5	20.3	6.7	-1.9	3.3
	Feb	4.4	20.7	44.3	21.2	6.8	-2.9	2.7
	Mar	3.5	20.8	40.5	24.7	7.5	-7.9	2.9
	Apr	4.0	22.3	42.9	20.5	8.5	-2.7	1.8
	May	4.1	20.9	45.4	19.6	7.8	-2.4	2.2
	Jun	4.3	19.5	46.5	19.1	7.9	-3.2	2.6
	Jul	5.0	20.6	48.7	17.1	6.4	2.1	2.2

cont'd . . .

		A lot better	A little better	Stay the same	A little worse	A lot worse	Feel-good factor	DK
	Aug	5.9	21.1	48.7	16.7	5.8	4.5	1.8
	Sep	4.5	21.1	47.7	17.3	7.4	0.9	2.1
	Oct	4.6	21.3	47.9	17.4	6.7	1.8	2.0
	Nov	4.6	18.8	48.1	18.7	7.1	-2.4	2.7
	Dec	4.7	20.3	46.4	18.7	7.7	-1.4	2.2
2000	Jan	4.2	20.7	46.5	19.5	6.8	-1.4	2.4
	Feb	4.0	18.9	44.6	22.3	8.0	-7.4	2.2
	Mar	4.0	17.2	41.0	25.1	10.5	-14.4	2.3
	Apr	4.3	17.4	43.1	23.2	9.6	-11.1	2.5
	May	3.9	18.3	46.2	21.0	8.1	-6.9	2.5
	Jun	4.0	18.0	45.0	20.9	8.6	-7.5	3.4
	Jul	4.3	17.5	46.6	20.1	9.2	-7.5	2.3
	Aug	5.5	19.6	45.8	19.1	7.3	-1.3	2.8
	Sep	3.8	16.4	45.0	21.6	11.1	-12.5	2.1
	Oct	5.0	20.1	46.6	18.9	7.2	-1.0	2.3
	Nov	4.4	23.6	46.4	17.1	6.2	4.7	2.3
2000	Dec	5.5	22.9	46.7	15.6	5.7	7.1	3.6

TABLE 16.2: EXPECTATIONS CONCERNING UK ECONOMY 1974–96

Q. Do you consider that the general economic situation in the next twelve months is likely to:

		Improve a lot	Improve slightly	Remain the same	Deteriorate slightly	Deteriorate a lot	Optimism factor	Don't know
1974	Jan	2	22	13	21	28	-25	14
	Feb	2	21	19	20	19	-16	20
	Mar	3	25	24	21	14	-7	13
	Apr	4	28	23	17	12	3	15
	May	2	28	24	22	12	-4	12
	Jun							
	Jul	2	22	20	24	17	-17	15
	Aug	1	21	26	24	14	-16	14
	Sep	1	20	18	20	17	-16	24
	Oct	2	20	18	26	25	-29	11
	Nov	1	17	20	24	28	-34	11
	Dec	2	8	13	26	40	-56	10
1975	Jan	2	19	16	26	26	-31	12

cont'd . . .

		Improve a lot	Improve slightly	Remain the same	Deteriorate slightly	Deteriorate a lot	Optimism factor	Don't know
	Feb	2	16	18	28	25	-35	11
	Mar	2	14	19	29	25	-38	11
	Apr	1	19	37	22	10	-12	10
	May	2	15	15	25	31	-39	12
	Jun	2	18	17	23	28	-31	12
	Jul	2	26	17	22	24	-18	10
	Aug	2	17	17	30	26	-37	8
	Sep	2	17	21	26	27	-34	11
	Oct	1	19	22	28	22	-30	8
	Nov	1	22	22	24	22	-23	8
	Dec	2	23	23	23	23	-21	10
1976	Jan	2	30	22	22	16	-6	8
	Feb	3	32	23	20	13	2	9
	Mar	2	24	27	20	15	-9	13
	Apr	2	36	23	20	8	10	11
	May	3	34	19	21	13	3	12
	Jun	3	35	22	21	12	5	8
	Jul	3	29	25	22	11	-1	11
	Aug	3	32	23	21	12	2	10
	Sep	2	22	23	26	17	-19	10
	Oct	1	9	17	30	35	-55	9
	Nov	2	19	25	31	16	-26	7
	Dec	1	17	20	27	24	-33	11
1977	Jan	1	26	20	27	18	-18	7
	Feb	2	22	25	24	18	-18	9
	Mar	2	18	20	29	20	-29	11
	Apr	2	16	26	26	19	-27	11
	May	3	28	23	24	12	-5	10
	Jun	4	27	22	22	14	-5	11
	Jul	2	22	24	28	13	-17	11
	Aug	7	28	23	20	12	3	10
	Sep	12	46	17	13	6	39	7
	Oct	8	41	20	14	6	29	11
	Nov	5	40	21	16	6	23	12
	Dec	6	40	21	14	7	25	12
1978	Jan	9	43	22	10	4	38	11
	Feb	6	40	23	12	7	27	13
	Mar	5	35	25	15	7	18	13
	Apr	6	38	24	13	6	25	14
	May	3	35	27	16	7	15	12
	Jun	2	24	33	21	7	-2	13
	Jul	3	24	32	19	6	2	17

cont'd . . .

		Improve a lot	Improve slightly	Remain the same	Deteriorate slightly	Deteriorate a lot	Optimism factor	Don't know
	Aug	1	29	29	16	7	7	18
	Sep	4	25	32	19	6	4	14
	Oct	2	22	28	25	7	-8	16
	Nov	1	18	25	31	10	-22	14
	Dec	2	20	25	31	11	-20	12
1979	Jan	1	12	20	30	23	-40	13
	Feb	2	16	17	29	23	-34	14
	Mar	2	17	26	26	14	-21	15
	Apr	6	25	22	14	4	13	29
	May	5	31	21	18	9	9	16
	Jun	3	18	15	26	28	-33	10
	Jul	3	20	13	30	26	-33	9
	Aug	3	22	14	27	24	-26	11
	Sep	2	19	15	28	25	-32	10
	Oct	3	22	21	24	21	-20	9
	Nov	3	20	15	26	26	-29	10
	Dec	2	17	14	26	28	-35	12
1980	Jan	1	13	14	32	30	-48	10
	Feb	2	13	16	28	33	-46	8
	Mar	1	18	15	28	28	-37	9
	Apr	2	20	20	28	23	-29	7
	May	3	25	18	23	22	-17	8
	Jun	3	25	17	22	24	-18	9
	Jul	3	24	17	22	27	-22	7
	Aug	4	27	17	18	27	-14	8
	Sep	3	22	18	23	22	-20	12
	Oct	5	28	17	22	22	-11	7
	Nov	3	26	15	22	27	-20	7
	Dec						0	
1981	Jan	3	24	18	24	26	-23	5
	Feb	3	26	19	21	23	-15	8
	Mar	2	23	18	24	25	-24	7
	Apr	3	29	22	18	21	-7	6
	May	2	28	22	20	20	-10	7
	Jun	1	22	20	26	24	-27	7
	Jul	2	21	24	23	25	-25	5
	Aug	3	25	22	24	19	-15	7
	Sep	2	31	26	22	14	-3	6
	Oct	1	20	24	26	22	-27	7
	Nov	2	25	23	23	20	-16	7
	Dec	2	23	25	25	20	-20	5
1982	Jan	2	28	28	24	12	-6	7

cont'd . . .

		Improve a lot	Improve slightly	Remain the same	Deteriorate slightly	Deteriorate a lot	Optimism factor	Don't know
	Feb	1	22	24	25	22	−24	5
	Mar	3	24	27	20	19	−12	7
	Apr	5	31	22	21	13	2	9
	May	4	35	23	21	9	9	8
	Jun	4	36	28	17	8	15	7
	Jul	2	31	28	20	11	2	7
	Aug	3	29	25	22	13	−3	8
	Sep	3	33	33	17	10	9	5
	Oct	4	31	26	19	11	5	9
	Nov	3	33	25	21	11	4	7
	Dec	2	23	32	23	13	−11	7
1983	Jan	1	24	31	23	13	−11	7
	Feb	3	24	27	27	13	−13	6
	Mar	3	33	26	20	11	5	7
	Apr	5	29	29	19	8	7	10
	May	3	43	25	13	6	27	10
	Jun	5	31	22	16	9	11	17
	Jul	4	37	26	18	8	15	7
	Aug	3	34	25	20	11	6	7
	Sep	2	29	31	21	10	0	7
	Oct	1	26	31	23	12	−8	7
	Nov	1	27	29	21	12	−5	10
	Dec	1	34	31	21	9	5	4
1984	Jan	1	31	29	20	10	2	8
	Feb	1	29	31	22	9	−1	8
	Mar	2	26	27	25	12	−9	8
	Apr	3	29	29	21	12	−1	8
	May	1	26	26	26	12	−11	8
	Jun	2	26	29	23	13	−8	8
	Jul	1	23	24	28	17	−21	8
	Aug	2	22	32	20	15	−11	9
	Sep	1	21	27	26	15	−19	10
	Oct	1	21	25	27	16	−21	10
	Nov	2	24	30	25	12	−11	8
	Dec	1	24	32	26	10	−11	7
1985	Jan	2	19	27	27	17	−23	9
	Feb	1	17	25	28	21	−31	7
	Mar	3	25	29	20	16	−8	7
	Apr	2	28	30	21	11	−2	8
	May	1	20	29	27	17	−23	6
	Jun	1	18	32	25	15	−21	9
	Jul	2	22	30	25	14	−15	7

cont'd . . .

		Improve a lot	Improve slightly	Remain the same	Deteriorate slightly	Deteriorate a lot	Optimism factor	Don't know
	Aug	2	21	31	22	16	-15	6
	Sep	1	21	33	22	13	-13	8
	Oct	3	22	30	22	14	-11	9
	Nov	2	30	27	21	11	0	9
	Dec	2	28	38	22	5	3	4
1986	Jan	2	18	32	27	15	-22	7
	Feb	2	18	30	25	19	-24	6
	Mar	3	21	32	22	16	-14	7
	Apr	4	24	33	20	10	-2	8
	May	3	20	29	24	15	-16	9
	Jun	3	20	33	24	12	-13	8
	Jul	3	24	32	21	12	-6	8
	Aug	3	16	34	26	13	-20	7
	Sep	2	19	35	23	11	-13	8
	Oct	3	26	32	20	11	-2	8
	Nov	2	27	31	21	10	-2	8
	Dec	2	24	33	21	10	-5	10
1987	Jan	3	23	31	21	13	-8	9
	Feb	4	29	28	18	9	6	11
	Mar	5	31	30	16	8	12	10
	Apr	5	33	30	13	7	18	12
	May	11	32	24	14	6	23	12
	Jun	5	29	26	12	6	16	23
	Jul	8	36	23	16	9	19	7
	Aug	3	29	34	21	6	5	6
	Sep	6	35	28	15	7	19	9
	Oct	5	29	32	16	7	11	12
	Nov	3	31	31	19	9	6	6
	Dec	3	29	29	21	9	2	9
1988	Jan	4	28	30	19	11	2	9
	Feb	4	31	27	20	10	5	7
	Mar	7	32	27	16	9	14	9
	Apr	4	31	26	20	11	4	9
	May	6	32	31	17	7	14	8
	Jun	5	33	32	16	7	15	8
	Jul	5	26	30	21	10	0	8
	Aug	3	24	28	26	9	-8	9
	Sep	4	25	25	25	10	-6	10
	Oct	2	23	28	27	11	-13	9
	Nov	2	22	30	27	10	-13	9
	Dec	3	21	28	28	13	-17	7
1989	Jan	3	19	31	25	11	-14	9

cont'd . . .

		Improve a lot	Improve slightly	Remain the same	Deteriorate slightly	Deteriorate a lot	Optimism factor	Don't know
	Feb	2	19	27	28	15	-22	10
	Mar	3	23	26	24	17	-15	9
	Apr	2	20	30	29	13	-20	7
	May	3	19	33	23	12	-13	10
	Jun	1	17	27	28	20	-30	7
	Jul	2	19	26	30	13	-22	9
	Aug	2	22	28	26	13	-15	9
	Sep	2	20	26	27	16	-21	8
	Oct	1	16	24	31	21	-35	8
	Nov	2	18	26	29	17	-26	7
	Dec	1	15	30	31	16	-31	6
1990	Jan	1	18	26	32	17	-30	6
	Feb	2	15	26	30	20	-33	7
	Mar	1	13	21	29	27	-42	9
	Apr	1	16	23	29	24	-36	7
	May	3	17	26	28	21	-29	6
	Jun	1	18	27	28	19	-28	8
	Jul	3	21	27	25	17	-18	6
	Aug	2	14	21	30	24	-38	9
	Sep	1	16	27	28	22	-33	6
	Oct	3	26	26	22	15	-8	8
	Nov	2	21	20	26	24	-27	8
	Dec	4	34	26	17	11	10	8
1991	Jan	2	20	25	26	19	-23	8
	Feb	2	23	22	24	22	-21	7
	Mar	3	27	25	20	17	-7	8
	Apr	3	36	24	19	11	9	7
	May	2	29	22	24	14	-7	9
	Jun	3	29	27	24	12	-4	5
	Jul	1	27	26	26	12	-10	7
	Aug	2	33	26	20	11	4	8
	Sep	4	37	26	17	9	15	7
	Oct	3	30	30	18	9	6	10
	Nov	2	34	29	17	8	11	9
	Dec	1	32	32	19	8	6	8
1992	Jan	2	25	32	20	11	-4	9
	Feb	1	24	32	22	11	-8	10
	Mar	2	31	31	16	5	12	14
	Apr	5	38	30	13	8	22	5
	May	5	43	25	14	8	26	6
	Jun	2	31	36	17	7	9	7
	Jul	0	23	36	23	12	-12	6

cont'd . . .

		Improve a lot	Improve slightly	Remain the same	Deteriorate slightly	Deteriorate a lot	Optimism factor	Don't know
	Aug	1	15	34	29	17	-30	5
	Sep	1	18	26	27	22	-30	6
	Oct	1	13	21	25	33	-44	7
	Nov	0	15	24	29	25	-39	6
	Dec	1	21	29	30	17	-25	3
1993	Jan	1	27	31	20	16	-8	4
	Feb	1	22	28	26	20	-23	4
	Mar	2	20	30	24	18	-20	6
	Apr	2	27	25	25	18	-14	4
	May	2	33	28	19	13	3	5
	Jun	1	28	33	23	13	-7	3
	Jul	1	26	32	21	13	-7	7
	Aug	2	30	31	21	11	0	6
	Sep	1	27	30	20	16	-8	5
	Oct	1	26	29	23	14	-10	6
	Nov	1	21	33	25	14	-17	5
	Dec	2	23	27	27	16	-18	6
1994	Jan	2	25	34	19	13	-5	8
	Feb	2	23	30	21	17	-13	7
	Mar	1	20	27	29	18	-26	5
	Apr	0	18	29	29	17	-28	6
	May	1	23	28	26	15	-17	7
	Jun	1	21	32	24	14	-16	7
	Jul	1	23	33	24	13	-13	6
	Aug	1	26	33	23	9	-5	7
	Sep	2	24	33	24	12	-10	6
	Oct	1	22	35	24	11	-12	7
	Nov	1	23	32	26	9	-11	9
	Dec	1	19	31	28	14	-18	8
1995	Jan	1	23	34	26	10	-15	7
	Feb	1	21	32	25	13	-16	7
	Mar	2	15	34	30	13	-22	6
	Apr	3	23	38	22	9	-6	7
	May	1	18	38	26	10	-17	7
	Jun	1	19	38	26	10	-16	6
	Jul	1	20	35	27	8	-14	9
	Aug	2	19	37	23	13	-15	7
	Sep	0	22	37	25	7	-10	9
	Oct	1	20	35	26	10	-15	7
	Nov	1	20	36	24	10	-13	10
	Dec	1	22	34	24	11	-10	7
1996	Jan	1	19	38	24	9	-14	9
	Feb	1	20	35	25	10	-14	8

cont'd . . .

	Improve a lot	Improve slightly	Remain the same	Deteriorate slightly	Deteriorate a lot	Optimism factor	Don't know
Mar	1	19	37	24	10	-15	9
Apr	2	19	33	24	11	-11	11
May	1	22	35	25	8	-2	9

CHAPTER 17
Specific Events

Most of the chapters in this book are concerned with reporting lengthy time-series. However, there have been a large number of specific events since the late 1930s that have been important at the time and that have had serious political repercussions. This chapter sets out Gallup's findings in connection with many of these events. The data include the public's responses to international crises, such as the Suez crisis of 1956 and the Vietnam War, and to more purely domestic events, such as the Profumo affair of 1963 and Margaret Thatcher's fall in 1990.

In connection with this chapter, two points should be stressed. The first is that a few of the events covered in the chapter passed so quickly that there was no time for Gallup or any other polling organization to go into the field and ask appropriate questions about them. An obvious result is that some of the findings are not as comprehensive as one would like and will inevitably leave historians, in particular, feeling somewhat dissatisfied. The second is that the best way of assessing the public's response to a wide range of events is not to ask people about the events themselves but to note how they respond to other survey questions, notably the standard voting-intention question and the two questions that ask respondents to assess the performance of the government in general and the Prime Minister in particular.

'Black Wednesday' on 16 September 1992, when John Major's Conservative government was compelled to withdraw Britain from the European Exchange Rate Mechanism, illustrates both points. The crisis came and went so rapidly that the opinion polls were able to conduct surveys devoted to it only after the event, though the results of those surveys are certainly revealing. But even more revealing are Gallup's findings in connection with voting intention, approval/disapproval of the government's record to date and satisfaction/dissatisfaction with the incumbent Prime Minister. As can be seen in Tables 1.1, 1.2, 6.1 and 7.1 above, the Conservative Party, the Major government and John Major himself all suffered sharp – in some cases, spectacular – declines in popular approval between August 1992 and October 1992. Anyone reading the tables, even without any knowledge of Black Wednesday, would inevitably surmise that some terrible event must have occurred during September 1992 to produce results as dire as these.

TABLE 17.1: SATISFACTION WITH GOVERNMENT'S CONDUCT OF THE WAR 1939–45

Q. In general, are you satisfied or dissatisfied with the Government's conduct of the war?

		Satisfied	Dissatisfied	Don't know
1939	Nov	61	18	21
1940	Feb	59	19	22
1941	Jun	58	30	12
	Aug	61	25	14
	Oct	44	38	18
1942	Mar	35	50	15
	Apr	50	38	12
	May	63	24	13
	Jun	57	26	17
	Jul	42	41	17
	Aug	45	38	17
	Sep	41	37	22
	Oct	49	35	16
	Nov	75	17	8
	Dec	75	19	6
1943	Jan	72	20	8
	Mar	76	15	9
	Jun	75	13	12
	Aug	81	12	7
	Nov	74	17	9
1944	Jan	69	16	15
	Mar	70	19	11
	Apr	75	16	9
	Jun	80	13	7
	Aug	79	13	8
	Sep	86	8	6
	Oct	81	12	7
1945	Jan	72	20	8
	Feb	77	14	9
	Mar	83	12	5
	Apr	86	9	5
	May	87	10	3

TABLE 17.2: DEVALUATION OF STERLING 1949

Q. Have you heard or read about the devaluation of the pound?
Q. Do you think that, on the whole, its effects are likely to be good or bad?

	Oct 1949	Nov 1949
Good	24	21
Bad	40	44
No effect	4	4
Don't know	28	27
All aware	96	96
Not aware	4	4

TABLE 17.3: THE KOREAN WAR 1950-52

Q. What is your main feeling about the situation in Korea:

	Oct 1950
Fighting should go on till North Koreans are beaten	50
United Nations should try to negotiate a settlement	41
Don't know	9

Q. Do you approve or disapprove of sending British troops to fight in Korea?

	Oct 1950
Approve	63
Disapprove	31
Don't know	6

Q. Do you think that the fighting in Korea will lead to a Third World War?

	Oct 1950
Yes	14
No	57
Don't know	29

Q. Do you think it is likely or unlikely that there will be further fighting in Korea?

	Dec 1953
Likely	22
Unlikely	44
Don't know	34

Q. If the Communists start fighting again, do you think we should continue to help the South Koreans?
Q. If the South Koreans start fighting again, do you think that we should continue to help them?

	Communists start	South Koreans start
DECEMBER 1953		
Should	43	16
Should not	31	57
Don't know	26	27

Q. Do you think that the United Nations should try to unify Korea or leave the situation as it is, with the North Koreans stopping at the truce line?

	Dec 1953
Try to unify	40
Leave	36
Don't know	24

TABLE 17.4: THE SUEZ CRISIS 1956

Q. Do you approve or disapprove of the way the Government has handled the Suez Canal incident?

	Aug 1956	Sep 1956
Approve	59	42
Disapprove	25	40
Don't know	16	18

Q. Some people say that France and Britain should have taken military action against Egypt immediately when Nasser seized the Suez Canal Company and not have wasted all this time talking. Do you think we should or should not have taken military action?

	Sep 1956
Should	22
Should not	65
Don't know	13

Q. Do you think we were right or wrong to take military precautions and step up our military forces in the Mediterranean?

	Sep 1956
Right	69
Wrong	21
Don't know	10

Q. If Egypt will not agree to international control of the Canal, what should we do? Would you approve or disapprove if we were to:

	Approve	Disapprove	Don't know
SEPTEMBER 1956			
Refer the matter to the United Nations?	81	12	7
Tighten up economic and political measures against Egypt?	58	21	21
Encourage pilots in the Suez Canal to leave their jobs?	23	55	22
Call another London Conference?	43	41	16
Accept Egypt's offer to enter into a new international treaty guaranteeing freedom of the Canal to all and let Egypt run the Canal with the help of an advisory board representing the Canal users?	47	34	19

cont'd . . .

	Approve	Dissaprove	Don't know
Give Egypt an ultimatum that unless she agrees to our proposals we will send in troops to occupy the Canal?	34	49	17

Q. If Egypt deliberately interfered with the free passage of shipping in the Suez Canal, should we take military action right away or refer the matter to the United Nations and only act with the United Nations' approval?

	Sep 1956
Take military action	27
Refer to UN	64
Don't know	9

Q. Do you think we were right or wrong to take military action in Egypt?

	Dec 1956
Right	49
Wrong	36
Don't know	15

Q. Having begun military action in Egypt, do you think that Britain and France should have continued until they had occupied the whole Suez Canal zone, or do you agree with their accepting the cease fire?

	Dec 1956
Should have continued	34
Right to accept	53
Don't know	13

TABLE 17.5: THE CUBAN MISSILE CRISIS 1962

Q. Do you think the United States should or should not take military action against Cuba?

	Sep 1962
Should	10
Should not	56
Don't know	34

Q. Do you think that Kennedy/Khrushchev has behaved wisely or not in the Cuban crisis?

	Kennedy	Khrushchev
NOVEMBER 1962		
Has	75	68
Has not	14	14
Don't know	11	18

TABLE 17.6: MACMILLAN AND PROFUMO 1963

Q. Do you think Mr Macmillan did or did not succeed in defending his handling of the Profumo case against his critics?

	Jun 1963
Did succeed	32
Did not	49
Don't know	19

Q. Do you think the steps Mr Macmillan is taking about the security side of the Profumo case are or are not sufficient?

	Jun 1963
Are sufficient	17
Are not	67
Don't know	16

Q. In your opinion, which of these statements applies to Mr Macmillan's handling of the Profumo affair when it came up in March this year?

	Jun 1963
Macmillan should have recognised the security risk right at the start and insisted on Profumo's resignation at that time	52
Macmillan was justified in accepting in good faith Profumo's statement that there was nothing wrong in his association with Miss Keeler	34
Don't know	14

Q. Some people say that Cabinet ministers should be able to lead their private lives as they wish, while other people say that their private lives should be above reproach. Which of these do you agree with?

	Jun 1963
Lead lives as they wish	35
Private lives above reproach	57
Don't know	8

Q. Do you think the Denning Report has or has not cleared members of the Government of serious misdemeanours?

	Oct 1963
Has	31
Has not	37
Don't know	32

Q. Do you think the steps Mr Macmillan took about security in the Profumo case were or were not sufficient?

	Oct 1963
Were sufficient	29
Were not	50
Don't know	21

Q. *Do you think Mr Macmillan and the other members of the Government were or were not justified in accepting Mr Profumo's denial of his association with Miss Keeler?*

	Oct 1963
Were justified	49
Were not	35
Don't know	16

TABLE 17.7: VIETNAM WAR 1965-72

Q. *Do you approve or disapprove of the [recent] American armed action in Vietnam?*

		Approve	Disapprove	Don't know
1964	Sep	41	33	26
1965	Apr	31	41	28
	May	37	36	27
	Jun	36	40	24
	Jul	34	42	24
	Aug	27	38	35
	Dec	27	37	36
1966	Jan	31	45 .	24
	Aug	31	49	20
1966	Dec	30	51	19

(The word 'recent' did not appear in the August and December 1966 question.)

Q. *If the US Government asks Britain to help in the war in South Vietnam what should we do?*

	Dec 1964	Apr 1965
Send troops	10	14
Send war materials only	17	22
Take no part at all	46	50
Don't know	29	15

Q. *Do you think the United States should continue its present efforts in South Vietnam, or should it pull out its forces?*

		Continue	Pull out	Don't know
1965	Apr	40	32	28
	Jul	33	33	34
1966	Jan	35	39	26
	Jun	33	39	28
	Jul	37	40	23
1966	Aug	35	41	24

Q. *Just from what you have heard or read, which of these statements comes closest to the way you, yourself, feel about the United States' war in Vietnam? The US should:*

	Sep 1966	Oct 1966	Jan 1967	Mar 1967	May 1967	Jul 1967	Oct 1969
Begin to withdraw its troops	42	35	42	41	47	45	54
Carry on its present level of fighting	17	24	18	28	15	15	15
Increase the srength of its attacks against North Vietnam	16	13	14	14	14	15	8
Don't know	25	28	26	17	24	25	23

Q. *Is Britain right or wrong to continue its support of US policy in Vietnam?*

		Right	Wrong	Don't know
1966	Jun	40	32	28
	Jul	33	38	29
	Aug	42	37	21
1967	May	38	42	20
	Oct	34	45	21
1969	Dec	28	43	29

Q. *The ex-President of South Vietnam said that America had broken its promises to South Vietnam, let it down and abandoned it to the Communists. Do you agree or disagree with his comments? A lot or a little?*

	May 1975
Agree a lot	22
Agree a little	24
Disagree a little	14
Disagree a lot	15
Don't know	26

TABLE 17.8: DEVALUATION OF STERLING 1967

Q. *Do you think that the Government was right or wrong to devalue the pound?*

Right	41
Wrong	37
Don't know	22

Q. *Mr Heath has described the devaluation as a defeat for Britain. Do you agree or disagree with him?*

Agree	45
Disagree	40
Don't know	15

Q. *In which of these ways do you think you and your family will be affected by devaluation?*

Cost of living will go up	85
Cut down on spending generally	39
Have to meet higher charges on mortgage loan or hire purchase	21
Cut down on spending at Christmas	16
May be unemployed	13
Cut in earnings	13
Give up plans for buying new car	10
No holiday abroad next year	9
Give up plans for buying things for the home	9
Give up plans for moving house	3
Give up plans for marriage	0
None of these	4

TABLE 17.9: COMMON MARKET REFERENDUM 1975

Q. Do you consider we were right or wrong to join the European Community (the Common Market)?

	Right	Wrong	Don't know
IN 1975			
Jan	31	50	19
Early Mar	39	45	16
Mar 5–10	37	42	21
Apr 4–7	43	38	18
Apr 9–14	46	36	18
Apr 17–21	42	38	19
Apr 23–28	42	38	20
Apr 30–May 5	42	42	16
May 7–12	45	37	18
May 14–19	46	39	15
May 21–27	44	40	16
May 29–Jun 2	44	36	20

Q. If the question in the referendum were 'Do you think that the United Kingdom should stay in the European Community (the Common Market)'?, how would you vote?

	Yes, stay in	No, leave	Don't know
Mar 5–10	52	36	12
Apr 4–7	57	31	12
Apr 9–14	60	26	14
Apr 17–21	57	28	15
Apr 23–28	58	30	12
Apr 30–May 5	57	33	10
May 7–12	60	29	11
May 14–19	61	29	10
May 21–27	59	31	10
May 29–Jun 2	61	29	10

Q. If you could vote tomorrow on whether we should stay in the Common Market or leave it, how would you vote or wouldn't you vote at all?

	Jan	Mar
Stay in	33	45
Leave	41	37
Wouldn't vote	12	7
Don't know	14	11

Q. If the Government negotiated new terms for Britain's membership of the Common Market and they thought it was in Britain's interests to remain a member, how would you vote then, to stay in or leave it?

	Jan	Mar
Stay in	53	63
Leave	22	20
Wouldn't vote	6	4
Don't know	19	14

TABLE 17.10: 'WINTER OF DISCONTENT' 1978–79

Q. To what degree do you think trade unions are controlled by Communists?

	Aug 1978	Jan 1979
A great deal	18	25
Considerably	24	26
Little	24	17
Very little	13	11
Not at all	6	8
Don't know	15	13

Q. Would you approve or disapprove if a law were passed which made it illegal for workers to come out on unofficial strike, that is, strike without the support of their unions?

	Aug 1978	Jan 1979
Approve	50	61
Disapprove	35	29
Don't know	15	10

Q. Do you think the country's industrial situation would improve, get worse or not change if we had a Conservative government?

	Feb 1979
Improve	38
Get worse	16
Not change	33
Don't know	13

Q. Do you think the current situation is or is not serious enough for the government to declare a state of emergency?

	Feb 1979
Is	52
Is not	34
Don't know	15

TABLE 17.11: THE FALKLANDS WAR 1982

Q. The Government have been criticised for being 'caught off-guard' by the Argentinians' invasion of the Falkland Islands. Do you think this criticism is justified or not justified?

	Apr 1982
Is	78
Is not	14
Don't know	8

Q. Do you approve or disapprove of the decision to send a British fleet to the Falkland Islands?

	Apr 1982
Approve	78
Disapprove	16
Don't know	6

Q. Do you approve or disapprove of the Government's action in general, following the invasion of the Falkland Islands?

	Apr 1982
Approve	67
Disapprove	24
Don't know	9

Q. *In order to regain the Falkland Islands, would you approve or disapprove of:*

	Approve	Disapprove	Don't know
APRIL 1982			
Attacking the Argentine ships and troops guarding the Falkland Islands?	61	32	7
Attacking mainland Argentina itself?	24	68	8
Cutting off all trade with Argentina?	86	9	5

Q. *In general, do you approve or disapprove of the Government's actions over the Falkland Islands?*

	Apr 1982	May 1982
Approve	76	71
Disapprove	18	24
Don't know	7	5

Q. *Do you think the Government has been tough enough in the negotiations over the Falkland Islands, not tough enough or about right?*

	Apr 1982	May 1982
Too tough	10	17
Not tough enough	24	27
About right	60	51
Don't know	6	6

Q. *Here are some statements people have made about the Falklands situation. Which, if any, of them do you agree with?*

	May 1982	Jun 1982
We have done everything possible to reach a peaceful settlement	58	66
We have done the right thing in invading the Falklands	64	65

cont'd . . .

	May 1982	Jun 1982
The Government was caught off-guard by the Argentinian invasion	65	64
We should have invaded the Falklands sooner	37	35
The lives lost so far are unacceptable circumstances	26	31
We should have continued to negotiate	28	23
We should put more effort into negotiations	26	23
In the long term the Falklands will be given to Argentina	27	22
We should invade Argentina	12	9
None of these	1	1

Q. *I am going to read out some statements and I would like you to tell me whether you agree or disagree with them. Strongly agree/disagree or only somewhat agree/disagree?*

	Agree	Agree strongly	Agree somewhat	Disagree	Disagree strongly	Disagree somewhat
JANUARY 1983						
I have a higher opinion today of Mrs Thatcher because of the Falklands War	19	20	11	18	30	2
The Government should have done more to prevent a war over the Falklands	38	29	4	16	9	4
We should continue to keep forces on a war footing in the Falklands even if it weakens our defence in Europe	19	35	5	15	17	9
It would make sense to try to agree with Argentina on the future of the Falklands	29	36	3	11	15	6

cont'd . . .

	Agree	Agree strongly	Agree somewhat	Disagree	Disagree strongly	Disagree somewhat
It is not worth £424 million a year from now on to keep the Falklands British	30	23	3	16	19	8
The Prime Minister was at least partly to blame for Argentina's invasion of the Falklands	19	28	3	19	23	8
There is no point now in raking over events in the Falklands	26	43	3	15	9	4
Mrs Thatcher has exploited the Falklands for her own political gains	28	22	2	15	26	5

Q. Have you read or heard anything about the sinking of the Argentinian ship, the General Belgrano *during the Falklands War?*

	Sep 1984
Yes	91
No	9

Q. All aware: From what you know about the incident, do you think the Government was right or wrong to order the sinking of the Belgrano?

	Sep 1984
Right	49
Wrong	31
Don't know	20

Q. All aware: Do you think that Mrs Thatcher has or has not told the whole truth about the Belgrano *affair?*

	Sep 1984
Has	16
Has not	65
Don't know	19

TABLE 17.12: MINERS' STRIKE 1984–85

Q. Are your sympathies mainly with the employers or mainly with the miners in the dispute which has arisen in the coal industry?

	Jul 1984	Aug 1984	Nov 1984	Nov 28– Dec 3 1984	Dec 5–10 1984
Employers	40	43	52	52	51
Miners	33	32	26	23	26
Neither	19	18	17	20	18
Don't know	8	6	5	5	5

Q. Do you approve or disapprove of the methods being used at present by the miners?

	Jul 1984	Aug 1984	Nov 1984	Nov 28– Dec 3 1984	Dec 5–10 1984
Approve	15	11	10	4	7
Disapprove	79	85	86	92	88
Don't know	6	4	4	4	5

Q. Do you think that the miners are using responsible or irresponsible methods in the dispute?

	Jul 1984	Aug 1984
Responsible	12	9
Irresponsible	78	84
Don't know	10	7

Q. On the whole, do you think that at the end of the dispute the individual coal miner will be better off, worse off or won't it make any difference?

	Jul 1984	Aug 1984	Nov 1984	Nov 28– Dec 3 1984	Dec 5–10 1984
Better off	12	12	12	13	10
Worse off	50	52	53	56	54
No difference	30	32	30	25	32
Don't know	8	5	4	6	4

Q. *How likely do you think it is that there will be power cuts this winter?*

	Nov 1984	Nov 28–Dec 3 1984	Dec 5–10 1984
Very likely	20	10	9
Quite likely	31	27	28
Not very likely	32	35	33
Not at all likely	14	23	26
Don't know	3	6	5

TABLE 17.13: THE FALL OF MARGARET THATCHER 1990

Q. *Mrs Thatcher has recently said that she would consider remaining Prime Minister until she is 70. Would you like Mrs Thatcher to remain Prime Minister until she is 70 or not?*

	Sep 1990
Yes	18
No	77
Don't know	5

Q. *If Mrs Thatcher were to stand down before the next election, who do you personally think would make the best Prime Minister and leader of the Conservative Party?*

	Sep 1990	Sep 1990
Michael Heseltine	17	30
Norman Tebbit	12	11
Geoffrey Howe	11	7
Douglas Hurd	4	6
Cecil Parkinson	9	4
John Major	2	4
Kenneth Baker	5	3
Chris Patten	1	1
Somebody else	6	3
Don't know	32	31

Q. Do you think that .... would or would not make a good Prime Minister?

	Would	Would not	Don't know
NOVEMBER 14–19			
Michael Heseltine	47	35	18
Geoffrey Howe	31	52	17
Kenneth Baker	8	70	22
John Major	21	55	24

Q. If .... were leader of the Conservative Party and Prime Minister rather than Mrs Thatcher, would that make you more inclined to vote for the Conservatives at the next election, less inclined or would it make no difference?

	Nov 15–16	Nov 17–19
MICHAEL HESELTINE		
More	33	27
Less	10	10
No difference	54	59
Don't know	3	3
GEOFFREY HOWE		
More	20	15
Less	20	19
No difference	56	63
Don't know	4	4

	Nov 15-16	Nov 17-19
DOUGLAS HURD		
More	10	11
Less	25	20
No difference	60	64
Don't know	5	5
JOHN MAJOR		
More	11	11
Less	22	19
No difference	61	65
Don't know	6	5
NORMAN TEBBIT		
More	11	10

cont'd . . .

	Nov 15-16	Nov 17-19
Less	28	26
No difference	58	60
Don't know	3	4

Q. As you probably know, Mrs Thatcher got more votes than Mr Heseltine on the first ballot, but not enough to win outright under the Conservative Party's rules. In your view, should Mrs Thatcher now contest the second ballot or should she stand down and make way for Michael Heseltine or someone else?

	Nov 17-19
Should contest second ballot	38
Should stand down for Mr Heseltine	27
Should stand down for someone else	31
Don't know	4

Q. Who would you like to see as leader of the Conservative Party and Prime Minister, Mrs Thatcher, Mr Heseltine, Mr Hurd, Mr Major or Sir Geoffrey Howe?

	Nov 21-22
Mrs Thatcher	22
Michael Heseltine	37
Douglas Hurd	11
John Major	3
Geoffrey Howe	12
Don't know	14

Q. Who would you personally like to see succeed Mrs Thatcher as leader of the Conservative Party and Prime Minister?

	Nov 23-24	Nov 24-26
Michael Heseltine	44	38
Douglas Hurd	19	12
John Major	27	37
Don't know	10	12

Q. And who would be your second choice if Mr .... were not elected?

	Nov 23-24	Nov 24-26
Michael Heseltine	15	18
Douglas Hurd	32	29
John Major	30	33
Don't know	23	21

Q. Do you think the struggle for the leadership has done the Conservative Party a great deal of damage, some damage, a little damage or no damage at all?

	Nov 24-26
A great deal	38
Some	34
A little	13
None at all	13
Don't know	2

Q. Which of the three candidates in the leadership election – Mr Heseltine, Mr Hurd and Mr Major – do you feel would be the most likely to reunite the Conservative Party?
Q. And which of the candidates would be the least likely to reunite the Conservative Party?

	Most	Least
NOVEMBER 24-26		
Heseltine	29	41
Hurd	23	28
Major	37	15
Don't know	11	16

Q. Which of the following phrases do you feel apply to:

	Michael Heseltine	Douglas Hurd	John Major
NOVEMBER 24-26			
Experienced	64	69	34
Cold and distant	17	34	12
Caring	34	33	46
Ambitious for himself	77	36	47
Strong forceful personality	70	19	24

cont'd . . .

	Michael Heseltine	Douglas Hurd	John Major
Cautious	18	58	43
Not to be trusted	36	23	16
Sincere	35	40	50
Not experienced	9	6	44
Warm and friendly	28	23	41
Dull and colourless	13	50	19
Willing to take risks	72	18	24
Not ambitious for himself	6	24	14
Uncaring	18	17	11
Can be trusted	34	40	48
Insincere	25	17	12
Far-sighted and imaginative	43	18	34
Weak personality	9	31	19

Q. *How do you feel about Mrs Thatcher's resignation? Are you, on balance, sad about it or pleased about it?*

	Nov 24-26
Sad	39
Pleased	48
Neither	12
Don't know	1

Q. *Do you think that on balance Mrs Thatcher was right to resign or should she have tried to stay on?*

	Nov 24-26
Was right to resign	74
Should have tried to stay on	24
Don't know	2

Q. *There is general agreement that Sir Winston Churchill, President John F. Kennedy and President Gorbachev have been amongst the great world leaders since the war. Do you think Mrs Thatcher deserves to be ranked alongside them or not?*

	Nov 24-26
Yes, does	59
No, does not	37
Don't know	4

Q. Which of each of the following do you think Mrs Thatcher has brought to Britain?

	Nov 24-26
More discord	60
More harmony	31
Don't know	9
More error	43
More truth	47
Don't know	11
More doubt	55
More faith	36
Don't know	9
More despair	55
More hope	36
Don't know	9

Q. People's views about Mrs Thatcher differ. On balance do you think she was good for Britain or bad for Britain?

	Nov 24-26
Good	59
Bad	34
Don't know	7

TABLE 17.14: GERMAN REUNIFICATION 1990

Q. From the point of view of the Germans, is it better for Germany to be divided or united?

	Nov 1989	Feb 1990
Divided	22	16
United	64	73
Don't know	14	11

Q. From the point of view of Europe as a whole, is it better for Germany to be divided or united?

	Nov 1989	Feb 1990
Divided	27	25
United	55	61
Don't know	18	14

cont'd . . .

Q. *How likely do you think it is that Germany will be united within the next 5 years: very likely, fairly likely, not very likely or not at all likely?*

	Nov 1989	Feb 1990
Very likely	24	56
Fairly likely	34	29
Not very likely	22	6
Not at all likely	12	2
Don't know	9	7

Q. *How likely do you think it is that Germany will be united within the next 10 years: very likely, fairly likely, not very likely or not at all likely?*

	Nov 1989	Feb 1990
Very likely	47	77
Fairly likely	32	15
Not very likely	7	1
Not at all likely	4	0
Don't know	10	6

Q. *How likely do you think it is that Germany will be united within the next 15 years: very likely, fairly likely, not very likely or not at all likely?*

	Nov 1989	Feb 1990
Very likely	64	86
Fairly likely	19	6
Not very likely	4	0
Not at all likely	2	1
Don't know	11	7

Q. *Assuming that West and East Germany were to be united and thinking of the long run, do you think that the united Germany would ally themselves with Western Europe, with Eastern Europe and Russia or be neutral?*

	Nov 1989	Feb 1990
Western Europe	36	39
Eastern Europe	7	4

cont'd . . .

	Nov 1989	Feb 1990
Neutral	34	35
Don't know	22	21

Q. Do you think that a united Germany would or would not pose an economic threat to Western Europe?

	Nov 1989	Feb 1990
Would	42	42
Would not	42	43
Don't know	16	15

Q. Do you think that a united Germany would or would not pose a military threat?

	Nov 1989	Feb 1990
Would	34	29
Would not	50	55
Don't know	17	16

TABLE 17.15: THE GULF WAR 1990–91

Q. As you probably know, President Bush of the United States has sent armed forces to Saudi Arabia and the Gulf to try to prevent an Iraqi invasion of Saudi Arabia. From what you have heard, do you approve or disapprove of President Bush's action?

	Aug 1990
Approve	85
Disapprove	10
Don't know	5

Q. *The British Government has also sent units of the navy and air force to Saudi Arabia to try and prevent an Iraqi invasion. From what you have heard, do you approve or disapprove of the British Government's action?*

	Aug 1990
Approve	88
Disapprove	9
Don't know	3

Q. *In any blockade of Iraq, should shipments of food and medical supplies be allowed to go through, or should they be stopped?*

	Aug 1990
Allowed to go through	57
Stopped	37
Don't know	6

Q. *Suppose the choice facing Britain and America were between an all-out military assault on Iraq and an economic blockade that might have to last for a very long time, which policy would you like to see Britain and America pursuing, the military assault or the blockade?*

		Military assault	Blockade	Don't know
1990	Aug 29–Sep 3	25	67	8
	Sep 12–18	27	63	10
	Sep 20–25	31	56	13
	Sep 26–Oct 2	28	60	12
	Oct 4–9	29	57	13
	Oct 10–15	32	57	11

		Military assault	Blockade	Don't know
	Oct 18–23	27	61	12
	Oct 25–30	29	61	10
	Oct 31–Nov 5	30	56	14
	Nov 7–13	33	57	10
	Nov 15–20	33	56	11
	Nov 21–27	31	58	12
	Nov 28–Dec 4	34	53	13
1990	Dec 4–11	31	55	14

Q. As you know, Britain and America hope to achieve their aims by means of an economic blockade alone. If after a period of time that policy looks like failing, would you personally be in favour of military action against Iraq or not?

		In favour	Not in favour	Don't know
1990	Aug 29–Sep 3	67	25	8
	Sep 12–18	61	30	10
	Sep 20–25	66	25	10
	Sep 26–Oct 2	63	26	11
	Oct 4–9	63	27	10
	Oct 10–15	60	31	9
	Oct 18–23	62	28	9
	Oct 25–30	62	29	9
	Oct 31–Nov 5	60	32	8
	Nov 7–13	60	29	10
	Nov 15–20	63	30	7
	Nov 21–27	63	29	8
	Nov 28–Dec 4	60	29	10
1990	Dec 4–11	61	29	10

Q. There are a number of different purposes for which British forces might be used in the Gulf crisis. Could you tell me for each of the following whether you support the use of British forces or not?

DSA   The defence of Saudi Arabia and the Gulf States
RIK   Restoring independence to Kuwait
TSH   Toppling Saddam Hussein's regime in Iraq
DI   The defence of Israel if attacked
PW   Protect the West's oil supplies

S   Support
DS   Don't support
DK   Don't know

		DSA			RIK			TSH			DI			PW		
		S	DS	DK	S	DS	DK	S	DS	DK	S	DS	DK	S	DS	DK
1990	Aug 29–Sep 3	86	10	4	84	11	5	68	26	5	66	22	12	87	9	4
	Sep 12–18	74	19	8	75	15	9	68	22	10	59	25	16	78	13	8
	Sep 20–25	74	17	9	76	14	10	67	21	12	61	23	16	78	13	10
	Sep 26–Oct 2	75	15	9	74	13	13	70	19	10	60	23	17	76	10	10
	Oct 4–9	75	18	7	75	16	9	67	24	9	60	25	15	76	15	9
	Oct 10–15	73	18	9	73	18	8	65	26	10	52	30	18	76	15	9
	Oct 18–23	69	21	9	72	19	9	68	23	9	48	30	22	73	17	9
	Oct 25–30	73	18	9	74	16	10	66	23	11	54	29	17	76	17	7
	Oct 31–Nov 5	71	21	9	73	19	8	64	25	11	47	33	19	73	19	8

cont'd . . .

		DSA			RIK			TSH			DI			PW		
		S	DS	DK	S	DS	DK	S	DS	DK	S	DS	DK	S	DS	DK
	Nov 7–13	72	20	8	72	19	10	66	24	10	52	31	17	72	18	10
	Nov 15–20	70	21	9	70	17	10	65	25	10	53	28	18	73	19	8
	Nov 21–27	71	20	9	76	15	9	65	24	11	53	26	21	72	17	11
	Nov 28–Dec 4	67	22	11	68	21	10	62	28	10	49	34	17	67	23	10
	Dec 4–11	66	22	12	69	20	11	62	27	11	47	33	20	69	20	11
1991	Jan 4–7	74	17	9	82	12	7	67	25	7	53	31	16	76	15	9

Q. If Britain and America did decide to use force against Iraq, could you tell me for each of the following whether you would be in favour of it or opposed to it?

FS   Firing at ships seeking to break the blockade
BM   Bombing military targets in Iraq from the air
BC   Bombing civilian targets in Iraq from the air
GT   Using ground troops to invade Iraq and Kuwait
CW   Using chemical weapons if the Iraqis use chemical weapons first
NW   Using nuclear weapons if the Iraqis use chemical weapons first

IF   In Favour
O   Opposed
DK   Don't know

		FS			BM			BC			GT			CW			NW		
		IF	O	DK	IF	O	DK	IF	O	DK	IF	O	DK	IF	O	DK	IF	O	DK
1990	Aug 29–Sep 3	78	18	4	75	20	5	10	86	3	74	21	5	32	64	3	26	70	4
	Sep 12–18	61	28	11	65	26	9	6	88	6	67	25	8	23	69	8	16	77	7
	Sep 20–25	63	25	11	67	24	10	10	83	7	65	24	11	24	67	9	22	68	9
	Sep 26–Oct 2	58	31	11	66	25	9	9	82	9	67	22	11	27	65	8	22	69	9
	Oct 4–9	62	28	10	65	26	8	10	83	7	67	25	8	23	70	7	20	73	7
	Oct 10–15	61	28	11	62	28	9	8	87	6	65	25	10	23	70	8	18	74	8
	Oct 18–23	61	28	11	63	28	9	9	84	7	63	26	10	24	69	7	19	72	9
	Oct 25–30	63	27	10	66	26	8	9	84	7	67	26	8	25	67	8	19	74	8
	Oct 31–Nov 5	61	29	10	65	27	9	9	84	7	65	26	9	26	67	8	20	72	8
	Nov 7–13	63	28	10	65	27	8	10	84	6	64	27	9	26	66	8	22	70	7
	Nov 15–20	63	26	11	66	27	7	7	86	7	67	24	9	25	69	6	22	71	7
	Nov 21–27	60	29	11	67	26	7	9	85	7	69	24	7	26	68	6	20	72	8
	Nov 28–Dec 4	61	28	11	63	28	9	10	81	8	61	29	10	25	66	10	19	72	9
	Dec 4–11	60	28	12	63	28	9	10	81	9	63	27	10	22	70	8	21	70	8
1991	Jan 4–7	67	24	9	76	20	4	11	83	6	74	20	7	33	60	7	36	56	8

Question in January 1991 read 'Using nuclear weapons if the Iraqis use nuclear weapons first.'

Q. *There are two views about the line that Britain and America should take, given that large numbers of Britons and Americans are now being held hostage in Kuwait and Iraq. Which of these two statements comes closest to your own view?*

If necessary, Britain and America should be ready to take military action against Iraq even if it means putting the
   lives of British and American hostages at some degree of risk
Britain and America should not under any circumstances take military action against Iraq if it means putting the
   lives of British and American hostages at some degree of risk
Don't know

		If necessary . . .	Britain and America . . .	Don't Know
1990	Aug 29–Sep 3	63	31	6
	Sep 12–18	58	35	7
	Sep 20–25	58	32	10
	Sep 26–Oct 2	60	30	10
	Oct 4–9	55	35	10
	Oct 10–15	55	37	8
	Oct 18–23	57	35	9
	Oct 25–30	56	37	8
	Oct 31–Nov 5	51	39	10
	Nov 7–13	55	35	10
	Nov 15–20	55	37	8
	Nov 21–27	56	36	7
	Nov 28–Dec4	56	39	6
1990	Dec 4–11	50	38	12

Q. *How likely would you say it is that a major shooting war will break out in the Middle East? Very likely, quite likely or not at all likely?*

		Very likely	Quite likely	Not at all likely	Don't know
1990	Aug 29–Sep 3	39	47	10	4
	Sep 12–18	26	48	18	8
	Sep 20–25	31	48	13	8
	Sep 26–Oct 2	31	49	13	8
	Oct 4–9	32	43	17	8
	Oct 10–15	27	48	17	8
	Oct 18–23	22	49	23	7
	Oct 25–30	24	50	19	8
	Oct 31–Nov 5	33	46	15	6
	Nov 7–13	40	44	10	5
	Nov 15–20	33	47	13	7
	Nov 21–27	35	45	14	7
	Nov 28–Dec 4	38	46	9	7
1990	Dec 4–11	25	44	22	9

Q. *If a major shooting war did break out in the Middle East, how likely is the possibility of it spreading to other parts of the world? Very likely, quite likely or not at all likely?*

		Very likely	Quite likely	Not at all likely	Don't know
1990	Aug 29–Sep 3	17	30	48	5
	Sep 12–18	16	30	47	7
	Sep 20–25	14	32	44	9
	Sep 26–Oct 2	16	26	47	11
	Oct 4–9	19	28	46	8
	Oct 10–15	16	28	48	8
	Oct 18–23	17	31	45	7
	Oct 25–30	16	29	47	9
	Oct 31–Nov 5	15	30	47	8
	Nov 7–13	16	30	45	9
	Nov 15–20	17	29	47	8
	Nov 21–27	14	26	50	10
	Nov 28–Dec 4	16	25	49	10
1990	Dec 4–11	15	29	48	9

Q. *Do you think the present crisis in the Middle East will be over quite soon, or do you think it is likely to go on for a long time?*

		Will be over quite soon	Will go on for a long time	Don't know
1990	Aug 29–Sep 3	20	72	8
	Sep 12–18	16	75	9
	Sep 20–25	14	77	9
	Sep 26–Oct 2	14	76	10
	Oct 4–9	18	73	9
	Oct 10–15	16	75	9
	Oct 18–23	17	75	8
	Oct 25–30	21	71	9
	Oct 31–Nov 5	24	66	11
	Nov 7–13	23	67	10
	Nov 15–20	25	67	10
	Nov 21–27	27	63	10
	Nov 28–Dec 4	27	64	9
1990	Dec 4–11	35	65	10

Q. *One of Britain's aims, as you may know, is to restore independence to Kuwait. To achieve that objective, do you support* .....

	Yes	No	Don't know
AUGUST 1990			
The imposing of an all-out economic blockade of Iraq?	81	11	8
The bombing of civilian and military targets in Iraq by conventional means?	38	46	16
The limited use of nuclear weapons on military targets?	18	72	9

Q. *Do you on the whole approve or disapprove of the British Government's handling of the Gulf crisis so far?*

	Sep 1990	Oct 1990
Approve	70	65
Disapprove	21	24
Don't know	9	11

Q. *If the United Nations deadline expires on January 15 and Iraq has not left Kuwait, do you think Britain, America and the other allies in the Gulf should:*

	Aug 1990
Try to free Kuwait by force	49
Give the UN blockade of Iraq more time to work	43
Don't know	8

Q. If there was a war in the Gulf, do you think it would last a few days, a few weeks, a few months or even longer?

	Jan 1991
Few days	6
Few weeks	24
Few months	32
Longer	30
Don't know	8

Q. If there was a war, should Britain, America and the other allies restrict themselves to trying to free Kuwait or should they try both to free Kuwait and topple Saddam Hussein's regime in Iraq?

	Jan 1991
Free Kuwait only	26
And topple Saddam Hussein	65
Don't know	9

Q. The Gulf crisis is sometimes compared with the invasion of the Falklands nine years ago. Do you think what happens in the Gulf is more important to Britain than the Falklands were, less important or are they of both the same importance?

	Jan 1991
More important	54
Less important	10
About the same	30
Don't know	6

Q. Taking everything into account, are you satisfied or dissatisfied with the Government's handling of the situation in the Gulf? Very or only somewhat?

	Jan 4–7 1991	Jan 31– Feb 4 1991	Feb 6–11 1991	Feb 13–18 1991	Feb 20–26 1991	Feb 25– Mar 1 1991
Very satisfied	47	44	39	43	48	55
Somewhat satisfied	32	35	36	32	31	25
Neither satisfied/dissatisfied	7	6	8	9	6	6
Somewhat dissatisfied	7	6	9	8	8	7
Very dissatisfied	7	5	8	9	7	6

Q. Do you think America, Britain and the other allies were right or wrong to launch an assault on Iraq once the UN deadline for Iraqi withdrawal from Kuwait had passed?

	Jan 4–7 1991	Jan 31– Feb 4 1991	Feb 6–11 1991	Feb 13–18 1991	Feb 20–26 1991	Feb 25– Mar 1 1991
Right	80	79	76	76	82	82
Wrong	15	16	18	18	13	13
Don't know	5	5	6	6	5	6

Q. If the present air bombardment does not cause Iraq to withdraw from Kuwait, would you support or not support the use of allied ground forces against Iraq?

	Jan 4–7 1991	Jan 31– Feb 4 1991	Feb 6–11 1991	Feb 13–18 1991	Feb 20–26 1991	Feb 25– Mar 1 1991
Support	81	82	79	78	82	79
Not support	12	11	14	15	12	10
Don't know	7	6	7	6	6	10

Q. Once Iraq has been removed from Kuwait, should the allies cease hostilities at once, or should they attempt to destroy Iraq's war-making capacity completely?

	Jan 4–7 1991	Jan 31– Feb 4 1991	Feb 6–11 1991	Feb 13–18 1991	Feb 20–26 1991	Feb 25– Mar 1 1991
Cease hostilities at once	34	33	43	48	34	29
Attempt to destroy Iraq's war-making capacity	54	58	44	43	55	55
Don't know	12	9	13	9	11	16

Q. Do you think that America and her other allies were right to dismiss the Iraqi peace initiatives out of hand as they did, or should they have taken them more seriously and considered opening negotiations on the basis of them?

	Mar 1991
Right to dismiss	73
Taken more seriously	19
Don't know	8

TABLE 17.16: 'BLACK WEDNESDAY' 1992

Q. How do you think the general economic situation in this country has changed over the last 12 months?

	Sep 1992	Oct 1992
Got a lot better	1	0
Got a little better	4	2
Stayed the same	17	9
Got a little worse	32	26
Got a lot worse	45	61
Don't know	1	1

Q. How do you think the level of unemployment (I mean the number of people out of work) in the country as a whole, will change over the next 12 months? Will it .....

	Sep 1992	Oct 1992
Increase sharply	31	44
Increase slightly	44	35
Remain the same	14	9
Fall slightly	8	8
Fall sharply	1	2
Don't know	2	2

Q. Do you think the Conservative Party has .....?

	May 1992	Oct 1992
Clear policies	54	35
Vague policies	32	55
Neither, both	6	5
Don't know	8	4

Q. Taking everything into account, do you think Mr Major/Mr Lamont handled the recent currency crisis very well, fairly well, not very well or not at all well?

	Major	Lamont
SEPTEMBER 1992		
Very well	6	5
Fairly well	28	25
Not very well	28	27
Not at all well	34	38
Don't know	3	6

Q. Do you think that, when the British economy does come out of recession, it will be in fundamentally better shape than it was before, or do you think it will have suffered serious long-term damage?

	Sep 1992
Better shape	15
Long-term damage	75
Don't know	10

TABLE 17.17: BOSNIA 1993–96

Q. Taking everything into account, are you satisfied or dissatisfied with the Government's handling of the situation in Bosnia, part of former Yugoslavia? Very or only somewhat?

	Feb 1993	Aug 1993	Jan 1994	1–6 Jun 1995	8–13 Jun 1995	Aug 1995	Oct 1995	Jan 1996
Very satisfied	5	4	7	4	8	2	6	7
Somewhat satisfied	33	28	26	26	27	20	29	31
Neither satisfied nor dissatisfied	19	21	16	19	19	20	23	20
Somewhat dissatisfied	26	27	25	27	25	30	24	25
Very dissatisfied	17	19	24	22	21	25	14	14
Don't know	5	0	2	1	8	2	3	3

cont'd . . .

Q. *From what you know about the civil war in Bosnia, who do you sympathize with more, the Bosnian Serbs or the Bosnian Muslims or the Bosnian Croats?*

	Apr 1993	Jun 1993	Aug 1993
Serbs	10	3	5
Muslims	32	20	17
Croats	–	4	3
All groups	9	19	23
None of them	21	25	25
Don't know	29	29	26

'Bosnian Croats' not included in April study.

Q. *Do you approve or disapprove of the use of British troops in Bosnia to protect humanitarian convoys?*

	Apr 1993	Jun 1993	Aug 1993	Jan 1994	1–6 Jun 1995	8–13 Jun 1995	Oct 1995
Approve	72	67	73	74	62	64	72
Disapprove	20	25	21	21	27	26	20
Don't know	8	7	7	6	11	10	9

Q. *If the British troops protecting the aid convoys suffered serious casualties, should we pull them out, continue to limit them to fighting back only when they are attacked or take steps to reinforce them?*

	Apr 1993	Jun 1993	Aug 1993	Jan 1994	1–6 Jun 1995	8–13 Jun 1995	Oct 1995
Pull them out	32	39	36	32	38	39	30
Limit	17	17	16	16	16	14	16
Reinforce	43	34	41	43	35	38	43
Don't know	8	10	6	8	11	9	11

Q. *From what you know, do you think it would or would not be possible for an international force – sponsored possibly by the UN – to enforce a peace settlement in Bosnia?*

	Apr 1993	Jun 1993	Aug 1993	1–6 Jun 1995	8–13 Jun 1995
Would	47	37	46	46	41
Would not	30	43	34	36	38
Don't know	22	19	20	18	20

Q. *From what you know, do you think it would be desirable or not to send in an international force to try to enforce a peace settlement in Bosnia?*

	Apr 1993	Jun 1993	Aug 1993	1–6 Jun 1995	8–13 Jun 1995
Would	61	50	57	75	62
Would not	22	32	29	17	24
Don't know	16	18	14	8	14

Q. *If an international force were trying to enforce a peace settlement in Bosnia, would you personally like to see British troops forming part of that force or not?*

	Apr 1993	Jun 1993	Aug 1993	1–6 Jun 1995	8–13 Jun 1995
Yes	67	64	69	75	62
No	22	25	21	17	24
Don't know	11	11	10	8	14

Q. *If an international force went into Bosnia to try to enforce a settlement, do you think it would have to be a very large force, or do you think a relatively small number of troops would be sufficient?*

	Apr 1993	Jun 1993	Aug 1993
Very large	68	69	69
Small number	17	14	18
Don't know	15	18	13

Q. *Do you think the civil war in Yugoslavia could lead to a wider war in the Balkans or not? The Balkans includes Yugoslavia, Romania, Bulgaria, Albania, Greece and part of Turkey.*

	Apr 1993	Jun 1993	Aug 1993
Yes	62	60	58
No	22	22	27
Don't know	16	18	15

Q. Do you think the civil war in Yugoslavia poses a threat to the peace of Europe outside the Balkans or not?

	Apr 1993	Jun 1993	Aug 1993
Yes	46	48	43
No	42	37	45
Don't know	13	15	13

Q. Overall do you think Britain and other European countries should be involved in the Bosnian conflict in any way or should we just leave the Bosnians to fight it out?

	Apr 1993	Jun 1993	Aug 1993	1–6 Jun 1995	8–13 Jun 1995
Should be involved	61	56	59	65	54
Should leave them	28	31	30	26	36
Don't know	11	13	11	10	10

Q. Do you approve or disapprove of the use of British troops in Bosnia for peacekeeping purposes?

	Jan 1996
Approve	65
Disapprove	28
Don't know	8

Q. If the British troops in Bosnia suffered serious casualties, should we pull them out, continue to limit them to fighting back only when they are attacked or take steps to reinforce them?

	Jan 1996
Pull them out	43
Limit	15
Reinforce	35
Don't know	8

Q. As far as you know, how many British casualties have there been in Bosnia so far?

	Jan 1996
Very many	1
A fair number	16
Very few	54
Don't know	29

Q. As the situation continues, do you think there will be very many British casualties, a fair number or very few?

	Jan 1996
Very many	6
A fair number	26
Very few	50
Don't know	18

Q. Do you approve or disapprove of the way Mr Major is handling the situation in Bosnia? Is that approve/disapprove strongly or somewhat?

	Jul 1996
Strongly approve	9
Somewhat approve	36
Somewhat disapprove	16
Strongly disapprove	7
Don't know	32

Q. Do you approve or disapprove of Mr Major's decision to send troops to Bosnia? Is that approve/disapprove strongly or somewhat?

	Jul 1996
Strongly approve	19
Somewhat approve	40
Somewhat disapprove	15
Strongly disapprove	13
Don't know	14

Q. Do you think the United Nations should use military force to settle the situation in Bosnia or should it stay out?

	Jul 1996
Yes, use force	46
No, stay out	38
Don't know	16

Q. Would you say that the British military effort in Bosnia has been completely successful, mostly successful, only somewhat successful or not at all successful?

	Jul 1996
Completely successful	3
Mostly successful	27
Somewhat successful	44
Not at all successful	10
Don't know	17

TABLE 17.18: KOSOVO 1999

Q. As you know, the NATO allies, including Britain, are currently taking military action against Serbia and Yugoslavia because of what has been happening in Kosovo. On balance, do you approve or disapprove of the action the NATO allies are taking?

	Mar 1999	Apr 1999	May 1999
Approve	58	72	67
Disapprove	33	23	28
Neither	3	2	2
Don't know	6	2	3

Q. Before the NATO military action began, do you think there was or was not enough public debate and discussion, including in Parliament, in this country?

	Mar 1999
Was enough	29
Was not	60
Don't know	10

Q. Do you think aerial bombardment on its own will be enough to force the Serbian leader, Mr Milosevic to grant autonomy to Kosovo, or will the NATO allies eventually have to consider using ground troops?

	Mar 1999
Enough on its own	16
Ground troops	70
Don't know	14

Q. *If the NATO allies decide they need to use ground troops, would you approve or disapprove of the use of such troops including British soldiers?*

	Mar 1999
Approve	52
Disapprove	40
Neither	2
Don't know	6

Q. *Do you think there is or is not a serious danger that the present fighting in the former Yugoslavia will spill over into neighbouring countries?*

	Mar 1999
Yes	73
No	20
Don't know	7

Q. *Which of these two statements comes closer to your own view?*

	Mar 1999
Recent Serb actions in Kosovo have been unfortunate, even tragic, but in the end they are really an internal matter for Serbia	23
Recent Serb actions in Kosovo constitute a humanitarian outrage and should not be tolerated by the outside world	69
Neither	3
Don't know	6

Q. *Do you think peace and stability to Kosovo is or is not worth the lives of any British airmen and soldiers?*

	Mar 1999
Is	51
Is not	40
Don't know	10

Q. *Considering all aspects of the NATO campaign so far, on balance do you believe that it has been competently or incompetently managed?*

	May 1999
Competently	48
Incompetently	44
Neither	2
Both	3
Don't know	4

Q. *Are you satisfied or dissatisfied with the leadership shown by Tony Blair in regard to the NATO campaign?*

	May 1999
Satisfied	66
Dissatisfied	29
Neither	1
Don't know	4

Q. *The Conservative Party has recently criticised NATO's handling of the campaign. Do you believe this criticism was or was not justified?*

	May 1999
Was justified	38
Was not	52
Neither	2
Don't know	9

Q. *Do you believe this criticism was or was not patriotic?*

	May 1999
Was patriotic	34
Was not	48
Neither	7
Don't know	11

Q. *NATO has ruled out the use of ground forces in Kosovo until a negotiated settlement has been reached. Do you agree or disagree with this decision?*

	May 1999
Agree	57
Disagree	38
Neither	1
Don't know	3

Q. *Tony Blair has said that he will not negotiate with the Yugoslav leader, Slobodan Milosevic, until Yugoslav troops have been withdrawn from Kosovo. Do you or do you not believe this?*

	May 1999
Believe	64
Do not believe	31
Neither	1
Don't know	4

Q. *Do you believe that NATO should or should not negotiate with Slobodan Milosevic before Yugoslav troops are withdrawn from Kosovo?*

	May 1999
Should negotiate	51
Should not	44
Neither	1
Don't know	4

Q. *Do you believe that NATO will or will not succeed in its objective of returning Kosovar refugees to their homeland?*

	May 1999
Will succeed	57
Will not	36
Neither	2
Don't know	5

Index

numbers refer to section and tables within sections